Life on Both Sides of the Wall

By Günther F. Skaletz

The Skaletz Family Coat of Arms

Life on Both Sides of the Wall
An Autobiography

<u>Author</u>
Günther F. Skaletz

<u>Editor</u>
Dianne Stewart

<u>Associate Editor</u>
Sheridan O'Rourk

Cover Design by *Günther F. Skaletz with assistance from Nicolas Prausa, Daniel Althaus, and Emiko Shekem*

Published by *Günther F. Skaletz, of GUES Enterprises*

Printed in the U.S.A. on acid free paper
www.gfskaletz.com
Ordering information:
1942 Ravenswood Lane, Manitowoc, WI 54220

FOURTH EDITION
GFMS
ISBN # 978-0-615-13820-6

WAR

Those who survived the war were left tragically
devastated, homeless, and with little hope.
During the war I learned to be self-sufficient and
how to survive, I also learned how to move on.

The most important lesson I learned
was that nothing is impossible.

FREEDOM

"Freedom is not free. Freedom has its price.
May this story of a boy born in Poland remind us that
one should never take their freedom for granted."

Günther F. Skaletz

LIFE

Life is but an ocean with its waves going up and down,
as is our life.
Some of us are caught in a tidal wave going nowhere but down.
I am nothing but the edge of the beach, being washed up by
others and joining in the waves of life.

FORWARD

"In the beginning . . . the earth was without form, and void; and darkness was upon the face."

Genesis 1:1-2

Writing in the first century was not easy. The ancient pen was a reed that was cut to a point, which needed continuous re-sharpening. The paper was usually animal skin. Ink was generally made by mixing soot with some kind of gum or glue. Writing legibly with a reed dipped in this kind of ink and applying it to parchment could be a difficult and tedious task. Writing a book could take years, however, in our 'novus ordo seclorum' (new order of the ages and present time), some people can accomplish this task in just a matter of months or even less in our computerized world.

To me the greatest challenge to writing is to make one's language and mind express our confused ideas, feelings and thoughts. Trying to write is very much like trying to put a Chinese enigma together. We might have a pattern in mind, which we wish to work out in words, but the words sometimes do not fit the spaces or many times when they do, they do not match the master design.

What drives me to keep trying is that I know that others have succeeded before me and I am not willing to acknowledge defeat. "There is no way to become original except to be born so," says Stevenson, "and although I may not be original, I hope sometime to outgrow my artificial uneasiness and compositions."

PROLOGUE

Life on Both Sides of the Wall depicts the central conflict of a man in a historic exception, which touches all people so closely no one can disregard it. The author's hope is to be able to inspire all who read this story.

Written by Günther F. Skaletz, *Life on Both Sides of the Wall* depicts the ordeal of a human soul caught in the conflict of life and death, the conflict of faith in God vs. material things, and the conflict of freedom vs. communism.

Millions of people will never understand how WWII has actually affected their families, their beliefs and values, and their faith. This book, *Life on Both Sides of the Wall,* translates these issues into the simplest, most gripping terms possible. It's the autobiography of a man who survived the Holocaust, the bombardment of Berlin and Magdeburg, his time served as a soldier in the German Wehrmacht, his capture by the Russians, torture, and interrogation by the notorious KGB, and his flight for freedom across East Germany, all by the time he was 20 years old.

Life on Both Sides of the Wall is a riveting book. Few who take it up will be able to lay it aside. In this book, you will meet a man who does not hesitate to disclose secrets that many men force themselves to conceal. It's the fascinating true account of a man who simply chose to survive in the face of incredible hardships and danger. In return, he has helped and encouraged thousands of young people to achieve their goals as he did through faith, hope, prayers, and hard work.

FROM THE AUTHOR

I am a survivor. How a man controls his own destiny when captive and helpless says a lot about him. Everything can be taken from a man but one thing, the last of human freedoms: to choose one's own attitude in any given set of circumstances, to choose one's own destiny.

In this book are the recollections of a time in my past that changed my life and my world forever. Many years have passed since all that, but at times, a great tide of memories will overwhelm me. Such as, the memories of not being able to be at home with my family for holidays or special occasions, not being able to play with school friends, or not being able to spend time on my grandparents' farm. There is not a day that goes by that does not remind me of those around me who suffered pain, anguish, and even death so I might survive.

In my teenage years, I wondered how I was going to change my life. My stepmother would often remind me to pray to find the answers I sought. She would tell me to find my attitude. I spent much of my life choosing my own attitude, often times carelessly out of conceit. In those instances, my acts of self-determination were mistakes, but thankfully did not result in any lasting harm to me or those around me. There are, other choices I have to say I have deep regret for having made. What I chose I did so to keep a balance in my life. A balance between good and bad, a balance between pride and regret, and a balance between liberty and honor. What I chose I did to survive.

My grandfather served as a Major in the German War of 1866 under the command of King William, my father as an officer in the Cavalry during WWI, and I served in the German Wehrmacht during WWII. The men in my family for almost two centuries were raised and educated to be officers, to go to war, to serve their country. My father and grandfather were my first heroes. They were not men of spotless virtue, but they were honest, hard working, brave and loyal all their lives. The respect I had for them has lasted throughout my life. They have been dead for many years now, but their stories and contributions still inspire me to live my life in a way I know they will approve.

My biological mother died when I was eighteen months old so I do not remember much of her, but I do know that her family members were farmers, devoted to their land; working the land with hands and horse, oxen and plows, hard working people and devout Christians. By the time WWII arrived, I realized how fortunate I was to have been raised in such a family. From both my father and stepmother I learned to persevere. My stepmother taught me resilience and that a positive attitude was crucial to survival. This inheritance has made an enormous impact on my life.

My family has always been a close-knit one, their ethos set in stone. Work, worship, pray, and waste no time. This all came to an end when our father came home from work one day in late August 1939 and our stepmother told him there would be war. Our lives were never the same after that. That was when disruption and anxiety invaded our lives.

Three years later at the age of fifteen, I was sent to a German youth camp to continue my education. It was hard work, not only did I attend school, but also I had to work on a large farm that the school owned. This was a heartbreaking emotional time not only for me but also for my stepmother. The last Christmas I spent with my family was in 1942. It was not until 1959 that I was able to return to my home. In 1959, I was finally able to embrace my parents and relish time with my sisters, Maria and Anna, and my brother Bernhardt. When we finally met, again we were all overwhelmed. The joy was indescribable.

The ravages of WWII left its mark on all of us. Our city was run over by the German Wehrmacht in 1939 moving on to Russia, and again in 1944 when the Russian army moved west to meet the United States forces in April of 1945 on the Elbe River. My father died on New Year's Eve, 1959. He left many questions I had unanswered; there wasn't enough time to pursue them. My father did tell me that seeing his family all together again was the highlight of his life. These words still resonate in my heart today and mean the world to me.

In those years when I was growing up without my parents, there was something very powerful and meaningful that motivated me and kept me going; it was the strong foundation they had laid for me. As I left home in 1942, my stepmother's last words were to "Never forget to pray." There was one other lesson she taught me: not to let life's constant disruptions break my stride, but to welcome them as elements that would enrich my life.

I was drafted into the German Wehrmacht at the age of sixteen and a half. I resisted its exertions, fearing its effect on my individuality, but as a prisoner of war, I learned that a shared purpose did not claim my identity. On the contrary, it enlarged my sense of self. I have seen examples of many brave men, especially my father who was wounded twice in WWI and nearly died of poison gas, proud of their singularity, but faithful to the same cause.

I left unimaginable horrors and destructions brought on by WWII as well as Auschwitz behind me. I became a migrant, not by choice. In such a life, some fine things are left behind and missed, but the bad times are left behind as well. You move on, remembering only the good. This book recounts some of my experiences and commemorates the people who most influenced my life and choices. What balance I have achieved is a gift from them and without them, I would not have been able to put this into written form. The faith instilled in me by my mother has certainly kept me going and helped me stay alive. I was at times homeless, miserable, hungry, frightened, and homesick. I often longed for the comfort of our home in Poland, and the love of my family, but all this was simply not possible to attain. These years of horror remain forever inside me. I hope that my story will not only be inspiring, but also informative and educational. It is all about survival, hope, faith, and optimism. It's not about being bitter, but taking responsibility for one's life. I believe that it's a good message to pass along.

GFS

ACKNOWLEDGEMENT

It takes many years and a great many people to shape a professional in any endeavor or in any art or technique. During my long career in the hospitality business, I've been extremely fortunate to come in contact with some wonderful individuals.

I want to take a moment to thank those innumerable people who made this dream a reality. Words cannot express the deep gratitude I hold for the mother who nurtured me, who taught me to read and write Polish, and who taught me to sew and cook. She taught me the importance of analyzing tastes on a plate as well as in a glass. This fostered my passion to enter this field.

I thank my father for sending me to Herr Kleinert and the Neumanns, who guarded me from harm's way, who in turn trained and taught me the finer art of culinary. I would be nowhere without the Duebners and Professors Pohl who cared enough about me to see that I went to college and made that dream a reality and to Herr Director Wachs and Monsieur Chevalliere who gave me my first real start in the field.

God's blessings on the unsung heroes who risked all to save my life and refreshed my soul along my arduous journey as I escaped the death train and escaped across the border into West Germany. Without these brave and caring people, I surely would not be here today.

Samuel Johnson, the great English lexicographer, critic, and author once said, "A man will turn over half a library to make one book." Fortunately, I did not have to do that. For the past five decades, I accumulated notes and facts that I knew one day would aid me in writing this book.

On one occasion, I had the opportunity to converse with then President L.B. Johnson and upon leaving his company; he insisted that someday I write a book about my life. It took me years to come to grips with my past and break my self-imposed code of silence, but I made a promise to him and now I have chosen to keep it.

My wonderful wife, Elaine, to whom I am very indebted for her untiring support and encouragement even at the cost of sacrificing our time together. Three years ago, she left a note on my computer screen and it still hangs there, it reads, "Now or never is the time." She is and always will be my biggest supporter and my best friend.

I thank my daughters Bettina and Anemone without whose encouragement I probably would not have started this project. I am grateful to my sister Anna and her husband for supplying me with invaluable details of my childhood, historical events, and pictures from that period and our life.

I acknowledge the resources and reference materials that provided me with specific facts pertaining to my homeland Poland and World War II. I thank my friends and the wonderful community of Two Rivers, for the continued support making this lifelong mission a reality.

Lastly, I need to thank my editor and friend, Dianne Stewart, who never gave up on this project even when it turned out to be more than either of us expected it to be. She did a magnificent job, in deciphering my enigmatic writing and thousands of notes, and in turning a daunting task into a finale. To my associate editor, Sheridan O'Rourk, a special thank you for proofreading the manuscript many times over and ironing out the rough spots. I thank him for his patience and expertise.

"Never give up on your dreams for everything is possible."
Mother

INDEX

"It is not who you are that counts, it's what you <u>do</u> that counts."

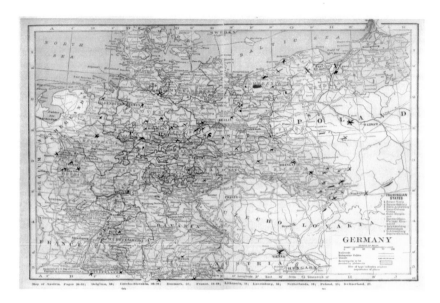

Escaping the Russian - crossing Poland
(1945)

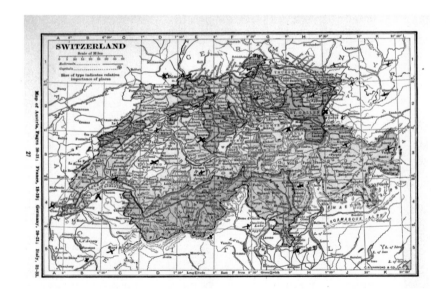

Switzerland (1953)

Auschwitz

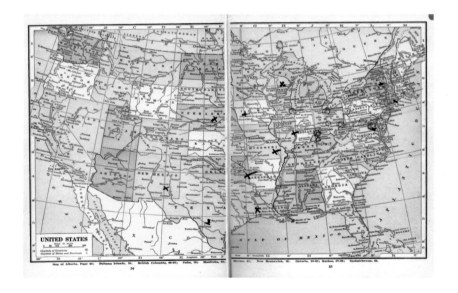

Crossing America

My father, Bernhard Skaletz
in World War I (1914-1918)

Brother Bernhard - pilot in the German
Luftwaffe (1942)

Me in World War II
(1939-1945)

My family in Poland (1929)
My parents, Bernhard and Anna Skaletz
sisters, Agnes, Maria, Anna; Brother
Bernhard with me on my father's lap

Grandparents' farm

Street, downtown Tarnowskie - Góry

Threshing on Grandparents'
farm - Poland

The remnants of grandparents' farm
after W.W. II

The gate to Auschwitz Concentration Camp with the
mendacious welcome "arbeit machtfrei"
(work will make you free)

My First Communion
I am nine years old.

My sister, Anna and me
Reunion after 34 years (Berlin 1997)

My father in World War I
(1914-1918)

My mother (whom I did not
get the chance to know)

My birth home -
coming home from school
Tarnowskie - Góry, Poland (1933)

Our lot - where once our home stood
Tarnowskie - Góry, Poland

My hometown

Tarnowskie Góry - Rynek

St. Anna Church
Our church
Tarnowskie - Góry, Poland

Kaiser Wilhelm Church - Berlin
Damaged by bombs
during bombardment

The seminary and convent
Tarnowskie - Góry

Winter in Poland

My father's Medal of Honor
World War I (1914-1918)
Now in my possession

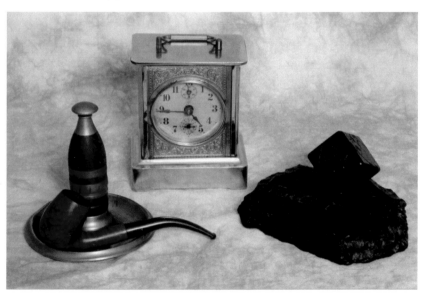

Our Father's clock, pipe, and cigar cutter
made out of World War I 36 mm. shell
and coal carving - out of Polish coal mine
(an inheritance of my father)

Helmstedt - West Germany
Ready to take off for college in Switzerland
with "My Bride" - a Horex Regina 400cm

Visiting sister, Anna, in Berlin

A good team - me and "My Bride" -
a Horex Regina 400cm
Cruising the counryside

My brother-in-law, Wolfgang and me
touring the country - Germany

The Racing Team (1954)
Me, friend George, and Wolfgang, my brother-in-law
Berlin - AVUS Race Track

My loving stepmother
Barbara Skaletz-Bartosch

Switzerland (1953)

Helmstedt - West Germany (1948)

The train that never came

Proud of his union, his church, and his profession, a Silesian coal miner wears a Solidarity badge and the Pope's picture on the ceremonial uniform of his trade. Sometimes called the aristocrats of the nation's working class, Polish miners are among the last groups in Europe to continue the centuries-old tradition of wearing trade uniforms on special occasions.

At a Polish coal mine entrance in Radzionkau before going down 1000 feet to the mine. From left to right: brother-in-law Wolfgang, me, and brother Bernhard.

Visiting Krakow, Poland (1959)
My brother Bernhard, me and brother-in-law Wolfgang on the Vistula River.
In the background is Wawel Cathedral

Graduation with professor - Dr. Pohl

Our first car, a Fiat Italian-built Topolino
(Photo 1959)

In Germany - Sprendlingen
Our condo is being built

Berlin 1994

Me after college (1954)

After graduation from college
Fernando Gonzales (Barcelona, Spain)
and me in 1954

Berwang-Tirol-Austria
1958

Omega watch was a gift from a Russian
KGB officer for saving his life (1945)

Helmstedt - Germany
The city that gave me a new start

In Tarnowitz - Poland (1959)

Visiting Krakow, Poland (1959) after 16
years. Brother-in-law, Wolfgang, me, and
brother, Bernhard. In the background,
Castle Wawel and cathedral

Crossing the Atlantic Ocean
(May 1964)

The roaring and tempestuous ocean

Dallas - Statler Hilton Hotel (1966)
Greeting German Chancellor,
Ludwig Erhard

German Chancellor Helmut Kohl
who helped me to find my lost identity.

The Berlin Wall went up August 13, 1961
and finally crumbled, after 28 years, in November 1989.

Returning to Berlin after 34 years. With my sister, Anna at the border line that divided West from East Germany. The Glienicke bridge where once Russian and American spies were exchanged. (1997)

President Ronald Reagan telling Russian President Mikhail Gorbachev - "Mr. Gorbachev, tear down this wall."

President
Lyndon Baines Johnson
at the Argyle
in San Antonio

The staff of the Argyle -
instrumental in
providing dinner for LBJ

President L. B. Johnson

AUSTIN, TEXAS

Dear Mr. Skaletz:

Thanks so much for your letter and your continuing
kindness and courtesy. Mrs. Johnson and I will not
forget your offer -- because we will always appreciatively
remember your past service.

We wish you much success with your new restaurant.

Sincerely,

Mr. Frank G. Skaletz
2811 Marlborough
San Antonio, Texas 78230

December 7, 1972

---

afternoon

March 26, 1971

Dear Mr. Skaletz,

I wish to say again how very
much everyone enjoyed the beautiful
Cocktail Buffet. Being able to have
such a perfect party makes Mrs. Ford
and me very happy that we are members
of the Argyle. You make all of this
possible — thank you!

Enclosed are some tickets to the
Battle of Flowers Parade and
Band Festival. We hope that
your family will enjoy them.

Sincerely,
Mary Louise Ford

SISTER OF: MRS.(GERALD) FORD

FIRST NATIONAL BANK OF SAN ANTONIO
GLENN BIGGS, PRESIDENT
231 EAST TRAVIS, SAN ANTONIO, TEXAS 78205

January 31, 1973

Mr. Frank Skaletz
2811 Marlborough
San Antonio, Texas 78230

Dear Frank:

With the passing of President Johnson, a happy
memory was brought back of his likeness and appreciation for the very able service you performed.
As a matter of fact, he recently mentioned to me
of your very able assistance and flair for having
a good party.

For the times you have served my family and me,
we are most appreciative and if we can be of any
assistance and support to you as you consider
various job opportunities, please be advised that
we shall heartily and enthusiastically endorse your
capability as a manager, a planner, and a "doer".

With every personal good wish to you and your family.

Sincerely,

Glenn Biggs
by bs

GB:bs

I worked here from 1954-1962, after graduation from college

Employee Feature

This month we take you behind the scenes and introduce you to a relatively new member of the Happy Hollow staff. Gunther F. Skaletz was appointed Chef by J.D. Clemmer on September 11, 1979. He brings with him an "impressive background of more than 30 years experience in chef and managerial positions."

Gunther is a graduate of Mark Graf High School, Tanowitz (Poland); the Gymnasium, Tornowitz; and the Hotel Management College in Lausanne, Switzerland. After holding chef positions in St. Moritz (Switzerland) and Frankfort (West Germany), he came to New York on an apprenticeship program in 1962 and then returned to West Germany for one year. He then came to Arlington, Texas, established his U.S. citizenship, and has held numerous management positions before accepting the job as Chef of Happy Hollow. His vast experience and expertise have already added greatly to the continental flair and appeal of many special club events.

In his spare time Gunther enjoys planning special menus and walking his dog. He tries to find time to go skiing at least once a year. Chef Skaletz, we contratulate you on a job well done.

Le "Chef"

Visiting sister, Anna in Berlin, Germany after 34 years. Brother, Bernhard on the right.

Family reunion in Berlin, Germany after 34 years

Mr. Delacy and me.
Tan-Tar-A Resort, Missouri
(1976)

Marriotts Tan-Tar-A Resort

The Coca-Cola Company
Foods Division
HOUSTON, TEXAS

ROBERT V. FEY
VICE PRESIDENT/GENERAL MANAGER
SALES AND MERCHANDISING

ADDRESS REPLY TO
P.O. BOX 2079
HOUSTON, TEXAS 77001
713-881-4411

April 5, 1977

PRINCE OF TAN-TAR-A

There was a kingdom by the lake,
    A multi-castled realm, Tan-Tar-A,
Many leagues from Kansas City
    And Saint Louis, with little nearer.

But self-sufficient was the kingdom
    On the shores of Lake Ozark;
In luxury, and every gourmet service,
    This fine hostel met the mark.

Then came along the Foods of Coke
    To stage a conference, nation-wide;
Precision service did they need
    Whilst in the place they did abide.

Many were their needs (and changing!)
    For food and beverage here and there;
'Twas a chore of great proportion,
    But quoth that good man, "Never fear!

Just you name it – we will do it."
    And we learned to place our bets
On the Food and Beverage Master:
    Diligent, conscientious Frank Skaletz.

And so to you, Tan-Tar-An Prince,
    Let this humble, heartfelt rhyme
Convey our thanks, confirm our judgement
    Of your quality: it is PRIME.

Warm best wishes,

Bob Fey

RVF:kj

River Falls Supper Club
(1987)

"Le Chef" in action
(2006)

With daughter, Bettina

The author and his grandson, Grant

Our Family

My wife, Elaine and me

At the Whitehall
Oklahoma City, OK
(1973)

Elaine and Günther

"May every nation come to know that war is the most terrible thing that can happen to its people."

—Günther F. Skaletz

The Beginning

No, I am not going back that far, I just mean my beginning. That's how it usually starts for all of us, doesn't it? My early and first recollection is growing up without a mother. My father struggled after the death of his beloved wife and his oldest daughter, Agnes. We struggled through the deep depression, which not only affected our country, Poland, but was sweeping through the entire world.

I was born in 1927 in Tarnowskie-Góry (the Tarnowitzer Hills), in Upper Silesia Poland, where the freezing blizzards swept in from Siberia making the winters unbearable. My first frustration came when I was still a little boy. One of my chores was to keep the huge fireplace stocked with wood when I was home. I would collect the kindling from a pile in the shed in our courtyard; I can still feel the sharp edges of the split quarters of pine against my hands. I was too young to have chopped the wood, but as I grew older, my father taught me how to do it. However, I was strong and able to bring in two logs at a time into our pine-planked kitchen where the large fireplace would devour them faster than I could bring them in. My older brother, Bernhard told me some years later that I would often cry like a little girl for having to do this task, although I don't recollect such a metaphysical profundity.

We lived in quite a large house, built circa 1676, constructed of native rocks and hand hewn beams which were exposed in all the rooms throughout the house. Its walls were at least sixty centimeters thick. This house originally had a thatched roof, but it was eventually replaced by a tar one.

While I have no early memories of my biological mother, I do cherish a family photograph where she is lovingly holding my sister Anna and I am sitting on my father's lap. I often think of my mother as a heroine; giving life to five children during an unimaginable turbulent time, shortly after the Great War (WWI). She lived through the great depression. Life must have been very hard. I do not have personal memories of my mother. I was eighteen months old when she went to heaven. I had three sisters: Agnes, Maria, and Anna; and an older brother, Bernhard. Agnes took over looking after us, since she was the oldest. It saddens me deeply when I think about my Agnes and how young she too died.

We lost her just six months after our mother passed on. Agnes was only nine years old. I never was able to find out under what circumstances she passed away, just that she left us entirely too soon. My sister, Maria told me years later that they thought Agnes died of a broken heart.

Our father did his best to provide for us. He worked hard during the depression to feed us and to keep a roof over our heads. With the passing of my mother and sister, the burden of daily care fell onto the shoulders of the next oldest, Maria who herself was only seven years old. She took care of my brother Bernhard who was four, me at eighteen months, and our youngest sister Anna who was a mere six months old. Somehow, we managed to survive these times.

With the eruption of the horrible World War II in September of 1939 and the subsequent invasion of our country, Poland by the Nazi army came the unimaginable and inexorable suffering and subsequent separation from my home and family. I gradually became aware of my true path. It has been a very difficult and arduous journey, but it has been a journey of hope, faith, and perseverance. It has always been my conviction that with God, nothing is impossible. I struggled and managed to survive the many precarious years that followed. It has been a daunting and long journey through which God guided me throughout these lonely and arduous years.

My Mother

Anna Ciedlik
February 22, 1894 to April 14, 1929

I was born to Bernhard and Anna on October 10, 1927. My parents were profoundly Catholic as was the entire region. Church was a large part of everyone's life at that time, and like many others, they rarely missed a Sunday Mass. By 1929, our family had grown to five children, the oldest being Agnes at age seven.

The Great Depression had Europe in its grasp as well as the rest of the world. My parents struggled to make ends meet. We were of German descent, yet we spoke and were educated in Polish. The Plebiscite of 1922 banned the spoken German language and we lived in fear of being found out. At the age of eighteen months I lost my mother, and within six months my oldest sister. When I was old enough, around my First Communion, my second oldest sister Maria told me that our mother was a very beautiful, caring, and hard working woman. She was always neatly dressed. She was a woman of stature; I must have gotten my height from my father's side of the family. The only images I have of my mother are those that my older siblings have planted there.

Years later when I was old enough to discuss our life back then with my sister Maria, she told me what it was like caring for us and our father during those hard times. I often wonder how five children could manage on their own, running a house without any of the modern day appliances we take for granted today. I marvel at the strength my two older sisters demonstrated to keep us together.

I went to a Polish school and was taught all the basics that all young children are taught. I recall vividly, Maria making sure I did my lessons and her teaching us to pray and how important it was that we continue to rely on our faith in good times and bad.

As I have mentioned, I was blessed with a second mother. Several years after our mother's passing, our 'Vater' (father) found a woman who was willing to raise and care for us; I was nine years old. It was quite a challenge even at that time to walk into a ready-made family. Her name was Barbara Bartosch. She had great compassion, patience, and love for our father as well as his children. Throughout this story, I will refer to her as either my stepmother or my mother; I think of her as my mother for she is the only one I really knew.

This wonderful woman proved to this struggling family that there was little she could not master. When she came into our lives, she relieved Maria, my fifteen year old sister from the pressures of having to care for the family. We had already lost Agnes, about six months after our birth mother had passed away. I always admired Maria, she never seemed to complain about the responsibilities that were thrust upon her at such a tender age. Like every child out there, we need our parents and I cannot even imagine what my life would have been like, had this woman not entered it when she did.

Our new mother worked tirelessly, to see to it that our father had his breakfast waiting and lunch ready for him when he left for work at five o'clock in the morning. She filled the role of wife and mother with grace and with a strength and tenacity derived from her faith and Christian upbringing. She raised us four children with love and discipline. She supported her husband's work. She made sure that we always had a hot meal to start off our day, our clothing was always washed and mended, and she saw to it that our homework was done. She was a teacher to us, a loving spouse to our father, a good cook, and an excellent baker; one of her best known desserts was a Polish favorite, Poppy Seed Cake; I never tasted one that could even compare. There wasn't much she could not or would not do. She made sure that we went to church on Sundays and performed our chores. I still think about our nightly suppers, all of us sitting around the table enjoying the Lord's blessings.

Her soft-spoken voice still resonates in my ears even after so many decades. She was truly an extra ordinary woman. She reminded us children to pray and respect other people as well as our selves. She was in many ways the 'pencil' in God's hand. She would never send anyone away who came to the door and asked for help, which happened quite often during the horrible war. She was a fragile looking woman and it was amazing to watch the energy soar through her small frame. It seemed she never stopped moving, she was always up before the rooster even had a chance to crow. No matter how busy or worried she was, she rarely let it show and her arms were always open to us; always there to protect us as well as admonish us as a true mother would.

One of her favorite pastimes was caring for her flower garden. She would grow long rows of flowers that were a glory to see. We had fresh flowers for every season and were the envy of many of her peers.

She loved to cook. Whenever I could, I helped her in the kitchen with many labor-intensive meals. We always had fresh vegetables from our own garden, which we all tendered lovingly for we understood its importance to our life in those times. Such bounty from the earth required unstinting effort, she often said 'One reaped what one sowed." She came from a farming family and knew how to work the land. We often worked long into the dark after school so nothing went to waste. She taught us how to preserve or can food. This was very important in those days when there was no refrigeration units. I learned the importance of salt; not only does it preserve and flavor food, but it disinfects what's been contaminated and prevents poison from setting into a wound. I said that my mother was a good cook, well she was but for one thing. Each morning we would have a hot bowl of oat gruel or 'haferschleim'. This type of oatmeal was not as refined as it is today and when you swallowed, it would often times scratch the back of your throat. Our mother would make it so thick that it would be almost impossible to swallow, but we were taught not to waste or want so we ate what was put in front of us. I am ashamed to admit that there were many mornings when on my way to school, I was not able to keep this hearty breakfast down and I would have to get rid of it alongside the road. I never told my mother this.

She was a wise woman. She possessed many qualities, too numerous to mention. Yes, she was our mother, my mutter, but to me she was more than that; she was my heroine.

Barbara Bartosch
November 30, 1896-September 11, 1969

She was my mother and I shall never forget her.

Mothers
Love them as in childhood, though feeble, old and gray
For you never miss a mother's love,
til she's buried beneath the clay.

I miss both my mothers, every day.

MOTHER

I once was alone in a dark circle of loneliness.

No one ever came to visit or to chat.

I was always on my own with no one to play with,

No one to sing with, no one to teach me my A,B,C's.

My mother never came, she died when I was still a toddler,

I never got a chance to know her and vater

was always gone to work.

Later my oldest sister Maria was the one who had to tell me

not to talk to strangers, but to me a stranger meant a friend

who would listen. Often after dark I'd sit in my room

thinking about the wishes I'd made that were all made in vain,

like my wish that my mother would come home and the wish

that my mother would play with me, but she never did.

My vater always thought I'd get by on my own,

my toys though not many were all the company I had on those

long long days and cold dark nights.

I am now grown up and think often of those lonely nights,

waiting for my mother.

Where I Grew Up

Tarnowskie-Góry Poland was the town where I was born and grew up. From my earliest memories, I recalled wondering what would happen to me when I got older. For most people childhood is a distant realm, a foreign territory long forgotten. For me, it's as close as the next heartbeat. Despite the hard times and difficulties surrounding my childhood; from the Great Depression of the 1930's to the subsequent World War II, I consider the recollection of my childhood with rich memories and indulgence. I keep these memories tucked away in a special place and only bring them forward to be relived when time and circumstances are conducive to proper daydreaming; now is such a time. I've always cherished those wonderful times of my childhood years.

My childhood coincided with the late 20's, 30's. I grew up in a multilateral-cultural community where Catholics, Protestants, Jews and Gypsies lived in harmony and peace. Everyone had their own problems and managed to live with the help of each other in this precarious time.

Tarnowskie-Góry set in the hills of Tarnowitz, in the south of Poland about forty-five kilometers south east of Krakow. For centuries, it belonged to Germany, but was eventually ceded to Poland in 1919 after the Great War according to the Treaty of Versailles, which was signed, by Britain, the United States, France, and Germany. Tarnowskie-Góry was wedged between two countries; Poland and Germany. Therefore, it was very difficult for us to visit or see our relatives: aunts, uncles, or cousins as much as we would have liked to. In order to visit them it required a pass to cross the border from one country to the other. Both my father and his new wife spoke both German and Polish and for a while found themselves in a delicate predicament. The Treaty of Versailles created some resentment among the people living in this affected area. My father had served in the German Cavalry Regiment under Kaiser William II from 1913-1918 as an officer. He was twice wounded in the war and nearly poisoned by 'yellow gas', found himself now on Polish ground. They decided to stay in Tarnowskie-Góry. When Germany lost the rights to Upper Silesia, it was a great blow to the German economy. Following the Great War, a run-a-way inflation set in more severe than in any other part of the post war Europe in 1922. The culmination of the inflation, however came in 1923 with a crisis of internal disorder and lack of unity. My parents had to cope with unemployment for the first time. Although my father had studied engineering and architecture at the University of Breslau in Silesia, Germany; he was still unable to find work.

Tarnowskie-Góry had become known in the 12th century, due to the large deposits of precious minerals, as the cradle of coal mining. It was the Mark Graf George the Pious von Brandenburg who eventually promoted and supported this industry. Legend tells that the first metallic silver was brought forth by a peasant in 1490. It was from that time on that mining settlers appeared. Nine mines were established near Tarnowskie and were called "Góry" or Hills hence the name was changed to Tarnowskie-Góry. It was a time of fast development. Mark Grave Jerzy von Hohenzollern decided in 1526 to support the growing city. However, all was put on hold by the 30 Year War from 1618-1648. Another set back came in 1867 when the plague hit this growing city. Tarnowskie-Góry later became the center of the Royal Academy for coal miners. It was here that a real classical secondary school was established with a seminary and agricultural college.

This region has a rich history; the Polish King, Jan Sobieski, marched with his army of 30,000 or more through the city to aid the city of Vienna, which was being besieged by the Turks. It was in this city and this region that Napoleon Bonaparte crossed with his grand army (450,000 men and 150,000 horses, wagons, heavy guns, etc.) in the spring of 1812 stripping the land of food, livestock, and draft horses as they marched their way to Moscow. Napoleon returned once again, this time in defeat and with a petit armee, working his way back to France in the winter of 1812. This region served many European countries, particularly to the Austrian Emperor Franz and the Czar Alexander of Russia on their travels from east to west and back. King August and Countess Aurora von Koenigsmark dined at the renowned Wine Stuben von Sedlaczek. It was also the German dichter-poet Johan Wolfgang von Goethe who traveled the long distance from Frankfurt-Main by horse and carriage to see the events which were taking place in Tarnowskie-Góry. While there, 'Goethe' wrote an epigram in the Golden Book of the city.

"Fern von gebildeten menschen
am rande des reiches,
werhilft bring zu licht?
Nur verstand und redlichkeit helfen.
Es führen die beiden schlüssel
Zu jeglichen schatz
Welche die erde bewart."

****

*"Far from the educated human heart on the edge of this
land who will help to find its treasures and will happily
bring them to light? Only understanding and integrity
will help. And only the two keys will lead to the treasures,
which the earth protects."*

There is no arguing about it, the most beautiful part of the world is wherever you grew up. Poland was and still is a nation of fighters; they have always defended their borders against greedy neighbors, especially Russia and Germany. Poland has never been a free country, and yet they strived to live in peace and harmony. We grew up surrounded by peaceful landscape in a friendly safe neighborhood.

Dirt roads were part of my childhood in the country nearby our town. I've got a hunch that society would be a lot better off today if so many of those dirt roads had not been paved over. Dirt roads build character, the people who lived at the end of a dirt road learned early on that life was a bumpy ride. We used to walk the dirt road to our school or to our farm. We learned quickly that bad words or hard feelings tasted like the dust from the road in our mouths and souls. We had very little crime on those roads, for the crooks were too lazy to walk and too scared of the dogs that often guarded the properties.

When there were dirt roads, people worshiped the Lord and their children, not their cars and possessions. Dirt roads taught patience. Dirt roads brought families together, when it rained we stayed home and had family time. Back then children enjoyed getting dirty for the sake of getting dirty. I remember walking in the mud after a spring rain with the muck squishing between my toes. Most paved roads then and now lead to trouble. Dirt roads lead to fishing spots and swimming holes. It is funny, I don't remember us ever having to lock our doors, except for in the summer when we would leave and didn't want to find another bushel of cucumbers or zucchini in our hallway. You always made a friend at the end of a dirt road.

To understand Poland, it is necessary to understand its past. The story of Poland is one of great sadness and tragedy. Poland has had several outstanding leaders and more than its share of shortsighted and incompetent ones who were instrumental in bringing this country to its ruin. Countries as well as people are forged by adversity. Over the centuries this country's people battled the Tartars, the Turks, the Teutonic Knights, Cossacks, Russians, the Prussians, and of course the Nazis; as well as its own leaders. Even in the darkest hours of Polish history, its people never gave up hope of restoring their homeland to independence. The final chapter of Poland's story cannot be written, since today's news will become tomorrow's history. Poland is a nation of faith. More than ninety-five percent of the population is Roman Catholic.

The war left factories and railroads un-operable. As Hitler's Wehrmacht forged their way toward the east, they ran over our country. The Nazi party gained national importance when big industrialists began to support it. When Hitler became the leader of the National Socialist German Workers' Party (NSGWP), he also began his plans for an Aryan Race (a pure Caucasian strain). The European countries were in turbulence for Hitler had sent a shudder of horror and turbulence throughout Germany and the surrounding countries. His armies marched relentlessly, devouring the innocent and peaceful that seemed to be a threat to his reign.

My School Years

Maria gave me my foundation for education. She saw to it that I received my First Communion and fostered my love for learning. I liked school very much and like many children back then as today, I had teachers who were a very important part of my life then and now. I attended a Catholic school. Since our home was bilingual behind closed doors, I learned both the Polish and German languages. By the time, I was nine I made it to the

Gymnasium, which was a different type of school, more structured; now my true early education began. Most of the teachers were extremely strict and demanded only the best from their students. One particular teacher would make us write a précis of a leading editorial in our local Polish newspaper and the task was to bring it down to fourteen lines. To say the least this was a dreaded assignment. As much as I disliked the project, it did teach me the art of the Polish language.

I liked school and had many friends, some of them Jews who lived in our neighborhood. I had a pretty normal childhood for those times, I played fussball, basketball, and tennis with homemade equipment like everyone else. I joined the school band and learned to play the drums, I wasn't very good, but I tried hard. The school I attended had a large range of courses, more than many schools at that time such as; calculus, trigonometry, chemistry, physics, Russian and Latin. What I liked the most was history and Latin. Our Latin teacher was a descendent from a White Russian family. We had a lot of recitation to do for this class, one such verse I remember is "De gustibus non est disputandum" (There is no use arguing). Also, "ordo or "ordnung" which has to do with a world dominated by God's inclusive order, if there was no 'ordo' there is a lack of discipline. I got to know the word and it's meaning quite well for it was a standard to live by in our home. The rector for the school was a tall imposing man with thick blond hair, very typical for a Pole, his name was Pan (Mr.) Maleczki. The rector ran a tight ship and we all knew it, often he would step unannounced into our classroom to observe the instructor as well as his students. One of my worst subjects was my penmanship. It was never good enough for Pan Maleczki, quite often I was given extra homework to improve my writing skills; I don't think it really paid off though, my wife Elaine still complains about my handwriting to this day.

History was taught by Pan Stefan Roglinsky, a stout gentleman who had a mustache which he would roll to a fine thin pin. I loved the smell of his pipe in the hallways and his wicked sense of humor. I enjoyed learning about the country in which I lived, Poland as well as the enigmatic countries beyond the Atlantic Ocean. Poland had always been a tormented nation, but despite all its troubles maintained an indomitable spirit. Poland traditionally produced brave patriots as well as fine artists from Koscivsko to Chopin, Paderewski to Magdalena Abakanowicz.

Our head master was Pan Zimkowski, a true character, right out of an old Polish novel. He was a smallish man, a little overweight, he wore a monocle complete with a silver chain that was attached to his vest. He was probably the most pedantic pedagogue (schoolteacher) I had ever come across. He left a huge mark not just on our education, but all over our school.

In school, if we were good, during the winter months, Father Paul would take us to a park where we would be allowed to ice skate for as long as we could handle the frigid temperatures. Many times he would skate in the center of our group with each of us (about ten of us) skating along side of him. Father Paul in his white vestments and us at his side gave an angelic look to the outing; afterward we would unthaw our insides with cups of hot chocolate at the concession kiosk.

Childhood Memories

Money during and after the depression was tight and it affected all who lived through it. Our mother was a good economist and budgeted our money well. She often stopped and picked up a penny on the street and I still do today. My life was simple and much like everyone else's around us. I came, I saw, I conquered; or so I was told. My sister Maria has told me that even at a young age I had an eager and self-asserting disposition. Everything I saw people do I insisted on imitating. I talked at a young age, expressions of happiness always covered my little face. These happy days did not last long, one winter day when I was quite young, I became very ill with a high fever, and I plunged into unconsciousness. Father was at work, we had not yet brought our new mother into our lives. Bernhard watched over me as Maria ran for the doctor. Finally, the doctor made it to the house. He sadly told Maria that he did not expect me to live. Maria even though only a young child herself prayed for me and let her faith guide her and our father through those strenuous hours. By the next day, my fever had passed and I was soon well enough to cause havoc around the house.

What fun we had when the circus would come to town, my brother and I knew we could find odd jobs around the circus lot which would provide us with spending money or help with home expenses. We distributed posters throughout the town and helped on the site while they were there. We were enterprising young lads, Bernhard and I; we often hung around the railroad terminals with our trusty wagon and would assist travelers with their luggage, sometimes we had more customers than we could handle, but we enjoyed the work.

It seemed like we never had time to get into trouble, or so I recall, I'm sure we did, what child doesn't. Our parents made sure they managed our time well with chores and lessons. There was always a garden or animals to tend to, fences to mend, and work to be done around the house. One of mother's favorite sayings was "Idle hands are the Devil's workshop." Therefore, our hands were always kept busy and our sauerkraut and pickle barrels were always full; what we didn't use we shared with our neighbors. One of my favorite 'chores' was to pick blackberries. It was a tedious time consuming job and it took a great amount of effort to not eat as many as you picked, the reward for bringing home two gallons of those sweet black berries was an extra dish of cobbler hot from the oven.

We were pretty self-sufficient with few exceptions. We grew everything we ate, we had a smoke house where there would always be one or two big hams hanging along with long ropes of sausages. Being a big family meant being able to fend and stand up for yourself. Sundays was usually a chicken dinner. Being one of the youngest, as a child I was not aware that there was such a thing as breast meat on a chicken. One had to pick quick to get the 'pick' of the platter. There was no refrigeration, so our dairy products were stored in a 'spring house'. In it we kept our milk, goat cheese, and butter cool by setting milk cans and crocks in the cool spring water that flowed from the ground.

In Autumn when the landscape was painted in rusty tones of red and gold and the huge chestnut trees were shedding their leaves, we would play in the chilling night air anticipating the first winter snow. My brother and sisters and I would take burlap bags and gather up all the leaves we could so we could lay on them and watch the clouds roll by until it was time to bring them inside the barn to be used as bedding for the goats.

I often dream of walking through the woods with my brother and sisters, sometimes it's so real I think I can catch the leaves as they are falling to the forest floor. I think back on the fun we had as innocent children sledding down our slopes clinging to each other in excited fear and anticipation, and thank God that I had those experiences that will never go away.

Winters in Poland were usually very frigid. It was common to find in the towns every few blocks or so a heavy wrought iron basket glowing with hot embers so that anyone who had to walk could stop and warm themselves before moving on, especially the older people.

I remember going to the 'sukiennice' or open market place in late spring and in fall where we would shop the local Polish crafts of beautiful ornaments, walking sticks, balloons, and what we enjoyed the most; sugarcane. The craft fair housed colorful carousels to ride on with their trademark music floating out in the cool light air. There was the unmistakable enticing smell of Polish food and pierogi wafting through the crowds making your mouth water. I can still taste the delicious confection of fried dough dusted with powdered sugar called 'paczki' which was such a treat for children as well as the adults. All around you could hear the sounds of Chopin concertos, non-stop polka dancing; I loved doing the Polish chicken dance. Folk singers and dancers from distant places such as Krakow, Warszawa, and the mountains of Beskiden or Carpathian, filled the spaces with their colorfully decorated costumes twirling this way and that, making everything so very festive. Storytellers wrapped us up in the legends of Poland, such as the story of Pan Twardowski or the 'Man in the Moon' who signs a deal with the devil to gain control over his domineering wife. In the end, Pan is rescued by two angels, but is denied entrance into heaven for disobeying God and is forced to remain on the moon. I especially enjoyed the highland sheepdogs that would perform their herding skills. These lively dogs were known to be hardworking and loyally devoted to their masters.

I remember the pilgrimages in May and October to Our Lady of Piekare in Upper Silesia, to commemorate the "Ernte

Danktag" (Giving thanks for the harvest) with our entire congregation being led by Father Anton Cieplic. I was an alter boy and would have to carry the cross. We would walk the twelve kilometers from our town to Piekare, praying and singing songs. To say the least, this would be an all day event. One could not help but come away impacted by this special event. In our school, before Hitler invaded our country, we were taught the mysteries of the rosary, the power of prayer, and the importance of family and our community. These are some of the wonderful childhood memories, which I hold dear.

I remember when I was eleven, we took a school trip by train to the city of Czestochowa, about forty kilometers northeast of our town. There we visited and viewed Our Lady of Czestochowa in a wonderful cathedral. If one wanted to get to the top of the spire, you had to climb over 860 steps, which I did, the view from the top was exhilarating and you could see the Jasna Gora Monastery about 25 kilometers away. In the cathedral was the most beautiful painting of the "Black Madonna". It is a shame that in the 15th Century, robbers slashed her face forever, damaging the what was and still is an unforgettable painting. This haunting portrait of the Virgin Mary was brought to the Jasna Gora Monastery in 1382, this icon has been credited with saving the monastery from anti papal Swedish invaders in 1655. After the siege ended, it was found that the monastery was the only fortification left uncaptured.

Our home was over three hundred years old and was built by some of the first settlers. Its walls were three feet thick and built out of native rocks. The huge hand hewed beams were exposed throughout the house. Its large kitchen was the center of the house, a room for plain folk. In it was a huge oven, which our father had built. It had four cast iron panes, which gave our mother a large space for cooking and for baking our potato pancakes. He had also installed a large built in vessel that would keep water hot for our use all day. He had also built a large oven that we stocked with coal. I told you, my father had studied to be an engineer. It was nothing short of ingenious, the work he did on the marvelous structure. On top of the oven was a flat three-foot square top where we could dry our wet clothing after playing in the rain or snow.

This was also the place where our big cat would often choose to take her nap. Each spring I would sit and watch the chimneysweeper that would come all dressed in his black suit and top hat, as he would work through the chimney cleaning out all the soot and ash. This stove had to be lovingly cared for since it was the soul and spirit of our home. In the middle of the kitchen was a large heavy wooden table with a long bench on each side of it for us children. Our father's place was at one end where he would preside over the meals in his large captain's chair; on the end our mother would observe our meals and manners. That table was never devoid of company, there was always laughter as well as Polish vodka for the adults. Aunts, uncles, close neighbors and friends were all part of our extended family. This was a happy time in my life. There wasn't much luxury, but there was so much togetherness, bursts of laughter over something someone said, tears falling over old memories. During troubled times I think about these memories and they ease my pain.

I loved our old house. Whenever I could I would wake up early to watch the milk wagon come clip-clopping down the street, sometimes I would doze off again to the creaking of the wagons as they moved from house to house.

In the kitchen was a flight of stairs no wider than a ladder actually, which led to two tiny bedchambers, which were tucked snugly under the eaves. There are times I still wish I could live in a house like that, a home centered around its kitchen.

This house was cozy, especially in the cold Siberian winter months. Its huge mantled fireplace was forever cluttered with items warming over the embers. The only room that actually had any heat was our kitchen. On cold nights our mother would heat up bricks in the oven, wrap them in towels and slip them into our huge feather bed. Bernhard and I shared a room as well as a bed so our joined body heat also kept us warm on those cold winter nights. We would have to chip away the heavy frost that covered our windows so we could see outside to witness the season's enchanting beauty. I savor the memories of snuggling under mother's feather bed while listening to the Siberian winds battering our old house. Our father rode back and forth to work on his bicycle, like most of his generation did, even in the winter. We would wait for him at the door, take the bike from his frozen fingers so he could go inside and warm up with a cup of Russian tea that our mother would have waiting for him before supper. There was no electricity, so after dark any work had to be done by either a petroleum lamp or candles. We also did not have the luxury of indoor plumbing, we had to use an outdoor outhouse. I hated using the small building in the summer because of the spiders, which would hang out waiting to drop down on you in your moment of weakness.

I remember a singularly severe winter in 1936. We had deep snowdrifts and the sun blinded us as it reflected off the smooth white surfaces. The day started out exceptionally mild, one would have thought spring was just around the corner. Anna and I walked to school enjoying the moment, but by mid day clouds had rolled in and a full blizzard was underway. School normally let out around two o'clock, but on this day we were still in our classrooms at five. We had to wait out the blizzard in the safety of the schoolhouse. There were very few telephones in our town, so there really was no way of communicating with our families to tell them we were safe and sound. We ended up spending the night in school, which was an adventure for us young children. The next day the snow was cleared away with horse drawn plows and men with shovels. School was canceled and we were sent home. The reward for this snow day was our mother's unforgettable chicken soup made with homemade kluski noodles. Many times on cold winter afternoons I find myself going back to those times and the aroma of chicken broth fills my senses and I can imagine my mother at the large table cutting the noodles on a floured board. As much as I enjoy cooking, I have never been able to duplicate her soup.

Many times, we would visit our grandparents' farm. While we were there, we would harness up the horses to our long sleigh, so they would get their winter workout. Grandfather would adorn the two horses with a set of brass or bronze sleigh bells and with each move the horses made they would jingle producing a lively sound. Sleigh bells served many purposes, they kept away predatory animals and alerted other horses and drivers to oncoming 'traffic'. Often times we would invite our cousins and enjoy a long sleigh ride through the countryside. It was an invigorating way to see all God's creation.

March in Poland is a fickle month. It will lure you in with a premature warm breeze and then can slam you with its icy Siberian blast and subzero temperatures as you go out. The sun often times is reluctant to come out for fear of being shooed away with clouds heavy with another load of snow that must be shed. For us children, March was a tug of war between clinging to the last of winter's snow fun and longing for the rituals of spring.

Even back then we had an 'ice cream man'. During the summer on warm afternoons we would wait for the sound of his jingling belled tricycle cart as it cruised the streets in search of hungry children in need of a sweet treat. Mother always set aside some ice cream money for us, a nickel for a cone. Looking back, I admire the patience this young man had as he waited for us children to make that agonizing decision as to what flavor would taste good that day. I remember that the ice cream man had lost a finger and thumb on his right hand, he told us that he lost it in a factory job, but he put a bright side to the story. The factory paid him one hundred sloty which he used to buy his wife a warm winter coat.

My parents worked untiringly and it was a rule that we work for our rewards. My brother Bernhard being two years older than me, had already proved himself to be a good worker so I was always having to live up to his reputation. I wasn't as strong as he was, but I did have determination. What I did have over my brother, was that I loved to run. My Friday duty was to run over to our stepmother's parents' house about six kilometers away to pick up a gallon of buttermilk. Our Friday dinner consisted of mashed potatoes flavored with sautéed golden brown onions, marinated herring and buttermilk made all the better when there was butter floating in it. My grandparents made it 'to order' and it was my job to churn the milk. This process took sometime for one had to move the dasher up and down until the butter started to float to the top, then the butter would be skimmed off the top, this butter would be lightly salted and pressed into wooden molds to be used in cooking and baking.

Christmas at Home

Christmas at home was a time when families came together to celebrate Christ's birth and as in most families, it was a very special time and tradition. There were no artificial trees, the trees were selected, usually a balsam fir, cut down by hand and decorated on Christmas Eve with real candles, homemade ornaments and tinsel. We created homemade garlands from the boughs of evergreens. Our mother made cookies and other little treats that would adorn our tree. I have always enjoyed the smell of a balsam fir. There is nothing like it to bring the Christmas spirit home. Everyone has beheld the excitement of the night before Christmas, so did we with what little we had. The best Christmas' were when there would be light snow falling and the ground turned powder white, not too much to hinder travel, but enough to make it feel like the holidays. On those winter nights, Bernhard and I would follow the town's lamp lighter as he moved throughout the city streets. His duties were to light the gas fired streetlights when it became too dark to see without light. He was a stout man who wore a uniform with brass buttons down the front of it and a novel looking brass helmet on his head. He had a routine that could be compared to a type of ballet. There were no wasted movements. He would first extend a long brass wand to the lamp in order to maneuver the hook that would release the latch on the square lantern that topped the lamppost. He would light the lamp casting a golden glowing circle that spread out below it. He would then close the lamp and move on to the next one all this took but a minute apiece and was such a thrill to watch.

Christmas at home was an intimate family occasion, since early times it had always been a very special day for children, I have to admit, of all ages. Back then this time was truly spent celebrating the birth of the Christ child. There were no gaudy store displays or garish accents, and it was a purer simpler time. Even though we knew what the day was representing, we did observe the tradition of Santa Claus. Even though no one had ever seen him, he was as real to us as our own parents were.

Not surprisingly, the Christmas dinner was an elaborate affair. Mother worked long hours to prepare it. One of the main items served was the Polatek an unleavened wafer that was shared in the house to symbolize that God was in the house. We had no television, no Rudolf the Red Nose Reindeer or It's a Wonderful Life, and we sang carols and enjoyed each other's company.

Our parish celebrated this blessed event for the true twelve days of Christmas. Starting on the sixth of January (Epiphany). Our parish priest would visit the homes of his congregation imparting a special blessing and marking the letters C, M, B (Caspar, Melchior, Balthasar) above the door of each of these houses. The receiver usually had ready a plate with special pastries and some tea for the Priest and his three Magi companions.

On My Grandparents' Farm

Whenever we could our parents would let us spend some of our summer vacation on our grandparents' farm. Both sets of our grandparents were farmers. Visits to them were always a special time for us children. We would take the train to Rosenberg or Kreuzburg, for each set lived in different cities. They lived in the German part of Poland and we needed passports in order to cross the invisible borders. The train ride alone was exciting for children our age. Anna got to dress up in her special velvet dress with its white collar and beautiful hat. We would get a window seat and I would open one for her, so she could look out and watch the scenery fly by. One time I did this, she stuck her head out and whoops, off flew her hat. Oh, she cried and cried; mother had her hands full trying to console her. Anna still remembers that and now we can laugh about it.

Our (biological) grandparents always met us at the station with their polished black carriage and well-groomed team of horses. As most people do, we named these magnificent animals (Max and Hans) for they were truly part of our family. The ride back to the farm was about ten kilometers and we enjoyed every minute of it, bouncing and rocking along the road enjoying the bucolic countryside in what felt like true luxury.

The farmhouse was cozy with its pinewood floors and crisp white walls. It sported a huge fireplace, which invited us into its heart. I remember my grandmother as being a gentle and loving person. Grandfather had a rough and robust exterior, but he was gentle with us children.

Grandfather taught me patience, for he always said that living in the country you had to be patient, for much of your time was spent waiting. You had to wait for the wheat to come up, the pigs to put on weight, the potatoes to mature, or the river to go down, the ground to thaw, the rain to come, for the rain to stop, you were forever waiting on the weather. Nothing is immediate; everything is in the process of recoming.

I loved his farm, the long stretches of farmland, the beautiful tracts of flax; its sea of purple flowers swaying in the wind. It's an unforgettable sight. This crop could be used to make almost everything from breads, cereals, to oil and more. There were cows, sheep, pigs, goats, chickens, geese, horses, and even turkeys. One was never dull on the farm; there was always something to do or to look at. Grandfather believed in not having anything on the farm that did not contribute to its overall economy. All the animals were carefully tended so the products derived from them were handled so to yield the maximum income.

Many idyllic summers were spent on the farm helping with the chores. Anna usually stayed with grandmother, while I spent my time with grandfather. Early in the morning, often before the rooster had awakened, I would hear the porch screen door springs shutting behind him and I would scramble out of bed and run barefoot after him, following him until sunset. He taught me that the soil is a living thing and it must be treated as such. Work on the farm was very interesting. I loved the sound of the rooster's crow, the sound of a blade being sharpened on the grinding wheel. My grandfather taught me how to split wood, he always said that wood heats you three times: when you cut it, when you stack it, and when you burn it. I helped him plow the fields; walking barefoot behind the plow that was pulled by horses, picking up fishing worms. I even learned how to operate the cultivator and spike tooth harrow even as a young child. I loved the sound of the hay wagons groaning under their loads.

Out of all the animals on the farm, I enjoyed the goats the most. They were inquisitive, mischievous, and quick. They could climb ladders and often got themselves up on to the rooftops. I loved to watch the cows; they often touched heads with each other, closing their eyes as if they were confiding something to each other. We got up early so we could feed the animals and get his team ready for the day's work. His hands were always busy; there was always something to do.

My main chore was to keep the horse stable clean, I didn't mind, because I liked the horses. I would clean the stalls and brush their coats until they shined. Like all cows, they grazed all day until it was time for milking. To get them back to the barn, grandfather stood near the big barn and cried out "co-pan, co-pan". No matter how far they were from the barn, they'd raise their heads and begin to slowly amble toward the barn.

On the rare mornings that I slept in, I would be awakened by the pleasant clop clop sound of the milkman's horse. He went around, collected the milk cans from the farms, and took them to the creamery. I remember to this day the first time he allowed me to turn the crank of the hand powered centrifuge (cream separator), to me this seemed to be the most powerful innovative tool in the world. It could separate the cream from the milk, which was used to make butter. Grandmother would then chill the buttermilk for a healthy summer treat.

At night, I would let the wind lull me to sleep. Often I would drift off as it built up a riotous symphony rattling the doors and windows like they were snare drums. I remember there being a gap in the roof somewhere which would send the sound like a flute through the house. I had a unique companion on the farm next to the goats, which I adored. There was a small barn owl which would perch in a nearby tree and hoot to me at night. I used to worry that he was lonely since no other owls ever answered his call, some nights he seemed so forlorn.

Like most of the people I knew, we didn't have indoor plumbing so roughing it on my grandparents' farm was no different from what I was used to. My grandfather used to recite this little ditty that he composed:

If you had to go awful bad and be mighty, bold
When the snow piled up and the wind blowed cold.
One thing about it, there's no lost motion
You don't go out till you get the notion.
You don't sit and read or linger long
You do the job and then move right along.

My grandparents were very religious. We prayed before each meal, giving thanks to the Lord for our bounty. On Saturday's we would brush and groom the horses and pull out the black carriage so we could ride in it after Sunday breakfast the six kilometers to church.

The Saturday trips to town were a special treat for us. I would get up early to ready Max and Hans for the trip, hooking them up to the wagon from the barn. Everyone rushed to get cleaned up and into good clothes before we piled into the wagon. We got an allowance from Grandmother based on the work we did. Bernhard always got a little more, because he was older and could do more chores. Grandfather would light his long curved pipe, with the sound of "Hoo-Ho" Hans and Max would pull hard on the harness, and we would be on our way. We hummed tunes as we rode along and enjoyed the scenery. The first stop for Grandfather was the lumberyard; he always needed some for repairs. There was a table saw at the far end and you could tell what the owner was cutting by the sound the saw made. A steady 'zip zip zip' meant he was cutting laths, a sustained whirring meant planks were being processed, and if the saw started out at a high note and droned down, we knew he was cutting two-by-fours. The lumber building was a barn like structure with two floors, it held his entire inventory; the array of materials was only matched by their diversity of textures and smells. Pickets drenched in creosote mingled a bittersweet odor with the tangy freshness that arose from bundles of cedar shakes. Asphalt shingles were gently abrasive and the oak paneling bore a finish as smooth as alabaster. The owner knew Grandfather very well and trusted me to look around without getting into anything. I often wandered into his crowded office and would begin nosing around. The walls were covered with colored prints and calendar pictures of scenes depicting the highlands of Upper Silesia and the Hohe Tatra a mountain range of Poland near the Czechoslovakian border. I never tired of looking at them. What I enjoyed the most though was the lumberyard's inner reaches the working area of the operation. After we finished and the wagon would be loaded, we would board the horses so they could rest and be fed while we finished our errands.

From there, we all headed over to the drug store to shop off the list that was sent by our grandmother. We would be quite excited by then for we would be able to buy an ice cream and make our selection of sweets from his wide variety of candies that he displayed. The eight-foot counter started at his medicine shelves and ended at the magazine and newspaper display. What wonders that counter beheld for us children! Jawbreakers, jellybeans, suckers, gumdrops, peppermint sticks, and licorice whips and there were dozens of other kinds of bulk candies for us to choose from. Candy filled the trays inside and in huge jars on top of the cabinet. I felt sorry for Pan Kolaski, the shopkeeper, for he was constantly cleaning that glass case of finger and nose prints put there by zealous children anxious to indicate their preferences. It took my sister Anna what seemed to be an eternity to make her selection; agonizing over the selection was almost as much fun as eating them.

After we finished our rounds, it would be time for lunch. We would step outside and the streets would be full of farmers and their wagons, everyone took this day to restock their supplies. We ate our lunch in the back of the wagon from a food basket packed by our grandmother, everyone brought one and by noon, the whole street looked like one big picnic site. By one o'clock it would be time to leave, sometimes if the load wasn't too heavy Grandfather would encourage Hans and Max to pick up the pace and we would all laugh and sing as we jostled down the road. We never missed the opportunity to marvel at nature as we rode out in the open of the wagon. We had no video games or DVD players in the back to keep us occupied, therefore we were always taking in what was going on around us. Grandfather often would remark that this was God's country and we needed to give thanks for it and relish it.

When it was time to return to our home, we were always sad to leave. Our father would take the train and spend the night on the farm, the next day we would all pile back into the wagon for the ride back to the train station. Usually in fall once school started everyone would have to write an essay about what they did during the summer and I always had something to write about.

I remember one occasion on my step-grandparents' farm I was asked to watch and learn how to milk the cows. A few days later, I was given two gentle cows to try my hand at milking. I didn't do too badly, in spring it was easy since they gave up their milk willingly, in summer as the flies and the heat got to them things got a little more complicated. They would constantly be swishing their tails back and forth to get the flies off them and often hit me in the back or side of my head. Sometimes I think they did it on purpose. One day the cows had gotten into the cockleburs and 'Jean' got tangled in them; she swished her tail full of burrs into my head one too many times and having had enough of her antics I divided her tail in half and tied it to her legs. I got back to my job of milking quite satisfied with my solution. Suddenly, the urge to swish became too much and the harder she tried to free her tail the more frustrated she got. Finally, she pulled free knocking me from my stool and ran from the barn bucking and kicking like a young colt. Needless to say, my bucket was on its side and I was on the floor laughing. Everyone came running to see what the ruckus was all about and had a good laugh over what I had done. The next morning Grandfather had to cut those burrs out and by the time he was done, she didn't have much of a tail left.

The last time I was able to visit all three sets of grandparents was in 1941, before the war made it impossible to travel. I never saw them again; all I have left are my memories of the times I spent on their farms and the life lessons I learned from them.

Man Carrying Bale

The rough hand closes gently on the load; out of the mind
a voice calls "lift!" and arms remembering well their work
lengthen and pause for help, then a slow ripple flows
along the body while
all the muscles call to one another "lift!'
and the bulging bale floats like a butterfly in June.
So moved the earliest carriers of bales and the same watchful
sun glowed through his body feeding it with light.
So will the last one move and halt and dip his head
and lay his load down and the muscles will relax and tremble …
earth you designed your man beautiful both in labor and repose.

Fräulein Jalowski

A short distance from our home lived an old lady, Fräulein Jalowski (a distant kin of the once German chancellor, Von Bismark), she was a retired teacher; my parents knew her very well. She lived alone in a big house and was unable to get around on her own, so she rarely ventured outside. She had a huge garden behind her house, but as much as she enjoyed it, she was unable to tend it; my stepmother and my siblings and I would go over and care for the garden. One summer my father built her a gazebo. On nice days, I would help her down the stairs, the two of us would sit inside it for hours watching the butterflies, and bees swoop from flower to flower gleefully humming their song.

One day she asked my mother if I would go to the general store for her and pick up a few items she needed. When I arrived at her home, I was allowed to enter by the front door which had a bell attached to it that would announce when someone came to visit. Visitors would find her sitting in a large 'queen-anne' chair where she could observe the comings and goings of her guests. When I entered that day, she called me by my middle name, Maximilian. I was to go into the room opposite the parlor to retrieve her purse. I had never been in that room before. It was an airless room, which made it seem extremely oppressive. I could smell that a fire had recently been kindled in the old fashioned grate. You could tell that the room was once very handsome, but it had fallen to neglect. There was a film of dust on every surface. The room seemed to have been stopped in the middle of a dinner or gathering. It was as though time came to a standstill.

The most prominent object in the room was a long table covered with a lace tablecloth. I remember there being a centerpiece of some kind on the table, but the room had been neglected so long that the piece was almost indistinguishable for the cobwebs, which hung from it. I recall cringing as I watched the speckled legged spiders running around on the beautiful lace cloth. For a moment I couldn't move. In the silent room, I could hear the sound of mice running behind the walls' wooden panels. The only thing that exhibited life was the swinging of the pendulum of the grandfather clock, which stood in the far corner. The sound of the clock's striking still resound in my head. I must have hesitated a bit too long in the still room, for I heard Fräulein Jalowski call out to me, her voice brought me back to earth. I quickly found her purse and rushed out of the room.

She handed me her shopping list and five zloty (Polish currency). Glancing at the list, I was surprised to notice a true luxury item on the list, kaffee-bohnen (coffee-beans). Most people could not afford real coffee beans and made their own roasted coffee beans from grains like rye or barley. My mother would roast her own 'beans" with a special recipe that only she knew.

My chore when I returned was to grind the beans for Fräulein Jalowski. She had a small wooden grinder, which I had to grip between my knees so I could turn the handle. I'd ground the beans before for her; she insisted only twenty beans at a time. She wanted her coffee to taste the same with each cup she made. Once I tested her and ground twenty-two beans. I sat back and watched her expression, as she tasted her fresh brew. To my shame, she called out my name and complained that the coffee was too strong; she scolded me for wasting those precious gems. I lied to her and told her I had done what she had asked and she called me out and made me promise never to do it again.

Over the months that I visited with her, I learned that she once enjoyed playing the piano. In her parlor was a grand piano. It was a piece of beauty with its heavy and ornately carved legs. Even as a young boy, I was aware that a Steinway, which is what she owned, was very precious and valuable. The piano had always fascinated me. It was my favorite instrument. To see it covered in layers of dust saddened me. One time when I ventured into the room, I noticed that there were two music books displayed on the notebook bracket. One was titled 'Mozart's Kleinenacht Musik' (Mozart's Minuet) and the other was the 'Third Movement of the Ninth Symphony, I loved this piece, it depicted God reaching for the hand of Adam in Michelangelo's vision of the creation. Beethoven wrote this piece when he was deaf. Fräulein Jalowski had to quit playing when the arthritis in her hands would no longer allow her fingers to caress the keys. She shared with me that even though she enjoyed Beethoven and Mozart; Chopin was her favorite composer. She loved music and taught me much of its history and beauty.

As I said before, she was a retired teacher. Her favorite subject was history. She told me many stories about Kaiser Wilhelm as well as stories about her travels to China and Africa. I could sit there for hours and listen to her. Her life was amazing. Sometimes when I had upset her for some reason, my punishment would be to walk her around the parlor. She would lay her hand on my shoulder and lean on me. We would walk round and round the room. You could tell that even though we may have been moving around the room at a painfully slow pace, the twitching of her hands and mouth betrayed that inside her body, we were running. If I tried to stop out of regard for her, she would chastise me that there was no need to rest and we would continue our laps. Many times, she would mumble words I didn't understand; she spoke French and German as well as Polish. We would continue this activity until she decided she had had enough. At that point I would walk her over to her chair, place her crutch by her side so she could move around when she needed to.

Without fail we visited Fräulein Jalowski two times a week. She had become a part of our family. One day late in the summer of 1939, we walked the short distance to her home. When we entered her home as we did on many occasions, we found her laying on the floor in the entryway. We rushed to her side; she was breathing, but unconscious. We did what we could to make her comfortable, getting her a pillow to put under her head and a glass of water for when she came to. When she finally woke, she couldn't speak. Mother gave her a drink and she asked where she was. As quietly as she woke, she again closed her eyes. We were all scared. There was no telephone, no way of calling 911 as one can today. Mother suggested that I run and fetch our family doctor. Before I left, we carefully lifted Fräulein Jalowski to her couch. Once I was assured she was situated I took off down the road. I knew where Doctor Koworoczak lived, about one kilometer from where we were. I ran there as fast as I could. It was the quickest kilometer I would ever run. Luckily, I found him in his office. I quickly explained what had happened and he agreed to come. He assured me he would come as soon as he finished with his patient. I pleaded with him to hurry and headed back. About an hour late, he peddled up to her front porch (he did not own a car).

His demeanor was serious when he assessed Fräulein Jalowski's condition. We children were asked to leave the room. The minutes ticked by painfully slow as we waited for some news good or bad from either our mother or the doctor. After what seemed to be an eternity, Doctor Koworoczak opened the door and addressed us, telling us that Fräulein Jalowski would be just fine. Mother enlisted Anna and me to stay with Fräulein while she and the others went and got her some food. Over the next few days her health improved and she eventually recovered.

I'm embarrassed to admit that I didn't like Fräulein Jalowski when I first met her. She intimidated me, but thankfully, I allowed myself to open up and receive her and found that she had much to share and even more to teach those who wanted to learn from her. Many times, I realized she tested me in some way each time I visited her and I thank her for taking an interest in me.

One of the most important lessons she taught me was punctuality. If I had a set time to be at her home or was to be somewhere for her, I had to be on time or she would find a way to 'teach me a lesson'. We fell into a simple routine. I would go and buy her coffee beans, grind only twenty and she would hum her favorite tune from Johan Strauss: "Nur, nur, nur du allein solst fur immer meine freude sein" (Only, only, only you alone shall forever be my joy).

She was a remarkable lady. She taught me right from wrong and on quiet days, we often would pray. We played chess and she would read to me from her small library. One of her favorite verses was:

"Goethe's Faust – Bergschloss"
(The Castle on the Mountain)
Da droben auf jenem berge
Da steht ein altes schloss
Wo hinter toren und türen
Sonst lauerten ritter und ross.

*****

(There yonder on the hill, there stands an old castle where behind gates and doors otherwise knights and horse would hide.)

It was comforting to hear her smooth German voice reading to me. We had to be careful, since it was forbidden by the Polish government to speak German in public. She reminded me often never to mention that she read to me in German. It was to be our secret.

My special world came crashing down in August, when my mother found Fräulein Jalowski had passed away in her sleep. My mother was concerned about how I would react to the news. I was miserable. I had lost my best friend. She had given me so much and had expected so little in return.

Over the next month, Hitler invaded our town of Tarnowskie-Góry, tanks rolled over our cobbled streets. My life had changed drastically. My mother did what she could to ease my pain. The lesson I learned was that "suffering is a test of faith...If God's love calls you in suffering, respond by self surrender and you will learn the mystery of love."

WW II Begins

Before Hitler invaded our town, it had a type of medieval feel to it. You could hear church bells toll and could walk in silence and without fear. Everyone living without prejudice and in harmony with each other. There were only three cars in the whole city and they belonged to the doctor, the butcher, and the cab owner. There was a huge and well manicured park. Within the city with thousands of flowers and many walkways leading in all directions, within it there were magnificent fountains which spewed water into the air then falling splat into the reflecting pools situated underneath. This idealistic atmosphere seemed to change overnight with Hitler's invasion into our quiet life on September 1, 1939; our lives were forever altered. Ravaged by war, people began to panic. Early that morning we heard the drone of hundreds of bombers which obscured the sun and detonated our unique universe with the explosion of bombs falling on our railroad yards between Poland and Germany as well as many other industrial targets. I will never forget that day, we were on our way to church. At first we thought it was just thunder, but when we realized what was happening we ran to the safety of the church only to find it empty but for Father Tadeusz Barczik who was kneeling before the alter. We stayed inside until we felt we could possibly make it back to our home. Before we left, Mother and Father Barczik talked together and with a prayer sent us on our way. It seemed like the exploding bombs were chasing us and nipping at our heels as we ran as fast as we could back home. I felt sorry for Anna who was nine at the time as she cried out with each thundering detonation. Only Anna and I were with Mother, while Maria and Bernhard had stayed home doing chores. We called out to them as we flung open the door and rushed inside the house, but there was no answer. Frantically, we looked for them and finally found them in the barn finding solace with the calming atmosphere of our farm animals. They had barricaded the doors with bales of hay in a futile attempt to keep the enemy out. I will never forget that fateful day of September 1, 1939.

Mother's clear headedness had us take shelter in our keller (basement), just in time to hear the unopposed Stukas (dive bombers) swooping down to unload their bombs. Our house was built with a solid rock foundation, yet that day it shook as though it were a bowl of jelly. I remember my mother sitting there with a calm exterior with her back against the wall, but I knew with the concentrated look that was on her face she was praying with all her soul that we would survive this horrible day. Our father was not home so we needed to rely on our mother's strength to get us through this. Many years later, she told us that she was in her twenties during World War I. She was all too familiar with the tragedies that would follow these events.

A few days after the first bombings, many people fearful of what might happen to them decided to leave the city, packing up their belongings and loading up handcarts and whatever other type of vehicle they had and moved on to what they hoped would be a safer location. The first ones to flee were those families who had political ties to the Polish government. We noticed right off that our Jewish neighbors too were gone. Quickly, news spread of the atrocities committed by the invading German Wehrmacht and the Jews were particularly being targeted. We asked our parents if we were going to leave and they said they had worked too hard to make this their home and they were going to stay. We put our trust in the Lord that he would watch out for us.

In the week that followed, the full impact of the war became apparent. Hitler targeted savage devastation through every means at the Polish people, their pride, its nationhood, and the culture. The Nazis closed the churches, schools and universities. They set fire to the Synagogue which was across from our home, and within what seemed to be moments, all our Jewish friends and neighbors vanished. German soldiers pillaged whenever possible. They targeted political figures in all walks of life by inflicting maximum humiliation and bodily harm. They arrested Polish professors, teachers, lawyers, and doctors.

This became a turning point in my life, I was twelve years old. Some mornings we were jolted out of our beds with horrific explosions. The four of us would huddle together in a room until we felt it safe enough to move to the basement. It frightened me to the core that this once bucolic town with dirt roads and peaceful atmosphere was being targeted for reasons unknown to us. For hours we would have to endure the heavy drone of planes flying overhead, waiting with dreaded anticipation for the inevitable explosions that would follow, shaking with fear sometimes I could not distinguish who shook more, me or the house. Despite these events, those who stayed had to maintain their lives as best they could. While there was work yet available, men and women went to their jobs. Gardens still needed to be tended or food would run out, livestock what was left had to be cared for or they would die. We did the best we could under the circumstances. It is amazing where those reserves of strength come from in times of trouble.

One day we stood in stunned silence as we watched our neighbor's house go up in flames. It was a beautiful structure and it hurt to the bone to watch it being reduced to ash, I had never seen such a fire. I could see tears rolling down the faces of all who watched this spectacle for we all knew, what treasures were being destroyed inside and felt it was such a waste. Of course, with a fire so near, we were afraid that our own home would burn. Mother decided that she couldn't stop it if it would start, since we had a black tar roof and wood throughout the house, so she made the decision for us to leave and go into town and if God had decided that our home was to burn it would do so without us watching it. When we returned that afternoon, we were relieved to see that it had been spared and gave a quick prayer of thanks. We helped out our neighbors in whatever way we could, so they could get back on their feet.

Our father at that time was working in a coal mine and was not able to get home to us for four days. He had been told to keep the mine running at whatever cost. Stores closed when supplies ran out for no more stock was allowed in to the town. Like I said before, we were pretty self-sufficient and had plenty of food in our larder to tide us over thanks to the frugality of our mother.

One day when we went into town, we came to the town square only to find that our schoolbooks were piled up and had been set on fire. It burned for days. Our lives changed rapidly. Everyone worked even harder to be supportive of each other and to help out in whatever way they could. Many times, I would stand and watch in awe at the endless stream of friends and neighbors fleeing our once peaceful city. Stories of labor camps and prosecution for trumped up crimes made everyone fearful. The Jews vanished one by one and eventually they were all gone. Many were my friends and I missed them terribly. The Hitlerism was soon imposed on all the citizens and we all felt the pressure of the SS who patrolled the streets without mercy. The war progressed quickly and Hitler's Blitz-Krieg over Poland escalated rapidly. More and more troops passed through our town, long freight trains loaded with tanks, heavy artillery trucks, and German soldiers. The war completely altered the course of men and the Polish nation. Families were destroyed and lost everything they had worked for generations to obtain, land homes, possessions, and most of all their freedom. Millions were refugees devoid of any hope of returning to their homes, much less staying alive. I only hope and pray that they are at peace and have an eternal place in heaven. All these events remain deeply etched in my memory. What took generations to build, Hitler destroyed in twelve years. To Hitler violence seemed the only obvious way to power.

Eventually, we managed to find some sense of order and after two months, the town found a way for us children to once again attend school. The Polish textbooks had been burned and the schools closed, so we were put into German schools; it was as though we were starting over. We had to read and speak German since Polish was forbidden. What helped us get through this, was the fact that both our parents spoke German as well as their native Polish. Academically I began to fall behind, most of my classmates were of German descent and the change was nothing to them. Socially, I was at a total loss, with all my Jewish friends having been taken from their homes by the Nazis. It is remarkable how a child can rebound under difficult circumstances and eventually I made friends with my new classmates.

It was now 1942, almost three years after Hitler's invasion of our country. Poland no longer existed. What had replaced it was a state of tyranny, despair, and hopelessness. Only small fragments of Polish families remained. Their lives destroyed because the Russians had permitted and encouraged Hitler to destroy Warsaw and their country. Poland was raped not only by Hitler's Nazi armies, but by Stalin's insatiable greed of power and material. Stalin stripped the country of its industrial and agricultural wealth, calling it war booty.

When I turned fifteen I found myself with no choice but to join the Jung volk or the Hitler Youth. The rules were strict and the punishments harsh. The Nazis had passed a law requiring all Aryan children to join this 'organization', just as their elders had been drafted into the Wehrmacht. Curfews were set into place and strictly enforced no matter where you were or what you were doing. Punishments were costly and harsh.

I was forced to take part in "land service' during the summer and fall to help farmers harvest their crops. Most of the younger men had been sent to war and farms needed the extra help. I left home and was barracked in a camp in the village. We took cold showers, performed vigorous exercises before being dropped off at whichever farm we were to work at for the day. I was lucky enough to be placed with a farmer in the town of Grotkau for we got along well. I was treated well by both him and his wife. The wife never called me by name, but always referred to me as 'mein junge' (my boy); both their sons had been drafted and they missed them terribly. I was no longer in control of my life and missed the daily interaction with my family and my service to the church as an altar boy. At the age of fifteen, I began to walk a path upon which I did not know where it would take me.

"Allein, und doch nicht ganz allein bin ich immer
in meiner einsamkeit"
****
*"Alone and yet not quite alone am I always in my great
loneliness"*

Children with Star

As hard as it was to imagine how many children had been forced into horrendous work and living conditions imposed by the Nazis, a whole generation was growing up without a spark of joy in their lives. These were the Jewish children, who through no fault of their own had lost their innocence and their childhood.

Jewish children were forced to have a yellow star sewn and displayed on the outside of their clothing. Many of these children were homeless and alone, forced to wander the streets scavenging for their next bite of food and a place to stay warm.

It is unthinkable even to this day how human beings can inflict this type of pain and suffering on the innocent and helpless. My parents were Catholics and were always concerned about other people who needed help. I remember one episode when a mother and her two children showed up on our doorstep asking for food. We didn't have much at this time for food was being rationed, but mother found a way to help them. There was another time when two Jewish families met up with us and after explaining their predicament we gave them shelter. For two days, we hid them in our basement while our father tried to obtain papers for them so they could go to Belgium, a country yet untouched by Hitler. We would have let them stay longer, but somehow the SS had been tipped out to the possibility of what we had done and our home was raided. Soldiers ran from room to room shouting for us to tell them where the Jews were hiding, they even checked our goat stall in the barn. They shouted at my mother and we all were crying, it was a traumatic experience. Finding nothing, they had to leave, but threatened that they would be back. That night the families left. I knew I could never tell anyone what we had done, we no longer knew who we could trust.

For weeks, we were the target of random searches, but they never found anything. One day they took our father away to an undisclosed location for several weeks. When he returned home he was a different man, he never talked to us children about what had happened to him; if he told our mother we do not know.

Not all Germans supported what Hitler was doing, not even his own armies at times, but fear can make you do things you would not normally do.

During one of my forced labor assignments, I came across two Jewish men who were hiding on a farm. I never told anyone for fear they would be killed, but the farmer was found out and the Nazis arrested him and his sons. At the time, we children could just not comprehend why this was all happening, I am sure that most adults couldn't either. Many times, we whispered to each other in the dark, whether we would be snatched from our family and homes like those around us had been.

We learned later that some of the Jewish families had been sent to the 'Ghetto of Lodz', a city approximately 100 kilometers from Tarnowskie-Góry. Maria by now had married a Polish officer and was living in Lodz. She wrote to us about having witnessed first hand the unimaginable atrocities committed by the SS and the Gestapo.

To this day, as I reflect on the past I can now summarize it with these three words: Painful, Promising, and Rewarding. It was through hope, faith, and prayer that I was able to work through the long dark tunnel of my past.

The war affected our home, the shadow of necessity never left our table and made us silent. Long gone were those carefree days of laughter. We had been rudely forced out of our childhood. The struggle for life got to us early; misery, shame, hatred, lies brought on by the war imprinted themselves on our souls and made us mature well beyond our years. Our lives became sad and painful our once closely-knit family was torn apart by these events. People became depressed unable to express themselves but through violence. Food was in ever-short supply and had been rationed. Every family was issued a ration book that they could use to purchase only items listed in the booklet. I remember many times, my mother having to leave groceries behind because she did not have enough or the right stamps to cover the cost of her purchases. You couldn't use real money, for it couldn't be tracked. This was Hitler's way of funding his army, he traded food for tanks.

Auschwitz

Leaving my home, my parents, my sisters Anna and Maria, and my brother Bernhard in April of 1943, I thought it would only be temporary. I thought I would be home by Christmas. I was much unprepared for the grief I felt when I realized this would not be the case. The night before my departure, my stepmother tried to comfort me as best she could. My parents assured me we would see each other again soon. This was something I had to do. They promised they would visit me in Auschwitz where I was to begin my apprenticeship as an intern in a newly built hotel; but I was inconsolable.

I cried for most of the night. The thought of only seeing my family on special occasions was hard. We were a very close-knit family having lost two members of it already; no one wanted to be parted from each other. I especially had strong bonds to my family and would be very hard for me to say goodbye when the time came.

However, the time came and so did the hour. It was a gray and cloudy morning. My father and I walked the three kilometers to the train station. My stepmother chose not to say goodbye at the station and stayed home. When we said our farewells, her soft gray eyes were over brimming with tears. She after all had taken on all four of us when our biological mother went to heaven. As my father and I walked through the so familiar streets of Tarnowskie-Góry, Poland; over the cobblestone-paved streets I couldn't help but take in the beauty of our renaissance town. Its historical buildings housed Napoleon Bonaparte in 1812 when he marched his troops toward Russia. Other kings and princesses dined at the renowned Sedlacek Wine-Stuben during their time in power. This was my hometown and I was reluctant to leave it. I wondered how long it would be when I would be able to see it and my family again; turns out it was sixteen long painful years. We passed my school the Mark Graffen School, named after the town's benefactor Mark Graf. This was before Tarnowitz was ceded to Poland centuries later and renamed Tarnowskie-Góry.

In too short of a time, we were standing on the platform waiting for the train to come. I took this time to take one last look around at the countryside as well as savoring the crisp early spring air. Our terminal was an impressive domed structure. Inside there were two restaurants where many important travelers from many different European countries dined.

In the distance, I could see the dark smoke spewing out of the huge locomotive, much like a monster eating its way toward the terminal. I couldn't help but reminisce about family trips my siblings and I along with our parents took to visit our grandparents in Rosenberg. We always took the train. So exciting and eventful these train rides were to us children. Our grandfather would bring his big wagon and his favorite team of horses (Max and Hans). We would sing songs until we got to their farm where we would spend a few days. However, this trip did not hold that type of childish excitement for me. This monster train would take me away from my hometown and my loved ones. It was a very sad moment in my life. My father and I spoke little as we stood together on the platform. I do not remember all that was said, although one bit of wisdom he imparted to me was to understand that through my life's journey I would be put through a series of tests, and most likely this being the easiest of all of them. He reminded me that the road of life is never straight, that suffering is essential to human survival; it makes us strong and helps us endure its many trials and tribulations. All too soon, the train conductor called for the passengers to board. My father and I embraced for the last time before I climbed up the stairs.

I was able to get a window seat where I could look out at my father. He looked worried and his eyes emitted sadness. He stood there in his black suit holding his homburg in his hands. The train let out a loud shrill from its steam whistle and slowly set into motion. As it increased in speed, I stood up at the window to continue waving goodbye to my father until his face faded away into the gray mist of that April morning.

I was saddened to the core to be leaving my home and my family and most of all the few memories I had of my biological mother. I was leaving my childhood and my friends behind. If I was to let myself think about all the bad times I had endured over the years to date, this adventure might find a positive aspect. I would be leaving the horror of Hitler's reign and its aftermath. When his armies invaded our country in September of 1939, their main goal was to persecute the Jews. Many of my friends disappeared. Hitler's men burned the synagogue across from our home. It was a beautiful structure. My father helped build it. Such devastation instills lasting memories into all who survive it.

Leaving home was not by choice, but dictated by the horrible WWII and the post war years that followed. My father made me promise not to give up. He always said that giving up was a sign of weakness. I knew I could not let my father down.

I was young; I did not even know where Auschwitz was. I knew it was about 75 kilometers from Tarnowskie-Góry and near the city of Krakow. We were told that the city was still occupied by the German Wehrmacht. All I knew is that I was leaving my home and family. My new guardian was to be Herr Kleinert, he owned the Stadt-hotel, a large casino, and an Inn.

What we didn't know and not many did was that there were concentration camps there. No one talked about this out of fear that the reign would soon affect our people. It was a frightful time for all of us. Were our Jewish friends alive? Were they in those concentration camps? Would we ever see them again? No one knew.

I had taken train trips with my classmates to Krakow, Czenstochowa and Kattowice; as well as our family trips to Rosenberg. This was the first time that I had been on a train alone. I sat 'alone' in the train compartment. Even though it was crowded in the train car, I felt alone. I passed the time watching the various groups of people; all looked worn and depressed. In large numbers, it was easy to see how the war had ravaged these people how they had to struggle to live, how little they cared about anything. It was sad to see this side of humanity.

I made myself think about my future. My education that would continue under the care of Herr Kleinert and soon I became anxious to get to my destination. The train stopped at each small town along the route. Around mid afternoon, we finally pulled into Auschwitz. I waited inside the car letting others leave while my boyish body trembled in anticipation of what lay ahead. Everything would be strange and new to me and I would be experiencing it without my family's support. It took some courage for me to leave the security of the train, but finally I made my way to the platform. I carried my luggage with me and stood there watching in wonder as people ran back and forth. People were everywhere; I did not know what to do.

I looked around trying to find someone who resembled the photograph my father had shown me the night before of Herr Kleinert, I did not see him. I decided to stay still and wait for him to find me. Suddenly a tall man approached me. I can still see how striking he looked in his black suit, pinstriped pants, silver tie, and homburg; he looked like an English lord. He walked up to me and asked if I was by any chance the boy from Tarnowskie-Góry by the name of Franz Skaletz? I told him I was he told me he was Herr Heiduck (Herr Kleinert's assistant). He explained to me in German that he had been sent to welcome me and to bring me back to the Stadt-Hotel.

He led me to a waiting limousine I was awestruck. I liked this man from the very first moment I saw him. He relieved some of the apprehension that had built up during the past few days. He carried my hard cardboard suitcase without any indication of my 'station in life'; I insisted that I carry my meager box of possessions therefore holding on to my life for a while in my own hands. He again welcomed me to Auschwitz as we climbed into the waiting automobile. I had never ridden in a motorcar before so this was indeed a grand experience.

It was only a short ride from the railroad station to the Stadt-Hotel. Once there Herr Heiduck took me into the lobby, I paused to take in my surroundings. It was simply beautiful and I was overwhelmed by its splendor. I thought I was in a different world, was I dreaming? Herr Heiduck, anxious to deliver me to his boss told me to follow him. We came to a grand set of door and I was told this was Herr Kleinert's personal office. Upon entering, we came up to his secretary a nice attractive woman sitting at a desk just inside the outer office area. She told us that we were expected and to go on in.

My guardian, Herr Kleinert also wore a black suit, white shirt and silver tie, the attire of a true hospitality businessman. He seemed to be very friendly as he warmly greeted me. After a brief orientation I was told that Herr Heiduck would be my immediate supervisor and that I would be staying at the Inn, but I would be working at the casino and when needed, here at the Stadt-Hotel. I think that all that I was experiencing helped me forget temporarily about leaving my family and home.

As our meeting was ending, the phone rang and he told me that his wife wanted to meet me. I had noticed a picture of a beautiful woman on the shelf behind his desk and had assumed it was Frau Kleinert. She was even more beautiful in person. Tall and well dressed she towered over me, all of six feet compared to my five foot one. She warmly welcomed me to their town and immediately I felt right at home. After a brief discussion between Herr Kleinert and Herr Heiduck, we left his office. In the lobby, I could not help but notice a number of impeccably dressed SS officers walking about, saluting each other as they passed in their tours of the hotel.

During the ride to the Inn, I was told that from here on, I would walk to work and to school and must learn my routes. I realized immediately that what I was to experience would have a great impact on my future. Herr Kleinert, a man of unusual stature would become my mentor and I his protégé. He would be responsible for contributing a great deal to my education and would help me in many ways. A new milestone was unfolding for me in a new city. Who would have guessed at this point in my life that events would haunt me the rest of my life.

The Apprenticeship and Internship

The day after my arrival in Auschwitz, Herr Heiduck came to the Inn to tell me we had to go to the police headquarters and report in that I had left Tarnowskie-Góry. It was mandatory by law that if any person moved permanently from one town or city to another that this person had to provide an affidavit from the previous residence to the police, failure to do so could have serious consequences. After all, Germany was a police state. At the police station my papers were checked and found to be in good order, I was now officially a resident of Auschwitz. From here, we went to the Chamber of Commerce so I could be registered as an apprentice. By noon we were done.

My father had signed my apprentice/internship contract before I left home. These formalities had to be followed so I could begin my tutelage under Herr Kleinert. Herr Kleinert was a master chef, German born, but he had lived several years in Paris before WWII. He was a graduate of the renowned L'ecole Hoteleire de la Scoiete Suisse, Lausanne, a college in Lausanne, Switzerland (specializing in culinary arts and hotel hospitality management). Little did I know that I myself would attend the same college several years later after WWII.

I learned quickly that Herr Kleinert was an indefatigable and vigorous man, always there for me when I needed him and always with a kind smile. He was unequivocally methodical, organized, and thorough in everything he did; and he expected no less from his subordinates. He knew all the facets of a hotel operation and food preparation. As the owner and director of the operation, he would spend considerable hours in the large and bright kitchen dressed in black trousers, crisp white shirt, yellow tie and snow-white chef's coat, and his toque (a tall chef's hat a symbol of a professional chef). He was a gifted and talented man. No task was too small or too big for him. He had a very distinguished form of speaking; he was larger than life. Many things he demonstrated to me became a part of my life. What I had learned over the course of three years became invaluable to me later on and he helped me make it through some very difficult and hard times in my life. Herr Kleinert was a man of impressive stature and his professional knowledge was unequalled in my aspects.

Working at the Stadt-Hotel at times under his supervision was an extraordinary experience. His constantly shifting degustation menu, always aimed to trump itself. He would often explain to his kitchen staff that elegant culinary meals should last for hours, when in fact they <u>need</u> to last for hours. Showing his culinary art, alternating between sweet and savory, hot and cold, familiar and worldly. He was truly a master of his craft. As a master in his craft, he could produce the finest dishes one can only imagine. Carrots turned into soft foam or mousse. Foie Gras into ice cream, tortoise into potage a'la 'lady curzon'. Herr Kleinert maintained a small laboratory at his Hotel where he would experiment with almost everything from centrifuges to cotton candy machines. He always looked for changes in cuisine art and demanded that food was not only well prepared, but needed also to be consistent. He mentioned it quite often and wanted his kitchen staff to know that culinary art is indeed a science.

He used to say to his staff that the 'foodies' of the world have always changed since the time of 'Auguste George Escoffier', the King of Chefs. Auguste was one of the greatest French chefs and that the age of discovery will never end. There was another comment Herr Kleinert made, "He who would become a good saucier must understand the importance of the ritual of the roux. The ritual of the roux adds a distinctive texture and taste to food you cannot get any other way.

As I stated before he was a very meticulous man, not only in his kitchen as the master chef, but also in his management style. He had impeccable manners and would never accept anything but the best from his staff. I slowly began to realize how fortunate I had been to be around such a man. He built a lasting legacy as the architect in the hospitality industry. However, he had to travel a very rough road during the Nazi regime, sans regret I suppose, to maintain his unfaltering image. It was unimaginable how this man could function as though nothing was going on around him, yet incorporating it all into his operation.

Frau Kleinert was not a very visible entity, yet she was able to always make herself known and felt throughout. She was a very well dressed woman and seemed self composed, yet once you got to know her, you would find she was rather shy. She always inquired about me and seemed to genuinely care for my well-being. She was wise enough to stay out of her husband's way when there were important functions at the Hotel. She knew he and we needed to focus. Some of these events catered to the higher-ranking SS officers, German Wehrmacht officers as wells as civilians.

Herr Kleinert was a legend in his own way. Working under his leadership was not only very educational but also very enlightening. He possessed an entrepreneurial ascendancy I have seldom seen before. However, Herr Heiduck mentioned that despite his reputation, Herr Kleinert had experienced some personal problems with the Nazis, who were constantly visible at the Stadt-Hotel and the casino. There were allegations that he was not a member of the N.S.D.A.P. (the German Nazis Party). Herr Heiduck said the nascent rivalry between Herr Kleinert and the Hitler's Nazis spilled over into the news columns, which didn't help him very much.

Even though Herr Kleinert owned the Stadt-Hotel, the Inn and the casino the license to operate these establishments was mutable by the Nazis government. Once I learned this, I noticed that Herr Kleinert never wore the 'Nazis Pin' on his lapel, as most of the businessmen did. Herr Heiduck told me the reason he didn't wear it was that he had nothing in common with the N.S. D.A.P. and did not want to waste any time pretending. His life was to manage his operation the best he could. He spent as much time as was possible with me. He seemed to be very concerned about my progress and how I was feeling. He helped me learn the German language. He also knew I needed to keep in contact with my family and tried his best to keep the communication lines open between us.

Slowly, I became used to my new surroundings and everyone was very nice to me. I worked three days at the casino and three days at the Hotel. At times, the hours were very long, but I managed to do the best I could. At the Inn where I had my room, there were people who were disabled former German Wehrmacht soldiers with missing arms or legs. Some of the tenants were displaced people as refugees as a result of the on going senseless and horrible WWII. I remember that there were three girls from the Ukraine who had been deported by the German Nazis as forced labor; their names were Olga, Nina, and Natasha. They did not speak German, but did speak a little Polish, which I understood. They worked at the Inn as chambermaids and soon became my friends. They looked after me similar to how my own sisters did. Herr Kleinert too was very fond of them and sometimes ate lunch with them.

Herr Kleinert had a certain panache that made people feel good. Another resident was a man named Pan Vitov from Ukrenia. He was a former professor at the Schtomir University. Prior to his deportation, he had a prolific life. He spoke German, Polish, and of course Russian. He worked at the Hotel's switchboard and in the mailroom. He was a fine gentleman. One of the things I remember most about him was his silver hair. It was so striking. Herr Kleinert treated his employees with respect and dignity. He had the innate ability not only to lead, but also to help people whenever possible; and he did both quite well. He inspired people when they felt low, he could easily build them up again. Whenever he was around, he increased the 'espirit de corps'. He was quite the man in many respects.

Things were going quite well and I had adapted to my new surroundings quickly. Don't get me wrong; I desperately missed my family and home. I was kept busy and at many times I would find that I had to reach down deep to realize I still felt homesick, I tried not to let it show. My days were long; in the morning, I attended school after which I reported to work at either the Hotel or casino. My days were so full I realized that I had little time for anything else, but also that my childhood was suddenly gone. My childhood dreams were gone as well. Things had certainly changed. Gone were the lazy days of chasing clouds and rainbows.

I remember a letter from home, which my father wrote to me. It was a long loving letter; I could tell I was missed. I loved seeing my father's handwriting. He had beautiful penmanship; his capital letters were like beautiful paintings. He wrote that he and my stepmother would come to visit in May and would bring me a second pair of shoes, which they had finally been able to afford. During the war, items like shoes and other commodities could only be purchased with coupons and sometimes saving up for items such as these could take up to a year. The letter raised my sagging spirit. The thought of them coming to visit was constantly on my mind; I could not sleep. My whole body was a tuning fork, suddenly struck by the news so sharply that it would not stop vibrating for the longest time imaginable.

I was homesick almost all the time, besides missing my family I missed going to church on Sundays. We were a very religious family and this made me sad. There were times when I had time to dwell on my circumstances I would find myself crying for the things I could not change. Yet I knew I had to move on.

One night just as I was falling asleep, I heard several shots close by. Following the gunfire, I heard shouting down in the street. I tried not to listen, but even after it all stopped, I could not shut out the echoing of the chaos in my head. I was very frightened and could not fall back to sleep no matter how hard I tried. Finally, morning came and with that new day, I couldn't wait to get to work at the Hotel. It was a Sunday morning and the maids were doing their morning routine. As I was leaving the Inn, I ran across Nina, we exchanged a few words in Polish and she asked me if I had heard the shots during the night. I told her I had, and she told me that she too was frightened about the events. I told her not to worry and to try to have a good day.

The walk to the Hotel took about twenty minutes. As I walked around the corner to the next block, I noticed two bodies lying on the ground face down in a pool of blood; they had been shot to death. The sight of the dead bodies to me was the most terrible thing I had ever encountered. I was terrified and wanted to run away, far away from this sight. My head was a ball of pain. I ran as fast as I could to the Hotel. As I ran, I came across several people oblivious to the sight I had just witnessed, I wanted to scream there were two dead people back there, but I held my tongue. I had had nothing to eat that morning and with the running and the trauma, I felt faint. I felt sick to my stomach; my head rang and boomed with pain, yet I continued to run. I finally had to stop because I could not go on. I took this moment to try to compose myself. Had I actually seen the bodies? When I got to the Hotel, I came across Herr Kleinert, before I could even explain to him what I had seen, he guessed something was wrong and asked me to tell him what had happened. I explained everything to him and he tried to console me the best he could. I could not get that vision out of my head. My life after that was just not the same anymore.

I struggled all day at work to get the image of the bodies out of my head. My co-workers did everything they could to pump up my spirits, but the only thing that gave me any hope at all was the fact my parents would be coming to visit soon. I harbored a childish desire that they would take me home with them. I thought that if I told them about the dead bodies they would have to take me away from here. I was exhausted by the time my shift ended. All the running and the emotional stress I had put myself through had just worn me out. Although I was tired, I had no desire to walk back to the Inn. Would the bodies still be there? As I came down the street, I could see that indeed no one had bothered to move the bodies. Why had no one bothered to have them removed?

As I entered the Inn, I sought out Nina and Olga. They had not been outside all day, but they did have a lot to tell me. Although they only spoke Ukrainian and a little Polish, we managed to communicate fairly well. They told me that around noon several SS soldiers searched through all the rooms of the Inn. I was frightened. I told the girls about the two dead bodies. Now we all feared for our lives. Soon my attacks of despair were acutely devastating. I did not want to go to my room, I felt abandoned. I wanted to go home, I wanted to give up, and I didn't want to be here anymore. Just as I was sinking to my lowest point I remembered the words my stepmother whispered to me before I left, she told me "Never give up, no matter what. Pray," I prayed a lot. I said goodnight to the girls and reluctantly went up to my room. A realization hit me as I sat on my bed that night; that I was not really lost until I actually decided to give up.

I couldn't help but be excited about the prospect of my parents coming to visit. Herr Kleinert was also looking forward to their visit. I enjoyed working for Herr Kleinert and knew he would give a good report to my father when they met again in May.

I may have been young and new to the organization, but it was easy to see that there was something going on. Herr Kleinert seemed at times not the same. His smiles became less visible and he seemed concerned about something. He looked at times quite haggard. I was worried about him. One day I saw him talking with two SS officers in the Hotel lobby, I could not hear the conversation, but no one looked at all happy. Something was not right. Was he in trouble?

The following night I woke again from loud gunshots very close by. This was to be another night I would not be able to sleep. I knew I should be able to get over seeing the dead bodies, but some how I could not get past it. When I was able to talk to Herr Heiduck about what I had seen and heard, he confirmed that things might be changing around the Inn. He didn't elaborate and I didn't think I should ask any more questions. One change was that Nina and Olga no longer worked at the Inn. They had been transferred to the Hotel along with me.

More than anything, I was looking forward to my parents visiting. Despite everything, I still enjoyed going to work. I helped the chefs in the kitchen prepare elaborate dinners and worked the large banquets, which were attended by high-ranking SS and German Wehrmacht officers. When Herr Kleinert was the master chef at the helm, there was no limit to the amount of courses that he would prepare. He inspired the other chefs. He viewed them as fine artists, rather than mere craftsmen. He once made a comment that I will never forget, "Confidence is a requirement of someone who works with flames." It was absolutely fascinating to watch him working in the kitchen as well as managing his staff and the operation.

I relished going to school, but I could see a change in the atmosphere there too. One day I was reprimanded for not being a member of the 'Hitler Youth'. The school went as far as stating I would have to join the Hitler-Jugend. My duties as an apprentice and the amount of homework and studying required filled my days completely. I wanted nothing more than to please my guardian with my hard work and good grades.

Something was indeed in the air. Even Herr Heiduck looked troubled. However, no matter what was going on in his life, he always walked me home if I had to work late and the walk home would be in the dark. Even though I knew I was not without friends here, I couldn't help but miss my brother and sisters and my father and stepmother. Since those couple of nights where shots rang out in the dark stillness, I lived in fear that this trouble would somehow find me.

I often thought about the fact that I had no friends outside of work or the inn. I didn't really have any friends at school; I missed playing soccer as I had at home. I needed companionship of boys my own age. I was extremely lonely.

The strange atmosphere seemed to permeate the whole operation. One day I noticed two Gestapo officers coming out of his office; their demeanor said that they were all about business. The day after I was able to talk to Herr Heiduck about what I had seen. He confirmed my suspicions and stated that Herr Kleinert was indeed having trouble with the Gestapo over the past few days.

Herr Heiduck allowed me to confide in him on other occasions and I decided to see if he would be receptive to my concerns now. I told him about missing my family and how excited I was that they were to visit in May, only a couple of weeks away. He said he was happy for me and was looking forward to meeting them. After our talk, he walked me back to the Inn. That night I cried myself to sleep; the place I called home was in trouble.

This late afternoon conversation would be the last one I had with Herr Heiduck. The next time I would see him he would be in the hands and at the mercy of the Gestapo.

Auschwitz 1943 – Arrested by the Gestapo

It was on April 28, 1943, this day remains deeply embedded inside me, when in the morning hours at approximately 8:30 a.m., while working in the Hotel kitchen, that we heard loud voices and the clatter of boots. Suddenly, the kitchen's doors swung open and several Gestapo officers stormed inside, they shouted, "Halt! Bleibtalle Still!" (Stop! Nobody moves!) They gathered all of us; about 24 were working at the time. We were taken to the Hotel's keller and were interrogated one by one. I was the youngest employee at the Stadt-Hotel, only fifteen and a half. The owner, Herr Kleinert, was not at the Hotel at the time of the raid, he and his wife usually arrived at the Hotel around 10:00 a.m.

The Gestapo officers called us dirty people, traitors, and undesirable Jews and demanded that we tell them the truth or face the consequences. The interrogations went on and on. There were some female employees among the staff and they started to cry, "We haven't done anything, let us go!" Nevertheless, the Gestapo officers became more belligerent and the questioning became almost unbearable. They demanded all our valuables such as watches, rings and our money. Around my neck I wore an aluminum cross attached to a light silver chain which my stepmother had given me before I had left home, but to my dismay they took that too.

From the very onset of the interrogation by the officers, I knew that I was innocent and had nothing to hide. When my turn came to be questioned, I tried to explain to the officer that I was innocent; many times, I broke down crying and begging them to understand. I tried to explain that I was only an apprentice and begged him to let me go. He only laughed at me and continued to shout at me about my political affiliation. He asked me why I did not belong to the 'Hitler Jugend' (the Hitler Youth). I tried to explain, but he cut me off and told me that they, the Gestapo would show me how to be a good citizen of the German Reich. I was told to step aside and face the wall.

Herr Heiduck was the next to be interrogated. Neither he nor Herr Kleinert belonged to the NSDAP (Nazi Party). Herr Heiduck was brutally beaten, until he finally collapsed. I stayed facing the wall and my heart sank with each blow to my dear friend. Herr Heiduck was a gentleman and I felt every blow bestowed on him by the Gestapo. How could they do this to him? To us? It was extremely hard to comprehend.

I silently blamed my father for sending me to Auschwitz, but he couldn't have known this was going to happen. He had made a decision that he had hoped would be the right one for me. Why were we being treated like criminals? Why were we being treated in such a barbaric manner? After about three hours, we found out that Herr Kleinert and his wife had arrived at the Hotel. They too were brought to the keller and were briefly interrogated. We were then told to follow several SS men outside. Waiting for us were several German Wehrmacht trucks. We were loaded into the trucks and then taken to the Auschwitz concentration camp. As I stated before, my parents never talked to me about these camps, they either did not know of them or had decided not to frighten me with the thought of them.

As we drove through the gates, I caught a glimpse of a sign at the entrance 'Arbeit macht frei' (Work will make one free). It was a mendacious promise; there was no such thing in the German regime. The sign was just a big lie. Once we were unloaded from the trucks, we were separated according to our gender and by age. Since I was the youngest at the hotel, I was set off by myself. How I felt at that time is very difficult to describe.

I heard officers yelling, while other just laughed. I heard someone say that the only possibility of an escape would come through the chimney. I did not know what that meant, but I was overcome with fear nevertheless. I learned quickly that there were three options available to me in the camp, option 1: work until you were exhausted; option 2: and if you could not work any more they would kill you; option 3: escape, but your chances of making it were near impossible.

I was commissioned to hard labor. One of my assignments was to work on building a road near the Autobahn. We marched there very early in the morning, we worked in the rain or scorching heat with very little food or water. When we were fed, it was mostly turnips and tiny rations of bread. Many men collapsed from either hunger, exposure, or from beatings. I worked along men from every lifestyle; there were political prisoners; some were Poles (affiliated with a resistance movement in Poland), some were Jews, and even Soviet POWs. The Polish political prisoners were treated worse than any other of us were. They were beaten until they couldn't stand and when they collapsed were taken away or shot. Amongst all this turmoil was I! I was just a boy, a teenager, just an apprentice at a Hotel. Now I found myself in an adult world of hate and torture.

Many times, I heard the SS guards shouting at the Jews that they had no right to be alive; but they didn't stop with just the Jews, they targeted the Catholics and priests also. Since I could understand and speak Polish I could communicate with many of my fellow prisoners, but I knew if I were caught, I would be severely punished. To say the least WWII and the Auschwitz concentration camp changed my life forever.

There were two men that everyone feared most; they were Rudolf Hess and the cold-blooded SS chief Heinrich Himmler. The cries from the prisoners under their torture still echo inside me. There was no happiness, no joy in the blue skies; we were totally ruled by the SS soldiers behind those barbed wire fences. We came to believe they ruled the heavens and all the earth with their ways.

It was during these days that I learned the power of prayer. I asked the Lord to deliver me, to give me strength to go on. I knew I had to keep my faith and with that faith, I would keep Him at my side. The realization that I was an innocent prisoner kept me going. I knew someday I would be let out of this hell.

Not only were we terrorized by the soldiers themselves; but also we had to fear their vicious dogs that were trained to attack upon command. There was no humanity in any aspect of our life in this camp. The soldiers were well trained to make sure we felt powerless and crushed under their tyranny and at times, it was inconceivable that people could survive through so much suffering.

I watched as men became increasingly thin and frail. They contracted diseases such as dysentery, beriberi, and malaria. Despite all, the guards still beat us at the slightest provocation and kept us underfed to keep us under control. Work was unbearable at times, in the heat with no protection, no rest. If you slowed in your pace, you were beaten. If your work did not progress as expected you were not allowed the meager water ration for the day. I remember well the guards laughing when men became delirious from lack of water. I remember thinking then and now, how people could survive, how the human spirit would not give up even in the most extreme circumstances. Each day I saw men fall by the side of the road or not make it out to the yard for morning roll call; they were either taken away or shot on the spot.

There were times even when someone would be assured of a beating from the guards, that you could still see kindness in their soul and hope in their eyes as was the case with one fine old Jew; he could hardly walk, was extremely emaciated, constantly being brutalized for not doing his share, but he was a wonderful man. Often, I heard him repeating the Lords Prayer to those who would listen, this gave me hope. It gave me a light at the end of this dark harsh tunnel. When my spirits were at their lowest I could always tell that there was someone always reaching for me, I believe to this day the Lord saved my life in that concentration camp.

Each day became a continuous struggle to stay alive. No one knew who would make it through the day and who would perish before the day's end. We were not allowed to talk to each other so we developed a sign language in order to communicate; we knew if caught, punishment was inevitable. Repeatedly I asked myself the question, why was I here? Would I make it out alive? Every day my conviction grew stronger and stronger, that I must remain patient and that the day of freedom would become a reality.

Nights were almost worse than the hard long days. At night you could hear the lamentations of the inmates so very weak, some very seriously ill, it was heart wrenching. No longer could you see even the faintest glimmer of joy in the men's eyes, there was only sadness and despair. Real life had ceased to exist. Men no longer talked to each other, many just sat there waiting for death to come. I wanted to live; I believed the day would come when I would walk out those gates free. I desperately wanted, needed to go back to Tarnowitz, to my home and family. I knew now it was not possible; with my stepmother's words in my head repeating endlessly to never give up, I made it through the nights and pushed forward each and every day.

One of the ways the guards would break up their day, was by having a group of men run or walk around in circles, and they would open fire gunning the men down for no reason, but sport. Everyone who lived through this ordeal I am sure has never forgotten these atrocities. Imagine the impact it has on an impressionable fifteen-year-old boy. What was the purpose to all this? No one had the answers.

Words from my youth resounded in my ears: "Do not lose faith; faith is what nourishes and sustains us even in the worst times. It allows us to endure." I prayed when I felt powerless and abandoned. They were the most difficult weeks and months of my life. My one value to the guards was that I could speak both German and Polish. At times I worked as a translator. When there were problems between the guards and the Polish Jews, they called on me to help as an interpreter. Many times I would go the extra step to try to smooth out the situation. My reward was the prospect of additional bread and sometimes being spared a beating, but even this ability did not guarantee my continued safety. What I appreciated most was the respect I received from my fellow inmates.

What we dreaded most was the rain. Even in inclement weather, we shoveled the heavy earth or loaded heavy rocks into trucks. Our clothing soaked through to the skin, our bodies weak from hunger we were often times pushed beyond our limits. Beatings and whippings were commonplace. All who were able worked as hard as they could in hopes of being spared. I felt sorry for the Jews, who were persecuted no matter what they did, but I could do nothing to help them except to pray.

Auschwitz was known for genocide; it was truly, utterly inhumane. The depth of these crimes needs to be remembered so they will never be committed again in any situation.

We were always hungry, but rain or shine, we were forced to work. The atmosphere was depressing, getting worse with each passing day. I often felt overwhelmed with emotions and loneliness cursing through me to my very core. I had witnessed the worst of humanity but I clung to the hopes of being free from all this pain. I knew I would never forget all I had seen and endured in my short existence here on earth. I asked myself many times why me? Why was I chosen? When would it all end? Was there anyone listening to my prayers and pleadings? I did not know the answers. To this day the memories, nightmares of what I had endured creep into my conscious and unconscious mind, but I have learned to live with the realities I have suffered in the hands of monsters who didn't know any better.

Never will I forget these inexorable nights filled with pain and horror, a pain that never has gone away. Never will I forget the cries of once brave men, the sight of once beautiful and full of life, barely clinging on, emaciated to the point of no return. Everyone knew the inevitable was that they would die in this camp. Every time I thought I couldn't take anymore I thought of my family and how I missed them and that, I knew they were praying for me too.

I welcomed each dawn. It proved I had made it through another night and would somehow make it through the day. I did not know what the day would bring, but I did know that I would be outside in the fresh air no matter how hard it was to endure, it was better than being locked in a cell or the ultimate alternative, dead. What I dreaded was the nights, the hot stale suffocating air in the barracks. Sleep started to elude me as the nights progressed. I knew I had to pull myself together or I would not be able to keep up my end of the work or survive during the day. With the lack of sleep came the inability to focus. My mind was splayed in all different directions. It took all I had to pull my mind onto a focused and precise goal, to survive and to endure.

I began to wonder what happened to the rest of the Hotel staff, I had not seen anyone I knew since we arrived in the camp. What had happened to Herr Kleinert and his wife and Herr

Heiduck? It was as if they just vanished. What would happen to me? I was alone.

During all those dark and lonely days, weeks, and months what motivated me most was my Christian upbringing, especially under the support of my stepmother. My suffering and the suffering of others that went through and survived and those that didn't can only be truly felt by those who went through it. No one can fully put into words these pains. The SS guards were tough on us, always forcing us to go faster and work harder, yet the trusties or 'kapos' were even worse. They would punish the men for anything and with anything so they looked good in the SS guards' eyes.

I forced myself to work each day and to give it everything I had no matter how exhausted I was. There were days I was light headed from lack of sleep and lack of food. In order for me to survive, I had to push myself past my known limits.

WWII was a different kind of war. Why or how did it get that way? No one should forget to what depths the human psyche can sink. To this day, I search for answers to these questions, I have read hundreds of books but I have yet to find a plausible answer or explanation for what happened during that war.

In mid October, I noticed a subtle change in the guards' attitude toward me. After the usual roll call, I was escorted by two SS guards to a building I had not been to before. I was taken inside to an office; there inside I was dumfounded to see Herr Kleinert sitting there. In the room too were three high-ranking SS officers and the two guards that had brought me in. They dismissed the guards and I was ordered to sit down. We had been in the camp almost six months and I was shocked at how Herr Kleinert looked haggard, thin, and bewildered. He was not the same man I was introduced to in April and had lived with for almost a month. This once strong willed take charge, impeccably dressed man was now ensconced in rags and looked beaten down. He managed to give me the softest smile he could without being noticed. I was told that the meeting was to be kept confidential; I could sense from the conversation between the officers and Herr Kleinert that there was something very significant going to take place. During this meeting, he was ordered to sign several documents. I had no idea what he was signing. It wasn't until several weeks later that I found out those papers were a declaration that all his properties in Auschwitz were confiscated by the Nazis regime and he no longer at any time or any place could own any properties. I did not know how this all came about, but within a few days after this enshrouded meeting I and all but three of the other employees were released after almost six months of hard labor, hunger, and maltreatment. Bruised and emaciated, but alive the others and I had escaped the pincers of the Gestapo and SS.

During those unthinkable months, I'd witnessed more horror than a human heart can imagine. I had lost considerable weight because of lack of food, poor conditions, no medical care; I walked out of the camp weighing in at 90 pounds. They had taken a great deal out of my early life, but they were not able to take away my faith and trust in my Lord. My future at this point was uncertain. I did not know what I was to do, what I did know was that I was sixteen years old, homeless but nonetheless, free! Herr Kleinert had left Auschwitz the following day for Berlin, but he had left behind an address for me. Within a few days after my miraculous liberation from the concentration camp, I was told that I would continue my education in Berlin, with the condition that I would join the 'Hitler Jugend' (Hitler Youth). I had been hoping I would be able to go home and visit my parents and family, but that was denied to me. Being a police state, I had to do as I was told and go where I was sent to go or suffer the consequences.

As much as I wanted to leave Auschwitz, I thought constantly about those unsung heroes, I was leaving behind. Those innocent people who died for no reason for any cause. I was grateful to the Lord for sparing me and answering my prayers. I knew in my heart that I could once again sleep without fear and that I was finally free. The unimaginable became reality and with that came freedom. It was truly hard yet heroic to realize the sacrifices Herr Kleinert made for us and to save his own life. I have always respected him for that. It was not until twenty-one years later that I was able to repay him for what he had done for me. He realized that no matter what conditions he was under, his staff at that time was innocent and endured much on his behalf. For those of us who had suffered under Hitler's regime knew him for what he was a man without dignity or respect for human life and a man with insatiable pride.

St. Bernard of Clarivaux once said, "Pride is a secret poison. It is an evil crucifying and disquieting all it takes hold of." Pride was Hitler's number one problem. It is a proven fact that the proud often end in despair. His pride made him realize the conclusion that the only way out was to commit suicide before the Third Reich collapsed. It was on April 30, 1945 that Hitler, half demented, shot himself; while his new wife, Eva nee Braun killed herself with cyanide rather than face the people.

Many times, I considered my situation hopeless and all I have to do is look back on my time in Auschwitz. The fact I survived is nothing short of a miracle. I often wonder if my outcome would have been different had Herr Kleinert not relinquished his properties, only God knew the answer to that.

I have been asked if I felt bitter or was angry, disappointed, or acrimonious about what had happened to me. Everything I have endured has made me a survivor; it has made me stronger I often wonder what I would be like if I hadn't lived through these times. The only thing I feel sorry for myself, is the fact I never actually new my biological mother, I want to believe that she would have instilled in me the same strength of spirit and faith that my stepmother had. The rest..."Je ne regretted rein." (I regret nothing.) My stepmother had told me once that no matter what happens that I was not ever to feel bitter, that bitterness would ultimately destroy me. Not to be bitter and to forgive is and was a difficult task. It took years to put this ugly time in my life behind me. I to this day believe in miracles, when I left that concentration camp I was witness to one.

Leaving Auschwitz for Berlin

After our unexpected and miraculous release from Auschwitz at the end of October 1943, I was told that I would be going to Berlin. I was to continue my education and apprenticeship at the renowned 'Café Sonneneck' located in Charlottenburg on Kaiser Dam. One condition I had to submit to; was that I would join the Hitler Youth, which was compulsory during Hitler's reign. I was to attend all the scheduled meetings and special gatherings.

Herr Kleinert left Auschwitz before I did, but before he left; he gave me a train pass to Berlin and instructions as to where I would find him when I arrived. I had directions to Café Sonneneck; I had never been to Berlin and the only thing I knew about the city is that it was the capital of Germany and the second largest city in Europe.

Berlin is approximately 720 kilometers from Auschwitz. I was relieved that this trip would take me as far away as possible from this city that held only ugly horrific memories for me. Auschwitz for me only held the smell of burned bodies and reminders of its odious torturers. I was extremely grateful that even if I was not going home, that God had answered my prayers and that he had kept my faith and hope alive during the darkest hours of my life.

I never accused or had the courage to question anyone about what had happened to me. I was full of gratitude for Herr Kleinert and all he had done to save us. As I stood again on the same platform where just six months ago I had arrived in Auschwitz, I was now waiting for the train that would take me away from it. Once again, I knew nothing of what lay ahead, but in silence and with resignation, I waited for the train to come and take me away to start yet another chapter in my life.

I remember vividly the gloriously sunny day, standing in the warmth waiting for the train to pull into the station. I was impatient to get away from this city and the memories that would haunt me the rest of my life. I boarded the train with unimaginable joy; my excitement grew inside me as the locomotive left the station. I left the thick and dirty smoke behind me as the train picked up speed and put distance between me and this awful time in my life.

I prayed over and over again and thanked God for giving me a new chance on life. I knew it would be a very long journey to my new home. As we traveled northwest, I realized that I would be passing by my home town of Tarnowitz and I realized how much I would have liked to see my family. I had missed the visit I was promised by my parents in May. I wonder what they thought had happened to me. It hurt to be this close to them and not be able to see them. However, as quickly as we neared it we were traveling away from it. The pain and loneliness I knew I had to put it away and learn to deal with it if I was to go on with my life.

I felt lost traveling alone with no one to talk to. I studied my fellow passengers and noticed there were sad worried mothers tending to their small children. There were older passengers who looked depressed and saddened by their circumstances. I saw no joy in any of their faces. The war had touched everyone even the children. It was a desperate time for all. To survive people had to suffer much just to maintain their daily lives. Food was in short supply and jobs were scarce. All around me I saw despair.

My spirits were lifted momentarily by the prospect that I'd be soon in a new home, with new adventures and experiences ahead of me. With each passing mile, I strove to put the brutality I had endured behind me. I did not want to carry this stone of cruelty around with me in my heart and soul. My childlike innocence still resided inside me and with this innocence; I knew I could move on with my life. I was tired and wanted to sleep, but I couldn't; my head was crowded with a million things. I struck up a conversation with an older man sitting next to me. He told me he was from Breslau (now called Wroclaw), and that he was on his way to Frankfort to visit his daughter who had lost her husband on the Russian front. He told me his town's history, which helped pass the time and the miles. He asked me many questions about what I had been through, even though the memories were fresh and maybe because of that I could not answer them because they were too painful to discuss. When the old man got off at Frankfort, he alerted me that the next stop would be Berlin. With a loud shrill prompted by steam from the engine we pulled away from the terminal and began to move faster and faster. If we were on schedule, we would arrive in Berlin around five o'clock in the evening. At this stop, our already crowded train took on even more passengers. An old woman in a babushka asked me where I was headed, I told her Berlin. She confirmed that we would be there in about two hours. As we moved along it started to get dark. I began to worry, how would I find my way in a strange city in the dark? As I sat there in the train car, I let myself think back on what I had endured and the fact that I had survived it and those that hadn't. I thought of all those innocent people who had been tortured and killed. With misty eyes, I thanked the Lord for watching over me and making all this possible, why was I allowed to endure these atrocities? I am sure it was to make me a better person.

I must have dozed off, somewhere at the edge of my consciousness I heard the conductor call out that the train was now approaching Berlin. I felt the train slow down and heard the snuffing and puffing of the train as it came to a complete stop. It was very dark and I found out the train was later than anticipated, the old woman wished me good luck, and with that, we parted company.

I stood on the platform of the huge terminal, the Bahnhof Zoo, it had cavernous halls, and I did not know which way I was to go. There were many exits and innumerable signs; I was simply overwhelmed and confused. I felt lost standing there watching hundreds of people rushing in all directions with a purpose and the knowledge of where they were going and needed to be. There were German soldiers roaming about, inspecting the trains (for they carried their equipment, WWII was at its peak, it was 1943).

I finally spotted two German police officers and I knew that with their help I would find my way out of the huge terminal. I was reluctant to approach them because of the experiences I had had with the Gestapo and the SS, but I had no other choice. I looked at them closely trying to study their faces to see if they would indeed help me. I found friendliness in their eyes and even as I struggled with myself to put my helplessness in their hands, I found I had no choice. I forced myself to take those steps and once in their line of vision I explained to them that I needed their help. I explained my situation and to my surprise, they were very willing to help me. They gave me directions and I was on my way. For a moment they assured me that, not everyone was bad.

I was to take the S-Bahn to Witzleben, which would take me to Charlottenburg. However, something had gone wrong and I missed my stop, now it was very late and I was even more confused. The size of the city was too much for me, I was just a small town boy, and with each passing minute, I was more frightened and frustrated. I was desperate; the conductor of the S-Bahn gave me new directions which would ultimately put me on the right path to my destination. I was finding out that the people in Berlin looked out for their fellow man, it was a nice feeling. After a long and exhausting day, I finally found the address I sought. By now, it was almost ten o'clock.

The Café was located in a secluded area, surrounded by beautiful buildings and the largest trees I had ever seen. I was to find out later that because of its setting it was an ideal meeting place for dignitaries and other famous celebrities from the city of Berlin. I also found out that it was only a half a block away from the headquarters of the German Hitler Youth, which was housed in a complex of buildings. Herr Kleinert was very relieved to see me. He was now the managing director of the Café. Once having gotten back under his protective wing, I knew that my life would become normal again. He showed me to my room, which I had to myself. He told me that I would continue my education as well as working as an apprentice in the kitchen at the Café. I could not wait for it all to start, I had an unquenchable thirst for learning, and I wanted as much of it as I could get.

I expressed my concerns about having to join the Hitler Youth, but he reminded me it was a condition of my being able to stay with him.

On October 10, 1943, I turned sixteen, but that was in Auschwitz. There was no celebration only hunger and despair and loneliness. I managed to put that behind me and I forced myself to look forward to my future. I wasn't hungry any more and I was slowly regaining my weight. I had an insatiable desire to learn and to please Herr Kleinert, but most of all I wanted to forget the painful memories of the past months and to find solace to my nagging loneliness and homesickness.

I found I was having some difficulty coping with depending on other people other than my parents and family. However, I felt a great debt to Herr Kleinert. He paid a tremendous price for the safety of his staff. There was no doubt that he was a man of integrity. Despite all he had been through, he had not lost his ability to lead and command his staff. I welcomed the familiarity of my surroundings and soon grew accustomed to the routine; I saw rays of hope for my future. I faced many challenges and hungrily consumed them as they presented themselves.

Herr Kleinert took time out of his busy schedule to take me on a tour of this city. Although, Berlin was a comparatively young city by European standards, it only dated back to the 13th century; it rapidly grew to become a booming cosmopolitan city. He took me to the Kurfursten Dam with its cafes and chic boutiques, and to the Brandenburg Gate. He took me to the Charlottenburg Schloss, which was built in the 17th century. We went to the opera house on the Unterden Linden and the National Gallery. The Unterden Linden ran from the royal palace to the Brandenburgertor, Berlin's social and official life centered around this area. This street was one of the finest and most spacious in Europe, nearly a mile in length it was lined with linden trees and it was beautiful. Berlin's population grew to be over four million; it housed a concrete stadium (which was built in 1936) and a sport field that could seat 100,000 spectators. This was the site where the Olympic Games took place in 1936.

Even as a teen, I valued all that I had seen and what lay at my fingertips. This city was inspiring. I soon began to feel comfortable with my new life, except for one fact; I had not heard from my family. Herr Kleinert made sure I was kept busy with school and work, he looked after my needs; food and shelter, but what he could not provide for me was the satisfaction of seeing my parents and family.

Little did I know, but my quiet life was going to change and change drastically. Berlin was shaken to its core when the bombs fell from Allied planes. The raids became more and more frequent shattering our tranquility and putting all our lives in jeopardy. Running for shelter when the alarm sounded became very frightening for all of us. I was to find out that the air raids had actually been going on since early 1940 and here it was 1943. Each night we were awakened by the sirens as the raids became more frequent. You learned to dress quickly when you heard the shrill sounds of the sirens; one was never sure where the bombs were going to fall and to get to safety we had to run down five flights of stairs to a shelter across the street. I remember one night while running into the night, looking up and staring in awe at the spectacle of the night sky full of flares that the planes were dropping illuminating the landscape as they dropped to the ground.

The glow painted a silvery magic sheen on the countryside in the fall evenings.

One evening we were caught by surprise by a particularly devastating raid. The sirens failed to sound and we were still asleep when the bombs began falling around us. The buildings trembled, the walls shook, and windows were shattered by the blasts. Befuddled by the noise and confusion I dressed as quickly as I could. I heard shouts from the floor; everyone was in a panic to move quickly, we ran into each other as we raced down the stairs and into the street to the shelter. While I was running to the shelter, a shard of shrapnel caught me on the chin and by the time we got to the air raid shelter my face was bloody. Hundreds of us huddled together in fear mothers and crying children, elderly people, men, and women of all ages. It was chaotic as we listened to wave after wave of explosions. Buildings began to tremble and the power failed in the shelter. People cried out. Chaos was all around us. Only after the second wave bombings and the drone of bomber planes above us did we finally hear the sirens screaming out into the night. I was to find out that this was not uncommon, many times the bombers could fly in undetected by radar. That is why the sirens did not go off with enough warning for us to get to safety. Eventually emergency lights came on which brought some relief to the chaos inside the shelter.

After what seemed like an eternity, we were finally told by the security guard that we were able to leave the shelter. Surfacing we witnessed the destruction of our little community. Our block was completely demolished, some fires still burned and would smolder for days. Beautiful villas were in ruins. Many people were dead or homeless. There was rubble everywhere. Many streets were impassible.

Bodies lined the sidewalks with hopes that someone could identify the bloated corpses. People walked dazed in the streets barely able take a breath for the air was dark and full of acrid smoke from the smoldering fires. Our building, the Café Sonneneck was spared somehow. Herr Kleinert resumed his operation and opened the doors to the public. I was put to work, but I could not concentrate, I wanted to go home, to run away. I was tired, so tired of everything. My chin was examined and I suffered only a minor injury; I was bandaged up and told to put it out of my mind.

I had hoped that once I left Auschwitz that the worst was behind me, but I was wrong. The raids continued, but in different areas of the city. Just about every night we had to be awakened to the sound of the sirens and rush to safety. I heard the bombs falling and could feel the buildings trembling even in my dreams. I would wake each morning to the thought of who had not made it through the night and to thank God that I had. All around me, all I saw was pain and despair.

One night in particular, November 22, 1943 I will never forget. We were awakened again by the sound of the air raid sirens. People poured in from all over the neighborhood. Tonight the bombs sounded very close, the noise was deafening. When the shelter was packed to its capacity, the fireproof steel door was shut and guarded by the shelter guard. Again and again, we heard the swishing sound of the bombs falling followed by the earth shaking explosions, which sent shockwaves through the building. One bomb tore the steel door out of its frame killing the guard who was standing by it. I realized instantly how lucky I was, I had been standing next to the guard and was spared. Hysteria ripped through the crowd. Children cried and women screamed, we all thought we would die. After the initial shock wore off I realized that my left leg and foot were bleeding the pain became unbearable. I found a place to support myself as another bomb exploded, the building trembled we thought our time had finally come. However, the building did not collapse. Another bomb exploded which caused our power to fail, the situation inside the shelter had become unbearable, yet it was better than being outside exposed to the raids. Some people had had the forethought to bring makeshift emergency kits with them from their homes. Candlelight eventually illuminated the dark room. A third explosion broke the water lines, causing water to pour in through the ceiling. We scrambled to stay dry. People stumbled over each other while a selected elder tried to keep order. He pleaded with the crowds to stay calm and to stay still. All the while, I could feel my shoe filling with blood. With the help of a kind man, I took my sock off my right foot and tied it under my left knee as a type of tourniquet to try to staunch the flow of blood; it helped somewhat, but I began to feel weak and dizzy I thought I would pass out, it took a lot for me to stay conscious. The man suggested that I loosen the tourniquet to let the blood flow a little and I might feel better, I did and it helped some. After an interminable amount of time, the siren sounded telling us it was safe to leave the shelter.

It was a miracle that we had survived this horrible night. Red Cross volunteers were on hand to help mothers with their children. I tried to walk and found that I couldn't. I called out to the volunteers and asked them to help me. At first, they did not realize what was wrong until I told them I had hurt my foot. I was told to sit down before I fell down. I was very pale and dizzy. An hour later, I awoke to find myself in the hospital. The attending doctor quickly realized that there was a problem with my leg, it was swollen, and my shoe would not come off. They soaked my foot in water to loosen the dried and caked on blood, my shoelaces had to be cut open. The examination proved to be in my favor; even though there was a lot of blood, I only had minor injuries; some cuts and bruising. I was given a larger pair of shoes to wear until the swelling went down. Two days later, I was taken to the homeless shelter. I could not quit thinking of the bombing and the aftermath of that fateful night.

It was surprising how the human spirit is able to rebound after tragedy. Even when faced with the horrors of war people eventually delve inside themselves and emerge with humor, love and their kindness intact. I also learned then that each of us possesses internal resources, which can help establish a firm foundation of personal respect and peace. With prayer and faith, I knew I would make it through all that was dealt to me. Despite my injuries, my spirit remained unbroken. This gift enabled me to release my doubts, resistance, and limitations to a higher power without hesitation. I knew that someone had been watching over me and had once again protected me from serious harm.

In the emergency homeless shelter, the volunteers were very helpful and went beyond their call of duty trying to locate my guardian, Herr Kleinert. How they were even able to find him amidst all the chaos was beyond me, yet after only one night, we were reunited. We were taken in a van to Kurfirsrtendam, where the Café Sonneneck was located; all I could see was destruction everywhere for blocks on end. Buildings where still either burning or smoldering emitting clouds of acrid dark smoke into the air. At the corner of Kaiserdam, the once beautiful complex of building was now reduced to rubble. Herr Kleinert and I stood where the café once was where famous and brilliant people dined and met, it was gone. From the still smoldering structure, water was now cascading down the interior walls from broken pipes. The entire ground level that housed the restaurant, which was once adorned with marvelous crystal chandeliers and a tasteful interior design, too was gone. The beautiful apartments on the upper level were reduced to a pile of bent steel beams hanging in grotesque shapes. We attempted to enter the building through the basement, but it was completely flooded. We joined many of the tenants outside the building. We realized that retrieving our belongings was impossible, anyway there was nothing left to salvage.

Buildings became message boards from survivors leaving notes for their missing loved ones, in hopes of being reunited. Most of the bombs dropped were incendiary ones; the explosions caused incredible fires. Other bombs were extremely powerful ones, which caused buildings to tremble and fall destroying everything in their path.

Each new day was filled with trepidation as to which part of the city would have been the target of the night's bombing. As the raids increased in intensity and frequency the more complacent, the citizens became. It almost became a way of life. If there were no sirens sounding people still thought about it all the time. Everyone suffered the same, everyone lost someone, or something in the raids, and it was incomprehensible how we lived through these times. As the days passed there was an exodus of people leaving the burning ruined city. Their world was one of fear and despair, there was no hope left. It was horrific; at times, the skies were completely obliterated by the heavy dark toxic smoke. My brief time in the city of Berlin affected my life psychologically in many ways. The childish view I had of my short life had been completely ripped apart. World War II was escalating and we did not know it at this time how it was all going to end.

At times, it was extremely hard to witness the sufferings of everyone around me. I believed that time heals all wounds and I knew with time and faith I would survive this horrendous ordeal.

That night in the air raid shelter has stayed forever etched in my memories. My innocence and freedom had long since been stolen from me; a sense of fear, loneliness, and sadness had invaded my entire being. There are moments in a man's life when the words he needs to pray are so deep within him that only God can hear them. The human being is the most adjustable living thing on the earth; therefore, life went on despite the hardships people had to endure day in and day out.

The B-17's or as they were known as the 'the flying fortresses' flew over Berlin and unloaded their cargo indiscriminately; British bombers dropped their loads mostly during the daylight hours. We lived in constant fear, our lives were forever changed. Mothers feared for their children, wives feared for their husbands away at war. It was a precarious time. One never knew what the next day would bring. Food was in short supply and became a rare commodity. There was always the chance that the power and water supply would be damaged beyond repair.

One had to admire the strength portrayed by those mothers. They had to put on a brave face for the sake of their children. They had to calm the fears of their children when they woke crying in the middle of the night when the sirens sounded or nightmare woke them. They had to scavenge to put food on the table and a roof over their heads. Their main job was to keep their children safe. I was amazed at how the elderly and incapacitated coped with all that was happening yet they saw to their daily needs with little or no complaints. It was humbling to me when I wanted to give up and find a corner to hide in.

I have always admired those people in Berlin, what they endured and the way they did became a part of my life. Fortunately, my stay in Berlin was a short one. I added my experiences there to the ever-growing chapters in my life and it helped me cope with my situation better than I thought I would.

When I hear the wailing of sirens today, it still brings back flashes of the horrible day and night bombings in Berlin. People paid a terrible price to survive and the mutilation of the soul was the highest price of all. Thousands of families were torn apart never to be reunited. Long treks of refugees were visible everywhere as they fled the city in hopes of finding a better safer life.

My apprenticeship in Berlin had been cut short due to the destruction of the Café. Everything was lost, the few possessions I had were gone, but I was alive and well. I wanted to go home, I felt lost in this city. I felt all alone. Herr Kleinert went to secure a new position for himself and us in Magdeburg about 140 kilometers southwest of Berlin, he told us he would send for us when he found something that would keep us all together. The Red Cross provided me with a train pass to Tarnowitz- Tarnowskie-Góry; I was beyond myself with excitement about the prospect of seeing my family for the Christmas holiday.

I stood on the train platform in the cold November night shivering as I waited for the train. As the time passed, I became chilled to the bone; I only had a light jacket. I must have looked uncomfortable because a stranger out of nowhere offered me an oversized topcoat saying, "Mein junge, das ist mein weihnacht's geschenk" (Take this, my boy this is my Christmas present to you). I was dumfounded and before I was able to say thank you, the stranger was gone. I looked all over for him, but could not find him. I think about this man nearly every Christmas season. The train I was waiting for never arrived. We were told by the stationmaster that the train tracks had been damaged and all trains going east were suspended indefinitely. I was devastated. I stood there in the frigid November night in one of the biggest cities in Europe without a place to go to. I did not know what to do. I soon noticed two people with Red Cross bands on their arms. I approached them and explained my predicament. An hour later, I was once again in the homeless shelter. The next day I was placed in an orphanage in order to free up space for families that needed to stay together. For days, I strove to comprehend that I was once again close to being with my family only to have it ripped out of my hands.

Berlin 1943 the Orphanage

At first, I was somewhat apprehensive about being placed in the home, but where else could I go? I was waiting to hear from Herr Kleinert and it was good to have a safe place to be and people to watch over me. The building was a former villa, which had once belonged to a wealthy Berliner businessman who had donated it to the city. The villa was old and our footsteps echoed in its cavernous hallways as we trooped down to the cafeteria like dining hall. The orphanage was filled with children of all ages, but mostly younger ones; there must have been about 120 boys in the home. Some were there because their parents were dead, while others were like me and were separated from their families and were waiting for the war to end so they could be reunited with them.

The walls were lined with the many portraits of children who had lived there in the past and the portraits of past superintendents. It was a catholic orphanage and the portraits looked stern and very disciplined, frozen in time. Did these faces hold the answers to the many questions I had that were piling up on top of each other? I desperately needed someone to talk to and to help me through my fears. I am not ashamed to admit that I cried myself to sleep many nights while I asked God to help me.

The nuns and Red Cross volunteers saw to our daily needs. They also did their best to hold classes on different subjects so our education was not entirely neglected. Father Daniel, a very gentle priest looked over all of us as a father would. He always had time to stop and talk to us and listen to our fears. He celebrated Mass in the basement; he made sure our spiritual needs were met as best as he could under the circumstances.

We waited for the raids to stop, but night after night, day after day the sirens continued to roust us from our beds and forced us to run for the safety of a shelter. We lived in constant fear; there was always the chance of imminent danger right around the corner. One day I was called to Father Daniel's office, I thought I might have done something wrong and was going to be punished. I had only been there a few days and was not sure if I had stepped out of line. Father Daniel asked me where I was from, where my parents were, if I had any family and I answered his questions the best I could. He asked why I was in Berlin and I explained that I was to be under the care of Herr Kleinert and working as an apprentice in his hotel under his management. I told him about the arrest by the Gestapo in Auschwitz and my time in the concentration camp. I told him that I didn't think my parents knew what had been happening to me, I was not sure whether Herr Kleinert had ever gotten in touch with them. Father Daniel was shocked to hear all I had been through at such a young age. He told me that he had singled me out because I looked troubled and he sensed I had been through a rough time. I still had that concentration camp look about me.

Father asked if I wanted to help out in the kitchen that they could use the help of someone who could work without being told constantly what to do. I jumped at the chance to be of help to the home. He was also aware that working in the kitchen I would have more of an opportunity to eat and would maybe put on some weight. I don't remember all of what else we talked about, but I do remember enjoying being able to talk openly about my feelings and troubles. I knew others had suffered so much more than I had, but inside I felt just as lost as they did. Father helped me hang on to my sanity and resolve to get on with my life.

My motto was "Not to give up." Through providence and constant prayer, I was able to leave Auschwitz, bruised but alive. I knew what had actually kept me alive was my faith, and without that, I would not be writing this book today.

Now that I had a purpose at the orphanage, I found myself helping the younger ones move to the shelter when the sirens wailed. Many times the bombs would be so close that they shook the building. As many times, as we had to run to the shelter we were always afraid. It still tears my heart out to hear children screaming in fear or pain. Raid after raid, we would sit in the shelter until the other siren would sound announcing that the tireless bombers had moved on to another city or part of the city. Usually, after that siren that released us would sound, we would sit their in utter silence giving thanks that we had survived another bombing raid.

It was amazing how much destruction could still be wrought when you thought all you had, had been destroyed. Most of our windows were shattered; glass was everywhere, in the halls and in our rooms. Each time we came out into the night, we could see even more buildings in ruins, burning, or reduced to a pile of rubble.

I was happy to put in my time at the orphanage by working in the kitchen. It kept me busy and occupied my time. I especially enjoyed looking after the younger boys. Doing all that helped take my mind off my own loneliness and homesickness. What amazed me most was that Father Daniel never seemed to sleep, he was always there for us; he would often stop by the kitchen to see how I was doing.

After each bombing raid, more and more children would be brought to the orphanage. Even though we were full to capacity, Father would always find room for the new kids even if it meant they slept in the hallways. The Red Cross provided beds, blankets, and whatever they could. The German Wehrmacht brought truckloads of milk, bread, and other food staples.

It was December 1943 and the raids continued, but thankfully in a different part of the city. It is hard to say thankfully, but for a while, we were spared. I often thought, how many more would have to perish. How much were we expected to endure? How much pain could a person go through before they became numb to it all and complacent. How much would this war change us?

Christmas was fast approaching, and I was still hoping to be able to go home to my family, but deep down I knew I would not be doing that. Reality was always there to bring me back to this insanity, so I allowed myself the reunion in my dreams. In my dreams, we had a wonderful joyous Christmas. The week before Christmas, I was once again called into Father Daniel's office. I sat down in his plain sanctuary, trying to think if I did something wrong. The simplicity of this room had a sense of warmth to it. It proved that Father Daniel wanted nothing for himself, and was only thinking of others. I focused on the crucifix hanging on his wall as he told me he had received a letter from my former employer, Herr Kleinert; he was in Magdeburg.

Magdeburg was a large city on the Elbe River, located approximately 180 kilometers southwest of Berlin. The letter stated that he was now the general director of the Roemer-Hof, a fine establishment in Magdeburg. Enclosed in the letter was a train pass for me to use to join him there, there was also a money order which Father Daniel was to cash and give to me as travel money. I was elated! It was hard not to get excited about it, even though things had fallen through in the past, but I was. I started to cry, but they were tears of joy. I had actually begun to think that he had forgotten about me, but he hadn't. I could not wait to leave this forlorn city and move on with my life. Even now, I do not understand how I could have been so happy to leave, yet feel an obligation to all those I would be leaving behind, especially the younger children who were so frightened. Nevertheless, I knew I had to go where I was meant to go. I thanked Father Daniel for letting me know about the letter, he was very happy for me and knew I had a better life ahead of me. He prayed with me that I would have a safe journey and told me to keep my faith in the face of any adversity.

That night we had another intense air raid. We were in the shelter of the building where we spent more time than on the upper floors or so it seemed. The sound of the bomb falling, the screaming children, and the shrill sirens filled the air as I spent my last night in Berlin. I got ready to leave the following morning with as little commotion as possible; I did not want the younger children to know I was leaving them. It hurt me deeply to leave them behind, I had become as fond of them as they had of me, and many called me their big brother. Before I left, I took a minute to thank Father Daniel once more for all he had done for me. A Red Cross volunteer took me to the railroad station the Bahnhof Zoo. I was aghast as I looked at the devastation of the city. I had not traveled far from the orphanage since I was brought there; blocks upon blocks lay in rubble. Wherever we turned, we could hear the cries of the homeless and helpless. Wherever you turned there were hundreds of people wandering through the burned out buildings searching for some memento they could salvage from their lives. I had to wonder if a person in this city would ever be able to breathe fresh air again, for toxic smoke filled your lungs with every breath you took.

From every apparent setback in my short life, I have managed to learn lessons and values from those who shared it with me. I learned strength came in every person young or old, I found that even in the worst circumstances there were people who could still find a human emotion toward their fellow man, I learned that everyone had something to offer someone if they took the time to look deep inside themselves. I would have to say though that the children I encountered left more of a lasting impression on me than any adult did. Where they were able to find their strength and the will to go on and at times remember that they were still children was beyond me.

As I waited for the train to arrive, I once again thanked God for looking out for me over the past month. I knew that without his intervention I would not be where I was today. My faith was my only comfort. Even though the cruelty, the terror, and the torrent of war had made my life insecure and precarious, God gave me a courageous spirit to go on. I believed that with faith, anything was possible. I will never forget a simple sentence that Father Daniel said to me as I left the orphanage, "A small grain of faith can achieve great things."

We ended up having to wait until late evening for the train to arrive. I spent the time waiting with the Red Cross volunteer, I learned he had lost two sons at the Russian Front; he had lost his wife and best friend during one of the bombing raids here in Berlin. What amazed me was that through all this hardship, he could not wait to continue giving to those less fortunate than he; he enjoyed immensely working at the orphanage. By the time the train pulled in, there were hundreds of people waiting to board. I stood amidst a sea of somber faces, their eyes filled with pain; their meager belongings at their feet and their only dream was to flee this city and the horror it represented.

In The Orphanage

I'll not fear the darkness of the night,
because "He" is always with me.
So many questions unanswered, so many tales untold
Walking around in circles, everything feels so cold
Trying to find the truth beneath the walls of doubt
Never realizing what lies within or what you may find

Sometimes you just jump in not thinking how you'd feel
I'm sure it will get you in the end
It always gets you in the end
I need to get away – Just a change of pace
Somewhere people love each other, that's my kind of place
I still hear sirens in the night;
see those shadows of faces on the wall
Hoping light will make them disappear
and hoping I'll find my way home.

Finally, we were allowed to board the train. Once again I was heading for a city I knew nothing about, to continue my education and apprenticeship with the only true friend I had, Herr Kleinert. The conductor looked at my train pass and asked if I was traveling alone and when I said yes, he just shook his head as if to say I should have been in the shelter of my family not traveling across the country alone. Something about his face and demeanor reminded me of my father, it made me sad.

It was nearly Christmas, and I could not help but think back to my childhood Christmases back home. I loved the fact that we had snow on Christmas Eve; our town would be blanketed in white fluffy drifts. At each stop, more people got on. The train was near its capacity; our compartment alone was jammed with people. An elderly woman got on at one stop and she looked exhausted and weary. She desperately searched for an open seat so she could rest, when she couldn't find one you could see she was resigned to stand until the train reached her destination. When I noticed her I offered her my seat without hesitation, she thanked me profusely and dropped into the seat I had vacated. I found a place where I could sit down on my pressed cardboard koffer and look out into the night at the stars as we sped across the dark countryside. I could not sleep, my mind kept recalling all I had been through, the concentration camp, the bombings, the orphanage the children, the nuns and Father Daniel.

The train stopped in Potsdam and more people crowded on to the already overflowing train. I had to give up my window seat, due to the fact there simply was not enough room in the car to sit on the floor without being crushed. At times it seemed like the train had slowed and we would be traveling forever as we forged our way westward. Despite all the people, the cars held an eerie silence it was unnerving. Everyone had their own troubles and thoughts to keep themselves occupied.

Soon the conductor called out that we would be stopping in the town of Burg. This town was northeast of Magdeburg and so far was untouched by the bombings I was fleeing. Burg was located on the Ihle, an offshoot stream of the Havel Canal. It was interesting to note that even though the town hosted major industries it had not yet become a target of the bombing raids, but alas, this would not last, it too would fall to the destruction of the war. In Burg, many people got off the train. The old woman, whom I had given my seat to, got off the train at this stop. I took advantage of her leaving to reclaim my seat, where I could sit for a while in relative comfort. As the train began to pick up speed, I was told that the next stop would be Magdeburg.

We had been on the train for a long time, and I mentioned to a fellow passenger that I was thirsty; he offered me a drink from his travel canteen. I was grateful for that little act of compassion. We struck up a conversation and I learned that we both were getting off at Magdeburg. He told me he was going to visit his son who had been wounded on the Russian Front and was now in a military hospital there. He too had lost his wife and now lived alone with his sister in Berlin.

Magdeburg 1943

The next stop came fast. We were at Magdeburg, on the Elbe River. I learned it was an important industrial center, railway junction, and major river port. It was an older city and was known for its river crossing which made it a major trading town since the ninth century. Magdeburg was also the leading supplier of heavy engineering goods and of industrial equipment (famous for its steel and heavy machinery). As the train slowly rolled into the terminal, the locomotive gave out its final exhausting and long poof and came to a complete stop. People began streaming out of the train hurrying in all directions.

As I stood in the vast terminal, I was overwhelmed by the size of it. There were crowds of people going about their business. I stood there watching and marveling in the differences among all those people who swarmed about me. People were smiling and laughing, it had been so long since I had seen truly happy people seemingly without any worries moving about. This was so different from Berlin; the war seemed not to have touched this community.

I had a few German marks; I was hungry and splurged on a hot chocolate and a sandwich. I remembered the instructions in the letter, I had received from Herr Kleinert; I was to look for a porter in a uniform bearing the name of the establishment in which he was working. I was to look for him at the main entrance of the terminal. After the long and arduous train ride, I needed to stretch my legs. I waited until the crowds thinned a little. As their warm bodies cleared out of the terminal, the cool night air seeped back in making me shiver. It was early morning and I was tired. I was tired from not only the train ride, but also from the past few weeks in Berlin, I really could not remember when I had had a good night's sleep. I made my way to the main entrance to look toward my escort. It didn't take me long to find him. He was an elderly man dressed in a flashing uniform; I soon learned his name was Gustav. I introduced myself to him. He was very polite and he immediately attended to my luggage, my simple cardboard suitcase. My eyes could not escape his looks as he appraised my precious possessions. He looked at my simple suitcase and asked me if this was all I had, I answered it was and with that we left the terminal. He took me to his small car and once inside it he welcomed me to Magdeburg.

As we drove through the city, I was dumfounded and amazed when I saw all its beautiful buildings untouched by the ruthlessness of the war. I saw beautiful cathedrals, an opera house, and many other fascinating structures of rich architecture. The man must have been steeling glances at me as we drove along, and finally could not resist asking me if I was all right. I said I was. I didn't tell him how strange it seemed to see these beautiful things so close to the war, but yet they seemed as though they belonged in a different universe. The ride did not take too long and before I knew it, we were pulling in front of the hotel.

I couldn't help but be a little apprehensive about calling another place my home, but I knew I would have to adjust for the sake of my apprenticeship and because Herr Kleinert was doing his best for me. I was infinitely glad to be away from Berlin and the horror of the past few weeks. Although, I did already miss the children, the nuns, the volunteers, and Father Daniel I was looking forward to my new life here.

I was greeted by Herr Kleinert. He looked a little sad and drawn I knew he was lonely. His wife was not released from Auschwitz. She was a Jewess and he had to leave her behind. The hotel was simply beautiful and I was once again a little overwhelmed by it all. He looked the same as always, impeccably dressed, his silver hair glistened under the crystal chandelier, which was suspended from the domed ceiling in the lobby. His caring expression was in his warm smile as well as in his eyes. He asked me many questions about what my life had been like since he left Berlin and I answered them as well as I was able to.

Finally, he realized I was tired and he called in his executive housekeeper to take me to my room. It wasn't very spacious, but it was comfortable. My bed was like sleeping on a cloud, it was made with light feathers and down. I even had a private bathroom. I slipped gratefully between the covers and was asleep before I could even say my prayers.

I did not wake until late the next morning and only then because I heard knocking at my door. Groggily, I made my way to the door and upon opening it found a young woman standing there. She had a message from Herr Kleinert that he wanted to see me. I quickly dressed and went down to his office. I was escorted into an elegantly furnished room. He asked if I had slept well, I told him I had, and that it was the best sleep I had had in a long time. He then asked if I had heard anything from my parents. I told him I had heard nothing since last November when I was supposed to be able to go home, but was not able to because the trains were not running. He was sad for me. Herr Kleinert commented that I must be starving; I didn't realize just how much I was until I smelled the aroma of the delicious meal he had prepared for us. By then it had dawned on me that I had not eaten anything for about 24 hours.

Over our meal, he explained that I would need a new wardrobe. This was a fine hotel and the staff's appearance was a reflection of its reputation, therefore very important. He explained that quite often businessmen and government officials dined and frequented the establishment and I must remember to be on my best behavior and to put my best foot forward at all times. He had already enrolled me into a classical secondary school and I was expected to study hard to catch up with my peers. After school, I would be helping out in all the different departments within the hotel. As he explained my daily duties, my mind wandered in all directions trying to absorb all he was telling me. Even I knew that he was trying to assure me that I would be too busy to be homesick, but all it did was make me reflect on my childhood and all its good times; my loving home and family in contrast to how hard my life had become. My life now was fraught with miseries, betrayals, and longings, which hung around me like a huge impenetrable dark cloud.

Over the next few days, I willed myself to focus on the present and I found that once I let myself enjoy my new surroundings and experiences my life did become a little better. I felt safe in this city. I had a comfortable room, great food; I liked my teachers and enjoyed my duties at the hotel. When I returned each afternoon from my classes and had finished my homework, I was to report to the executive chef – Herr Reuter by 6 p.m. sharp. Chef Reuter wore his 'toque (tall pleated chef's hat)' as a sign that he was a professional chef. He gave me my nightly assignments; sometimes I helped prepare meals while other times I washed dishes. I worked until 10 p.m. when I would fall exhausted into my bed.

For the first time in my education, I was made fun of by some of the other students. They said I talked funny. My native language is Polish and when I explained to them that I had only been speaking German for four years, they backed off me a little. I explained to those who asked about my brushes with the war, although I didn't go into detail, it seemed to satisfy their thirsty minds, and I was able to put my energies into my studies. I had begun to make friends of my own age, which I had not let myself do over the past year. They pressured me to stay and play with them after school, but I had to refuse stating I had a job. Others wanted to know why I wasn't a member of the Hitler Youth. I was a member briefly in Auschwitz, but after all I had been through, I was in no hurry to rejoin the organization. Herr Kleinert knew my feelings regarding this and hadn't pressed as of yet to make my decision.

When I told Herr Kleinert about the comments, he said not to worry about it. Not many kids my age worked and the Hitler Youth was a good outlet for them. Joining would be in conflict with my working since they met in the afternoons, on weekends and on some holidays. He had hoped that since I was working, I might be overlooked.

I was making good progress in my apprenticeship. I was taking extra classes to make up for what I had missed and if all went well I would graduate in October of 1944, almost a year ahead of schedule. There were times when I got frustrated with having little or no time to myself. Herr Kleinert was always watching out for me and every once in a while, I would be allowed to go to the movies. This was my time to escape reality in the make believe world there in the dark. I was to be home by 10 p.m. and if I was late, I had to face a scolding by Herr Kleinert.

The last letter I had received from my brother Bernhard, stated that he was serving in the German Air Force. Even though I was busy and wanted free time to myself, when I had those precious free minutes I instantly was homesick. It was not as though I was being mistreated under Herr Kleinert's care; I just needed to be with my family if only for a little while.

In the hotel, Chef Rueter took me under his wing as his assistant. In the kitchen, I worked with mostly female cooks, since all the fighting age men were off to war. I got along well with them, which made me comfortable in my duties. I was taught that a good chef is well organized, that food had to have just the right balance, and to always remember that cooking was an 'art'. Chef Rueter stressed that food had to first be pleasing to the eye and then to the palette.

In school, the pressure to join the Hitler Youth was increasing with each passing day. When I expressed my concerns about this to Herr Kleinert, he explained that it was a condition of our release. He had been forced to join the NSDAP (Nazi Party) and that I had no other choice but to join, the Hitler Youth.

It was now 1944, Christmas had just passed, so had the New Year and it was another one away from my family. Although, I had to admit, it was easy to fall in love with this city and its people.   Its rich heritage and beautiful architecture was mesmerizing. In school, I was taught more of the city's history. There was the Cathedral where Emperor Otto I was buried (he founded the city of Magdeburg), the Monastery of Our Lady (which was an architectural marvel in its Romanesque style), its huge bridges which connected the two parts of the city were also marvels of the day. One of my assignments given at the end of a semester was to write an essay. I was a little apprehensive about it, but I knew I would do my best despite my poor command of the German language. We had to write about something meaningful, I wasn't sure what I should write about. I asked Herr Kleinert for ideas, he advised me to write from the heart and my experiences, but to be careful what I wrote about.

I turned in my essay along with everyone else. Several days passed until one day the teacher laid my essay on my desk and announced to the class that if I was willing, he wanted me to read it aloud. The class sat in silence as I stood up next to my desk with my paper in my hands. My body shook and the paper trembled as I tried to focus in on my words. My essay was a portrait of my love for my parents, my brother, and my sisters. It painted a background of my life in a small city in Poland. It highlighted my memories of my grandparents' farm. I colored in the blue skies with sorrowful regrets of not having enough time with my birth mother and my oldest sister. The edges of my paper were filled in with growing up in the Great Depression. I filled in the spaces with the truth about going to bed hungry and frightened. I painted in the foreground with lessons my stepmother taught me and how she loved me like her own. She taught me values, respect, and honesty. She taught me to be kind to others and how to keep our faith. As I finished my paper, I realized I had tears rolling down my cheeks. Instead of being ridiculed by my peers, they broke into a sincere applause. Even our teacher who was a member of the NSDAP and who was a stoic man who showed few soft emotions had tears welling in his eyes as he surveyed his class. I felt I had won the respect of my classmates from that day on. Herr Kleinert asked me how things went at school, because he knew how anxious I was about this project, but when I told him what had happened he was truly proud of me.

As much as I liked school and my work at the Hotel, I disliked being part of the Hitler Youth. I had to miss a meeting and was severely reprimanded by the group leader, my punishment was extra duties.

Weeks passed and so did another winter. Soon it would be spring break and final exams. As each day passed, hopes were dashed when I failed to receive any mail or word from my family. I knew the war in the East was far from being over and that worried me a great deal, but one had to be careful about voicing aloud ones opinions. I kept a secret journal where I could write down my thoughts and fears. Writing in it allowed me to "talk" to my family and to write down things I could not find the way to say in person to those around me. No one knew where it was hidden, not even my closest confidants Olga and Nina the two Ukrainian chambermaids. Even though they did not speak German, they did speak Polish and Russian, so we were able to converse. They looked after me well, by keeping my room neat and my clothes clean. We met secretly so we could talk about our lives and families. We had a lot in common. Even though I had them and the kitchen staff, what I lacked was a father figure to confide in. Herr Kleinert was good to me, but his time was often taken up with the demands of running the hotel and negotiating with high-ranking government officials and this left little time for me.

It was mid April of that year, when I arrived home from my classes, that I was met by the concierge who informed me that Herr Kleinert wanted to see me as soon as I arrived at the hotel. I did not think I had done anything wrong, but nevertheless I was nervous as I entered his office. He welcomed me as always with a sincere good afternoon, but I could tell there was something in his tone that I had not heard there before. We spoke briefly about my upcoming exams and the written exam I was to take for my apprenticeship. After a long pause, he stated that a letter came for me. Immediately I asked with elation, if it was from my parents.

He said no, that it was a letter from the Ober Kommando Der Deutshen Wehrmacht (the High Command of the German Army). It was my conscription. At first, I thought he was joking, but deep down I knew Herr Kleinert would not joke about such a thing. I was to report for a physical examination at the Wehrmacht headquarters. I was devastated. My world had collapsed with that single piece of paper. What was going to happen to me? Would I even be able to use my education? What did my future hold now? I was only sixteen and a half years old. Herr Kleinert comforted me the best he could and I spent the night staring into the darkness.

The next day I told my teacher about the directive and that, I was to report in two days. He too had served in the wars and felt great compassion for me as well as many of my classmates who were also summoned. We were excused from classes.

The day came when we were to report at the Wehrmacht headquarters, I could see that I wasn't the only one who was scared. We were given our physicals and were instructed as to what we could bring with us, which wasn't much. We were to report to the train station at the end of April, only three days away.

I spent those days saying goodbye to all those I had grown to love Olga, Nina, Chef Rueter, the kitchen staff, and of course Herr Kleinert. With tears streaming down all our faces I again had to leave a place I had come to know as home. I walked slowly to the terminal taking time to ingrain all the beauty this city had to offer into my soul. I wanted never to forget my time here or the people who I was blessed to know and love. As I walked along, I found I was still in denial about what was happening. I wanted to finish my education, I had worked so hard to catch up so I would be able to finish ahead of schedule and I wanted to complete my apprenticeship, but now all that was nothing more than a shattered dream.

Looking around the station I spotted a German Wehrmacht Information kiosk, I went over to it and asked the officer where I should be. He asked to look at my papers and he directed me to where I was to report. He was very kind and helpful. I found the spot where we were to wait and I stood amongst a group of boys the same age as me. The only real difference was that many of them were laughing and singing German Army songs. I was surprised with how many wanted to join the Wehrmacht. I was not ready to be a soldier, nor did I want to be one. For those who took their membership in the Hitler Youth seriously, this is what they had been preparing for. Our papers were checked and double-checked; we were given our train passes and told to wait on the platform. I found myself standing on the same platform waiting for the train that brought me here four months ago, the same train that would be taking me away from my 'home'.

I still could not believe this was seriously happening. I was really going off to war. My world had caved in around me; I was beside myself with fear. I could not believe I was on my way to boot camp to learn to be a soldier. I let my mind go back to all that had happened to me over the past year and I found so little joy to carry me through what I would now be facing.

The train finally rolled into the station. As I looked into the windows, I could see it was already crowded. Someone whispered that it was a 'war' train now. It had grown dark and it had become chilly on this early spring evening. The train spewed out its acrid smoke from its coal-burning locomotive into the night air. The train's shrill whistle cut through the tension on the platform as we were told to start boarding. Those that had relatives there with them said their goodbyes. I stood there alone and watched this heart-wrenching scene unfold around me. We no sooner found a place to sit, when the train began to pull out of the station. There was no looking back as we picked up speed and disappeared into the mist like a ghost in the night. Silently, I said my goodbyes to Magdeburg and its people for I knew I would never be back.

Leaving Magdeburg for Boot Camp

I found myself sitting next to a man in uniform. I asked him his rank and he told me he was a staff sergeant. On his coat he wore two medals with pride: Das Eiserne Kruez (the Iron Cross) and Das Verwundeten Zeichen (the Purple Heart), both awarded to him for gallantry. The citation said something to the effect of "Devotion beyond the realm of duty." This reminded me of my own father, who too had these same honors bestowed on him when he served in WWI. This staff sergeant asked me where

I was going, I told him, and that I was on my way to Lunenburg Camp. He asked my age and when I told him, he just looked at me and sighed not saying another word. I could tell he was proud to be a soldier, but I could tell he was sad to see the youth around him being drafted into this horrible way of life. He swayed with the motion of the train, but his sway seemed to come from within, almost as if he was in mourning; something from his soul trying to get out, to escape.

After about an hour, the train stopped in the city of Hameln. I noticed that the station was roped off to one side. In that space were more draftees. German soldiers were issuing final instructions as the boys families stood on the other side of the rope looking on. I could see in this group not all were happy about going to war. Some discreetly wiped away tears as quickly as they formed. Some broke ranks to get that last kiss or hug from their loved ones. I turned away from the sight. I knew I would see my share of unsolicited pain once I was out of boot camp and had no desire to watch this sadness unfold.

As we got rolling again, the soldier next to me suddenly got up and moved to another car. Maybe he didn't like being around civilians, maybe he could not bear the thought of wasting the young on this war, maybe he just needed to be alone with his thoughts. War can make even the strongest most courageous solder sad inside. As I recount the events of that night, I think about how scared I was. How I dreaded what lay ahead of me. It started to rain, it seemed as though the angels were crying for us. I remember the sight of the lights flickering in the windows from homes lining the tracks and how they momentarily illuminated the faces of all of the young soldiers to be on that train.

After a while, the soldier returned to his seat next to me. I watched as he groomed his mustache with his fingers and lit a cigarette. His dark eyes found mine and I turned away for I could see the death behind his eyes and that made me uneasy.

The flicker of lights as we pulled in Hanover denoted that this must be a bigger city than the last stop. We witnessed the same scene as we did at the previous stop. It was late at night and there were hundreds of men waiting to board. The staff sergeant who had been sitting next to me left the train, as had many others of its passengers. In the background of the station there was a huge banner attached to the wall, which read "Deutschland Über Alles" (Germany over all). Hitler wanted to conquer the world, but this was confutable. I learned that the German Wehrmacht on the Russian front was crumbling and the casualty count was high. Hitler needed more soldiers and the young boys, especially those that were in the Hitler Youth were his last hope.

These stops continued all night and before long, the train was crowded to its capacity. Some sang or chanted "Deutschland – Deustchland Über Alles (Germany – Germany over all), those that sang also couldn't wait until they could put that soldier uniform on. All I could think was God help them. Amidst the din and apprehension sleeping or even catching a catnap was virtually impossible, the night wore on.

I couldn't help but wonder when I would see my family again if ever. I knew if I wanted to survive, I would have to look deep within myself to find the strength I needed to make it through this. I had had my own hopes and illusions about my future, but those dreams were now shattered.

My orders were to report to Münster, in Westphalia. As we neared it, I asked the Lord for his protection. A new day was dawning as the train finally slowed down and the locomotive gave out its exhausted blast of steam. As we pulled along side, the platform I looked out at the crowded noisy station and thought that this was home for me for at least a while. From Munster, we were taken to the German Wehrmacht boot camp. Most of us had already been traveling since early the previous day, when we finally arrived at the processing station at dawn the next morning.

Boot camp changed our life over night. Many of the boys like me, were only sixteen years old, the oldest being eighteen. I had a hard time imagining that at sixteen and a half I was going to be trained to be a soldier. Reality of our situation set in quickly. The next morning as we stood outside, barely awake in the chilly spring air before our sergeant as he yelled at us and trained us on when and how to say "Yes, Sir!" After what seemed to be an eternity of this repetitious lesson, we were told to report to the supply area where we would be outfitted with our gear and uniforms. We all felt like we had been knocked off balance by the bizarre tumult of angry men shouting insanely about underwear, flip-flops, and boots; they made it seem like our survival depended on these mundane items. We learned the army lingo quickly and learned fast to answering with "Yes, Sir!"

Wake up call was at five o'clock in the morning to the sound of our 'unteroffizier' (sergeant) shrieking at us to get up. Many times, it felt like we had not slept at all. Cold showers shocked our bodies to life and we were then off to breakfast; after which we were handed over to the drill instructors. Over and over we would repeat the basic movements on how to handle our rifle, where our hands were to be placed and at what angle it was to be held in our arms. We practiced crawling along the ground, by noon we were filthy, sweaty, and wrung out.

Often times the staff sergeant would watch our drills and point out those of us who needed extra practice or make snide comments about how hard all of this was on us 'young' boys. We were made to shout "Ehre!" (Honor!) "Courage, commitment to the Reich and Führer-Adolf Hitler!" "Kill, Kill!" "Sieg Heil! Lange lebt der Führer!" (May he live long!) This haiku was ingrained in our young brains. We were shouted at for every instruction and if we tried to relax. We were taught a completely new set of terminology for our new way of life; windows were 'bulls eyes', our beds were 'racks', and the lane that divided the barrack's bunkers was called the 'Drill Unteroffizier's Highway' and when he was on it, we had better be off it. Even the simple task of making a bed turned into a team project. We were in constant fear of our crazy sergeant. It was stressed that when he said something, we had better jump and to do it quickly and right the first time. If we didn't work hard enough, we drilled through until evening without breaks or meals.

None of us knew how to march and we were not let to forget it. We were called 'infants'. Because we had to be taught how to march like German soldiers. When we were allowed to eat our meals, we were not allowed to talk whether we were in line or sitting at the tables. The only thing we were allowed to utter was "Danke" (Thankyou) for whatever food they put on our tray. Even during our meals there was no respite. The sergeant circled the tables and lectured us as we ate. We grew tired and confused. We were to do things fast and many times we were pulled in different directions at the same time. Many times, we were told that by the time we left boot camp; we would all breathe, think, look, talk, and walk alike.

One time while marching, a recruit rolled his eyes in dismay and must have moved his head. The always-vigilant sergeant was instantly at his side. He pulled the boy out of formation and shouted into his face as to what his problem was. We were scared for him and for us. The boy quietly said he was not cut out for army life and didn't think he could do it anymore. He started to cry. The sergeant asked him if this was the worst day of his life and Edward, the recruit, nodded and replied with a "Yes, Sir!" The sergeant addressed all of us. He said that there had been 10,000 recruits who have felt like us and that they all walked across the parade ground and graduated and became loyal soldiers to the great German Reich. He told us to be proud to serve this country.

Edward, who later became my friend, was put back into formation and we continued on with our drill. Over the next eight weeks, he looked like he would crumble at any minute. Many times, he confided to me that he did not think he could take the stress. We were told by the sergeant that tears wouldn't cut it, which at some point every recruit breaks down, but they always pulled themselves back up to carry on.

The camp itself was set outside a small town called Munster Lager. It was set in a remote area away from homes and the town itself. We were completely isolated and had to depend and rely on the camp and its staff for our training, well being, and survival.

Besides the physical instruction we were given, we also attended classroom sessions. The classroom was an open bay at the end of the barracks. We sat on the cement floor and were taught from a book called 'Knowledge', this was the one word title of a guide we were given on our first day of instruction. We were to carry these little white booklets everywhere we went. It didn't take long for its white pages to turn brown as it soaked up our sweat and the dust we carried with us everywhere. We were to study it in our off time, of which we had very little. We were to learn the order of the ten people who where in command and what their role was; but mostly we were to learn all there was to know about the Führer, of the Great German Reich was. I remember there were two crucial pages called the "Customs and Courtesies" and we were to memorize them. One key phrase that sticks in my head is the definition of knowledge. Knowledge is Power. We were never to forget it.

For the next eight weeks, every order we heard was to be executed immediately. For those entire two months, we trained and drilled every waking moment. During this time, we were never told when we would actually have to use any of this training. We were still boys, we weren't really soldiers yet, just trained puppets. Our identities had been stripped away and we were a jelled unit. Everything we had belonged to the German Wehrmacht, we had nothing to call our own. All we knew was that we were trained to fight and we were too young to do so.

My friend, Edward, the recruit who told our sergeant he could not go on, proved to be a godsend to many of us in the barracks. He had the intelligence to teach those of us a little slower to catch on the tricks they wanted us to know, he had the physical strength to help us whenever we needed the extra boost. The contrast between us was amazing. He was this hulking mass of boy and I was this wiry little boy that could not speak out for himself. I myself thought at times of giving up, running away from it all, but where would I have gone? I could not have gone home to my parents and would never have been able to face Herr Kleinert if I defected from this army.

Once again, I felt very lost, but what got me through the tough times was prayer. My faith and trust in my Lord gave me strength to go on and to face each day as they came. Each morning we were awaken by the now familiar voice of our drill sergeant. Each day we were even more tired and exhausted from drills the day before. Each day we were assured in no uncertain terms that we would be made into soldiers or we would die once we were sent into action.

Soon the time came when we actually were allowed to fire our rifles. We were taken to an open rifle range for basic training on our weapon. The range was located behind a wooded area of the boot camp about ten kilometers away. We hiked this distance in full gear every day. I knew I would have a problem with this area of my training. I had been taught not to do harm and it was evident that when I saw harm happening to others, it affected me deeply. Where I was allowed to depend on Edward in the barracks, we were separated at the rifle range. I had been using him as a buffer between the officers, and myself now I had to face my fate alone. I was assigned to a new platoon and told to pay close attention. We hit the range as early as six o'clock in the morning. Our instructor took great pains to explain the importance of our weapon and how we handled it. There were four common sense rules we had to live by when we had that rifle in our hands, they were:

Treat every weapon as if it were loaded
Keep your finger off the trigger until ready to fire
Keep the weapon on safety until you intend to fire
Never point the weapon at anything unless you intend to shoot it.

Then we had classes on Introduction to the Infantry Marksmanship, followed by Fundamentals of Marksmanship, then Introduction to Positions, and finally Shooting Positions. There were three common elements to any shooting position that were drilled into us: relax our muscles, use the bones in our bodies (not our muscles) to support as much of the weight of the rifle as possible, and to fire at the natural point of aim; this is the point on which the rifle sights settle when the first two conditions are realized. I wasn't very tall nor big so just holding the rifle at point made my arms shake. Aiming it took all my concentration, and shooting it jerked my body and head backward with such force I was sure I would injure myself. One session the drill instructor saw this reaction to the force of the weapon and ordered me off the range. He screamed at me insanely as he handed me over to a special instructor who took me to the pit for a little wake-up call after which I was forced to run for five kilometers in full gear.

Each day was the repetition of the day before. Fatigue set in and I often wondered if I would make it through the training. I wasn't alone though. When I looked around me, all I saw were boys; we weren't men or soldiers, we were just kids some of us not even through school yet. One day a new instructor was introduced to us, he was a veteran SS sturmbannführer. He was a tall slim man with a sarcastic manner. Immediately we could tell he was a true Nazi. We quickly grew to fear his discipline. Rumor had it that he had been wounded twice on the Russian Front, he walked lamely on one of his legs making him unfit for combat.

We were told that due to the huge losses the German army had suffered both on the Russian Front and in Africa, Hitler needed to replenish his armies and the only option he had left was to start recruiting the youth of Germany. This new commandant took over our company and our training. He was adamant that he would teach us to shoot with the emphasis on the final kill. We would be able to shoot while sitting, standing and prone to the ground. We were taught how to adjust our aim for the weather conditions and the wind. Every day began with a five-kilometer run and the twelve-hour days ended with us falling exhausted into our racks. This hard training regimen was because they needed us trained and ready to go in a very short amount of time. We tried hard to impress this new kommandant whether we did or not, we rarely knew.

If we failed to impress him, which I did on several occasions resulted in a trip to the 'pit'. The pit was filled with wet sand and sand fleas. The punishment was often pushups into the sand of the pit. The fleas took advantage of the activity and eagerly bit at whatever exposed flesh they could find. If the offender missed his platoon's departure from the training site, they were forced to run and catch up with them while carrying their full gear. There was one occasion when we were at the shooting range and it started to rain. We were to get into our ponchos so we could continue our lesson. I had trouble with mine and could not get it on over my pack. The sergeant shouted at me calling me names and finally ordered me out of the formation. The rest of the platoon was told to move on without me. I was told to perform my pushups and while I was doing them, he asked me my age. When I told him, he commented that it was a shame that I had been neglected in my upbringing and that I had to forget who I was before and to realize that I was now at their mercy and I would at some point realize that and do it their way and if I didn't, it was assured that I would die.

Our lives began to revolve around our rifles. This piece of metal was to become our best friend. It was to become our only means of survival. We had to master it and in doing so we would master our lives; and ultimately to the glory and victory of the Führer and the German Reich. The mantra we shouted when given these speeches was "Sieg Heil! Sieg Heil! Sieg Heil!" We were to shoot true before our opponent had a chance to shoot us, we had to kill first or be killed. We were taught to kill blindly and without hesitation.

One day our lessons included bayonet fighting. This meant being face to face with the person, we were obligated to kill. I knew I would have a hard time doing this, but I was required to sit through the sessions and demonstrate the skills taught to me. The sergeant used pugil sticks to simulate bayonet-fighting techniques. It was a daunting experience. The duels were short, but very violent. Many times, I found myself lying on my back in the mud looking up at my attacker. Only the strong will survive in matches such as these. After each session, I was humiliated in front of my peers by the instructor; he never failed to point out that I was weak, immature, and too timid. I felt I let my platoon down. Would they be able to count on me when the time came? I did not know if I could actually do what I had been trained to do when the time came.

At night I cried into my pillow, I was so homesick I thought I would burst into a million pieces from the aches inside my heart. I felt that the whole world had abandoned me. Often, I wondered where they found the men that they put in charge of us. Were they insane? Were they criminals? They never simply talked to us, they always screamed or shouted their orders. There were times when we just did not think we could please them and after a while, the verbal abuse was just as painful as the physical punishments they laid on us. The drill sergeants never seemed to sleep, the nights became shorter with each passing day. We were never alone, never without someone watching our every move. To punish us even more or to keep us off our guard, we were taken out on night marches through impossible terrain in the dark. We were not allowed to show our frustration or emotions, which put us, all on edge. One day I was pulled out of ranks and told that I was not measuring up to the unit's expectations and he threatened to have me sent up to a special unit where my training would only take place at night. I was frightened of this possibility to the point that I forced myself to do the very best I could even when I thought I could no more. It worked, after a few days I was once again called out and told that I had improved and would remain with the unit.

Over and over again, we were told that we must become men and soldiers. We needed to remember that we would be fighting 'real' soldiers and it would mean that we needed to kill or be killed. We were reminded that we were not alone; that countless others had gone before us. No power was more fickle or more of a force to be reckoned with than the field of battle. This was a treacherous one in which only the well trained would survive. The survival of the German Reich rested on our shoulders.

New lessons were given in map reading and using a compass. Fearful lessons in gas torture (chambers) provoked nightmares after the day's activities. Remembering the experience in the gas chamber still causes me to break out in a sweat. Individually, we would don our gas masks and enter the room. The tear gas would be released, we would have to take off and put on our masks over increasing time periods. It truly was torture, not letting ourselves take a breath. When we finally were allowed out of the chamber, tears would be running down our faces, mucus from our noses and eventually we would vomit from the stench and effort it took to perform the task. Over all we made it through the exercise pretty well.

We were taught to be ever vigilant. We had to be mindful of the conflicts that would unfold at any given moment and we needed to watch the shadow of our enemy. Our marches were stepped up with the added weight in our packs and increased distances sometimes up to 35 kilometers in the heat of the early summer. We were pushed to and beyond our limits to break us and to make us able to face the next day with hopes it would be easier. We were shown how far we could be pushed and still manage to survive, it was meant to make us more confident in our conditioning. It was amazing to see how we had changed over the past few weeks, I was beginning to see signs of maturity in myself and those around me. We were far from being men, but we were becoming soldiers. The last few weeks were devoted to putting the finishing touches on our training. In mid June of 1944, I was deployed to a highly classified unit.

A Green Recruit

When it came time to write this chapter I had a difficult time and mixed emotions about undertaking the task. The longer I procrastinated about it the more reluctant I became and yet my inner voice told me that my soul needed relief from its horror which had been holding it captive for seemingly unending years. The reality I'd seen touched me deeply and directly.

I knew I had to face my fate, I was forced into the war along with thousands of other teenage boys; all we had were our prayers, our faith and hope that we would come out of it alive. I relied on what I had been taught as a child, to take one day at a time and to never lose my focus and faith. As I reflect back on those days, I freely admit that there had to have been a divine power looking over me and shielding me from harm, it was truly a miracle that I survived the war.

After making it through boot camp, I was now a "green" soldier, very young and with no experience in the real art of warfare. To top it off I was even more homesick than ever. Letters from home never came, I never heard from my parents at all, even though I had written them on three different occasions since my conscription. It made me very sad and depressed at times, but my daily duties kept me going. When Herr Kleinert answered my letters he wrote me long letters of encouragement and sent notes from everyone about how I was missed at the hotel. I missed them too, he made sure I knew that his door was always open to me and when the war was over he definitely wanted me to complete my education under his tutelage. Knowing that gave me a great deal of comfort and needless to say lifted my sagging spirits.

As I said in the last chapter I was assigned to a highly classified unit with experienced soldiers who were in charge of an underground depot of Hitler's Secret Weapon, the V-I Flying rocket and the V-2 rocket. V-weapons or vergeltungswaffen (revenge weapons) were called Hitler's wunderwaffen or miracle weapons. Our objective was to guard these wunderwaffen with our lives twenty-four hours a day, seven days a week. In addition to these v-weapons there were innumerable JU's 52 the Germany's most dependable Luftwaffe transport air craft (a workhorse), which also required a twenty-four hour watch. There were two air strips for the planes to take off and land which needed to be constantly maintained and repaired. Sometimes these airstrips needed to be repaired quickly when the British bombers would do their best to break it up. We were in charge of seeing that those repairs were made and that the planes would be able to land and take off at a moment's notice. On one such occasion, an air raid leveled the living quarters of this camp which housed the Luftwaffe pilots and ground troops; this required us to quickly rebuild everything just so we could carry on our normal routine in camp. We worked around the clock in the rain and mud in order to get it done. Our army rations were low, I needed a new pair of boots, but food and supplies were delayed. We lived on tuna fish and rye bread and I would have to continue to work in wet feet until our supply truck showed up. Supplies did not come regularly, many times they were delayed due to air raids, lack of transportation trucks, or simply no one to deliver them; so we had to improvise. It was not a simple life.

There was never a lull in our duties. The air strips were in constant need of repairs due to the never ceasing bombing raids. It was a constant battle. The raids shattered our days as well as our nights, the lack of sleep did not help our moods. Morale in the camp had begun to deteriorate and the weather did not help any. There wasn't much time for recreational activities, except for our routine exercise. We were on duty 24/7, always on alert, sleeping only a few hours before going on guard duty. Occasionally, someone would break into song and we would half heartedly join in. With the constant threat of attack literally hanging over our heads no one felt in a jovial mood. Losing our friends or comrades was very depressing. After a while you learned not to get close to anyone for fear the next minute they would be gone. The dead and wounded were replaced with new ones, mostly young men who quivered in their boots and cried at night. Each day was an unpredictable one. We never knew when one's turn would come, it was a cruel way to have to live. You might wonder what happened to my friend Edward, from boot camp. He was sent to a different unit; I often wondered what happened to him with the way he started out. I never saw him again.

Many times we would be out on the airstrip and a group of British Spitfires would swoop in and fire at us. All we could do was drop to the ground and hold on to our helmets and pray we would survive. On one raid, which only lasted a few minutes, it killed four soldiers and wounded many of those in camp. I helped carry the wounded and bleeding bodies to the medical area. It forced you to grow up fast. The sight of young men lying there helpless on the ground, their faces covered with blood, or whose arms or legs were missing, or having to carry those lifeless bodies back to our compound was the worst and saddest time of my life.

Our wehrmacht was fighting on three fronts; in Russia, western Europe, and in Italy. The tide had begun to turn when Field Marshall Paulus, commander of the sixth army surrendered at Stalingrad in late January 1943. This enabled Stalin's army to push the crumbling wehrmacht into retreat. Hitler's Third Reich was in peril. A constant stream of Allied bombers flew over Germany's cities: Berlin, Hamburg, Dresden, and Koln; in Hamburg alone, over a million citizens fled to the countryside. Thousands of homes were destroyed as the bombers dropped their deadly cargo over Hamburg, I wondered about my aunt, who lived in Hamburg during that time.

It was June 1944 when we got the news through unconfirmed rumors that an invasion was taking place in France by American troops. Hitler wanted this news kept under wraps. We were not even allowed to mention the word "invasion". On July 20, 1944, I was assigned to guard duty which meant I was to circle the compound. It was a beautiful summer day, when from nowhere planes were droning above us and dropping their deadly cargo and pulverizing us with a barrage of fire. The casualties were high and so was the damage to the aircrafts. Two pilots who were checking their JU 52s were killed when their planes were hit by bombs which instantly exploded. These explosions sent huge mushroom shaped plumes of smoke and fire into the air. Some of the pilots were killed and many airplane mechanics were severely burned. We spent a most miserable day and night trying to rescue men out of the fires. We lost two men out of our company, they were overcome by smoke and charred beyond recognition. We found them the next morning. I had just gotten to know them. They were new to our unit. They were from the Hitler Youth, just young boys.

On this day there was an attempt to kill Hitler. Many of his entourage were wounded, but he managed to escape unharmed. We heard that Hitler had ordered a massive witch hunt for the people behind this attempt on his life. Among those who were arrested was a Colonel Claus Von Staufenburg. After his short "trial" he was shot. Others were tortured, tried, and hanged. Field Marshal Erwin Rommel, a highly decorated officer, was forced to commit suicide to save his wife and son from the notorious Gestapo.

The Nazi leaders were committed to sharing the Führer's fate. The German people and we soldiers were still hopeful. Despite everything, Hitler was still respected as someone above and beyond the common person. The complexity of the war was enormous. Despite all that we were enduring, the horrible war went on. On the surface there were still reasons for optimism as the war went on. The reason for this optimism by many hard line German Nazis was that they still believed that Hitler and his cronies could win the war. How well the German wehrmacht performed and how outstanding the troops fought was never talked about. We didn't get to hear any news and if we did it was mostly propaganda. Everything was kept quiet or downplayed. Little was said about D-day, even though it was well executed and became the turning point of WWII. Millions of lives were already lost and millions of families were homeless and displaced.

The wehrmacht's fighting was unparalleled, yet we were losing ground on all three fronts. German soldiers gave it all they had, yet they were not making any progress. Mostly due to lack of supplies; chiefly ammunition, guns, tanks, fuel supply, heavy army trucks, not to mention the lack of food. Hitler was forever making changes to his leaders on the lines. He didn't trust his generals and when you make drastic changes like that it creates mistrust and misdirection of ideals and goals, which in turn racked up huge amounts of casualties as well as losing their hold on terrain, which men fought so hard to earn. We had lost control of the war. Women were forced to work in factories to produce ammunition and all the necessary equipment needed for the troops. We were told to improvise when and wherever possible. We utilized our resources to their fullest potential. We never left anything behind.

We made our own repairs to our vehicles and treated our personal effects as though we would never get them replaced. We were not to waste ammunition. We were to make certain we had someone in our sights before we pulled the trigger. This forced frugality has stayed with me all these years; I never pass up the opportunity to make something useful from someone's discarded possessions. Germany was caught up in nearly six years of war and was struggling to survive, yet we were not willing to give up.

I was only twelve years old when Herman Goring, Chief of the Luftwaffe, publicly stated that not one enemy bomb would fall on Berlin or any German city. Obviously, this promise was not able to be upheld. I had lived through countless air raids and the concentration camp and was very fortunate to have survived when so many hadn't.

On July 21, 1944, the day following the attempt on Hitler's life, I was assigned to night watch. I was terrified. There were fifty-five of us "green" soldiers posted about fifty meters apart from each other. We would walk our post, meet up with the soldier on either our right or left, exchange the password of the night and repeat this process all night. Security was very tight. A full moon peeked through the clouds, shining just enough light down upon us to illuminate our area of watch. During one of my tours, I noticed a shadow along my peripheral vision; pulling my rifle from my shoulder, I yelled, "Halt!" I demanded our camp password and got no response from the shadows. I heard shots in the near distance. I was too scared to fire my own weapon, but my shouts brought soldiers from all around me to see what was going on. A search of the area proved no one was there, I was removed from my post.

Our unit was placed on high alert due to our huge arsenal of weapons, ammunition, and the V-I's we were in constant threat of an attack. It was a dangerous time. Since the plot against Hitler, our officers had been replaced by SS officers. Hitler was forced to re-organize his leadership and especially his inner circle of trusted advisors. Fearing a possible sabotage attempt we were always under the scrutiny of the SS officers. We had to watch what we said to each other, even things said in jest. The SS officer's goal was to protect and guard this highly dangerous compound at whatever cost. They were deeply devoted to this country and most of all to Hitler. Nothing else mattered. They were willing and ready to sacrifice their lives, sans regret. Their conviction was that the war would be a victorious one; even though we as soldiers were taught to believe this same philosophy we did our part with grim bitter determination.

It didn't matter to Hitler nor Himmler how many soldiers died fighting a losing battle. The stream of dead bodies never stopped. It was a time of unimaginable pain and sorrow. Mothers, wives, and children were left behind to struggle daily to survive without their sons, husbands, and fathers.

Since the attack on Hitler, the power of the Gestapo and the SS had gotten out of hand. No one who was arrested, whether it be a soldier or an officer had a chance to protest. There usually was no appeal or trial by jury. The Gestapo made the final decision. Hitler demanded it this way. Over the next several months as many as 5,000 people were killed by his inner sanctum. Hitler trusted no one.

Wounded on the Eastern Front

On October 1, 1944 most of my unit, about two hundred men, were sent to the Eastern front, I was one of them, but not knowing where we were going was scary. We were all worried. The Russian army was making great progress and had broken through the zone of German defenses. Hitler more than ever depended on us new recruits which were mostly his Hitler Youth. We were now being sent into the most searing and intensive infantry fighting in the theatre of war. Our unit traveled by train, though we did not know our final destination, we did know we were being shipped east. There were rumors that we were going to the Baltic Sea Region. Two days later we were in our new deployment area approximately forty kilometers south of Königsberg (formerly East Prussia).

On October 4, 1944 a thick fog hung over the lake near our camp and lingered there most of the day. Without warning Russian guns opened fire along with heavy artillery which we thought would never end. It was a long and very frightening day. The fog turned into a heavy rain turning the already horrendous conditions into a mud bath. The heavy Russian artillery guns would not stop. They just kept hammering in our direction. Nine men were killed and seven were wounded. We were outnumbered. The only thing we were able to do was take our wounded with us as we back peddled, leaving the dead to hopefully be retrieved another day. Our captain, Hans Rulisch, demanded that we must take all our wounded with us. This instilled in us a semblance of humanity. We made our way through what at first seemed like an impossible terrain, which came out in a small village where we found German Red Cross trucks. They relieved us of our injured and we set up camp alongside their fire under their makeshift shelter. Refreshed somewhat, we were able to move on.

The German command began to withdraw our troops, which saved many lives, but with our withdrawal came the Russian troops right on our heels. Our command needed more men, but the resources to draw from were dwindling. We were running low on ammunition and we had no other choice but to retreat.

October had always been my favorite month of the year as a child. I couldn't help but take time to reflect back to those times when the nights got quiet and we were allowed to rest. October at home meant time at my grandparents' farm. The colors of fall in my hometown were at their peak in October, the brilliant colors painted the countryside; there was beauty everywhere. Now, wherever I looked I only saw ugliness and despair. October was also the month in which I was born.

We were pushed further back by the advancing Russian troops, which to us never seemed to rest. The Russians were constantly penetrating our defensive lines and had captured thousands of German soldiers. It was common knowledge that once you became a prisoner of war by the Russians, your chances of survival were very slim. Our orders were to kill as many advancing Russians as possible. What jeopardized the war effort was Hitler's preoccupation with his situation which took his focus off the real issues of the war and his refusal to accept the need for an organized withdrawal.

Our supply of rations, clothing, equipment, and ammunition by the German Luftwaffe was doomed. Our uniforms were in tatters and we were surviving on scant rations of bread and horsemeat. The Junkers-JU 52's the so called workhorses of the

German air force could not provide all the necessary supplies to all the compounds set up over the country. It didn't help either that we were constantly being shelled. Our equipment was in bad shape making it virtually impossible to maintain any state of morale.

It was difficult to comprehend the entire situation we'd been living in. Every day we witnessed more of our comrades falling to the enemy's attacks. We all thought about our families and prayed for their safety along with ours. We were fortunate to have a fine SS captain leading our infantry at that time. He seemed to care about us, but at the same time he demanded only the best from his men and pushed to achieve it. He reminded us of our oath to the Führer and to the German Reich; to be obedient and to serve our vaterland. Deserters would be executed.

I remember one disastrous stand, we were positioned in our trenches at the edge of a village, our captain coordinated and prepared for an attack of an advancing Russian infantry brigade armed with dozens of tanks. I caught the eye of the captain, fear registered in my eyes, and after he issued the final orders for the attack he assured me he would always be in front of me. With that we moved out. Our attack failed and many men were killed along with our fine captain. There wasn't much time to grieve. You learned to take losses in stride and you grieved silently inside as you marched along, or dug your ditch. You had to think about those of you who had survived an attack and how you would survive the next one. The SS captain who stepped in as his replacement believed that if you left your soft underbelly show, you would not make it through this war. It was his way of life that he instilled in us.

The strength of the Red army forces was too overpowering, yet a surrender at this point was out of the question. We retreated as fast as we could and sought to join up with a nearby German troop. The face of this horrible war had changed dramatically. We moved on without rest, our spirits were broken, our hopes of winning this war had vanished. I have no doubt that the collective prayers of our platoon kept us alive. There was no chaplain in the unit; Hitler did not believe in the church. He believed if we were going to pray it was to be to him or his efforts. We were to be completely devoted to the Führer. As defeated as we were, we were not ready to give up. Somewhere along the lines we had begun to show the maturity and dedication of real soldiers; loyal to his country and the war effort.

I still wake at night to the images of hundreds of faces of men in pain. These images still haunt me after all these years. I see the faces of all the young boys killed in action for a war we couldn't win. I have been asked if I ever killed anyone; to my knowledge I never did, and if I did, I hope I never find out. I've seen more human blood than a person should have. Piece by piece our defenses disintegrated, our garrison sought what safety it could while in flight, our situation was rapidly becoming hopeless. Somewhere along the way I realized I had turned seventeen, there was no celebration, no well wishes only the devastation of the war.

The main objective of the Soviet forces was to isolate as many German Wehrmacht units as possible. Fortune smiled on us and we were able to find a way out of the Soviet's army pincers and continued our retreat westwards finally reaching the relative safety of larger concentrations of German troops. Despite the fact that we were constantly losing ground and innumerable lives, our commanders expected us to continue to fight and defend the German Reich to the bitter end. We were constantly reorganizing and digging into new trenches for cover. The heavy rain made marching through the glutinous mud irksome and strenuous.

On quiet nights when we weren't being directly attacked, we could sit back and observe the flashes of fire and warfare in the distance. Many times too if the night was too quiet we waited on pins and needles for something to happen. One relatively peaceful evening, our objective was to recapture a road which would enable us to replenish our supplies. We tore ourselves from the mud one by one and bundled onto the road, diving toward a dark opening on the other bank. Machine gun fire shot past us out of the darkness. Bullets cracked sharply over our heads. We quickly rolled into the opposite trench and moved as fast as we could down the road. Lights flashed around us turning our dark night into one full of brilliance and fear. Bursts of fire came from everywhere followed by a sharp whack of an explosion. The hillsides shuddered and the earth trembled around us. We didn't have time to find cover, we could only lie flat on our stomachs and pray the shelling would miss us.

In our eagerness to move on, we had inadvertently run right into a Russian resistance. We had no hope of even scratching the surface on this barrage, therefore our efforts inevitably came to an end. To avoid being trapped we retreated as fast as was humanly possible. On October 18, 1944 we found ourselves pinned down again by the Russians just outside the town of Gummbinnen in East Prussia. During that firefight, I was hit in the head by an object and was knocked unconscious. I woke up in a German army hospital three days later. I had a serious, but non-life threatening injury to my forehead. I was expected to recover.

Later I was to learn that I was now many miles from my brigade. How I got here? I did not know. The hospital was in Kunersdorf near Frankfort-Oder. The hospital itself was an old school house which had been converted to deal with all the injured soldiers. The wounded were brought in daily and the dead removed quickly to make way for the never-ending tide of casualties. Limited supplies and understaffing made the conditions appalling. Although my injury was not life threatening I would carry a scar on my forehead as a reminder of that night for the rest of my life. Each night as I went to sleep I thanked God for looking down on me and helping me survive. During my time in the hospital I witnessed unimaginable horrors of the human condition ravaged by this war. I saw young boys and men missing their arms or legs crying out in pain. It was unbearable to see them lying hopeless in the beds in pain, calling for their mothers or fathers to comfort them. After a few days, all I wanted was to get out of this depressing place. I recovered without any complications and was soon to be released and sent to another facility until I was ready to either be shipped back to my platoon or home. I was beside myself with joy when I was told I would be sent to Magdeburg-Elbe, this was as "home" for me as it could get without actually going back to Tarnowitz. I left Kunersdorf, November 10, 1944, I left behind the images of young boys and men with little hope. Men with injuries they would have to live with the rest of their lives.

I truly realized how fortunate I was to be able to walk out of this hell. I forced myself to sit with some of those injured souls and I listened to their dreams of being with their families. I knew just as easily as they were hurt, I could have been one of them. WWII was a horrible war, one without mercy. Only those who were there or lived through it can understand the ramifications of it. "Jamais Plus La Guerre!" (No More War!)

On leave in Magdeburg 1944

I was very happy to be in Magdeburg, the city which I had adopted after I left Berlin in December 1943. I was relieved to see that the city had remained untouched by the bombings and had retained its claim to being the 'Pearl' of the Romanesque Road.

I was sent here to finish my recovery and made great progress thanks to the walks in the fresh air and the relaxed atmosphere. I enjoyed those walks of the city, observing its inhabitants going about their business without fear.

I anxiously awaited my new orders from the OKW (German Army High Command). In the meantime, I was given the okay to go home if I wanted too, but that was impossible since that part of upper-Silesiea was under heavy Russian army artillery fire. With the soviets rapidly moving westward, going home was out of the question. Instead, I got permission to temporarily return to the Romer Hotel and Herr Kleinert.

I could not wait to walk into his office and when I finally did, he welcomed me with open arms and honored my request to be put back to work in the area in which I excelled – the kitchen. A pleasant surprise awaited me when I realized that my younger sister, Anna was also working there. I was to learn that my parents had sent her there before the fighting took over Tarnowitz. I enjoyed each day as truly 'borrowed time'. I knew that at any moment I could get torn away from this place and time in my life and back to the realities of the war. My family now consisted of Herr Kleinert, Anna, the Ukranian chambermaids, and the hotel staff. I was content as I could have been given the circumstances.

Soon it would be Christmas. Having spent time away from the pleasantries of life, I enjoyed watching the townsfolk shop for just the right gift for the loved ones in their lives. Although, the stores weren't stocked with the usual merchandise since everything was being rationed, a person could find almost anything they wanted on the black market.

Even though this would be my second Christmas away from home; I did feel blessed that I had Anna there and was with the people I felt most comfortable with. I was grateful to God for allowing me to survive. I was grateful too for my comrades in arms who laid their lives down for those they loved and the country they loved so we could carry on.

Just before Christmas on an evening I haven't forgotten, the restaurant was packed when we heard sirens. At first, we assumed there was a fire close by, but the sirens sounded again even louder than before. Everyone stopped and looked at each other. A policeman stepped into the lobby and advised everyone to take cover, Allied planes had been spotted and we should prepare ourselves for a bombardment.

Panic ensued, china and glassware fell to the floor as tables were overturned as people rushed from the hotel. Herr Kleinert did his best to calm his patrons with little result. We both had been through this and we knew that moving to safety with a calm head was the best scenario. Some of the customers stayed and we put them into the hotel's shelter. The chef and his staff along with myself and Anna shut down the kitchen, turning off the gas and electricity to eliminate the risk of fires. As quickly as we moved we did not quite make it to the shelter, as the first bombs fell to the ground. Explosions shattered the night.

I was devastated that this fine city with its architecture and history was no longer safe. These people had never witnessed this devastation and were dumfounded by its affect on their city and their lives. It was very frightening to hear the swooshing of the bombs as they ripped by us and found their target. No matter how many times you lived through this, it made you cringe wondering when one would find you. The building shook and trembled on its foundation. We prayed it would hold together and not collapse around us and bury us alive. The raid seemed to last forever, having been through this before, Herr Kleinert had stocked the shelter with candles and blankets so instead of sitting there in the dark we at least had light and could comfort each other until the terrifying experience stopped. After what seemed an eternity, the sirens finally sounded which allowed us to leave the shelter. The night was illuminated by the yellow white flames which devoured the buildings. It was astounding to find that our hotel had been spared while others around it were demolished. The dry wind that evening fed and fanned the blaze and we could only watch in disbelief.

When day break finally arrived we opened our doors to business and offered aid to our neighbors. We listened, watched and prayed for those carried away in the never ending stream of ambulances that cruised our segment of town. People quickly accepted that this was a condition of war and went about salvaging their lives from the rubble without lamentations. The anticipation of Christmas was squelched by this onslaught of violence, there wasn't anything to celebrate.

Herr Kleinert attempted to run the hotel as he always did, but people were afraid to be out of their homes at night. During the day we were busy, but our nights were as desolate as a tomb. We moved into January and I had yet to hear anything from the OKW. Herr Kleinert assured me not to worry, that the army knew where I was and when I was needed again they would let me know. I am sure that since he was still technically my guardian, that he didn't want to see me rushing back into harms way; he cared about all his employees that way.

Rumors informed Anna and me that the Russians had now moved out of our hometown and we had not heard any news of or from our parents. Russian troops were now headed to Berlin and before we knew it they would be in Magdeburg, I was recovering nicely, albeit a few headaches. I had been given medication for them and would surely have felt better had I had a chance to relax instead of working in such a fast paced environment, but I enjoyed being busy and was able to put those episodes behind me without much trouble. If I would have been forced to lay around all I would have done was wallow in my homesickness, at least here I had friends and Anna, I had something to keep my mind occupied.

Magdeburg Destroyed

Even though I was helping out at the hotel while on leave, Herr Kleinert assured me that all my effort would be accredited to my apprenticeship. The day of January 14, 1945 will forever remain indelible in my life. It was late in the evening when we heard the ominous and shrill sirens again announcing an air raid. No one had forgotten the raid just three weeks ago. Herr Kleinert immediately shut down the kitchen, turning off the power and immediately asked his patrons to leave the dining room and seek shelter. We had just enough time for us employees to hustle down to the shelter in the basement when we heard the first bombs exploding.

Even in the basement we could hear the immense drone of the bombers above us. More bombs fell, the building shook. As the attack continued, I silently asked myself how this could be happening again. Around me some of the staff had started to cry, some had even become hysterical. Herr Kleinert had his hands full trying to restore a sense of calm so the situation would not get out of hand. When the power inevitably went out, we were glad we had lit the candles upon entering the shelter in anticipation of this. Soon we noticed that the shelter was filling with acrid smoke, we began to cough and breathing became very difficult. Herr Kleinert was confident that the hotel wasn't on fire, that it was just the bombs burning outside.

I had experienced intense raids in Berlin as well as on the front and in a short time I realized that this was going to be a long extreme night. This was pure hell, the bombings seemed to go on forever. I couldn't help but wonder how many innocent people would be hurt or had to die before this nightmare would end. It was only a matter of time till the impact of the explosions would cause our water pipes to burst; when it happened the water began to flood our shelter. We frantically looked for a way out and we figured the quickest safest way was to bust through the wall into the adjacent basement. With a heavy hammer we created a hole big enough for us to crawl through.

Choking on the toxic fumes, we resigned ourselves to the fact that the hotel was indeed on fire. We struggled to stay calm, what we didn't know was that the hotel's upper floors had collapsed and our escape routes had been cut off. In order to breathe we needed to create a filter and covered our mouths and noses with our shirts or jackets. We scrambled through the hole, but once on the other side realized too late that we had forgotten our only source of light, the candle; no one wanted to go back, so we sat in the dark and collected our thoughts. Some of the employees started to panic including my sister, Anna. No matter how I tried, I could not console her. We tapped our way around the room to find places to sit and to find the exit. In the darkness we could only sit in horror while we listened to the walls and floors crashing in above us.

We were jolted out of our stupor when a large section of the ceiling caved in on us. Somehow, we found our way out of the chaos. Climbing over the debris we regrouped outside, only to find that two of our co-workers had not made it out; Olga the Ukranian chambermaid and Maria who worked in the kitchen. All around us buildings were being devoured by flames, cries of helplessness resounded through the night air.

Herr Kleinert was concerned about the two missing women. Several of us started to comb through the rubble where we had last seen them. Despite the immense heat from the flames our fear made us cold to the core and we struggled to stay warm. The flames illuminated the night sky and provided an eerie light to work in. We were at the point of exhaustion when we finally heard a female voice call out, "Helfen, Helfen! Sie uns bitte!" (Please help, help us!) We were given renewed strength to pull apart the beams, bricks, and plaster. Anna began to cry again, but this time they were tears of joy and frustration. Quickly, we removed brick after brick, lumber, and steel beams. Olga called out that she couldn't move. She told us she thought Maria was dead. We worked even harder to get to them, in case there was something we could do for Maria. We finally found them bloody and trapped under a section of the stairs. Herr Kleinert and I climbed down to the trapped women. We tried to revive Maria but to no avail. We concentrated our efforts on Olga. Her legs were trapped under a heavy steel beam. To this day, I don't know how the two of us managed to move it. It must have been all the adrenaline pumping through us. We half carried her to the opening and with the help of the others brought her out to the open crisp air of the night. Herr Kleinert did not want to leave Maria. He went back to her and in a short while determined that he had found a pulse and we quickly moved away her trappings and carried the unconscious woman to the opening and she too was lifted out. We were worried that so much climbing around on the precarious conditions would cause the wreckage to shift and trap us, we decided the best course of action was to get out and come back another time, during the day so we could see what we were working in.

In the midst of all this danger we thanked God for helping us out of the nightmare that had threatened to capture us all. We had the opportunity to thank God again, as the night air filled Maria lungs, pushing the smoke clear and allowing her to regain consciousness and with some assistance she was able to stand. Herr Kleinert led us in prayer. Not knowing how seriously either woman was hurt, we knew we should find medical help for them. We knew as we turned away from what once was our home that a miracle had emerged from a night of holocaust.

We slowly made our way down the street to the public shelter a few blocks away. We weren't sure how we would get there. This underground shelter was near the Elbe-River; everywhere we looked we saw nothing but flames engulfing this once magnificent city. Buildings crumbled around us in the aftermath. Streets were blocked by the avalanche of debris making us alter our escape route. There were no rescue workers, we were left to fend for ourselves as were the hundreds of others that swarmed around us. There were no police or soldiers to direct the streams of survivors who were now flooding the streets hampered by the obstacle course of downed and broken power lines, burning cars, and over turned street-cars. Our goal was to make it to the bunker where we hopefully would be safe. Many times we felt hemmed in. Smoke made visibility poor and breathing difficult; with every breath we took, we tasted soot and dust. We knew our only hope was to climb over the mountainous debris in front of us in order to stay on course. Our concierge and our cook, Hans was assisting Olga over the pile when she collapsed, we rushed over to help her. Herr Kleinert suggested that it might be better if we just carried her, so we could continue on as quick as possible. A couple of the men volunteered and we moved on with genuine urgency.

Anna hung onto my hand on one side of me and Maria had hold of my other hand. At one point, I noticed that Maria was having some difficulty breathing, but she managed to keep up. At one point, I must have dropped Anna's hand and in a blink of an eye, she was gone. I called out for her, but through the din my voice did not carry far. I could not see her anywhere. In panic I called for the others to come back and told them that I could not find Anna. Frantically, we searched the carnage around us only to be jostled by the hordes of people running past us. I refused to leave the spot I had last seen her in hopes that she would find her way back to us. Herr Kleinert reminded me that Anna knew where we were headed and that we needed to think of ourselves first and move on to safety as buildings continued to crumble around us.

As we moved on, we passed by those who had succumbed to the fumes. Was Anna lying among them? This thought flashed across my mind like a lightening bolt. Herr Kleinert ordered us to keep moving. We had just passed the city hall with its awe inspiring towering spire when it seemed to collapse to the ground like a flow of lava. We were fortunate to have made it out in time. The street was narrow and we would surely have been killed or at the very least trapped until help could find us.

Relief swept over us as we neared the bunker. At its huge entrance were a few policemen trying in vain to control the never ending stream of refugees. The bunker was already brimming with lost souls. None of us had any possessions, we were just lucky to be alive. I had a hard time rejoicing, since I still had not caught sight of Anna anywhere. Once inside we were able to get help for both Olga's head injury, which turned out not to be serious and for Maria who just seemed to be suffering from smoke inhalation. Once Olga's head had been bandaged she softly said to us "Spa-see-ba" in her Russian tongue (Thank You.) We desperately tried to stay together as many weaved their way through us in search of their loved ones and families. I have to admit I was guilty of the same as I searched through the throng for Anna. Depressed I finally found a spot to sit and allowed myself to break down. I cried until a Red Cross volunteer found me. She asked me all sorts of questions and I told her what had happened. She promised she would do whatever she could to help me find Anna.

Rumors spread that thousands of people had perished in that last bombing. Wherever we turned around, people were praying and crying over their loss. One old woman stood out from those around her, in one hand she fingered a rosary while she prayed and in the other hand she held a photo of a young man. An old man was being comforted by volunteers, he had lost both his wife and his daughter. It broke my heart to see these the tears streaming down their faces. When I composed myself I checked on Olga and Maria. Once I had assured myself that they were all right I went off again in search of my sister. I asked dozens of people if they had seen anyone that looked like her. Frustrated and despondent I stopped and simply asked God to help me find her and if that was not possible to watch over her and to keep her safe.

Morning came and along with it, breakfast of sorts for those who were hungry: milk, hot chocolate and sandwiches. The untiring efforts of the Red Cross volunteers were amazing, they did what they could to comfort the young and old alike and gave medical attention to those who needed it; they never seemed to rest, there was always someone there to help and always someone who needed it. Later that day a priest made his way through the bunker. He talked with those who needed consoling. When he had made his rounds, he blessed all of us and asked us to join him in prayer. We prayed for the homeless, the injured, the sick and the destitute. He asked us to pray for those who had perished throughout the city. He left us and I never saw him again.

As I took in all the devastation around me, I became more determined to find Anna, no matter what it took. I knew deep down that she was alive. Herr Kleinert shared my concern, after all he was responsible for both of us and he too searched the bunker for her. With no place to go, we were allowed to remain temporarily in the shelter. I was happy about this, because Anna knew where we were heading and I was sure she would find her way to us if she was able. As our second day came to a close we were once again subjected to the horrifying droning of B-17s along with the blaring air raid sirens which announced yet another bombing run. This already badly battered city of Magdeburg was to be targeted again. Explosions accentuated the chaotic atmosphere of the bunker. More people pushed their way into this crowded enclosure. The Red Cross had finally caught up, but now they started over calming the new refugees and tending to those who needed help.

The next day we talked with those who were closest to me, the other employees at the hotel and we set out with renewed hope in search of Anna. We combed the streets, many parts of the city still burned, the devastation was immeasurable. We visited the two other bunkers but with no luck. Only one person was able to give us a lead, a Red Cross worker asked if we had gone to the hospital. In our state of mind we had not considered that possibility. The hospital was only five blocks away and at almost a run we covered the distance in no time at all.

Once at the hospital, Herr Kleinert found the administration office and asked if they by chance had a young girl matching Anna's description. Relief swept over all of us when we were told that a young girl had been admitted unconscious with a broken nose and a minor head injury. Our prayers had been answered once again, when we looked in on her and found that the young girl was indeed our Anna. It was another miracle! God was indeed watching over us. We went back to the bunker and were told that due to the sheer numbers, that some of us needed to be evacuated to a nearby village of Mutzel. Before we left the city, we decided to go back to what was left of the hotel in hopes of salvaging something of use to us but there was nothing left. All there was, was a pile of smoldering rubble and dangerous debris.

It was sad to see the dead lying there as a testament to this savage unforgiving war. Before we left the city, Herr Kleinert contacted a business couple in Berlin who were willing to take in Anna, I supported this idea knowing that she would be cared for, when I was called back to active duty. I was grateful and amazed that he could arrange this in such a short time.

With a heavy heart I reluctantly said goodbye to Anna and helped put her and her meager belongings onto the train to Berlin. While the rest of us waited in what was left of this once beautiful train station, I couldn't help but recall how it looked just a year ago; this beautifully crafted building with its domed canopy, was now a grotesque shell of what it once was. If one tried hard enough you could just make out the ghostly images of carefree laughing patrons milling around a prosperous city without a care in the world, but once you blinked – reality chased those images away and replaced them with the hard brutal truth of those ravaged by the war.

The Red Cross was somehow able to outfit us with a few pieces of clothing and food for our 35 kilometer journey. The first leg of our exodus landed us in Genthin on a cold afternoon on January 18, 1945. The train did not go the last eight kilometers needed to get us to Mutzel, so we needed to walk. As soon as we left Genthin, it started to snow which in a short amount of time developed into a full blown blizzard. There was no shelter to be found along the country road on which we traveled. We were fortunate to have secured a large luggage wagon from the train depot and decided to take refuge under it. This makeshift shelter did give us a brief respite from the biting wind. We huddled together, relishing each other's body heat. When the blizzard began to let up, we thought it best to move on. We wanted to make it to Mutzel before night fall. After a short while the sun appeared, its brightness glaring off the fresh white snow blinded us as we walked along.

Once we arrived in the village, we really didn't know where we were supposed to go. A local farmer suggested that we find the village mayor. We must have presented quite a sight, the twenty or so of us looking half frozen in the late afternoon light. The farmer took pity on us and offered his barn as a place for us to rest and warm up. We gladly accepted the accommodations. We desperately wanted to get out of the blowing freezing wind. The sun started to set and no one wanted to continue on. After we got settled in, Herr Kleinert asked me if I wanted to go with him to find the Burgermeister (mayor). When we found him, he was unaware and unprepared to receive us, but promised he would do his best to see that our needs were taken care of. We made our way back to the barn and were delighted to find that the rest had made a comfortable sleeping place for us to spend the night. I found a spot for myself and could not help, but let my mind drift back to happier times playing in the hay barn on my grandparents' farm.

The barn provided us with a much needed respite from the air raid sirens, the bombings, and the smoke filled air of Magdeburg. Our situation was not one we would have chosen for ourselves, but without it was better than what we had left behind us. Only God knew what lay in store for us tomorrow. The next morning we found that the Mayor had contacted the Red Cross in Genthin and soon a German army truck showed up with food, supplies and necessities. Our next matter of business we had to attend to was to register with the Mutzel police as was required by law. Several days later we all walked back to Genthin and caught the train back to Magdeburg to see if there was anything we could salvage from the ruins of the Roemer Hotel.

Eight days had passed since the last raid, we came across many people sifting through the rubble hoping to find even the smallest token of their previous lives. We moved some of the wreckage and came across the tables and chairs that once seated the elite in the hotel's restaurant. After a while our arms and hands ached to the point of not being able to lift another thing. We decided it was fruitless to continue this endeavor. We had hoped to possibly find survivors in the rubble, but what we did manage to find was four charred bodies lying together. This was a gruesome sight, an image that would haunt me for many years. Our spirits were low and our adrenaline had given way to fatigue.

As we walked back to the train station, we noticed many handmade posters and messages posted on buildings which left directions for the lost so they could be reunited with their families of friends. We came across an elderly man sitting on the ground against a burned out building, he was sobbing into his hands. We asked if there was anything that we could do for him and he informed us that he had lost his wife, daughter and his two grandchildren. He felt lost, he said he didn't know what to do. As we talked with him, our voices and conversation drew his neighbors to him and they took over trying to console him. After a bit, we realized we were no longer needed and moved on.

Years later I came across this phrase and I feel it summed up this time in our life very well.

How very fragile a life can be,
So easily broken, so very hard to mend

I never went back to Magdeburg, a city I at one time called my home. I learned that some forty years later, Anna and her husband, Wolfgang did go back once to visit. I have never had the desire to do it. I would have rather had the last images of this once magnificent city to have been in its beauty, but instead the last memories I have of it are ones of ugliness, of man's inhumanity to man. You can't rebuild that natural beauty. For years I have tried to push these images from my memory and only to focus on the way this city was when I first entered it all those years ago, maybe with the writing of this book I can finally do that.

Mutzel 1945

Three days after returning from our unsuccessful scavenger hunt in Magdeburg, an army truck and three SS soldiers pulled up and escorted me back to the army headquarters in Genthin. When I left the village of Mutzel it was not of my own choice. I had an obligation to fulfill and it was heartbreaking for me to once again leave those that had become so important to me. I had to leave Herr Kleinert a man I truly respected for all he sacrificed for his employees, his true family. I thought at this time I would never see him again, but I did see him two more times; once in 1946 in Berlin, and again in 1964 in Frankfurt – Main West Germany, right before I immigrated to the United States; this time he needed my help. As we said our goodbyes, he whispered to me to keep praying and he hoped we would meet again and we embraced.

After the registration formalities at the army headquarters, I was issued a new uniform, boots, and soldier gear. I was examined by the doctor who needed to confirm that I had fully recovered from my head injury and after a brief consultation I was found fit for duty. My new orders sent me to a compound outside Genthin where I was to retrain for combat duty. My new commanders were SS officers, immediately I knew I had to show my strength and reserves if I was to survive this. During my time as a civilian, I had heard news broadcasts over the radio. I knew that the war had escalated on the Eastern front and that the Soviet armies were pushing toward Berlin. Hitler was in desperate need of soldiers and all around me were green young boys with their heads filled with visions of serving the Third Reich. Hitler did not care in whose hands he put his rifles, only that they were able to carry them, shoot straight and willing to kill as many of the 'enemy' as possible.

The spirits in this German Wehrmacht camp were surprisingly high and the SS were still hopeful to win the war. No one at that time would have dared to voice their opinion for fear of being shot for doing so. The war was in Stalin's favor, it was Stalin who now wielded his incredible power and who moved his armies toward Berlin. Hitler's once mighty Wehrmacht posed no threat to Stalin and the road to Berlin was wide open.

In February, I was sent with several soldiers to a camp near Brandenburg. We had not been told our exact mission, but we were soon to find it out. Once we were settled in, we found there were barracks filled with Polish prisoners of war. These prisoners were being used by the Germans as forced laborers in a nearby ammunitions factory. During my registration in Genthin, it was found out that I had a good knowledge of the Polish language, which is why I was sent there. I was to be the interpreter between the Poles and the German officers.

It became clear that I was indeed being of service to both entities. Better communication meant better treatment, less misunderstandings, and more work being accomplished.

The weapons that were produced in this factory were the Panzer Faust – a powerful anti-tank weapon. Its production was closely monitored by the Germans. The vast factory was in operation twenty-four hours a day, seven days a week. The machines never stopped spewing out a never-ending supply of Panzer Fausts.

Hitler's confidence in a successful outcome of the war was based on a variety of factors: He depended on his vengeance weapons (V-I and V-II), Vergeltugs waffen, hopeful astrological forecasts, and a few personal convictions. He no longer trusted his generals who were losing ground constantly on the Russian front to the Soviet armies. Much of my knowledge of the war at that time came from the prisoners in this camp. I was amazed at how much I learned from those seemingly helpless and freedom deprived men. They often told me more than I wanted to know and if I had reported this to my superior officers, the men would have been shot for it. I remember when the prisoners first began to trust me, they told me that the Soviet marshal Zhukov's forces had reached the Oder River only two weeks prior and were moving on to the city of Frankfort. It was obvious that Zhukov's goal was to get to Berlin. They also told me of a radio speech from Hitler, which made the promise that his military situation would soon turn around. I didn't know even at that time how they were able to come by as much information as they shared with me and I didn't ask.

I felt helpless in my efforts to help these men when it came to their treatment. The factory was guarded and ran exclusively by the SS soldiers, which did not always bode well, for the prisoners. Many times, they were deprived of food, water, and even sleep. Many of them looked emaciated and near death. The only help I could give them was through my translating and then too I had to be careful of what I said.

With the now rapidly advancing Russian army, we learned that these prisoners would soon be evacuated, but to where I had not been able to find out. I remember very well having a conversation with two of the men when they recounted to me some of the horrible events, which they had witnessed before the German soldiers took them as prisoners of war. Many men had been captured and sent east to Russian labor camps, just as many had been outright murdered. Women of every age were raped. Both men and women were beaten and robbed of their possession: rings, watches, even the shoes on their feet. Thousands had died of hunger or cold on the roads fleeing the Russian army. Homes were pillaged and whole villages were burned to the ground. No one was safe from the Russians. In the face of this terror, some German men chose to shoot their wives, children, and committed suicide rather than be tortured or have to submit to the Russians.

I learned many many more stories from these prisoners each one more heartbreaking and sad than the other. At times, I felt like I was one of them. The Soviets had completely liberated their country, punishing the Poles and sweeping now through Germany leaving a trail of millions of tears and homeless families.

Eventually the rumors about the evacuation of the Polish prisoners became a reality. Trainloads of prisoners were transported at the end of February to an undisclosed location. The day before the evacuation, I'd been able to make contact with some of them and wished them a sad farewell. For a short while, we had become like comrades of life. Since my mission as a Polish interpreter had ended, I was sent back to my unit in Genthin and eventually to Mutzel. Many nights I thought of those stories of those who were brutalized, raped, and tortured; the helplessness of these innocent people made and makes me very ill to this day.

The Secret Mission to Potsdam

Potsdam was once a town of East Germany, the headquarters of the Bezirk (District) of the same name in the German Democratic Republic. It is situated on the Havel River adjacent to the southwest border of Berlin and approximately 155 kilometers northeast of Magdeburg.

Shortly after midnight in early spring of 1945, I was ordered by my "unteroffizier" (NCO) to report to the compound's commanding officer. I found him waiting for me in his small office. Without any long explanation, I was told that I was to be sent on a very special and absolutely secret mission. The communications between our unit and the Befehlstab in Babelsberg, Potsdam were poor or nonexistent. After I was briefed on the mission that awaited me, he told me how important it was that I accomplish it. The destination was the "Schloss Cecilien Hof in Babelsberg on Lake Griebnitz near Potsdam. On the commander's desk lay a small leather pouch, a 36mm pistol, a laminated map, and next to the wall a bicycle. The commander told me to prepare to leave at four in the morning.

I went back to the barracks, took a short nap, and was at the commander's office again at four o'clock sharp. He reminded me that I needed to be at Cecilien Hof by noon. As I set out from the small village of Mutzel it started to rain, the weather turned cold but I forged my way kilometer by kilometer to reach my destination of Schloss Cecilien Hof. My mission was to deliver the sealed messenger pouch, which contained classified interintelligence information to the German Wehrmacht commanding officer in Potsdam. I had strict orders to avoid any contact with other German outposts; I was to use only by-ways rather than the main roads. If someone detained me, I could use whatever force was needed to escape and to complete my mission. If anyone was to attempt to get hold of my pouch, I was to destroy it; the pouch contained a special detonation device.

I was pushing myself hard to make it to Potsdam for my expected noon arrival time. The exertion and the inclement weather made me feel somewhat faint, but I was determined to traverse the 125 kilometers in record time. I passed through a small village and took notice of a beautifully built church; I could not resist its allure and stopped there to take a small respite. I felt chilled through to the bone and was exhausted. I parked my bike next to the entrance and to my surprise the heavy, beautifully carved portal was not locked I ventured inside. I was awestruck by the magnificence of this church, especially by the altar; its intricate carvings and statues reminded me of our church in my hometown of Tarnowskie-Góry. It was a weekday and I was the only one in the church. I felt a little frightened being in such a beautiful place without anyone else around. It was very still inside; I could hear myself breathe. I looked around and not seeing anyone, I knelt down in one of the pews and began to pray. Suddenly, I heard footsteps. The steps were not of a soldier, but turned out to be the parish priest. He told his name was Father Karl Robinski and assured me that there was no reason to be frightened and asked if there was anything, he could do for me. He noticed that I was shivering and that I looked tired. He offered me some hot tea and invited me into his library. It was a small cozy room, adjacent to the church in which he had a fire burning. The warmth from the fireplace felt good and soon seeped into my body. He quickly made some tea and served it with lemon; now I was warm on the inside as well as the outside. He struck up a conversation with me, asking me some questions that I could not answer given my circumstances; overall, we had a nice cordial conversation. He asked where I was from and when I told him, his weary eyes lit up like the embers in the fire. He told me he was from Krakow on the River Vistula. We had been conversing in German up until then and immediately we switched to our native tongue, Polish. My polish was a little rusty, since I had not spoken it for some time, but we got on well. When I noticed the time, I realized that I had to end our visit and continue on my way I had about sixty-five kilometers left. As I stood to leave, Father Robinski asked if I wanted something to eat along the way, I told him I had some crackers and tuna fish (which I had grown to hate), he quickly made me a cheese sandwich for which I was extremely grateful. As I was mounting my bicycle, he disappeared inside and reappeared with a pair of mittens. Since it had grown quite cold, he knew I would feel better if my fingers were not stinging from the cold. The generosity of strangers has never ceased to amaze me. Before I left, we said a prayer for my safety and he sent me off with a "Go with the Lord" and made me promise that I would stop when I passed through on my way back to Mutzel. Into my hand, he pressed a small card, which he asked that I read when I needed comfort. It read:

"Show me your ways, O Lord, teach me your paths;
Guide me in your truth and teach me,
for you are God my Savior, and my hope is in you all day long."

I treasured this little card during the turbulent time of war, but somewhere along the way, I lost track of it, but the words are forever ingrained in my soul.

When I left the church I felt like an entirely different person, the sanctity of the church the encounter with Father Karl, the hot tea and pleasant conversation were comforts I had not felt in many months. For a moment, I had completely forgotten all the pain, the loneliness and homesickness I constantly felt, at some level I was a little ashamed that I could easily forget what I had been through, but again, I felt hope that I could someday completely get past these hurts and the losses I felt.

As I rode down the roads I passed a long line of German tanks, artillery guns and hundreds of soldiers marching on foot; their faces were tired and you could tell at a glance that they were exhausted. With every step, you could see the pain and fatigue radiate through their bodies and to top it off it had begun to rain again. I struggled valiantly with the downpour, which was coming down like a torrent. I passed what seemed to be endless regiments and motorized equipment. It occurred to me that Hitler's Generals were trying to assemble their forces for their final senseless counter attack.

I had little time to think about what I was seeing, my mission was to deliver the pouch no matter what it would cost or take. If I failed, even because my body would not let me continue would constitute desertion and I could face execution. This thought alone kept me peddling on my way. It took all I had to go on. I consulted my map and was relieved to find that I had approximately ten kilometers to go. I knew I could make it, but I prayed that God would show some mercy on me and make it stop raining. No sooner was the prayer past my lips when the torrent slowed to a drizzle. I made good time even though I had to use the back roads and had to stop occasionally for water; people were very friendly and were always eager to help in whatever way they could.

Glancing at my watch I nervously realized that it was almost noon; looking into the horizon, I could just make out the steeples of what had to be Potsdam. I arrived at the heavily guarded compound of Schloss Cecilien-Hof at about 12:30. I was told to stay where I was by one guard and was asked for my credentials and password by another soldier. After examining my "ID' I was taken to a courtyard where I could leave my bicycle. Two soldiers stayed with me while a third went inside to announce my arrival. He returned shortly with two more soldiers and a captain. I was escorted inside debriefed and taken into the kommandant's office. I handed him the sealed pouch and he immediately left the room. I had to relinquish my weapon and was taken to another room for a brief questioning. Following this meeting, I was allowed to refresh. I took a deserving bath and was furnished with a clean fresh uniform and a good solid pair of boots. My uniform and boots were completely soaked through and I would have surely gotten quite sick if I had attempted to return to my camp in them. I ate a hardy meal with some of the other soldiers and realized I was the youngest one of the group in which I sat. After lunch, I was taken yet to another room for instructions for my return to Mutzel. I was again given the sealed confidential classified pouch with a message for my commander; my weapons were returned to me. I was given the same directives for my return as I was for the delivery to the Cecilien-Hof. I was sent off with a light ration of food and was told to go directly back to my unit. I left the compound at 2:15 in the afternoon with a prayer and started on my trek back.

Berlin- Sister Anna

After I left the compound, I had to make a difficult decision. Although, I was given direct orders not to detour in my route, after a bit of deliberation with my conscience I chose to disobey those orders and decided to seek out my sister Anna who after having to leave Magdeburg was now living in Berlin. I had an address for her; she was living with a business couple and was attending an academic high school there. I could not pass up this opportunity to try to see her. I looked on the map and found that Berlin was only about thirty kilometers northeast of Potsdam, according to my calculations it would take me less than two hours to get there. I took the AVUS; which was a long and straight piece of road where before the war, they held car races. I had to be careful, however, there were traces of the German army everywhere. Long envoys of heavy tanks, artillery, guns, hundreds of trucks loaded with German soldiers were on their way to Berlin for the final battle of that besieged city. I was concerned that I would not be able to get to Berlin because of the traffic. I was determined to get through, I had come this far. I was grateful for all the activity; I passed by the convoy without attracting too much attention.

I was familiar with this route. What bothered me though was the change in the scenery. The once beautiful landscapes, homes, and villas of prestigious bankers, business magnates, movie moguls, that lined the boulevards now lay in ruins and rubble. The last time I was in Berlin, I was considered an orphan and had spent time in the orphanage there until Herr Kleinert summoned me to his new place of employment in Magdeburg.

I was anxious to see Anna; she was my only link to our family. It had been over a year and a half since I had heard from any of them and I hoped Anna had some recent news of them. I knew my brother was serving in the German Luftwaffe and to my knowledge was flying the ME-109 fighter jet.

Along the way I talked with some of the officers and soldiers I rode along side of. A German Unteroffizier explained to me that Berlin was under heavy artillery attack by the Russian army from the East, this explained why I was hearing thunder yet the skies were clear. Another time when I stopped to adjust my bicycle seat an officer asked if he could help me, I told him I had it covered. We talked a little about what was happening in Berlin and he informed me that this was going to be a tough battle and that it would probably be Germany's last stand. Berlin was completely surrounded by the Russians and it was only a matter of days when it would fall into their hands and control.

With some trepidation, I entered the city and at around four o'clock found the address where Anna was living. She was not at home and so I ventured over to the store she told me she was employed. The owner's wife called Anna out front and we warmly greeted each other with a hug and a kiss. This was the first time that she had seen me in my uniform and was a little taken a back by my appearance. We were as giddy as kids. The owners having noticed the time locked up the store so we could all have a nice uninterrupted visit. I learned that they too had a son, who was serving in the army. I explained to them that Anna was the only one in the family that I had had any contact with and they sympathized with me. They made us some sandwiches and hot tea, which I welcomed very much. I had taken on a chill again with the night coming on and having been wet most of the day. They asked what brought me to Berlin and I briefly told them and explained that I could not stay long. The owner, Herr Riedel, told me that he respected my mission, but could see no reason for me to return to my unit in Mutzel. He told me that the Red army had already rolled into the eastern part of Germany and that our town of Tarnowitz was now in the hands of the Russians. I already knew that they had surrounded Berlin. It was all very difficult to comprehend.

Everyone knew that the fight was over and it was just a matter of time. Herr Riedel tempted me again to stay with them by saying he would give me some of his son's civilian clothes and I could stay with my sister. I reluctantly stated that I could not become a deserter and had to finish my mission. I knew in my heart that I would never be able to face my father if I deserted my duties. To vanish would mean that I would be on the run forever and I would not entertain that idea. I knew I had to return to Mutzel. With much heartache, I said farewell to my sister. With tears on both sides, we said goodbye after a heartbreaking hour visit. I left Berlin the end of March 1945 and would not see her again until October of 1946. As I rode back down the road out of the city, I knew no matter what, that in order to live with myself I had made the right decision to leave Berlin and return to my unit.

Returning to my Unit

It was dark by the time I left Berlin and I knew I would be traveling most of the night in order to get back to Mutzel, I was expected back at my unit by five o'clock in the morning. Taking one last look at my map, I faced approximately 150 kilometers. On the road out, I had to traverse among hundreds of fleeing refuges: their possessions and their children in tow. They were in search of somewhere safe. I had to wonder, did that place even exist? It was well known that Berliner people were respected for their daring and indomitable spirit and courage, but even they could no longer take the relentless bombings and witness the devastation of their homes and lives.

The power of the war made thousands of those innocent people homeless and hopeless. The face of a great nation was now in total destruction. What I saw in the faces of these people was utter despair, pain, sorrow, and despondency. I silently prayed for them as I traveled along knowing in my heart that God would watch over the innocent. I hoped deep down that Anna would be safe where she was or that Herr Riedel would take whatever precautions were necessary to keep her safe as long as she was with them.

I realized as I rode along that I was happy to see the German strength on that road, it gave me hope. I could hear loud explosions behind me and turned back to witness the illuminated night skies above that magnificent city. I could see the huge fireballs rising above the city. My heart sank and I started to panic with thoughts about my sister's well being. I was torn on whether or not I should return and rescue her, but I prayed that she would be fine and forced myself to turn around and continue on my way. The road was completely clogged with tanks and trucks; I heard the voices of commanding officers giving orders to their men. I needed to make up some time, I realized that I would have to get off the main road and take the unfamiliar back roads so I could move on my way unhindered.

It grew later; I desperately needed some landmark to assure me I was heading in the right direction. It was quite late when I finally passed the city of Brandenburg. I knew I had passed this city on my way to Potsdam and I felt reassured that I would make it back to my unit. However, I had pushed my body past its limits. I was tired and exhausted. My back had begun to hurt from the hours spent bent over on the bicycle. I needed to rest. I had just passed a small hamlet, noticed a very dense patch of pine trees, and thought that it would provide ideal cover for me to take a short break. Once off the bike I walked to the grove of trees and found what looked like a comfortable spot to sit down. The fallen pine needles made the ground feel like a soft pillow. It was very peaceful in that little patch of trees. The wind blowing over the treetops created a symphony in the grove. I allowed myself to relax and for a little while felt peace. I took this opportunity to pray that Anna was and would be all right, I prayed for my family back home, and I prayed that I would continue on my journey undisturbed. I had always believed in the power of prayer and from my experience felt, it indeed worked if you believed and kept your faith. There is a bible passage that reads;"If thou canst believe, all things are possible to him that believeth." Mark 9:23

In the distance, I could hear the noise of the rolling trucks and tanks. The number I had seen over the past two days were as innumerable as the pine needles upon which I now sat. I closed my eyes and whispered into the night sky "Pacem in Terris: (Let there be peace on earth). Soon, I realized that the pain that had been plaguing me in my back had went away. I was no longer tired, but I was hungry. I searched my pack and found that I did have some bread left and a little water. With this to sustain me, I mounted my bicycle once again and took off. It was now well past midnight, but as I passed village after village I knew I was making good progress. I recalled my promise to Father Karl that I would stop at the church when I passed back through, but the sound of German voices put that thought out of my head. I stopped to listen what the soldiers were saying and realized that they were searching for some missing soldiers. Deserters! I decided I did not want to be confronted and questioned so I chose to alter my course, to get off the road and headed through an open field. I discovered a narrow road, which seemed to lead in the direction I needed to go so I took that. I decided to look for the church again. I soon found the beautiful building and upon trying the front door to my dismay, it was locked. I checked the time and realized that it was five o'clock in the morning. I went around to a side entrance and that too was locked. I had just about given up when I heard the sound of mooing from the courtyard. I walked toward the cow barn and a voice called out asking if someone was there, I answered back not to be afraid and an old man came forward. He seemed to recognize me, having seen me the day before talking to Father Karl. I told him I wanted to say hello to the Father and the man seemed distressed.

He told me that right after I left the day before, some SS soldiers came and arrested Father Karl. The caretaker had locked up the church for fear it would be vandalized and was waiting to hear word of the priest's safety. The whole village was wary of strangers and of being pulled in for questioning. I was in shock. I was dumfounded and could not speak. The caretaker went on to say that Father Karl had a practice of helping German soldiers in the past, and probably without his knowledge, his actions had been watched. All the time we talked the man looked around him nervously and pulled me inside the barn so we could continue with less chances of being caught. Hitler had publicly stated that he had no use for priests, what he needed were soldiers. Hundreds of priests and other clergy had been arrested, tortured, or put to death. Their churches were looted or seized, universities and high schools were closed. The Nazis carried out savage mass punishments, public executions and imprisonments for sabotage and for as little as listening to Allied radio stations. That is how Hitler wanted to silence the peace loving people of his country. The man asked me questions that I could not answer. I told him I had to return to my unit. When I explained where it was located, he told me I had about forty kilometers to go. He invited me in for breakfast, but I told him I had to get going. My stomach betrayed me and upon hearing, the hungry growl it gave off I was forced to stay and have a quick breakfast. His wife made us some 'Gehrurte-eier und pfankuchen' (scrambled eggs and pancakes). I ate with relish and after thanking them, quickly made my way down the road.

It was now almost twenty-six hours since I had slept last and knew my commanding officer must be wondering where I was. I knew I would have some explaining to do and was not sure of what I was going to say. I forced my legs to keep pumping, my eyes to stay focused on the road, and my mind focused on completing this mission. I passed by some German soldiers and one shouted out to me to watch out for the SS forces. I searched for a side road and found one that was too narrow for army vehicles, but seemed just right for someone on a bicycle.

Around seven o'clock the skies darkened over and thunder rumbled on the horizon. A cold rain swept across the open plain. I knew I was in for a soaking and looked around for some sort of shelter. I spied a cemetery, which had a small chapel inside its gates. I knew I was late and should not be stopping, but the rain was coming down harder now and I took cover under the trees. Under the dark skies, I looked out at the gravesites with winged angels to my right and granite crosses scattered about. It was an eerie feeling. Standing there, I could not help but think about my own mother and older sister, gone so many years now. I thought about all the survivors to these dead and about how these people died. After a while, I realized that the rain had stopped enough for me to venture out to the gravestones. I wanted to pray for my mother. As I passed the chapel, I heard voices, turning I saw two men in cloth caps crouching under a cypress tree by the wall. They didn't seem to notice me and soon walked away from the spot. Looking over I noticed a freshly dug grave covered with a tarpaulin and felt so sad knowing that another person had been laid to rest.

As I pushed my bicycle out the gates, I encountered a stillness in the air as well as inside myself. According to my map and compass, I wanted to go west and should pass the town of Kade and Wustelwitz, which should bring me close to Genthin. As I passed the town of Wustelwitz, a truck loaded with soldiers stopped in front of me and the Unteroffizier got out and warned me to watch out for SS men who were stationed about three kilometers down the road. He said they were ruthless and had just executed three deserters in front of his men. Again, I knew I had to change my course; the detour I knew would cause me further delay.

I was pleased to note that the weather had changed for the better and the sun's warmth smiled down at me through the clouds. A soft warm breeze pushed me from the east and felt good on my back. As I passed Genthin, I looked up at the clock tower and to my dismay saw that it was already nine-thirty in the morning and I had another ten kilometers to go. As I rode along the countryside, I marveled in the tranquility of the cows grazing in their pastures, the strength of the chestnut trees that lined the roads, and the promise of the coming spring.

Exhausted but with renewed purpose I spied the steeple of St Agnes Church in Mutzel, I had made it! My mission had lasted thirty-one hours. Round trip I had traveled three hundred and twenty-nine kilometers, crossed eighteen major cities and innumerable small towns and villages. I was pleased with myself that I had completed this mission successfully. I was asked for my password at the compound gate and was escorted inside to see the kommandant.

I handed the pouch over, surrendered my pistol, hand grenades, the map and the compass. I explained my encounters and the detours I was forced to make and it seemed to appease the kommander. I was released and allowed to take a much-needed rest.

Mutzel the end of March 1945

After the return from my mission to my surprise, many of the soldiers I knew and had gotten along with well were no longer at the compound. A soldier's life is unpredictable, one never knew what the next day had in store; you went where you were needed. There were a great many new soldiers, and the majority of them were very young boys. A fresh shipment of Hitler's youth. I felt old compared to these "green" recruits

Our current commander was a stoic and true Nazi SS Sturmbannfuher. I was questioned once more about my mission and I was dismissed. However, two days after I returned from my mission, I became ill. I collapsed during an early morning drill and was brought back to the barracks. There was not a doctor permanently stationed at our compound and I was administered to by our first aid field soldier the best he knew how. I was unable to stand or walk, my head spun and my body ached as it had never before. Since there was no infirmary, I was to be taken to the next larger town, which was Genthin, to the Wehrmacht hospital there. My condition baffled my commander and myself since I had no symptoms when I returned from the mission. As I waited for the transport truck to arrive, I must have passed out. The next thing I remember was waking up and looking over at an elderly nurse who was sitting by my bedside.

I was asked many questions, some extremely personal, others very painful or difficult to answer. I liked this nurse and did my best to be helpful and truthful in my responses to her. After I felt a little stronger, I was able to talk to her about my family and my life experiences so far. She seemed genuinely concerned and listened to my ramblings. The nurse had that kind of look that most mothers have when they care about their children. Her eyes were a deep blue and soft, they emanated something that is difficult to describe.

The nurse told me that at first, they were not sure what was wrong with me, but eventually they diagnosed that I had some digestive problems and pneumonia resulting from my laborious journey and exposure to the elements. I had lost a lot of weight in a short amount of time and it took a toll on my body. With rest, I was sure I would recover. The nurse said she would do her best and I trusted her.

Over the days that followed, I learned that the hospital was full of truly suffering German soldiers some with missing limbs. It was horrible. Sleep was often interrupted by the lamentations of these wounded men and boys.

By His providence and the care of this wonderful nurse and the doctors at the hospital, I started to recover much faster than anticipated. I watched in wonderment as these untiring angels of mercy worked day and night to fight for and save the lives of these brave men. The combination of prayer, medication, and genuine caring of the staff had everything to do with my remarkable and relatively speedy recovery. Despite the surroundings, all the staff radiated a cheerful demeanor, which managed to lift many troubled souls. The doctor assured me I would recovery completely and should plan to be discharged in a few days.

On the day I was allowed to leave, I looked around for my guardian angel, but could not find her. I had to leave without ever telling her how much her kind spirit managed to lift mine. A week after returning to my unit, we were heading east. Our company was reorganizing now and getting ready to face the westward forging Russian army.

As I said, we had a true SS kommandant. He was forever filling us up with the glamour of stopping the Russian forces with whatever forces it took, even if it meant giving up our lives for the Reich. He exuded great authority, was convinced that we must, and would stop the army. One could see that there was little humanity left inside him. He reminded me of what I had read about Himmler, the head of the SS. He was cold blooded and unpredictable. Human lives did not matter to him very much; soldiers were just numbers.

We knew things were not going well with the war. Our unit's supplies and food were sparse, our uniforms were in need of replacement, and our boots were in poor condition. Normal people, every day soldiers could see the realities of the war, but these SS commanders were blind to what was actually happening around them.

I had recovered from my illness and was feeling better with each passing day, despite the insufficient food and little sleep that soldiers get during the war. What nagged me most was the thought of my little sister Anna in Berlin and my parents in Tarnowitz. Each day that passed without me hearing from them weighed heavy on my mind and heart. It was now April and we were getting ready for the first wave of the Russian army. More German troops were brought in and to my astonishment; most of them were young boys from the Hitler Youth. Where did they find them? It saddened me to watch these young boys grow up tough in this type of environment. Most had fathers or brothers in the war, knew what to expect and what was expected of them. They started out frightened and wanting to go home, but it didn't take long for that thin layer to be replaced by one harder and tougher in order for them to survive. Those coming up through the ranks of the Hitler Youth were accustomed to the strict discipline of army life that is what the program taught them, to take orders and do what they were told to do without question. Now that Germany was fighting for its life, the importance of following orders was even greater than before.

We were aware how desperately the 'fatherland" needed us, so we did all we were asked to do without complaint or backtalk. I was now under the reign of a different commanding officer, another tough SS officer; obviously, Hitler did not trust his army officers and Himmler did not trust the German generals. The eastern front rapidly and exorably crumbled before the Russian advance that stopped before the gates of the city of Berlin. The kommandant reminded us once that we soon would be facing the advancing Russian troops. We were approximately 119 kilometers from Berlin. Our goal was to stop the advance, which was only three or four days away. It is hard for me to describe what we felt as we anticipated this confrontation and even hard to describe having lived through it.

The following days were raw; we dug in to our moats and waited for the inevitable. Suddenly out of nowhere, three RAF (British Royal Air force) Spitfire planes spotted us and they swooped down for an attack. In the chaos that ensued, several of the Hitler Youth members were killed by machine gun fire; others were severely wounded. After the planes disappeared, the wounded and dead were carried away. The attack was over as quickly as it began. As I scrambled to safety, I came across a young officer who had been hit, he lay sprawled in a ditch and cried out when he saw me "Can you believe this? I survived major battles on the Russian front only to die in a minor skirmish as this." There wasn't much we could do for him except to comfort him and close his eyes when he died.

We honored our dead the next day with a simple church service. We sang the traditional song of farewell to dead heroes 'Ich Hatt' Einen Kammeraden…' (I once had a comrade, a better one you cannot find) It was a simple yet moving ceremony and it made our 'green' recruits quickly face the reality of this war. It made them realize that this was not a game anymore. Shortly after this attack, we had our first deserters. Apparently, death had come too close for some and they fled only to be caught by the SS field police. The boys were taken away, they were not returned to our unit, we never saw them again. Our kommandant warned us that deserters would be shot on sight. It was a quiet night in camp.

We worked around the clock in order to prepare for our ground confrontation. We struggled against the elements whose purpose it seemed was on the side of the Russian army. Without notice, we would one minute be in a complete white out and the next in drowning rain. Sharp winds cut through our worn out uniforms like razor blades. Our fingers were forever numb with cold we had no heat in our barracks. The only warmth and shelter we really had was in our ditches. As soon as we felt we could not get any colder, the sun would cut through the clouds and we would be blinded by its rays and engulfed in the warmth that radiated down. We never had time to lament or praise the weather; we needed to be constantly vigilant so as not to be caught off guard by attacks.

One day our commandant came out of his heated hut and announced to us that the Russians had taken control of Berlin and its army was pushing on westward. We could hear the bombardments from the artillery cannons in the far distance.

The SS was now completely in charge, Heinrich Himmler, the head of the SS, worshiped Adolf Hitler from the very beginning. He was a man of great organizational skills with a passion for perfect record keeping and a heart as black as his schutzstaffel uniform, which was adorned with emblems shaped like double lightning bolts perfect symbols of the terror and suddenness with which they swooped from the night to arrest their frightened victims. His power in the Reich was tremendous, only Hitler reigned above him. German generals had all the reason to worry; the SS (the only hope in possibly winning the war) was now in charge. However, their military once so powerful was now failing. The Wehrmacht and Luftwaffe were showing grave signs of weakness and were falling apart. Even the U-boats, once feared on the waters in the early stages of the war, no longer controlled the oceans.

We worked from dawn to dusk reinforcing our line of defense with little rest. The enemy had the overall control over the air and despite our efforts relentlessly bombed German cities and our supply routes whenever possible. We were facing the unimaginable and most crucial times of this horrible war.

Berlin Under Siege - 1945 the Devastation

On the onset of WWII Herman Goring, Chief of the Luftwaffe publicly stated that not one enemy bomb would fall on Berlin. The Royal Air Force made more than thirty raids on this beautiful city in 1940 alone, and to make it worse the attacks grew in intensity especially when the United States entered the picture. From the first British air raid on August 25, 1940 until April 20, 1945, the city was blasted with more than 76,000 tons of explosives and incendiary bombs. The city was hit from the ground forces too, as Soviet heavy artillery during the last ten days in April 1945, concentrated about 40,000 tons of shells on the city of Berlin. I had good reason to follow the statistics of this mind-boggling war, my sister Anna still lived in Berlin. I worried about her constantly, when I had last seen her in March it was extremely hard for me to make the decision to live up to my obligations and leave her to the fate of the Russians. Would she be found? Would she be hurt? Killed? These questions constantly nagged at me, but what was I to do?

Most public buildings had been brought down or badly gutted during the war, especially in this final battle in Berlin. The Reichstag was reduced to a gaunt wreck and it was very difficult to identify the many ministries, embassies, and once handsome office buildings on the Unter Den Linden. The cathedral erected in 1893 was badly damaged, as was the old 'schloss', the ruins of which were later cleared away by the East Berlin authorities. Berlin suffered a great deal of casualties, many were never accounted for. A census taken in May of 1939 reported a population of 4,332,250 people, but according to the census of October 1946, its population had dropped to 3,189,400. During all the chaos many had fled the city leaving behind all the destruction, the loss of great architecture, and the memories of lost loved ones. With the capture of Berlin, the Russian armies moved westward toward the Brandenburger Canal and Elbe River. Germany had plunged even deeper into a desperate situation. Germany's people were ravaged by hunger, disease or had been trampled by hostile armies. The countryside was awash with roving bands of laborers and displaced people many of them intent on robbery and revenge.

General Eisenhower crossed the Rhein River with his armies and liberated the western part of Germany. General Patton's forces at Moosbury in Bavaria pushed toward the east during the final days of the war.

One night as we slept in our trenches we were awakened by the drone of flying RAF's and the flashes of light from the flares they dropped on our compound, seconds later we were scrambling for cover as the bombs started to fall. When everything was over we had many casualties, among them were new green recruits and our SS officer commander. The next morning as we were getting organized we heard in the distance the clatter of tank tracks. We were now under the direction of a young officer who shouted with a tremble of fear in his voice, "that the Russians were coming!"

The Russians had taken us by surprise; our scouts had misjudged their relation to us. We were not prepared, we were out of ammunition, and our supplies were non-existent. How were we going to fight back? With each explosion another deep crater was created, meters deep right in front of us. Under cover of heavy artillery fire we scrambled out of our collapsing trenches and scurried out of the village for what we hoped would be safer cover. In the distance I could make out a couple German Wehrmacht half-tracks smoldering on the outskirts of the village, they had been the target of shelling. Once we regrouped we realized we had lost a great deal of our platoon. Twenty very young, very scared boys were all that remained. We looked around for the young SS officer who had been forced to take command the day before, but he was nowhere to be seen.

As the shelling subsided, we took stock of our situation and we were surprised to hear sounds from a nearby shelled German tank. We investigated the noises and miraculously found two of the crew had survived the attack. We quickly dragged them out of the tank and made a litter so we could take them with us to our next stopping point about five kilometers away. I am sure that the most fearful time of a soldier's life is to be wounded and along with your enemy all around you, hoping that the one who finds you will help you even if it is the enemy.

After checking in with a nearby unit, it was evident that no one knew in which direction we were to go. The NCO finally made the decision to go west, and we did as fast as we could. After a couple of kilometers, we came upon a German truck in which we could put our wounded. No matter how fast we moved the Russians were forever on our heels. Fresh rounds flew over our heads. The heavy artillery fire kept us scurrying for cover, in no time our faces and clothing were covered with mud and blood.

I am ashamed to admit that we begged for food from the farmers we came across. I am even more horrified to confess that if they did not help us out, we looted their belongings and dwelling to find what we could use to supplement our non-existent supplies. We were exhausted and none of us felt as though we could go on. We came across a village. Most of the houses had white sheets hanging from their windows, but not a soul was in sight. There was evidence of recent fighting; smoldering army trucks blocked streets and the smell of gunpowder was in the air. We looked around and came across a partially damaged barn, hoping to find some food storage but all we found were a few hungry cows huddling in the corner out of fear. We searched the adjacent farmhouse but could not find anyone. We went back to the barn with the intentions of killing one of the cows when we heard someone call out, "Ist dort jemand?" (Is there anyone there?) "Bitte tuensie uns nicht weh!" (Please don't hurt us!) We told them to come down, that we wouldn't hurt them. Two older men climbed down from the loft. One explained that his wife and two daughters were hiding up there too. They told us that they were hiding from the Russians. We learned later that they had two sons in the Air Force and were worried about them, because they had not heard from them in over a year.

We cautioned them that it wasn't safe to hide in the barn, since the Russians had a reputation of burning them down. We suggested that a safer place would be underground. They indicated that they had a root cellar and we agreed that that was probably a better place to hide. They were so grateful for our help that they sent us away with a feast of smoked ham and rye bread; we felt like kings. As we said our farewells, we secretly prayed that no harm would come to them or their farm. Our NCO wanted us to get to Magdeburg about thirty kilometers away. The hellish barrage of shelling forced us to travel mostly on our hands and knees, we crawled crater to crater to make a smaller target.

For the last three days it had been raining, making the thought of getting any sort of rest impossible. The next night while we were in our trenches trying to recuperate from the previous night's battle. The Russians started with a heavy bombardment on the northern end of the town. The main road itself had an enormous crater filled with rainwater in its center. There were minefields on one side and a steep hill on the other; we could not see the Russians and had no means to which we could retreat. Rubble from the destroyed homes created an obstacle course through which we had to navigate, there were no roads to steer us through the town. Every once in a while you would see a German tank creeping along trying to find a way through the twisted steel, masonry, and the huge craters some of which were probably twenty meters wide and eight or so meters deep. The whole town was in ruins. It wasn't wise though to follow the tanks since they made an easy target for the Russians.

There was not much fighting going on, not even the officers made any attempt to fire at the approaching Russians. The Russians sprayed machine gun fire into the air above us and sometimes into our ranks. Bodies fell to the ground, it was horrible. We felt helpless our morale was at an all time low. Somewhere along the way, we heard a voice calling out from depths of a vast pile of debris. With our bare hands, we frantically tried to dig down to the trapped men, but with the heavy shelling from the Russians we had to abandon our efforts in order to save ourselves.

We were hampered by the rain as well as the shelling. We were so wet, we could no longer feel our uniforms, and it was as though we stood naked there in the streets. Our equipment refused to function due to the conditions, especially our radios making communication impossible. There was no moon to guide us as the night became darker, so we stumbled single file with each man holding onto the shirt of the man in front of him. The rubble over which we walked had changed to the consistency of dough making each step a struggle. Every surface was slick with this gray slime forcing us to move at a snails pace to keep our footing. Many times, we had to rescue a soldier who had slipped into the many massive craters along the way. These moments sapped our already depleted energies, but we would not leave anyone behind.

Our goal was to make it to the next day, we did not expect any reinforcements to assist us, and we were on our own. The only light that shown that night was from the Russian bombardments, the explosions went off all around us, we knew we were hemmed in and that it was just a matter of time. We hoped we could get to the Elbe River. It was only by the will of God that we made it to the village of Dorf. It was an immense relief to see that there were no destroyed homes. The farmers gave us food and space in their barns to rest in order for us to face another day.

One never loses the images of their war torn comrades mutilated by artillery shells and bullets. It is sad to think of those men lying lifeless on the desolated fields, alone with no one to acknowledge their deaths. It took all our effort not to fixate on who was falling around us, but rather to focus on where we were and where we needed to be. The din of artillery fire was so great that it was impossible to communicate with the rest of our troop so we were on our own until we could catch their attention or get closer. When we finally were able to regroup, our troop had dwindled down to a mere nine men; we had lost eleven in the blink of an eye.

As night fell, we knew the darkness would provide us cover, which would allow us to reach the Elbe River and Magdeburg. Our small group was determined to stay a step ahead. The notorious Russians hated the Nazi-German soldiers and did not always conform to the Geneva Convention, which offered some protection from hardship to POW's. Exhausted from the effort to keep moving and lack of sleep, we literally fell into the town of Gerwish, about 15 kilometers southwest of the Magdeburg. We found a large concentration of German soldiers holding up there. We all had the same goal in mind and that was to get to the Elbe River and Magdeburg. We found out that it would be impossible to cross the river since the German Army had blown up the bridge, after they realized that much of the town had fled in a human swarm of thousands of people crossing it to find a safe haven. We seemed to have reached our limit.

What was left for us to do, but to surrender to the Russians! The thought of being captured was unbearable. The Russian army moved very rapidly towards us with shots coming from all directions. They shelled us with rocket-propelled grenades in addition to heavy artillery guns. We returned their fire as best we could, but without adequate stores of ammunition, our guns were soon silent. We were not to retreat upon orders of Hitler; we were to fight until the bitter end. Upon the command of our SS fanatical officer, "Sieg Heil!" we left our trenches running towards the oncoming Russians. We fought with bayonets, grenades, and when necessary our bare hands; the outcome was often decided by the determination of the soldiers involved. The first to fall was the SS kommandant followed by many many others. There were wounded and dead soldiers everywhere. Young boys who should still be home playing in their backyards, crying for help and without it, dying. After the barrage, the Russians were within fifty meters of us. At one point a Russian jeep with three soldiers in it, drove directly into our ranks, yelling out "Achtung!" (Attention!)

On April 28, 1945 we were told to lay down our arms, we thought we were so close to being free, but the worst was yet to come. We were captured and forced to witness the debauchery of the Russian soldiers. They broke into homes, raped the women, killed the livestock, and killed without provocation anyone who stood in their way. The soldiers seemed to take a great deal of pleasure in intimidating us. We stood in fear for our lives as they ranted and raved around us. I am not able to tell you the day of the month or week that this happened, but every minute detail of what happened is forever etched in my memory.

The Russians

They announced to us that we were now prisoners of war. We were told not to move. For some reason one of our comrades raised his hand as if to ask a question and a Russian soldier instinctively raised his machine gun and opened fire, severing the man's arm from his body. The spray wounded several other soldiers and panic broke out among us. They fired more rounds, this time into the air. Russian trucks drove in around us penning us in. We all wanted to survive so with extreme effort we calmed down somewhat. Fear shook our bodies as we waited for their next move.

More and more Russians came, some singing in jubilation. We, the Germans, were supposed to conquer the world. Hitler bragged that he would build huge German farms on Russian soil and that he would bring <u>freedom</u> to all nations and would liberate all the oppressed, this would not come to pass. As the endless stream of Russian trucks, tanks, and soldiers flowed towards us we were made aware exactly where we stood. Most of the enemy moved on leaving only 50 or so men to decide our fate. It was somewhat comforting to see that their soldiers did not look any better than we did. Their uniforms were shabby and you could tell that they had had very little rest. What was dangerous about this was that their nerves were on edge and any wrong move would prove disastrous for us.

We were told to form six men rows. It was very difficult to imagine that we were under the Russian control and at their mercies. The situation among us was very tense. Somewhere inside me, I could still hear the voice of my mother telling me <u>not to give up</u>. With that ingrained message, I hung on to my determination to live. Surrounded by machine gun armed soldiers, we were ordered to march. We were forced to leave our fallen and wounded comrades behind.

We were at the mercy of the Russian army. Marshal Stalin had accomplished his objectives and that was to conquer the German Reich. I knew my faith would help me survive anything that came my way; I had promised my stepmother that I would do what ever it took to come home again. Prayer, hope, and faith gave me strength. As we marched along, we faced an unexpected problem; the Russians had to keep us in check as we made our way through the mangled remains of the town. We were required to constantly stop, move on in small groups through narrow gaps in the debris; many times, we were forced back under cover when rogue German snipers fired at the Russians. It cut us to the quick when the Russians returned their fire silencing the oncoming assaults almost immediately. After one such attack the Russians pulled out three of our unit at random, lined them up and shot them dead. This scene flashes back at me still to this day. When feasible, we were forced to walk with our hands on our heads, which made traversing the terrain even harder.

We pondered whether we were marching somewhere to be executed or if we were on our way to a prison camp. Still as we marched along, we would be showered with a barrage of bullets from those who believed in Hitler's lunatic rantings. I felt sorry for the Hitler Youth who had been brainwashed into believing his whole philosophy, it was sad to see them still with the determination that they would win this war. Everyone was on edge, including the Russians, we never knew who was lurking behind or inside a building waiting for the opportunity to shoot at us; but we marched through the night. The wet weather had turned bitterly cold as we trudged along the muddy remnants of the roadways. We must have marched twenty-five kilometers and with each step, the temperature dropped to near freezing.

We came upon a small village, there was no movement, and it had a ghost town like feel to it. We had marched for so long without seeing any living thing, that when a dog trotted out from between some farm buildings it jolted us awake; one of the guards shot it. I could not help but wonder where every one was. Were they dead? Had they fled into the woods? Or were they hiding in their homes? We passed by a large factory, which had been totally demolished. We later found out it was a German ammunitions factory. Along side this building was a smaller one with very little damage to it, the guards ordered us to stop. Our men, who had had nothing to eat or drink for nearly two days just simply collapsed, there was a brief scuffle from a few who had reserves of strength (probably pent up nerves) that caused a commotion. The guards fired a few rounds into the air and they calmed down. We were told to get on the ground while they checked out the building. We sensed that something may not have been right and we held our collective breaths as the minutes passed.

It was getting dark, but we were able to make out the sight of several trucks coming down the road. They pulled up by the factory; there must have been at least twenty-five trucks. Russian soldiers poured out of them, there must have been a few hundred. Almost a thousand men, where had they all come from, were holding us captive. We were told that we would get a ration of food and water if we remained calm. A few minutes later, we were told to stand and were to move in an orderly manner toward one of the trucks where we were given a chunk of bread and some water, this was like manna from heaven, and I thanked the Lord!

After we had eaten, we were given permission to relieve our selves under heavy guard. After we were through we were once again told to sit or lay, but not to move around or we would be shot. The night had become extremely cold and we quickly found out, that by huddling together somewhat we could share each other's body heat. Some managed to sleep but some of us just rested. Every time I felt myself drifting off, a new round of explosions and shootings would go off. I think that the guards enjoyed jolting us awake by yelling their commands into our ranks. I found that I was sitting next to an older soldier who had a habit of talking in his sleep, it always fascinated me, but chilled me at the same time when he would call out "Fight, Fight, Fight!" he even dreamt of war. During the day, we would talk and he had told me stories of his family and how he missed them. About how he was forced into the Wehrmacht, but lately he had been talking about trying to escape. I cautioned him about making such an attempt into the unknown and if he failed, the consequence would be death.

The next day as we were sitting there quietly, we were suddenly in the midst of a hail of gunfire, our comrades were falling around us. I was scared my nerves made my body quiver all over. The old soldier was sitting next to me mumbling a prayer, I joined him praying "Lord, please help us, don't let anybody die." This war was supposed to be over. The Russians charged at us, we could see hundreds of them rushing towards our huddled mass. They swung at us with their machine guns yelling "Stoy! Stoy!" (Stop! Stop!) A nearby soldier cried out that he was dying, there was more shouting. Machine gun fire filled the air. Finally, all was quiet. The wounded were taken away. We could not understand what provoked this exchange, we had no weapons, we were doing what we were told to do. Eventually, it came out that a few of the German soldiers had tried to run. The futile attempt prompted a very important lesson; we would surely die if someone tried to escape again.

As we sat there, I noticed that the man next to me had suddenly changed. His demeanor was one of a lost person, his eyes became glassy, and he had become unusually quiet; at times he resembled a mere block of marble. When we became too cold to sit, we were allowed to walk a bit, albeit in a circle and only a few men at a time in an attempt to generate some body heat. Every now and then, I could see tears on the faces of those around me. It is said that soldiers do not cry, yes they do if there is still some humanity in them. There were times the old soldier would look at me as though he needed desperately to tell me something, but dare not. I knew he wanted to run, to be free, but he could not will himself to make that first move.

Night fell again, and yet more Russian trucks pulled in to our encampment. We were ordered to lie down and not move. It was near freezing. With minute shifting, we inched our bodies closer to each other to share what little heat they gave off. A soft pale moon reigned above us among the silvery shining stars. Strangely, it was very serene. Loud voices from the Russians would occasionally penetrate the still night. At some time during that long night we managed to fall asleep. I remember waking to the dawn flaming up along the horizon in a truly majestic glow of radiance, it was another miracle that I had lived to see another day.

My Quest for Survival

Day three in the POW camp, my bones ached from lying on the cold damp ground. When we were ordered to march, some of us could hardly get up, we were exhausted, and our bodies were stiff from being out in the cold for so long. We were told to report to one of the abandoned ammunition factories to register, we stood in a long line and tried to stay warm through the slow process. They asked each of us our name, age, army unit, and place of birth; and we had to relinquish all our belongings. We emptied our pockets; they took our watches, rings, wallets, anything of value. When it was my turn, I thought for sure they would see how scared I was, my whole body was quivering. When I had to empty my pockets, the only thing I had to give up was my small diary. The officer scanned through it and handed it to another soldier who studied it a while. I was ordered to leave the room. I was a little fearful of its contents being in the enemy's hands. The book contained the names of the cities I had been sent to, there were strategic places of Wehrmacht troops had engaged in battle, as well as my secret mission to Potsdam. The diary also contained entries about Auschwitz and my hometown in Tarnowskie-Góry. I was distraught that this precious book was in the enemy's hands. I was taken to another room by two soldiers; in it were eight soldiers and a major. After the major had scanned my diary, he made me explain the entries; especially those in Polish. When I did not follow his request, I was told to undress so they could go through my pockets and look for hidden compartments. As I stood there shivering with cold and fear, I watched in dismay as they confiscated the little money I had - a few deutschmarks. When they finished with my clothes, I was subjected to a body search and finally allowed to get dressed.

The officer seemed to empathize with my situation and asked me some questions with a more mellow tone in his voice, it was as though he had a job to do and he was sorry it was going to be bad for me. He asked me how old I was, where I was from, and why I was in the Wehrmacht. I explained to him that I was drafted by Hitler's decree at the age of sixteen-and a half. He listened to what I had to say, but without any comment to me directly, he told the guards to take me outside to the rest of my platoon. I don't think I had even allowed myself to breathe while I was inside, because once outside in the air I gasped for breath and thanked God for getting me through what could have been a disastrous ordeal. I was upset that they had taken everything I owned, but I was grateful that they had not taken my life.

After everyone had registered, we were told to go over to the food truck and we would be given something to eat, another chunk of dry rye bread and more water. The morale in our group was at an all time low. During this ordeal I had met up with a POW a few years older than me, we had talked some before we registered and I looked for him now since everyone had passed through the building; just before dusk I saw him on the other side of the compound. I worked my way through the mass of soldiers to meet up with him; he admitted that he had been looking for me all afternoon. The day before when we had talked, I told him about my sister Anna and how I wanted to see her again. His comment to me was that I would, it wasn't what he said that made a chill run through me, it was the way he said it.

Day four in the camp, five big Russian trucks arrived delivering huge canvass tents. We worked all day putting them up. We were grateful to finally have a 'roof' over our heads. We hadn't finished a moment too soon; upon completion of the last tent, the dark ominous clouds released their torrential deluge. We waited out the storm inside the tents and pondered our fates. The nights that followed inside those tents provided the much needed rest for all the POWs. The tent also allowed us to generate the heat needed to keep us warm. The Russians never failed to amaze us, by providing us on night five with blankets in which we could wrap our bodies. Day five also delivered to us our first warm meal in almost a week. It was a simple cabbage soup and very dark rye bread; even though it was a simple fare, its warmth spread through our bodies like lava from a volcano.

The next day we were ordered to clean up the demolished factory next to our tents. We did not have any equipment, but we were forced to pick through big heavy steel beams and piles of rubble. Eventually, we came to the large pieces of machinery. It was hard backbreaking work. We worked from six o'clock a.m. until usually six o'clock p.m. with one meal break in the shift. When we were allowed back into our tents, we collapsed exhausted into our makeshift beds. As we dozed off, we could sometimes hear the distant sounds of rebel gunfire in the distance; every once in a while, it would be answered with a fireball fired into the night in the direction of the shots.

Each day was the exact duplication of the day before, the only break in the monotony was if someone was caught talking; when this happened the offender was taken to the other building and severely beaten. Occasionally, we would see a fellow POW crawling out of the building because he could not stand to walk. There were many times I used my knowledge of the Russian language to my comrades' benefit and mine. They did not know that I could speak all three languages, which gave me an advantage. One day jubilant shouting and singing disrupted the calm. Guns were fired into the air. From their shouting, I learned that the war had ended. They shouted through their PA system that the Germans had surrendered, the Russians celebrated their victory! I looked around at all the former soldiers huddled near me, I say "former' because a soldier is only a soldier when he is fighting and there is a war to fight. We were now truly prisoners of war. I could see the depression in their faces and the fear in their eyes. Their spirits had been broken. I took a moment to thank the Lord for delivering me from the jaws of death.

Now came the uncertainty of our fate. For the millions of men and women who participated freely or against their will, the consequences of their actions were in the hands of the Russians. The defeated were punished and the victors were rewarded. What was to be our punishment? We did not know what was ahead of us. Our future in this POW camp was certainly unpredictable and given our unhealthy state only God knew when our hour would come.

Rumors circulated around the camp that we were going to be transported to another location as soon as transportation became available. Many thoughts ran through my head. Would I survive the next stage of my captivity? Would I ever see my parents and family again? I had youth on my side; most of my fellow captives were older men. I had strength and conviction that I would make it. I knew I had to keep fighting, praying, and hoping. I also had a burning desire to be free. I had lost a lot of weight, but I kept fighting and hoped for better days to come. With enthusiasm and passion, I looked forward to each new day. Despite the circumstances, I never failed to thank God for letting me see a new day dawn.

We no longer heard the cannon shots in the distance; it was almost too silent without the drone of planes overhead or the sound of explosions on the ground. Remember that older soldier who scared me with his eerie silence? Well, one day he finally broke it. He came over to me and started to talk to me about his family, he was so lonely and so worried about his loved ones that he scared me with his talk and what I feared he was going to do.

One night the silence was broken by several rounds of machine gun fire, this was their way of breaking us. Another form of punishment was to walk in circles, round and round we went. We do not know why they did it, but we knew it made them feel in control. Our meals consisted of heavy dry bread and a tin can of lukewarm thin soup. One day after our meal instead of being able to return to our tents, we were told to stay outside. As we were made to stand there, we could only watch with dismay as the clouds became darker and the wind began to pick up. We were not even allowed to take cover when the rain turned into pellets of hail that bit into our skin on that cold afternoon. That same afternoon we were split into two groups in order to make our large group more manageable.

Russian trucks rolled into camp, it was obvious that we were going to be moved. I somehow managed to stay with my friend, the older soldier. He had me almost convinced to escape when the time was right and I wanted to stay near him to make sure if he did try to run, that it was with the least amount of risk giving him or us the greatest chance of making it. There were about two hundred and fifty men in our group, but the Russians split us up into smaller groups as we were loaded into the trucks. To our surprise, only about half of us were soon moving out of this camp. We were weak, during the long daylight hours we were forced to remain upright, it was only when it became dark were we allowed to lie down. When we were able to see outside, it was disheartening to see the overwhelming numbers of dead German soldiers lining the roadways.

On the upside, it gave us a degree of satisfaction to see the Russian soldiers in tattered uniforms and in the same state of despair as the rest of us. It was evident that they too were short on supplies, at some level wanted to go home, and for their part in this war to be over. I noticed that we were passing the small village of Moser, which was not far from Magdeburg. In Magdeburg, we were told that the American and Russian troops met at the end of the war. As we passed the village, we heard shots coming our way apparently from snipers or the small factions of diminishing German forces that evidently had refused to believe that the war was over. During one such ambush, the Russians were able to capture one of the shooters; they brought him close to the trucks, ordered us to remain inside them, and as a lesson to us, executed him. It was sad to see these instances of insanity happen, but it reinforced their hold over us. Our future depended on the mood of the Russians. Under heavy guard and with machine guns pointed, we were now ordered to leave the trucks and to march.

Many times over the past couple days, I noticed that the Russian soldiers seemed to be hovering close to the older soldier, Hans, and myself; we had been caught talking. When I had a chance, I whispered my fear to Hans that I felt something was not right. Later that day, the guards came back and ordered the entire group to sit on the ground. Hans and I were taken away from the group; we were taken to a nearby tree. Several guards joined them, I begged them to let me go, but instead they tied me with my hands behind my back to the tree. They removed my boots and tied my feet to the tree. I felt for sure that I was going to die. They took Hans back with them, leaving me there shivering and crying for help. The group was moved away from me, I thought for sure they were going to leave me behind. As the night fell, I got colder and more frightened. During the night, I was startled awake by the sounds of gunfire from the direction in which the Russians had gone; I knew deep inside me that they had shot Hans. The next morning a farmer found me unconscious, so I was told. He cut me loose and took me to his home, gave me food and shelter and allowed me to rest, so I could recover from my ordeal.

The farmer and his wife were wonderful caring people; I know deep in my heart that they saved my life. I stayed with them a few days, they had lost their only son to this senseless war, and I did not have the heart to leave them. They provided me with clothing and a pair of boots, to this day I cannot imagine having lived without their care. It was a miracle!

There were many difficult and close calls during WWII; Auschwitz, the bombing raids on Berlin and Magdeburg, but the worst situation I'd faced was when the Russians tied me to the tree and left me to die. I recovered from my ordeal quite well. Finally, on May 7, 1945 an unconditional surrender was signed at Reims France, making it official the war was finally over. I was a free man at last. Before I left this humble farm home, I was asked if I wanted to stay, but I had to move on. They had filled a sack for me with food and necessities I would need to see me on my way. As we said our heartbreaking goodbyes, there were tears being shed by all. I did not know where I would end up; I just knew that I at some point wanted to get back to Genthin, which was close to West

Germany and true freedom. I never saw this wonderful brave couple again, but they have to this day been in my daily prayers. They are two of hundreds of unsung heroes that aided many refugees and soldiers throughout the war. I know there is a special place in heaven for them and those like them.

WWII - 1939-1945

Each war has always unleashed terror, destruction, pain, and death of innocent people. War has always resonated despair and hopelessness. The many tragedies and disasters, which the war brought on its people, occurred almost daily. No one is ever prepared to handle the aftermath of a war or disaster of any size. Germany was left mostly with women and children, and older people, many of the men had gone off and died in this horrible war. Those left behind were despondent and in despair.

History tells us that it has always been a struggle for humans to live a moral and peaceful life. It has been so in centuries past and will be so now and in the future. The sacrifices that these people made regardless of their country during the war will remain a timeless tribute to the world.

Those maimed by the war were doomed like wandering spirits to float around the edges of our consciousness. These were those who paid the price and were shunted aside, they were the war's refuse. The message they bear from war is too painful for us to absorb. I had first hand knowledge of this through my own family; my father, brother and uncle were pushed aside as they dealt with their physical and emotional battle wounds and struggled with the inner horrors that tormented them daily. The only ones who understand war are those who have lived through it. If we really understood, what war does to our minds and our bodies it would be harder to wage. This is why the true essence of the war is hidden from the public; politicians do not want us to see the suffering, the wounded soldiers, the innocents lost. The maimed are carefully hidden in the wings while the bands play its majestic march. War stares out at you in the faces of the orphans, the crippled, and those plagued by diseases. I have seen the effects of war first hand and sixty years later, it still is as fresh in my mind today as it was then.

WWII has had a profound and lasting effect on my life, leaving deep scars on my soul. It left me without the warmth of my parents' love, without a home, and without a future. Homeless and hungry I forged my way back to life again. Although there were times I wanted to give up, but I had promised my mother that I would fight and that was a promise I was sure I would keep. In 1945, the world to me was a sorry place. During WWII, the trails of tears were endless. Only those who were amongst those innumerable refugees can understand how painful it was to be a refugee. Over the years, I have come across chronicled accounts of some of their experiences, yet it is evident that millions of others have held it inside and have tried to get on with their lives. As I write this chapter with the world news on in the background, I see devastation all around the globe, people uprooted or having to flee their homelands in an attempt to find a safe haven for themselves and their families. Countless people have been chased from their homes in the former Soviet Union as a result of ethnic conflicts and the demise of the soviet state. The trails of tears still exist and no one knows when it will end. What is truly sad is that the number of refugees and displaced persons is even higher now than it was in the worst years of the war.

Every day we were faced to relive this nightmare caused during Hitler's reign, every day we are forced to repeat the stories, to those who don't believe, of the holocaust and to relive the horror of the inhumane treatment. One day, every generation will realize and believe that there were innocent people victimized and sacrificed for a country they believed in. My goal of this book is to acknowledge these events and some of the innumerable people and to let them know that their efforts were not in vain.

Surviving WWII

I suppose that the face of WWII is in this book, it is almost impossible not to see it. Innocent people suffered and died who never even looked their attackers in the face. In 1945, Germany was a sorry place. Hitler's "Blitz Krieg" did not work! All it did was bring destruction, pain, and sorrow. Millions were left homeless by senseless bombings of their cities. If you had never lived through seeing the Flying Fortresses at work, it was an awesome fear inspiring sight; they could take down apartment blocks in seconds; reducing the buildings to ruins of pipe and mortar and brick burying everything inside before you had a chance to even think of what was going on. It is truly hard to imagine how difficult the war was to live through if you haven't had to walk around pools of blood, or sit and listen to the wailing of a frightened child who has lost his or her world in a blink of an eye. I wanted to shunt the memories of the war, to crumble them and throw them away, but I could not. It is almost impossible to completely block those images out. Hundreds of books have been written about the war baring their souls. I hope they did it to tell the world their stories and not just for monetary gain. The world should use this phrase as their mantra "Jamais Plus La Guerre!" (No More War!)

I served in the war and shared the ordeals of wartime with thousands of young innocent boys and along side seasoned war weary veterans, I was one of the few who lived to see the dawning of a new day. World War II has had a profound and lasting effect as well as deep scars in my life. Simply stated, it left me with nothing. The ties to my family were gone. I was demoralized mentally and physically, I had to struggle to survive.

For those first few nights after the war ended, I could not help but think of Hans, whose only dream was to go home to his wife and two daughters; I never saw or heard of him after that night we were separated, I know in my soul he was killed by the Russians that night. I could have stayed with that farmer couple who had rescued me, but my goal was to go home to my parents and sister, Maria in Tarnowskie-Góry in Poland, the only obstacle in my way, was that I did not know how I was going to do it. I had not seen my parents in almost two years and little did I know that it would take me another sixteen years to finally make it back to my hometown. This was the reality of war; millions of people suffered the same fate as I.

The day I left that wonderful couple, I was given directions on how to make it back to Genthin and from there on to Mutzel. I knew I had to be on the look out for the Russians as I started my journey of approximately 35-40 kilometers. I was unsure whether I could walk the distance in my current condition, but my military training of being forced to go on even when I did not think I could take another step, helped me face each new milestone. In order to avoid the Russians who had staked out nearly every town and major roadway, I decided my best course of action was to stick to the country roads. This turned out to be to my advantage since they passed by small villages and farming areas where I could ask for assistance without fear of being turned in or turned away.

I was familiar with Magdeburg, having worked and lived there and if I had to go on to Mutzel I knew the village Burgermeister would help me out. I would have liked to go to Berlin, but that was out of the question. I wanted to find a place where I could be safe and free. I hoped in Mutzel that I would meet up with some of the employees from the Inn and then I would not be as alone as I felt at this moment. As I walked along, I took this opportunity to thank the Lord for looking out for me and getting me through everything that I had endured. By mid afternoon, I had walked about twenty-four kilometers with about twenty more to go before I got to Genthin. Suddenly a northeast wind started to blow and in the distance, I could see some ominous clouds beginning to form on the horizon announcing that a storm was imminent. I moved as fast as my already tired legs permitted me to go, I was in open country and I needed to find shelter before the weather changed. Even in the barren countryside, I had to be wary of rogue Russian soldiers who were pilfering farmers and raping the women. By now, the sun was long gone and a fierce cold wind had started to blow. I listened to the groan of the trees being whipped back and forth, as I passed by them. The horrific wind had now reached an intensity that mirrored that of a raging wild beast. I had no one to talk to; there were no homes or shelters along the stretch that I was walking, only wide-open fields sporadically dotted with trees. I did not have any warm clothes, only those that I was wearing. Bolts of lightening zigzagged across the skyline. As a boy, I had always been fascinated by lightening, but being out there exposed to the elements with no means of escaping it, made this lightening storm extremely frightening. The thunder was like the explosions of bombs over Berlin or Magdeburg. Thunder shook the very ground upon which I walked and lightening so bright that it momentarily blinded me. The storm had developed into a torrent, torturing my body almost to its limits. I bent my head against these onslaughts and pushed onward. Every step I took now on the muddy road was calculated to ensure I would not end up laying on my back in the muck.

Finally, the storm broke and a light rain was falling I tried to catch rain in my mouth for I felt dehydrated, my canteen was empty and I could see no other homesteads in front of me. The clouds moved out and eventually a silvery fog spread over the countryside making visibility poor along with the chilly night, the elements made the walk very austere. I vowed to keep trudging on, but I had already come to the conclusion that I would not make it to Genthin that night, I was soaked to the bone, and I needed shelter in order to give my exhausted body a rest and regain my strength. I prayed as I always did that God would show me the way and I knew he would not let me down, he had helped me so many times in the past. At the end of the long and dark tunnels of life, there is always light, but you will never see that light until you walk down your dark tunnel. In the eerie blackness of the night my stomach reminded me that I had not eaten in a while, my provisions provided by the farmer's wife were gone except for a small chunk of bread in the sack I carried over my shoulder.

In the dark, I felt lost. I suppose I was letting myself become too frightened to focus on where I actually was. I was disorientated. In the distance, I heard the howling of dogs, I knew this was a good sign, where there were dogs there were people. Somehow, I was able to pick up my pace; I guess I walked about another kilometer when lights came into view on the horizon. Physically, I stopped and asked myself if it was safe to approach the lights, were there Russians there? I asked God for guidance, something inside me told me to go on, that everything would be okay. Soon I came upon a huge barn with other buildings around it. As I approached, I spooked the dogs, who took to howling to alert their owners. Cautiously, I kept walking toward the buildings as I came nearer I could hear the dogs start making their way toward me, out of the darkness I heard a voice call out "Kommzürück! Kommzürück!" (Come back! Come back!) Nevertheless, they knew their job, and they kept coming with teeth bared, growling deep in their throats. I knew enough to stand still until the person who called out reached me and regained control of his dogs. To my relief it did not take long to make out the shape of an old farmer.

I called out "Guten Abend Herr!" (Good Evening Sir!) The farmer relaxed somewhat and locked the dogs in their pen. He explained that the dogs where his only protection against the Russians who were constantly terrorizing the farming community. He was surprised to see a civilian. He had expected to see a Russian soldier snooping around looking for something he could carry off with him. I listened to him talk, but I was shivering from the cold and wetness of my clothing, I did not want to seem demanding or rude so I stood there as politely as I could and listened to him talk knowing he would realize my situation in good time and would give me aid. We walked into his cow barn and he told me of his losses with tears in his words, I couldn't help but once again be awed by the strength and resilience of these people who had no stock in this war, but were suffering its effects and would be for years. After a bit, we heard his wife call out to him asking where he was. He called back that he would be in soon. As we walked to the house, he told me of his neighbor's encounter with the Russians. When asked for cows, he refused and was shot, and his wife was raped. I was so disturbed by all this that I actually wanted to move on, but he refused and as I walked into the warm kitchen, I realized that I was in no condition to stay out in the cold night. The farmer introduced his wife, and she kindly demanded my wet jacket, cap, and rucksack.

Without a second thought, another place was set at the table and she laid out a wonderful meal for us. We talked about all the suffering of the innocent; there was so much pain and sorrow in their stories. It was heartbreaking to hear of the pilfering of the Russians even from those who had nothing left to take. They insisted that I spend the night and were amazed that I had already walked over thirty kilometers. When I told them my final destination I was relieved to hear that I only had about seven more kilometers to go and I would be walking into Genthin before noon the next day. I woke up refreshed, the soft warm feather bed felt like I had slept on a cloud; it took a great effort to pull myself out of it, it was the best sleep I had had in a long time.

The farmer's wife had hung my clothes next to the huge stone fireplace and they were dry and warm to the touch. Over breakfast, we talked about the war. My plan was to set out that morning for Genthin, but the farmer voiced his concern over my condition and asked if I would consider spending another night with them, I let my body make my decision for me and I accepted their offer. He mentioned that he had to cut wood and set out, feeling in the way I offered to help him and followed him out. I have to admit I had not cut wood since I was back home in Poland, and was somewhat clumsy at it at first. I felt truly inadequate as I watched this seasoned farmer swing his axe. I relished the fresh country air, the pleasant company, and the hard work. Before we knew it, his wife called out that it was time for lunch. After the hearty meal, I took a moment to thank God for leading me to this couple and for once again saving my life. Our afternoon chore was to clean out the cow barn. At one time, it had housed over thirty cows and some sheep, but after the Russians had raided their farmstead, there were only two cows left. This chore as strange as it sounds brought back fond memories of time on my grandparents' farm. I always enjoyed my visits with them and the good hard work, which needed to be done.

It is strange, but I still hear his laughter over some funny thing that was said, how long had it been since I had heard someone laugh out of merriment and not to strike fear in a person. We talked about their boys, lost to the war and how they missed them. We talked about how he was going to plow the fields with cows that were not trained and not meant for this type of work. It sounded like a daunting task, but one of necessity. I ended up spending three days with this couple and after expressing my utmost sincere appreciation I told them I would not have peace until I reached my destination. The farmer gave me directions to Genthin and asked me once again to spend more time with them, but I had to move on. They found me a pair of boots and the wife stuffed my little sack with food and canteen with water. With an emotional farewell, I set out on my last leg of my journey. I did not want to leave and with a tired "Aufwiedersehen!" I set out. It was May 19, 1945 when I set out on a balmy beautiful spring day for Genthin. As I walked along, I saw other farmers, pulling teams of oxen through the fields. A sign some distance down indicated that I only had about three more kilometers to go. I rested in a small cemetery and ate a small lunch. Walking around reading the tombstones, I could not help but reflect on the fact that my birth mother and oldest sister were in a cemetery like this in Poland. Silently, I bemoaned the fact that I never had the opportunity to get to know them, but I had a wonderful stepmother that I hoped I would have a chance to see again. It was mid afternoon as I entered the town.

The last time I was here German soldiers occupied it, now it was in the hands of the Russians. I had to be vigilant to avoid being arrested. I was apprehensive of being questioned; I had no papers to identify me and had no real reason to be in this town. I managed to slip into the city limits without being detected or drawing much notice. I could see Russian trucks everywhere. At first, I thought I should have stayed at the farm. I wanted to continue on with my life, but I knew I could not do it here, there was too much going on. I asked a passerby if he knew how to get to Mutzel. To my relief he gave me directions with little question. It was late afternoon and I had about seven more kilometers to travel. I lost valuable time navigating the town to avoid any Russian patrols, but I was soon on the road out of Genthin and heading toward Mutzel. My hopes were to run into some of the Inn's employees. With luck, some had stayed there. I hoped that the town Burgermeister would remember me and could help me out. Immediately upon entering Mutzel I looked him up, he indeed did remember me as one of the evacuees from Magdeburg last January, he directed me to where I could find some of my old co-workers.

Once I found them, we had a bittersweet reunion as they caught me up on the whereabouts of some of those missing. Olga, Natasha, and Maria were gone; I was disappointed that we could not all be together. The first night I spent with the Burgermeister and we sketched out what I would do now that I was there. The next day he took me back to the farmer who had cared for all of us that fateful night in January and I became his farmhand. I thanked God for giving me another chance at life, good people to work for, and good friends around me. For the first time in what felt like ages, I was looking forward to my future with a sense of optimism.

The Aftermath

During the horrible war there was heroism shown by ordinary men and women doing extraordinary things. These acts often went unrewarded, but they did them with pride and honor. What is sad is that not only did we not have time to watch the sunrise or set, because we were focused on what was threatening our life at every turn that we often failed to say thank you to those who helped us along the way.

Surviving WWII became a quest for freedom and a safe place to live. At times, even though times were daunting, I managed to keep my optimism high. I often thought of all those who were left without their loved ones, homes and businesses and still managed to struggle on with their new lives, that it made my stumbling stones seem like pebbles.

The war had created great bands of nomads who wandered from town to town looking for work and a place to settle down. The destruction of the war left few flourishing businesses that could afford to hire help and no way of making a living. The orphanages were bursting with homeless children who had no one who could take them in. Hitler's war was nothing but deception from the onset. It had sucked in other countries into this swirl of destruction. Hitler traded food for cannons. He lost sight of the common man even when the realization hit him that it took more than the power of tanks to win a war. Hitler wasn't the only one. There was also Benito Mussolini, the fascist dictator who was obsessed with the war and who wanted to dominate the world. Those who had objected to the war were eliminated either through execution or sent to labor camps. Few sent to those camps ever came back.

Millions were forced to watch their churches, synagogues, their towns and livelihoods go up in flames. The war had created far reaching social and economic implications. There really was no way to escape this war, even though it was actually over. The war was doomed to go on without an end in sight. World War II was history. With a great deal of effort, I have moved on, but the memories remain. Everything has its price and WWII had its own in the loss of lives and freedom. Children died of malnutrition, many were diagnosed with health problems due to lack of food and poor living conditions. WWII has been heralded as one of the deadliest wars of all times.

The stress of the war had affected me tremendously; it was a time of despair and loneliness. Each day I was separated from my family seemed an eternity. Surviving the war was a daunting task and without my fervent prayers, faith, and the support of the many people along the way I would never have survived it. I can only summarize this with the following:

He watched over me at all times
He helped me when I was lost
He helped me rise when I had fallen
He found me in the pasture when I was homeless
He removed my chains when I was a prisoner
He gave me drink when I was thirsty
Fed me when I was hungry
He found me a home
He gave me freedom

All these things He did for me and it is my conviction that with God nothing is impossible. There were many choices and decisions I had to make such as; how was I to finish my education? How would I go about finishing my apprenticeship? Would I be able to support, live, and feed myself? Would I ever have anyone again who cares for me? These and so many other issues plagued me daily. Some people said to give up, to let nature take its course, but I had the strength and conviction instilled in me by my stepmother never to give up. All those who told me to give up were wrong. I knew I was going to have to create a workable plan or course, which I would follow or reach for. I had to face the fact that I was a person in need and to ask and accept and be grateful for help when offered to me from strangers, I was able to see my dreams come true and I rose to every challenge put in front of me.

I had always been intrigued by this Psalm: "By the labor of your hands shall you eat." I remembered it because of what my father used to say to us children, "If you don't work you don't eat." He was a wise man. Sadly, the war had created a fracture in our family and it's still there after all these years.

Mutzel – East Germany 1945

I was fortunate that the farmer, Herr Farber, took me in as his farmhand. The farmhouse was rather small; barely enough room for the farmer and his wife and two daughters; Gerda (17) and Theresa (15), but they found a place for me in a small room next to the granary adjacent to the cow barn. I did not mind. I considered myself very blessed to have a place I could call home albeit only temporarily. I was to help the Herr Farber with the plowing since the Russians had confiscated his horses. I looked forward to the hard work. It would remind me so much of my time on my grandparents' farm. We hooked up his team of oxen so they could help pull the heavy plow and we set to work.

For the first time in a long time I did not have to worry about where I would find my next meal or where I would sleep; to have found myself in this situation was a very precious gift. Countless people struggled for the simplest of staples to get by; I shuddered to think of all the children and those unable to make their way suffering without while I had so much. When people suffer through these types of circumstances it can either make them stronger or break them completely. Only time would tell. World War II was finally over, but the true struggle, the struggle for survival had just begun.

I was now eighteen years old, on my own and over a thousand kilometers from my home and family; I did the best I could to keep what I had. I prayed for the strength to keep up with the chores the Herr Farber needed me to do and it gave me consolation when I felt low to know that someone was looking out for me. I simply took one day a time. Herr Farber was a soft-spoken hard working religious man; his wife was a wonderful woman, who even through lean times was able to put food on the table for her family and myself. Each meal was preceded with a heartfelt prayer for the bounty laid before us, and the ability to face another day. I was offered pay to work for this family, but I was just grateful to have a place to stay where I could lay my worries to rest for a while.

No matter how busy I was, my homesickness would creep into my thoughts. I wondered how my family was and if they had any idea how or where I was. I did my best to brush these worries to the back of my mind and tried to focus on my future. I enjoyed the daylight hours where I could lose myself in my work. It was the nights I dreaded; the darkness allowed my loneliness to take over.

I was amazed at how well I was able to keep up with my chores having not done this kind of work in some time. Although, I remember vividly one morning when I found it impossible to walk, I was frightened had I contracted something? I did not know, but without fanfare, my aches and symptoms disappeared and I was able to get up as though nothing had happened. Even though I had to share my nights with the sounds of rats scrambling for scraps of food, I would not have changed my living quarters for anything, I was comforted by the sounds of the cows lying in their stalls, and the smell of the hay, and it brought back good memories. I found that with each passing day my spirits rose, I knew I wanted to survive and I would not let myself give up! The Lord was my inspiration, no doubt about it. I focused on my future and asked God to help me find a way that I could find my parents again and be reunited with my family, I knew some day that this would come to pass.

After Herr Farber and I became more comfortable with each other, we would often sit down and talk about the horrors he had seen and heard about the Russians as they marched through their small village. The Russians brought liberation from the Nazis, but they also dealt out a great deal of pain and suffering, rape and destruction. What had not been burnt or destroyed by bombs and artillery shells, the Russians put their hand to it. They pillaged farms for their livestock and grain stores whenever they could. A year or life's work could be gone in a matter of hours. He told me of one farmer who had lost his horse to a raid only to find it standing in his yard two weeks later badly beaten with open wounds, but its will had brought it back to its home. The farmer told me about the treatment all the villagers had to endure. The Russians treated all civilians poorly. Many of the Russians were uneducated, untrained soldiers they had a specific mindset and acted with evil intentions toward anyone that got in their way. Just the fact that this family had felt the need to hide their two daughters under the kitchen floor for two weeks in a cold cellar in order to keep them out of harms way is unthinkable.

One rainy day in May of 1945, as we sat down for lunch we heard the voices of Russian soldiers in the yard. At that moment I believe our collective hearts stopped, the two girls started to panic, we were able to calm them down, and not a moment too soon; the Russians barged into the farmhouse with their machine guns at the ready. One of the soldiers stepped forward and said something in Mongolian. I knew some of the Russians were Mongols and I was not able to speak their language, this put us at a definite disadvantage, I had hoped to be able to control the situation by being able to understand what they wanted. They stood in the kitchen, two filthy men in tattered uniforms, from the smell of their breath and clothing I could tell that they had been drinking. They looked at the women in the room and then at the farmer and myself, they pointed a gun at my chest and even without knowing their language, I knew they would kill me to get past me to what they wanted. I told them to leave the women alone. Without a thought, they started to beat and kick me. The women became hysterical, crying, and screaming. I found myself lying on the floor with my arms pinned down by one of the men while the other pulled my boots from my feet. After they got what they wanted they let go of me, I jumped up and yelled that they had no right to do this, that the war was over and to get out! They just grinned at me and before leaving the house; one came over and spit in my face as well as that of Herr Farber.

When would they decide that enough was enough and leave us all alone. The war was over, they had no authority to pillage and terrorize us anymore; when would it all end. One of them surprised me by calling out in German "Woman, you muss kommen!" They wanted to take the women with them, I wanted to throw myself in front of them to save them from what I knew would eventually happen. Summoning up my courage, I stepped forward shielding the farmer and his wife and daughters. I asked the soldiers in Russian if they were hungry or needed food to take with them, I figured if I got them talking or thinking of something else they might calm down. It did not work; they commanded again that the women would have to come with them. Frustrated with me, they asked me who I was. I said that I was a Polak and they had no right to do what they had planned to do, that the war was over and they were to leave. I was scared like a whipped dog as I stood there face to face with these rogue soldiers. I stood my ground, I knew their tactics, they figured they could frighten people into giving in; they were seldom stood up to. How I lived through that day remains an enigma to me, once again God was looking out for me. I knew that they had a reputation for torturing or killing those who were in their way. I knew that what they could not take with them they often destroyed so no one could come along after them, and reap a booty that they felt they had the rights to and to destroy the will of those left behind. I knew that women who were taken away were often beaten; stripped and raped only to be left in the snow along side the roadways and left to die.

When the Russians finally left and the dust had somewhat settled, we all fell on our knees and thanked God for this miracle. It was a harrowing experience. We watched them leave through the window. I was relieved that no one was truly hurt except me, I had some cuts, scrapes, and sore ribs, but I was able to stand there in the kitchen with a slight smile on my face as we all looked at my bare feet. Oh well, it wasn't the first time I had been bare foot and I was sure I would manage somehow. The farmer had been hurt in the tussle, but his wounds were not serious. We hugged and they thanked me repeatedly for my bravery. They called me a hero; I didn't feel like one, I just did what I had to do. "In the shadow of our lives, we must trust God."

I was rewarded for my bravery with a room inside the farmhouse, the two girls moved into one room together. Later that night as I lay shaking in my bed, I realized that God had given me the strength and courage to do what I did that afternoon and I prayed I would never have to live through that again. To this day, my imagination forces me to feel the point of that rifle in my chest and I break out in a sweat thinking that all he had to do was pull the trigger and it would have been all over. I know that the Lord had a reason for me to live and for that, I am a lucky man. Every day I prayed and gave thanks to the Lord for what he had done for me and for those around me, I thanked him for getting me over the hurdles and obstacles in my way and for each day, I was able to face with a new lease on life.

We all quickly recovered from the trauma of that afternoon. Over the next few days, I learned that they had had a son who at the age of twenty-two was killed at Stalingrad in 1943. Many times Herr Farber asked if he could pay me, I replied that I should be paying them. I had a clean wonderful home to live in, my own bed with a goose feather bed, I felt like I was in heaven with all the luxury I was living in. I stayed with this family for two months. I mostly enjoyed working with the team of oxen. They were strong and could pull the heaviest plow with ease. I seemed to have a rapport with them and it seemed they understood me.

I had endeared myself with the village Burgermeister with my ability to speak Russian. I often was the interpreter with the Russian Kommandant when talks were happening. The town respected the Kommandant. He had restored a semblance of order among his soldiers and although there were incidents such as what had happened with us, they were rare. With my help, I opened communication lines between the Burgermeister who spoke no Russian and the Kommandant who only spoke broken German. With some effort differences that had been left to simmer were smoothed out and everyone was relieved that they were able to share ideas and concerns. It was a time consuming job, but one I enjoyed. I began to hold great status in the eyes of those who knew of what I was accomplishing. I was often asked to spend time with the Kommandant and like most Russians he celebrated with vodka and would often offer me a glass of the potent liquid, not willing to offend I would accept and be one of the 'boys' for a while. The majority of the Russian officers I came in contact with were extremely cordial and very friendly toward me which allowed me to be at ease with my status. I must admit I had been a very industrious young man; I had a tough time refusing those who requested my help, so I was at times spread thin with giving support to those around me who requested it.

Things began to improve in this small village. The Russian Kommandant was very concerned that incidents such as what we had endured on the farm would not continue to happen. When we talked about the episode, he assured me that if the soldiers had been under his command, they would have faced harsh punishment and even possibly execution.

I enjoyed working on the farm, tilling the soil with the team of oxen often brought back memories of my time on my grandparents' farm at the age of ten. I had always enjoyed and still do today spending my days outside in the fresh air. I have always felt a special connection with nature. The independence I feel when working in the soil prompts me to hum my favorite songs, pray, or just reminisce about simpler times. Even when I felt at my lowest, I took solace in the fact that I had not lost my family to the war, just contact with them. I was whole in body and spirit and had a future ahead of me, so many others did not. Although, I was content with my present situation there was always an ever-present sheen of anxiety about me. My current concern was that I was now over eighteen years old and had not yet finished high school and I had no immediate way of finishing my education. The more I thought about it, the more it bothered me. My head started to spin with all the ideas running around inside me. I wanted to go home; I wanted to get back to Poland, but when? How? My main concern was if something would happen to me, who would notify my family, would I die alone like some crushed miserable insect? I knew I needed to change my situation, I needed to pick up my life, and I needed to be free!

Several weeks passed and the farmer's wife made note to me that I needed a haircut. I could not remember the last time I had had one. Mutzel was too small to have a barber, but Herr Farber knew of one in Genthin. I was too ashamed to admit I had no money, but Herr Farber understood my circumstances, gave me several German marks, and loaned me his old bicycle so I could ride over to Genthin. I flew down the road for those eight kilometers as free as a bird, I felt like I had been let out of my cage after being held captive for years. I couldn't help but sing out my favorite tune by Johann Strauss " Nur, nur, nur du alien solst fur immer meine freude sein" (Only, only, only you alone shall forever be my joy). I was stunned to have this beautiful day broken by the sound of a child crying. I had just passed some low growing shrubs and circled back to see if I could locate where the sound had come from. Finally, I found the source, a small boy lay in a dense patch crying his heart out. The sobs were so heavy that he had a hard time forcing words out. I became even more alarmed as I noticed among the smeared dirt and tears, his face was covered in blood. It took me several minutes to calm him enough to extract him from the foliage. As I got him upright, I figured him to be about four years old, how had he got here? I was only about two kilometers from Mutzel and thought that the best course of action was to take him back to the village. My haircut could wait. Somehow, I got the boy to balance himself on my handlebars and took him back to the farm. I explained to the farmer's wife what had happened. There were no homes close to where I had found him and up to this point, he had not said a word. The girls came in and asked their mother what we were going to do with the boy, and she simply said we would care for him until we found out to whom he belonged. When Herr Farber came in from the field, he was surprised to learn that I had not gotten to Genthin and even more surprised at our houseguest. He seemed content enough to let us fuss over him, but no amount of coaxing could get him to tell us who he was or where his parents were. We fed him and found him a place to sleep with the intent of visiting the Burgermeister the next morning.

Early that next morning the farmer's wife and I went into town, explained what had happened to the Burgermeister and the three of us went to the police station and officially reported what had happened. They assured us that they would do what they could to find this boy's parents and in the meantime if we were able to care for him to keep him until they contacted us. Well, there was no way the farmer and his wife were going to let him be taken into an orphanage and the matter was settled.

The next day I headed out once again for Genthin so I could get my much-needed haircut. I followed the directions given to me by Herr Farber and found the barbershop. I had to wait my turn and as I waited, I realized that I was now the focus of all their attention. They knew they had not seen me in town before and that I was a stranger, what made it even stranger to them is that I was a young man. There weren't many young men to be seen having so, many lost to the war. When it was my turn in the chair I couldn't help but marvel at all the different colors of hair clippings on the floor; red, black, brown and now my blond locks were being added to the mix. Barbers seem to think they have a right to ask a mélange of questions once they have you under their clippers and what are you to do but answer them. He asked me where I was from, what I had been doing, and where I was living. I told him about the farmer in Mutzel, but he did not know him. He asked what I had done before the war and I explained that I had worked in a restaurant. Excitedly, he told me he knew of a place that was looking for help and that he knew the owners. The barber liked me and when I asked what I owed for the cut, he would not take a cent from me. As I left, he pushed me to ride over to the Schützenhaus and I promised I would. It was a little past noon as I rode down a beautiful chestnut lined street to the restaurant. I was a little taken aback as I stood in the street and looked at the stately estate with its huge garden dotted with dozens of chestnut trees. To my dismay, the wrought iron gate was chained and padlocked. I called out "Is dort jemand?" (Is anyone there?) I called out several times and no one answered. I looked around and found a rock with which I could pound on the gate, it woke up the dogs, and finally a window opened on the second floor of the inn. A man leaned out and yelled at me to go away. I called up to him that the barber had mentioned something about a huge event coming up and wondered if he needed any kitchen help. He shouted down to me asking me what kind of experience I had. It felt awkward to be having this conversation in the middle of a street, but he seemed to be reluctant to come down and invite me inside. I yelled back up that I could do anything or whatever was needed. This must have impressed him and he called down to say I would need a white shirt and black pants and shoes. I told him I could get them and asked when I should come back and he told me to be there that Saturday at noon.

I was flying through town on eagle's wings as I skidded to a stop in front of the barbershop to let him know how everything went. I thanked him for helping me out and he was happy for me. All the way back to the farm I wondered how I would tell my 'family' that I would be working in town. Over supper, that evening I explained to them about what had happened and they were sad and happy for me at the same time. They knew I would not stay with them forever, but we all became quite a close-knit group. I told them I had a slight dilemma, I needed dress clothes. We were able to come up with a pair of blue trousers, a dark gray shirt, and a pair of shoes from their son's closet.

Before I knew it, Saturday was here, I was a little apprehensive as I walked through the gate at the Schützenhaus, this time the gate was open, and I did not have to shout for someone to open it up. I found my way to the large kitchen and asked one of the first women I met where I could find the owner. She told me to go around the corner and I would see his office. I found him easy enough. I introduced myself as Franz (I had decided to use my middle name), he looked at me with disappointment and asked why I was not dressed in the uniform needed to work in his establishment. I nervously explained my circumstances and he seemed to understand. He explained that there would be only Russian soldiers and officers at this Gardenfest and that I would be serving food and beer. I was a little concerned with serving a large group of Russians, but I felt I had a good rapport with the local Kommandant and that thought put me at ease. I worked hard that evening, but to my betterment. My tips were enormous, and well they should have been, the Russians had looted the banks in town and had vast reserves of cash and were not afraid to flaunt it. At the end of the night I went to Herr Neumann, the owner, to report my tips earned; he told me I had done well and he took the money. I went back to the farm disappointed and empty-handed. I was to report for work again the next day, which I did. I worked there all day and in the afternoon I once again was to take care of a group of Russians, once more I made a great deal in tips. My feet were killing me, the shoes I had borrowed from the Farber's dead son were a bit too small, and I fervently hoped the night would end soon. I was tired and my head resounded with the never-ending singing from one particular boisterous group of soldiers. I found the owners Herr and Frau Neumann in the large kitchen, once more, I emptied my pockets for them. Herr Neumann left the room, returned with a bucket from the night before, and handed it to me. He told me the money was mine that I had earned it. He was surprised that I had reported all that I had earned and had kept the wages from the night before to see if I would hold back anything on my second night. He was relieved at my honesty. That night late on Sunday, he offered me a full-time position with his inn. I immediately said yes!

As I peddled home, I was wondering how I would explain my job offer to the Farbers and how they would react to the news. The next morning over breakfast, I broke the news to them. They were very understanding and thanked me for all that I had done for them, especially for the episode with the Russian soldiers. I went to the Bürgermeister and the village Kommandant to thank them for all the help and trust they had given me. I told them I would be relocating to Genthin and they thanked me for all the help I had given them. The Russian Kommandant surprised me with a salute as I was leaving his office. It made me feel proud of all I had done.

Except for one visit from Gerda, the older Farber girl, I never saw that family or heard from them again. I thanked the Lord for steering me to that farmhouse for without their help I would not have been able to make a new start on my life. Their help provided me a renewed belief in hope, patience, perseverance, faith, and most of all prayer. I enjoyed working for the Neumann's, I had my own room and enough food, and I was never hungry again. I had money that I could spend on anything I wanted to. Times were tight and most of the stores only stocked the basic staples to get by, but someone with connections could always get what you wanted on the black market. For the time I was content, but my inner turmoil was always simmering just below the surface. I wanted desperately to continue my education, I knew I could not do it here in a communist environment; I needed to make a change, but I did not know how I was going to do it.

Berlin – Hohenneuendort

While working at the Schützenhaus late in the summer of 1946 I received a letter from Herr Kleinert, my former employer and guardian. I had not expected to hear from him again and wondered how he had even found me. We had completely lost contact during the last months of the war. However, with Germany being a police state we had to register whenever we changed residences or towns. Herr Kleinert stated in his letter that I must find a way to finish my apprenticeship, which had been interrupted because of the war and my conscription into the German Wehrmacht. He reminded me that I had a binding agreement with him to finish my apprenticeship and my schooling. He also informed me that he was now the owner of a large restaurant and cinema located in the Russian sector of Berlin. I was so glad that Herr Kleinert had not forgotten about me and was concerned about my future. I liked my job at the Inn and I liked the people with whom I worked and I knew they cared about me. Leaving them would be very difficult. The only consolation for me was that Herr Kleinert wrote that he had found my sister Anna. Even though the thought of seeing Anna was alluring, I had some apprehension about returning to Berlin. Berlin had been divided into four sectors: Russian, U.S., British, and French.

Herr Neumann immediately noticed the change in my attitude, one evening after the Inn closed, I sought out Herr Neumann and asked him if he could spare some time to talk with me about my dilemma. I went up to his apartment on the second floor. I told him about the letter and let him read it. Frau Neumann was there too and after finishing reading the letter he took off his spectacles raised his long eye brows and said to me "Mein junge, du hast keine wahl." (My son, you have not much choice.) He went on to lament that as much as they liked me, we all knew I had to continue my education and to think of my future. There was no future for me in Genthin and they both encouraged me to think of what I wanted to accomplish and do whatever it took to make it.

I knew I would miss Frau Neumann once I left the Schützenhaus. She was a wonderful woman, a good cook and a great baker. Before I left, she somehow managed to bake a cheesecake especially for me. This may sound trivial, but the ingredients for this rich dessert were hard to come by and it was a treasured delicacy. During my years in the hospitality business, I had tasted many cheesecakes but this one has always been one of my favorites.

I dreaded the day in which we had to say goodbye. It was an extremely emotional farewell, their final words were "If things don't work out, that I was always welcome to come back to the Inn." It was comforting to know that as I left the Inn that I had a home to come back to if something did not work out. A sea of tears was shed that day by the staff as well as Frau Neumann. It was heartbreaking for me to leave those who had become like family to me. I had packed my few possessions into a cardboard 'koffer', which I had bought on the black market. I chose to walk on the opposite side of the street to avoid any contact with the KGB on my way to the train station.

I was a little apprehensive about the train ride from Genthin to Berlin. I was looking forward to seeing Anna again and of course working for Herr Kleinert again, but I was worried about what awaited me there. As we entered Berlin, I was shocked to see all the devastation everywhere I looked; there were piles and piles of rubble and ruins. It truly was a depressing sight to behold. Doubts began to overtake me, had I made a mistake coming here? Would I find Anna? Everywhere I looked, I saw vast images of the aftermath of the war. In Genthin, there were signs of the war, but one almost had to look for it. Once in Berlin I had to switch trains to one, which would take me to the suburb of Berlin, Hohenneudorf, which was located in the Russian sector. It was almost dark as I came upon the brightly illuminated theater and restaurant. The area had sustained very little damage from what I could make out that night. I quickly found Herr Kleinert. He had changed little since I last saw him. Still dressed impeccably in a black suit, snow-white shirt, silver tie, and with that ever-present smile. Despite all he had been through, losing his wife while in Auschwitz and his son he still managed to smile. He used to say, "If you don't smile, your customers will not come back." How right he was.

It was as if I had never left, he welcomed me back with open arms, and he got me settled in for the night. The next morning he introduced me to his staff. Everything had been arranged, I would attend classes in the morning, and in the afternoon and evenings, I would work in the kitchen or the restaurant. He already had me registered at the police station. My immediate future was all mapped out. There was a couple also working in the restaurant, Herr and Frau Meier. They both were once teachers and during WWII, the teachers were forced to belong to the NSDAP and now those same people were considered criminals, and the Russians would not let criminals teach. They were lucky to be alive. Herr Meier worked as a waiter and his wife worked in the kitchen. They were a wonderful couple, Herr Kleinert had arranged that I was to live with them. I was delighted. The Meier's lived within walking distance of the restaurant. They owned a small home near a wooded area. My room would be in the attic with a small window (like a dormer) overlooking the woods. The Meier's worked hard but had a difficult time making ends meet. Very often, they needed to turn the heat down in their home while they were gone and we would have to return home to a cold house. Being late fall the nights got quite cold. Since the war the energy supplies, coal, and fuel oil were in short supply. There were nights where Herr Meier and I would sneak into the woods and cut down seedlings to burn in our small wood stove after we dried them in the basement. We had to be extremely careful when we made these night runs, if we were caught, we could face prison time for what we were doing. Many times, we would all sit around the small stove telling each other horror stories about the war while we did our best to get and stay warm.

On one of my first days off, I took the opportunity to seek out my sister Anna. Even though it had not been that long since I had last seen her, it seemed like an eternity. Our first reunion was very emotional. After that, we never let a free moment go by without arranging to get together. Anna was good to me, she mended my socks when I wore holes in them. She worked in a bakery and when others had to buy fresh bakery with government stamps, she sometimes slipped me treats before they were disposed of.

Since the war, food often times was in short supply, so when one had a chance to come upon highly sought after staples, they took advantage of the opportunity no matter what the risk. Many people went to bed hungry and worst yet were starving in the streets. Many times children lacked the basic food needs such as milk and even the simplest things such as bread. Unemployment was high, there were homeless and hungry people everywhere doing what they needed to do to survive. Berlin had the motto that "Ein Berliner wird immer alles überleben" (A Berliner will always survive.) When President Kennedy visited Berlin in June 1963, he publicly stated that he was a Berliner. The crowd listened to his speech and felt hope.

I knew just how fortunate I was to have a place to live, food to eat daily, and a job. I was very grateful. Working and attending school for the time being, chased my homesickness away. By now it had been almost three years since I last seen my brother and older sister and my parents, and I did not see a way to see them anytime soon. I did my best to make Herr Kleinert proud of me in my scholastic endeavors as well as in my apprentice role. Since I had turned eighteen, Herr Kleinert was no longer my 'guardian' but it did not stop him from wanting me to finish what I had started.

One day just before Christmas 1946, I was working in the kitchen with Frau Meier, when two men dressed in dark suits rushed into the restaurant and arrested Herr Meier and took him away. Frau Meier ran after the men begging them to leave him be, that he had not done anything. We watched dumfounded as they bundled him into the back of a black automobile that was parked in front of the restaurant. Herr Kleinert asked that I take her home. Once there she sat next to the wood stove and cried; I did what I could to console her, but nothing I did helped. I too was frightened by what had happened and I was afraid that they would come for Frau Meier, she too was a former teacher during the Nazi time.

The next day I went to Anna and told her about what had happened. She advised me to be watchful and careful in my daily duties. Even though she was younger than I was, she was wise beyond her years, having lived in this atmosphere for the past couple years. She warned me to be careful about what I talked about and with whom I talked. There were special interest groups sniffing about for information and leads to finding ex-Nazi high-ranking officials. Herr Kleinert had never succumbed to the threat of having to belong to the communist party and he paid a high price for it.

The following day after Herr Meier's arrest, I went with his wife to the police station to find out where her husband was being held. No one there knew where he was. We were able to learn though that the East German government supported by Stalin had unleashed a manhunt for all former Nazi Partei members. Rumors had it that often those arrested never came back home. They simply vanished. Innocent people constantly were victims of senseless violence and would be doomed to die in vain. We had to be constantly careful of whom we thought were our friends, for the KGB did not wear badges stating who they were to the world. Living there during those times was living in a time of constant fear.

It was now almost Christmas and we still did not know where Herr Meier had been taken. What did they hope to gain by arresting this old man was beyond me. It was a shame that this intelligent man had been forced to give up his teaching position to work as a waiter, now he was suffering alone somewhere for no reason at all. I comforted Frau Meier as best I could by praying with her when she felt lost or low. One day after my classes, I reported for work as usual in the kitchen expecting to see Herr Kleinert who usually was in there around two o'clock working on the night's menu and preparations. I was surprised to have a man approach me and inform me that he was the new manager, I was given no explanation as to what had happened to Herr Kleinert. The man asked me my name and walked away. I stood there in shock trying to comprehend what had happened while I was away at school. I learned from one of the cooks, that before noon four men came in and escorted Herr Kleinert outside and hustled him into a black limousine; right after that this man came in and announced that he was the new manager.

I could not help but wonder if I would be the next one arrested. As the afternoon progressed, I started to panic when I realized that Frau Meier was no where to be found, I just about made a scene when I realized it was her day off and she was probably at home. As I worked, I kept praying to myself that the Lord would watch over me and that I had to stay strong. I couldn't help but wonder whom Herr Kleinert had allowed into his confidence that turned on him. I couldn't wait for ten o'clock to roll around so we could close the restaurant. I rushed home to the little house in the woods, to find Frau Meier waiting for me with anxiety written on her face. She could sense that something had happened and I quickly recounted the events that had transpired. When I was through, all she could do was mutter, "Oh mein gott!" We both prayed that night with hearts full of fear. I feared not only for myself but also for my sister. I knew it was late, but I had to go to my sister, Anna's. I quickly navigated the dark streets and frantically pounded on the door where she lived with the bakery shop's owners. The owner finally opened the door and asked me what was wrong and why was I at their door so late at night? I was shaking so bad that I could not talk, they invited me in, and once Anna got up and came to the room, I was able to calm down enough to tell them what had happened. I told them of my fear that I might be arrested next, and that I had come here to take the opportunity to say goodbye to Anna in case it happened without me ever seeing her again. I knew in order for me to be safe, I had to get out of Berlin.

We talked until after one in the morning, I arrived back at the Meier's home around two o'clock. In the early morning hours, I told her I did not intend to return to the restaurant and feared for my safety. I explained to her that I felt it was not in my best interest to attend school any longer here in Berlin and that I felt it best that I return to Genthin. It hurt me to tell this already distressed woman that her one confidant was running away from her. I had some money saved which was enough for a train ticket. I could see the sorrow in her eyes as she slowly came to realize that I was right in making the decision I did. She watched as I packed my meager possessions in my cardboard suitcase. Sixty years ago, I left this poor woman on her doorstep and I can still see her standing there in silence watching me walk away from her.

Once more, I was a fugitive. I knew I could go back to Genthin, Herr Neumann said I could return if things did not work out. I left Berlin early Christmas Eve day 1946. For the past three years, I had not celebrated this holiday as most did. There was no joy to be drawn from this day, no family, or friends to be close to, no gifts to open or to give. Once again, I was on a train facing a new challenge in my young life. As the countryside slid past the train windows and the dawn began to form, I reflected on my childhood Christmases the warmth of the fires, the warmth of family love and I wondered if they thought of me as much as I thought of them. I cried that morning on the train as I reminisced about all I had missed. By the time the train pulled into the train station at Genthin, I could not wait to get off it and back to my 'home'. I practically ran down the chestnut lined avenue that led me to the Schützenhaus. It was Christmas Eve evening as I rushed into the Schützenhaus to the warm shouts of "Look Günther is back!" Herr and Frau Neumann welcomed me back like the prodigal son; who was lost and had found his way home. Frau Neumann hugged me and welcomed me back home. How comforting this was and I was overcome with emotion.

I was not to see Herr Otto Kleinert again until 1964, when we met by chance just days before my official immigration to the United States. We ran into each other in Frankfurt, this time he needed my help, but I will talk about that later.

Genthin 1945 - The Arrest by the KGB

It all began on a day in late July 1945. I had been working at a large inn called Das Schutzen Haus in Genthin, a city located on the Havel Canal, southwest of Berlin, southeast of Magdeburg An Der Elbe, where the Russian army and the American army met before WWII finally ended in May. At that time, I was not quite 18 years old. One day without any warning a Russian army truck rolled into the inn's huge chestnut tree dotted garden. I had been working in the kitchen and through the big window; I could see the Russian soldiers spilling out of the truck. At this moment it never occurred to me, that these soldiers would minutes later arrest me. In the past few months, I had seen hundreds of Russian army trucks. I had no clue that among the group of soldiers were members of the KGB. dumfounded, by all that was going on outside I quickly looked for the owner of the Schützenhaus, Herr Neumann.

However, before I was able to locate him I heard the loud voices of the soldiers shouting and yelling behind me, "Stoy! Stoy!" (Stop! Stop!) I was told not to move. I heard an officer yelling, you can easily tell the difference between an officer and a run-of-the mill soldier, by his ubiquitous pistols in carefully polished leather holsters, the flashy red epaulets embroidered with silver stars which indicated the officer's rank garnished their uniforms, along with the jingling that came from their chests from the bronze and gold medals they wore. This officer shouted "Voht Ohn!" (There he is!) Pointing at me, "Vohteh tat cheh-la-vek!" (That's the man!) "Voht Ohn!" with that they arrested me and another older man who worked at the inn as a maintenance man. I was not allowed to say good by to Herr and Frau Neumann, who were so kind to me; giving me a place to live and work. They were all I had at that time in my life. The KGB shoved us into the truck and drove off.

Minutes later, we were taken to the Russian's commandant. We were taken to different rooms and shown a paper, which said, 'Arrest Odobryayu' (Arrest Approved). The building in which we were taken was a large villa not far from the inn at which I worked. No one would have suspected that this beautiful home was the headquarters of the KGB. To say the least, I was terrified the whole time I was under arrest, the soldiers' machine guns were never out of sight. After a brief interrogation by a non-commissioned officer in regard to my name, date of birth, and place of birth, I was taken by another agent who was carrying a large bundle of keys. The man used two of his keys to open a door in the 'keller' (basement) and pushed me inside. I found myself in a stinking suffocatingly airless and dark room.

As the door shut behind me with a loud noise, I began to think that this must obviously be a mistake and that they would realize it and release me. My head was spinning; suddenly I heard a voice coming out a far corner of the room. I could not understand him and asked him to repeat himself. He asked me who I was and what they had done to me. The voice seemed to be that of an older man. I asked where he was and he told me he was in the corner. Carefully and with some difficulty, because of the darkness, with hands outstretched I inched my way to the other side of the room. I asked the voice were we were and he replied in a voice filled with pain, that we were in the 'sobachnik' (doghouse), that was Russian prison lingo for a cell.

Using the cold moist walls to guide me, I was finally able to sit down and asked the man then why he was here. He told me that he was accused of being a former Nazis Partei member and had been in this sobachnik for over a week with very little food and very harsh treatment. He said he had done nothing wrong. This only added to my bewilderment as to why I was in such a place. I too felt I was completely innocent of whatever charges they had against me. Did someone denounce me? I couldn't concentrate. The man made a comment that I must be a foreigner, I asked him how he knew, and he replied that he could just tell. I did not respond. Seeing how upset I was he didn't insist on an answer either. He told me to get some rest and that we could talk more in the morning. He wanted to know what time it was, but I was unable to tell him because it was too dark. Even though it was somewhat warm in the room, I was shivering. My mind was running wild. What would happen next? What did they want of me? Will I have to stay here long? I couldn't focus. I tried to sleep, but it eluded me. Over and over these questions raced through my mind. Morning seemed like an eternity away.

Finally morning did come. The only way we knew it was when the guard came to the door rustling his keys and yelling "Eed Yom-t'yeh!" (Let's go!) My bones were aching from lying and sitting on the concrete floor all night long. With the light coming in through the open door, I was finally able to see the man in the corner. His face was swollen and covered with crusted blood. He was unable to get up by himself. I had to help him. We were led into a room with several stalls where we could wash our faces in a long tin basin. The water was icy cold, but it made me feel better. After a few minutes, the guard led us back to our cell. The guard brought our breakfast, which consisted of about a half a kilogram of dry black bread and some water. I was hungry, but I had no desire for food. The long night did nothing to ease my devastated state of mind. The door shut and once again, we were left in darkness.

My companion asked me what I was accused of; I told him I had no idea. One question crowded out all other thoughts. Why was I here? I felt like I was trapped in a bad dream. I could not pay attention to the questions he was asking me; I was tired, but I couldn't fall asleep. Exhaustion finally overtook me and I managed to fall asleep anyway. I had not slept long when the guard opened the door and took my cellmate away to either his hearing or another interrogation session. I must have fallen asleep again, because I was jolted awake when the guard came in to get me. He said it was my turn. With his machine gun, he led me into the hallway. In the hallway stood a younger KGB guard who was holding a printed sheet of paper in his hand. He asked me my name,

I told him and he took me up to the second floor of the villa. In a large room sitting behind the desk sat a man in his forties with graying hair and a 'sarmatian' moustache. He was wearing the uniform of a KGB captain. The guard that brought me to this officer handed him the piece of paper, which he signed. The guard left me standing in the middle of the room. The captain scrutinized me for a minute or so. He asked if I knew why I was there. I was so scared I couldn't utter a sound, he repeated his question, and I finally said no. His response shook me to my very core, "There is no room for parasites in the Soviet system!" he said in a loud voice. He told me that he was my interrogator and wanted to know what language he should speak to me in: German, Polish, or Russian. I told him German. He asked me why not Polish since I was born in Poland. I was shocked that he knew so much about me. I hoped he would answer the question that consumed me, why was I there? He handed me a piece of paper, he told me to read it and sign it, and on it were my charges.

- You are accused of belonging to a counter-revolutionary organization
- We have reasons to believe that you are collaborating with such an organization

The captain reminded me that these were serious charges. I took a deep breath in relief, this was a mistake, and I felt confident and better about my situation. I told the captain that there was a misunderstanding and that I had nothing, whatsoever, to do with these allegations. He yelled at me, "there is absolutely no misunderstanding at all, we have all the proof we need and you'll be better off if you admit everything honestly!" I repeated again that I was innocent of these charges. He came back with the fact that I had served in the German army "duetsche Wehrmacht'. I replied that I did, but not voluntarily, only by conscription as millions of other Germans had to. I reminded him that Hitler's Wehrmacht invaded our country in September of 1939 and the Polish became Germans under his rule. Obviously, he lacked some knowledge of those tumultuous times. As were many Russian officers, this man was very arrogant and did not like to be corrected. The captain exploded in anger. His voice was sharp as the blade of a sword and his eyes were shining. He called me a liar.

I knew that any wrong move or body language on my part could trigger an outburst of punishment.

In the midst of all this tension, I suddenly remembered a phrase from a Latin class 'Ne grubit sekudantam' (Never be rude to seconds). This seemed to calm me enough to answer his questions. He asked me repeatedly where I was born, I answered in Tarnowskie-Góry, Poland. He asked me why I served in the German Wehrmacht and what my rank was. During the interrogation, he would remove his pistol from his belt and play with it in front of me. This instilled great fear in me that he would misinterpret some movement or tone and shoot me. In order to make me break down, two soldiers started to beat me with their fists. It was excruciating. I often felt like dying than continue this harsh inhumane treatment, just to end the pain that was being inflicted on me. The captain repeatedly yelled at me to tell the truth or suffer the consequences. Repeatedly, I told him I had nothing to do with these allegations. The beating continued, seemingly bored with it all the captain put the paper in a folder and called for a guard. Speaking in rapid Russian, he said " Eed'yom-t'yeh! Ehtohf'yo!" (Let's go! That's all!) That was the end of my first day of interrogations.

The Interrogation by the KGB and Sentencing

I was taken to a different sobachnik I was a little upset that I would not be spending more time with my original cellmate. It dawned on me that I had not seen the maintenance man from the inn that was arrested with me; it was as if he just vanished. This cell was no different from the one from the previous night. I couldn't believe what was happening to me, I knew I had not done anything wrong! I was exhausted and tired, but when I tried to sleep, I couldn't. I was hungry, but was not given anything to eat. I did manage to find a corner so I could support and relieve some of the pain in my back caused by the beatings.

I knew it was night by now, but I didn't know the time. Sitting in the dark and musty room the same thoughts ran through my mind, why was I there? I prayed and prayed that someone would come and help me. My head was spinning, I felt sick to my stomach. I do not know how long I sat there, but when the guard came to get me, I found I couldn't get up. "Eed Yomeyeh!" (Let's go!) The guard turned his flashlight on, pointed the beam at my face, blinding me completely and shouted again, "Eed Yomeyeh!" (Let's go!) It took all the strength left in my exhausted body to get up. I was then taken to another room on the second floor. Climbing the stairs was almost impossible; all my bones were in pain. One of the guards with a machine gun at his side snarled "Mach Schnell!" (Move faster!) The guards opened a door and pushed me into the room. Behind the large desk sat a different KGB officer. He asked if I knew why I was there. I said I didn't know. "The KGB does not arrest innocent people." was his curt harsh reply.

This young officer insulted me in the vilest manner. He used language which I do not care mention and proceeded to tell everything they knew about me. He told me that after searching my room at Das Schutzehaus, they found more evidence, which pointed to my belonging to an organization that had collaborated with certain people. Again, I told him that this was all a mistake. This earned me a beating from one of the guards. I tried to think, what do they want of me? What will happen next? How long will I have to stay here? I pleaded with the KGB officer, "For heavens sake, I have done nothing wrong. I have nothing to do with these allegations." The officer's face never changed, he kept a stoic expression. His curt response was that I should sign the confession and everything would be over.

After hours of interrogating, I was taken to yet another room in the keller. This time my upper body was stripped of clothing by the guards and my arms tied up above me to a beam over my head. I was ordered to step into a basin filled with cold water. This basin had water flowing into it constantly so it would always stay full and cold. The pain from the frigid water was indescribable. This method of punishment continued for three days for about four to five hours each day. The result of standing in the cold water, even after all this time has left me with pain that no medicine can ease.

During a subsequent interrogation session I was struck and punched, so hard in the face that it left me with two broken teeth that later had to be replaced with a bridge. All during these days and nights, my main concern was survival and when it would be over. I had survived the Second World War, the holocaust of Auschwitz, the bombardments of Berlin and Magdeburg and the war as well. I had no home; going back to Poland was virtually impossible. When I came to Genthin, things had begun to look up for me. I had the job at the inn, the owners were good to me, I had a place to sleep and food to eat, and people that respected me. I considered myself very lucky. Now, I was in the hands of the KGB. All this was incomprehensible; from the very onset, I knew that I was innocent. The KGB interrogators would not believe me.

Once again, I was forced to endure the cold-water torture. My body was one mass of pain. Exhaustion overtook me and I slept. A guard's shouts woke me from the only peace I could find, the darkness of my mind. "Eed Yomt'Yeh! Eed Yomt'Yeh!" (Let's go! Let's go!) They told me to get up, but I couldn't. My entire body was in pain; they dragged me out of the sobachnik and forced me to walk. I had not eaten for two days and I was weak from pain and hunger. My mind screamed out, just kill me! How much more torture were they going to put me through. The whirlwind inside my head would not stop, that in itself was torture. Inside I chanted: "Amo, amas, amat, amanus, amatis, amant," (Around, around, around until the end of time) the great mantra. I prayed as much as I could, "Please God have mercy and help me!"

My life was evidently no longer mine to control. It was in the hands of the KGB. Something inside me would not let me give up. I knew that God had helped me out so many times in the past, that he would not let me down now. I knew all I had to do was keep faith and hope with God and I would endure.

The guards could see that I was too weak to walk on my own and now they supported me from both sides. They too had orders to make sure I got to my destination. This villa had many rooms, I was taken to another room that had large windows, and it was dark outside. I was apprehensive as to why I was being brought out during the evening; usually the interrogations were done during the day. The KGB officer behind the desk ordered me to sit down. This had not happened during any of the other interrogation sessions. The officer looked at me with a stoniness that would make you shiver and not dare say anything wrong. He sat behind his desk and stared at me completely impassive. After a while, he got up from the desk and walked around the room. This made me extremely nervous. While walking, he would ask me if I knew why I was there and if I was ready to confess. Again, I told him that I had nothing to confess and that I was innocent of all the allegations against me. He got angry and called me a liar and a 'persona non grata'. He gave me another chance to confess. If I confessed now I would get a lesser sentence, he promised me. The officer told me he had the power to invoke clemency if I confessed to my crimes. I knew and could tell that he was ravenous for my confession. He reminded me that he could avert my sentence to hard labor for a long time.

I was tired, I couldn't think, I needed to rest. The officer sat down, looked at his papers, and said that he would no longer waste his time with me and that I would have to face the consequences. Looking out the windows, I could see another day dawning. How would this day end, I thought to myself. The officer leaned over his desk and shouted. "This is your last chance to confess! Do you understand?" I answered by remote, "Sir, I am innocent. I have not committed any crime." He told me I had made a terrible mistake by not making an effort to make a confession. He called for the guards, as they were cuffing me he shouted, "I'll be seeing you!"

The KGB were good at eliciting confessions. They gave their captives little or no food, little sleep, and of course the ultimate cold-water torture. I pleaded with my eyes for them not to chain me up again, but sadly, they just laughed at me. I was not down in the keller too long this time before they brought me upstairs to the interrogator's office. This time the door slammed shut behind me. I was terrified. I was ordered to put my hands behind my back. The guards were told to leave the room. The room was deathly quiet. Tension made my body hurt more than it already did, because I could not get my muscles to relax.

The officer took out his pistol and placed it on his desk. He lit a cigarette and began to leaf through some papers. After a minute or so, he started chatting with me asking who I was and how I had come to East Germany. All this I had explained to whoever asked me the questions, at least twice a day. They knew this information, they just wanted me to slip up and not tell them something correctly or add something new to my answers. My heart began to pound and I felt like breaking down. His manner soon changed to formal, but polite. "This is your last chance to make a confession," he said. I answered again that I had nothing to confess. Once again, I was told that the KGB does not make mistakes, that they had evidence against me. He held up my 'arrest odobryayu' (arrest approved). This paper was also the 'protokol doprosa', which included my last name, date, and place of birth, etc. He asked me if I would admit to being guilty of belonging to an underground organization. I told him I had no connection whatsoever with them. He told me I was foolish to hold out. I started to repeat my remote response about being innocent, when the officer erupted out of his chair and banged his fist on the desk knocking his inkwell and glass of tea to the floor. "Now I see what a dangerous character you are! Whom do you think you're dealing with? The German police?" He shouted. "The KGB will bring you to your senses soon enough!"

After this outburst, I was ordered to go over and face the closest wall to me. I stood there for about two hours. I was then ordered to turn around and approach his desk. The officer with great patience said to me, "You are a rational human being. Listen to my advice, confess. Name the persons who recruited you. Tell us the nature of your assignments, and where you meet your co-conspirators, and the activities you've participated in." Again, I told him that I was innocent. That I had not been recruited by anyone. "You're lying!" he shouted once again, leaping up out of his chair. Frustrated he rang a bell for the guard. They took me back down to the sobachnik. Once inside I was beaten with kicks and whippings. Barely conscious they left me lying on the floor.

For the next week, this went on two, sometimes three times a day; mostly at night, always the same questions. After one brutal episode, I lay on the cold cement floor in agony. When the guards came in this time, they knew I could not walk and dragged me into the interrogation room. This time the officer threatened to have me beaten to death if I did not confess. I told him there was no point in tormenting me any longer, that my story would not change. This set the officer into a rage. I was taken back down to the keller.

Ravished by hunger, I wondered dully how much longer I could go on this way. My will and faith kept me going when my body could not. I knew a turning point would come; I would either be released or killed. I had little respite from the torment. The keller door opened and there stood the KGB officer and his guards. I was put into a straight jacket and dragged out of the sobachnik like a sack. They took me into a large room and this time there were three officers seated at a long table. There was a Russian flag off to one side and five Russian soldiers stood on each side of the room. This seemed to me to be some type of military tribunal.

The officer in the middle made an opening statement by asking me questions in German; covering the same material that every other officer had. He asked if I knew why I was there. I told him what I had been told and that I was innocent of the charges. I was told once again that I would not have been arrested if there was no evidence against me. Once more, I stated my innocence. This time his reply was. "Good, in that case we can start talking seriously." I did not know what to say. My body language must have indicated indifference and he rebuked me but indicating that these were serious allegations and that this was absolutely my last chance to make an honest confession. There was nothing to confess I told him.

The officer closed his folder and the three of them got up and left the room. They returned a short time later. After they were seated, one of them asked me if I had anything further to say. I barely opened my mouth, when the officer who seemed to be in charge interrupted me by saying," We know all that, enough." I tried once again to profess my innocence, but once again was silenced. The three officers conferred for a short time and they seemed to come to an agreement. The officer in charge read the following: "Ten years in isolation, under severe regime! However, due to your age and condition, you are sentenced herewith to five years hard labor."

The whole trial lasted about thirty minutes, but to me it seemed a lifetime. I had no one to fight for my rights or to speak on my behalf. When the verdict was read, the ten guards saluted the tribunal and led me from the room.

These events are still vivid in my mind sixty years later. His last words to me still echo in my ears. It makes me think of what Plautus once said, "Homo Homini Lupus" (Man is like a wolf to men).

Two machine gun armed men took me to my cell just a few feet down the hall. It was not a very large room and it was full of other men who had been sentenced by the same tribunal. Fourteen men altogether, among them were laborers, a lawyer, a doctor, and an engineer; I was the youngest one there. I was just a boy; they were all my father's age. I started to cry. They tried to console me. I repeated over and over; five years, how was I going to survive it. IT was all very hard to believe. The week had been long, painful, and extremely draining.

I thanked the Lord for getting me through it; I knew he would not let me down. I knew he would get me through my sentence if I only kept faith in him. The following morning all of us in the room were taken by truck, under heavy Russian escort to a labor camp near Genthin. We were not allowed to talk to each other. All we could do was look out into the streets and watch with envy the people going about their business, seemingly without cares or worries. My chief concern was to stay alive. I knew no matter what happened, I would not give up. I was sentenced to five years of hard labor for a crime I did not commit.

In the Russian Labor Camp

Once in the camp we were assigned our quarters, which were just primitive dilapidated barracks that were apparently abandoned by its previous occupants, the German Wehrmacht. We were sleeping on wooden floors lined with straw. I began the slow process of recovering from my maltreatment and beating as each day passed. Most men in camp were all quite old and showed concern for me. I was very thin and must have looked emaciated. There was a roll call each morning and at the end of each day. These were conducted by the camp commandant. We were reminded that should anyone attempt to escape, he would be shot. Again, the words of Plautus I'd learned in our Latin class came to mind, "Homo Homini Lupus" (Man is like a wolf to men).

Almost all the prisoners in this camp were Germans; however, there were a few men from Austria. One of them was a doctor, his name was Karl. He was a fine man, likable features, good looking with silver hair. He told me he had served during the war in the SS unit before being taken prisoner and brought to this camp. The camp administrators used Karl as a doctor to us only when there was no one else available. He looked after me, sometimes sharing his bread ration with me. I admired this man, who was an intellectual, but did not hesitate to get his hands dirty like a common laborer. He worked with apparent ease and without complaint. After a while, we got along like father and son.

Our assignment was to dismantle a nearby German ammunitions factory. We went to work the day after our arrival in camp. I felt somewhat safe amongst the older men, compared to the time of the interrogations.

Our daily routine was as follows: we were given about 21 ounces of bread; in the barracks, this was a newcomer's ration for three days. After that, the size of your portion depended on your ability to meet your work quota. In the morning, we were given two hundred grams (7 ounces) of 'haferschleim' (gruel), which was consumed quickly. Eating was always done in a hurry. A gong would sound before we could even finish our water, and it would be off to the factory. We would leave the barracks reluctantly and assemble outside for the roll call. Usually it was still dark when we marched out the gate. The ammunitions factory was about two kilometers away, and we would have to march there rain or shine, always under heavy guard. Our tools were stored in a large wooden shed outside the factory. Only on rare occasions were considerations given to our safety while we worked. The high quotas set, did not allow safety measures to be taken. One's food ration was more important than life and limb.

To meet the quota, we had to work and move fast. Constantly, we were watched and guarded by machine gun armed Russian soldiers. There were usually two or three Russian or German engineers who made sure all parts were properly placed into the boxes provided and loaded on large trucks that transported the parts to the canal near by.

Not only the humans suffered severe conditions, so did the animals. The horses were used to drag the huge wooden crates to a central station. Those poor horses usually lasted no more than a couple of months. The horses had quotas to meet also and there was little or no care given to them. Death usually came from exhaustion and emaciation, all ended up in the camp kitchen.

As I said, I regained my strength quickly enough despite the small rations of food and water. With the generosity of the other prisoners, who shared their food with me and helped me when they could, I was soon able to keep up on my own. During the course of work we were not allowed to speak to each other, however, at the camp barracks, the men called me 'der kleine kumpel' (the little guy); I was only five feet four inches tall. My dream was to be six feet two, but that never materialized, I stopped growing at five foot six. I remembered what my father told me some years back, "Mein sohn, the height, or size doesn't make the man, it's what's inside a man." I remembered these words whenever I got down on myself.

It was surprising how quickly one got used to the hard work and the sullen surroundings. The hardest part of being in that camp was the constant thought of what would happen next. I knew very well that to try to escape from the camp was virtually impossible. With guards, watching every step it was inconceivable one would even survive such an attempt. Every move we made outside the barracks was not without permission and done as quickly as possible for fear of repercussions.

One day there was a very serious accident. One of the older men, Herr Karstadt, (the maintenance man from the Schützenhaus) sustained a very bad contusion on one of his legs. A large heavy part carried by two men slipped out of their hands and crushed his leg. The man had been like a father to me and I was very concerned about his condition. The guards kept everyone back; they loaded him onto a stretcher and carried him away. This was the last time I saw him. From here forward I strived to be extremely careful, it was apparent that any accident could get me taken away.

Shortly after, a new commandant terrorized the camp. He worked us past the point of exhaustion. The only way you could get 'easy ' work was to be ill, but that was risky. Weekly, the sick were taken to the infirmary and the next week replaced by new prisoners.

The march home (the camp), we thought of it as home because we had nowhere else to go; was always the worst part of the day. It was usually long after the sun had set and the guards, fearing that it would be dark before we got inside the gates, would force us to run. We had to run through a wooded area, stumbling over roots and logs. If you fell, there was the risk of being run over by those behind you or punished by the guards. Karl was always there to look out for me, to make sure I did not fall behind.

There were times, after our meager supper, when Karl and I would walk inside the fenced courtyard and talk about our lives. He had many stories about his experiences as a student in the University of Vienna. His father was a banker, his mother had been arrested by the Gestapo because she would not cooperate and eventually died. He had a sister who he believed still lived in Vienna.

During one evening's walk Karl, who was ordinarily so sober-minded, confided in me that he planned to escape. I was dumfounded. His plans struck me as utterly fantastical and I had a very hard time convincing him of their futility. Although he never complained, he told me he was constantly plagued by back pain and that the pain at times was unbearable. He began smoking the strong Russian cigarette called a 'makhorka'. He said it would relieve his pain somewhat. He refused to see the camp doctor.

One morning when we all lined up for roll call, I was instantly aware that I had not seen Karl when we were exiting the barracks, and I could not see him in the courtyard. We usually stood together and this particular morning he was nowhere to be seen. The commandant, First Lieutenant Kovalosov called the roll and discovered to our dismay that five prisoners were missing. Within seconds, the camp's sirens shrilled through the early morning's silence. Guards were running from everywhere in the camp. Pointing their machine guns at us, they shouted at us, "Fascists, bastards, whore-son's, etc!" There was always abuse from the guards, but after this, it was unbearable.

The thought that Karl would leave me cut me to the quick. The fact that I had lost yet another father figure devastated me. My friend, my confidant, my supporter was gone. Once again, all I had was the Lord to look out for me. That afternoon, the commandant informed us that two of the prisoners were dead, two were wounded, and one was still missing. I prayed that the one unaccounted for was Karl. That night I realized that I had to pull myself together, keep my faith, and keep praying. I owed it to my mother who told me when I left home, almost three years ago, "Mein sohn, you must remember to never give up!" Many times, I had thought about dying, but I knew I could not let my mother down.

Even though we were short these men, the quotas did not change. The guards inflicted abuse if we did not meet our agenda for the day. The security inside and outside the camp increased dramatically, losing a prisoner was disgraceful to any commandant. Sometimes the abuse on the way to our work site took such a toll on us, it was as if we had put in our hours before we had even started.

One day a man got his arm crushed. His cries were heartbreaking to hear. The guards carried him away and we never saw him again. Most accidents happened late afternoon when most men were tired from exhaustion, lack of food, and abuse. We all knew how important it was to stay alert, but the general apathy was so great that after a while you stopped thinking of the danger. Unfortunately, your body would scream for rest, even at the price of injury or death.

Before Karl left, he had told me that he heard once the ammunitions factory was completed, the camp would be transported with the machinery to Russia. This was why he wanted to escape, he said he would rather die or be shot than banished to some remote Siberian village. His words tormented me. Was it worth living as a slave of Stalin's socialism? Would I ever be able to live free again? What would become of me? Even in my darkest moments, I would not let myself give up. I knew I had to keep my faith.

After the escape, punishment for the smallest infraction became very severe. Often times when we made our way back into camp, the commandant would be waiting to ask the brigadier how much work had been completed. If the results were satisfactory, he would say nothing, but woe to us if we failed to meet his expectation. His insults would follow us inside the barracks and our rations would be cut in half.

After evening roll call, we would rush into the kitchen to quickly eat our paltry meal, return to the barracks to lie down and give our bodies the rest they so longed for. On most nights, I would cover my head with my coat to drown out the noise of the other men. The guards fearing another escape would often disturb us during the night to do body counts. Constant interruptions put us on edge and did nothing to help our already deteriorating conditions.

The rumors of the camp closing became real. I realized too late, that I should have joined Karl when he offered me the chance to escape. One morning we found out, as we stood in the torrential rain during roll call, that another man had attempted to escape. Guards with machine guns surrounded us while they searched for this man. Eventually, they brought around a body for us to see; the man was dead. Down deep, we all hoped he had made it, but the sight of him did nothing but drag our already sagging spirits into the mud in which we stood. Somehow, during the course of the day, we found out that the man had committed suicide rather than be shipped to Siberia. It was common knowledge that once you were there, your chances of survival were very very slim.

I knew I wanted to survive, I knew I would not survive if I were sent to Russia. I concluded that I too must try escape. I had to find a way to be free. The question was how and when. Life at the camp became almost intolerable. The guards seemed to take pleasure intimidating us. Malady among the prisoners was rampant. Daily we saw sick or injured prisoners carried away, never to see them again. Some prisoners pretended to be ill to avoid deportation to Russia.

One night after a long hard day of working in the factory, I went to bed exhausted. I must have fallen asleep immediately. In my dreams, I felt a strange anxiety and I woke up. In front of me stood one of the prisoners reaching toward me as if he were about to strangle me. I asked him what he wanted. He said he knew who I was and that I had been sent to kill him. I sprang up from my sleeping mat while the other prisoners tried to over-power him. A struggle ensued which alerted the guards. They took the man away. The next morning we learned that the man suffered from a persecution mania and had been taken to a hospital.

The work at the ammunitions factory was almost completed. The long halls were practically devoid of heavy machinery, which had been packed in huge containers and crates ready for shipment to Russia. The commandant told us that within a day or so our work would end.

On the Russian Death Train

It was at the end of September 1945. We were transported under heavy escort by Russian guards to the train station of Genthin in the city, which was my home for a short time before all this happened. Someday, I hoped I could return to Genthin to live. The train that would carry us to our next destination was equipped with passenger cars that had been outfitted with wooden benches and the windows reinforced with steel bars. One by one, we were taken from the transport trucks and led into the train. We were given provisions that were to last us two days:
About 22 ounces of bread, some dry salted fish and four lumps of sugar. There were over 120 men; they packed us into the train cars like cattle. Two guards stood at the end of each car. We had to sit quietly. If we talked to each other, it could only be whispers.

Everyone was wondering where they were going to take us. Some of us tried to find out by asking the guards, but none of them would answer us. We waited for hours inside the stifling train while they loaded the freight cars with the equipment from the factory. The railway workers looked at us with curiosity and pity. Many people passed by the windows with hopes of seeing someone they knew and had loved. Some women were known to search the train stations for weeks after hearing that their husbands had been arrested.

These stories made me think of my own family. My father and stepmother, my sister, Maria in Poland; my little sister, Anna living in Berlin; and my brother, Bernhard who was a POW in an unknown place. I had seen Anna in March of 1945, but where was she now? Were they all in good health? Were they even alive? Something inside me told me they were all well. As I sat there in the heat, I wondered yet again, what would happen to me. Where were they taking us? My mother's voice came to me again and told me not to give up, that my faith would keep me alive. Her voice never left me; those words did indeed keep me alive. I knew my time to be free would come and I would be ready when it did.

Finally, our cars were coupled with the passenger train. When we hooked up there was an eerie silence in the cars, no one said a word. I could see how desolate most of the men were. Heartbroken, unreachable, without hope. Our future was not our own to decide. Enviously we watched those outside who were able to move about at liberty. Those lucky souls who could chat with friends, sit at the railway café without fear. Most had no idea that they too without warning could suffer this same fate. 'The locomotive's shrill whistle made my heart contract. The train was leaving the city, where I had hoped to put down roots. I was leaving the people I knew: Herr and Frau Neumann the owners of the Das Schutezen Haus. Everyone murmured the same questions. Where were we going? Would we ever be coming back? We were all in the same emotional state; some had tears rolling down their cheeks. I had always thought that men did not cry, but yes, even the toughest were crying.

I watched as the train passed through towns I knew. We were traveling east. Next to me sat a farmer, he was rather short; broad shouldered with a round face, a Kaiser moustache and blue-grey eyes a typical German peasant. He told me that he had refused to give up his last horse to the Russians and was sentenced to five years. He feared for his life and his family. Would he ever see them again? It was heartbreaking to see this old farmer crying. Outside it rained, the train whipped through the countryside, the scenery became a blur.

Exhaustion overtook me; it made me sick to my stomach. My head was spinning; my entire world was leaving me as swiftly as the train was leaving the last home that I knew. I knew I had to get a hold of myself; I had to focus all my energy into my plan to escape. I prayed silently for the Lord to help me, to show me a way out of this situation.

I must have fallen asleep; the guards' shouts woke me with a start. "Stoy! Stoy!" (Stop! Stop!) One of the prisoners had fainted or became very ill. We were not allowed to help him. The guards pushed their way through the men and made sure none of us moved as they took the man away. It was an extremely tense moment.

We passed through several small towns and eventually through the larger city of Brandenburg; I had been there in March 1945. It was late afternoon when the train pulled into the Potsdam station. We were just outside of Berlin in East Germany. The train was shunted onto a sidetrack and our cars were detached from the rest of the train. As we were loaded into Russian trucks we were reminded not to try to escape, those that tried would be shot. We were taken to another train station, but I could not see its name. All we could see was a locomotive and five plain freight cars. We were to get out of the trucks and join the other prisoners that were kneeling on the ground by the train cars. By now, it was getting dark and starting to get cold outside. Surrounded by guards with machine guns, we knelt there in silence for about two hours. Finally, a Russian officer appeared and told us we could stand up. We were told to line up in rows of four and march toward the train. As we approached the officer, we were to call out our first and last name, our patronymic, date of birth, why we were arrested, and our length of sentence. We were taken one by one to a very small building. We were stripped and searched, no orifice was left undisturbed. At one point, the inspector stuck his fingers so far down my throat that in reflex I pushed his hand away. This brought on a verbal attack against me from the officer.

It was late evening by the time they finished searching all of us and we were taken to the freight cars and made to climb aboard. They were able to fit about fifty men to a car. The floor was covered in straw and there was a large pail in the corner for our bodily needs. Despite all this, our fate was still better than the abuse, the intensity of the interrogation sessions, and the confinement. We had each other to console and support in whichever ways we could. With a loud noise, the door to the freight car closed. There were no windows; we were in utter darkness. We all yearned for sleep.

The dark allowed my mind once again to wander. Would I ever be able to contact my loved ones? Would this inhumane treatment ever end? How was I to escape? I knew I could not share my thoughts or plans with anyone. All I could do was wait, pray, and hope for an opportunity to present itself to me.

Late that night we finally left that unknown train station and by early morning, we were passing through Berlin. Did my sister still live there? Was she well? If we tried hard, we could see glimpses of the city through the cracks in the car walls. The debris, the rubble, piles of sand and dirt left behind were the battle scars of bombs and mines; leaving forever the reminders of this horrible war. No longer could you tell that just two years ago in 1943; this was one of the largest cities in Germany and renown for their chic and fashionable shops, and now at least sixty percent of it had been destroyed.

With each passing hour, my thoughts raced around the fears that I would never see my sisters Anna and Maria, my father, mother, or my brother ever again. Pain engulfed me. The drone of the train helped me block out everything else but my desire to escape. I kept track in my head the towns we passed through so I knew where we were. After Berlin, came Frankfort An Der Oder, I'd traveled this way before when I went to Auschwitz in 1943 to continue my education, I was in Berlin the following year to finish my education, I was familiar with this area. Shortly, after passing through Frankfort, the train stopped in what seemed to be the middle of nowhere. We could see no buildings through the cracks. When the train began to roll again, it became apparent that we were being shunted to a side track.

The guards opened the heavy sliding doors, blinding us with their powerful flashlights. They stepped back quickly as the stench from the boxcar assaulted their senses. We were warned again that if anyone tried to escape, that they would be shot. We were ordered to stand up. It became clear that we were to empty our waste buckets and lay down fresh, albeit musty straw, which was brought to us. After we finished, the guards came along with large boxes and placed them on the ground. We were called by name to accept our ration of dry bread and water. It took about thirty minutes or so to feed everyone, and we enjoyed every minute of the cool night air. When we were finished, we were once again loaded back into the freight cars and soon were traveling across East Germany.

The car was quiet; every man had his own thoughts and pains to deal with. I on the other hand was formulating my escape plan. I prayed to God that I could carry it out, and that once I was free I would know where I was going and that I would get there safely.

The day before the now east moving train passed through Poznan, which meant that we were now crossing Poland. From time to time, the locomotive's whistle would give out a loud shrill puffing and snuffing sound, which only the engineer could interpret; it broke the monotony of the clacking of the train wheels.

The situation in the boxcar became almost unbearable. As we moved on, I continued to read the names of the towns we passed through. The next time we stopped a new day was dawning. We again heard the guards approaching as they unlocked the doors. They shouted for us to stop and to stay put. The sun and fresh air created a panic like state inside the boxcar. We needed to get out, and we needed to breathe. Shots were fired into the air to remind us who was in charge as the men jostled in anticipation of being let out of the freight car. The shots seemed to restore a sense of order and we were able to do as we were told. We emptied our waste buckets and were given an even smaller portion of dry bread and water. We were starving, tired and emotionally exhausted. We knew they did this to break our spirit, to keep us weak so we wouldn't try to escape. I knew my chance would come and I had to just bide my time. I knew that I had to keep up my strength and my faith in order for me to fulfill my plan to escape.

The Escape

If an escape was at all possible, my goal was that it should happen on Polish soil and not in Russia. My time was running out. We were quickly heading toward the Russian border. To escape from Russia would be virtually impossible. I had to make my move soon; there was no other option.

It became apparent that many of the prisoners were very sick, some even dead by the stench in the freight car. We could not move, we were packed in there like cattle. It was inevitable that many would die before the train reached its destination. We stopped once maybe twice a day to be fed. We were given lukewarm inedible 'kapusta zupa' (cabbage soup) and a chunk of heavy dark dry bread. What I would have given for a bowl of my stepmother's cabbage soup. Her soup got us through some hard times when food was hard to come by.

The men had named our train the death train; I knew it was imperative that I find a way to escape soon. When I was able, I positioned myself as close to the doors as possible; for several reasons: I could breathe clean air, I could see outside, and I was nearer my point of escape. In those dark hours I repeated from memory my favorite psalm, psalm 23 chapter one verse four; "Even though I walk through the valley of the shadow of death, I will fear no evil, for you are with me; your rod and your staff they comfort me."

One crisp night, as I sat there listening to the monotonous clicking of the train wheels, I thought I heard the sound "I wish I could be free, I wish I could go home', resounding over and over again in my ears. I could see the moon peeking through the slow moving clouds in the dark night sky through a louver in the freight car door. The wobbling of the train matched the sensation in my stomach as I waited for an opportunity to present itself. Suddenly, the rhythm of the wheels changed, now they said "What will come will come, what will come will come." I heard the shrill whistle of the train and we began to slow down. I looked through the louver in the door, but could see nothing, no homes, no buildings only darkness. Most of the men were either unconscious or sick and they were unaware of what was happening.

I had shared my secret with only one other person, Franek Nikolensky. We had become friends and agreed that we needed to get off the train. He was an older man. A schoolteacher in a Ukrainian village. He had been arrested during the German occupation and sentenced to ten years in a labor camp. Franek had family in Warsaw and he too had a burning desire to be free. As the train slowed, we sought each other out, in case we were able to make a run for it we knew we could not hesitate. We had been in the boxcar for three days, we were exhausted and malnourished, but we knew we could run if we had to.

Finally, we stopped. I hoped fervently that we were still in Poland. The guards opened the freight car doors. We asked them to remove the dead bodies, but they ignored our request at first, until their supervisor told them to take the bodies out of the car. They hit us with the bright beams of their flashlights, temporarily blinding us. The armed guards stood ready at the open doorways.

My body was fraught with tension, I was bathed in sweat. In the distance a very loud sound pierced the night, it sounded like a cannon shot. It echoed through the quiet, triggering the guards to panic and leave their positions; they all ran toward the locomotive. This was our chance! I found Franek and we jumped down out of the boxcar. Some of the guards must have realized that they had left us alone and turned around. They opened fire in our direction yelling for us to stop, but it was too late. With every ounce of strength we had, we ran out into the darkness. We ran back down the tracks relishing every minute of freedom we were handed. After a bit, the guards quit shooting in our direction. We stopped running. Franek explained that we could not let ourselves become too unfocused, we had to compose ourselves and figure out what we were going to do next. We lay down on the ground to make ourselves less visible to the guards. I forced myself to believe that the guards hadn't actually seen us jump from the train, that they had just fired in the direction to scare the prisoners. I was petrified. Franek on the other hand was very lucid; he sounded very self-assured as he quietly tried to calm me down. It took every ounce of strength I had to compose myself. I could not shake the sound of the machine gun fire from my head. In my panic, I thought Franek had left me; my heart beat thick, my head grew hot; all I could hear was the sound of gunfire. I whispered Franek's name and he replied that he was right beside me. With his encouragement and strength, I was able to get up again and we continued to run down the tracks.

As if to light our way, the moon peeked out of the clouds and sent a ray of light down upon us to guide our escape. The light gave us hope and strength, to me it was almost as if God was looking down on me and fulfilling His promise to help me in my time of need. Our spirits were lifted. Those that have heard my story often ask where I found the strength and courage to actually jump. War does that to people; it makes you find courage where you least expect it. You find ways to exist and survive even under the most deplorable conditions. Even though we could no longer hear any shouting from the direction of the train, we knew we had to keep going to put as much distance between us and the death train as possible.

We were not exactly sure where we were, but we knew the last town we had passed was Elblag, which was not far from the Gulf of Danzig and the Baltic Sea. Franek wanted to get to Warsaw, which was south of us to be with his family, and I wanted to get back to Genthin. Franek tried to persuade me to come with him and settle down in Warsaw, but that is not where I wanted to go. I had come this far; I wanted to get back to the people who had been so kind to me, Herr Neumann and Frau Neumann. The night was fading away rapidly; we were able to pick out trees in the horizon and headed toward them. As we turned down a dirt road, the sun made its appearance. The warm rays of majestic beauty awed us momentarily. Our stomachs growled in protest and we knew we needed to find a farmer who would give us aid in order for us to go on.

We had already made mammoth progress in our flight for freedom, but the only way we could survive was with the help of those who had no real reason to help us, except through compassion for our fight. As we silently walked along, I thanked God for letting me see this day and for helping us in our time of need. I couldn't help but remember the words of the German playwright, Bertolt Brecht, "Today, nourished by yesterday and proceeding into tomorrow." With great anticipation of what the day had in store for us, we moved on. I gave myself up to the warmth of the sun and thanked God that He had allowed us to live and see this day. In the distance, we could see a few buildings; our excitement began to grow. We cautiously moved on, wary of every noise. We were not sure which areas were occupied by the Russians and did not want to be caught off guard. At this point coming onto habitation we would have rather it had been night instead of broad daylight.

World War II had just ended and several dozen Russian divisions, which translated into thousands, and thousands of armed soldiers heavily surrounded Poland. Poland disliked the Russians immensely because of the oppression and persecution they dealt out freely to those that opposed them. The Poles are deeply religious, honest, hard working, proud people with morals; we knew if we approached them, they would help us out in our time of need. I grew up here, I knew these people. Franek knew them too and we were sure we would find someone to render us aid. As we neared the buildings, we could see the remnants of what the war had left behind. Huge burned out tankers, charred and shredded German army trucks, buildings burned down, it was awful to see the destruction and desolation of this once proud country.

By one of the buildings, we saw an old man walking hunched over. We wanted to get his attention, but did not want to startle him. He looked up and noticed us walking toward him. Franek called out, "Pan-Pan Gospodarz!" (Mister, Mister Farmer!) "Prosba?" (Please can we talk to you?) He told us to come closer. I listened as Franek and the old man talked, my head swam, was I dreaming? Was this really happening? It appeared that the farmer would indeed help us; the years of war and oppression had not made him jaded to his fellow man. He called for his wife to come out of the house. He assured us that everything would be fine and invited us to come inside. It felt good to be speaking Polish again with such a nice couple. It lifted our spirits. It rekindled the spark in me and renewed my hope that I might make it back to Genthin. The depth of what this meant to me was only apparent to God and myself. I was dazzled by the couple's humble yet cordial hospitality. I remember everything so vividly; them visiting with us and providing us with food and shelter for the night. They never complained about the tragedies of war they had survived, but they told us their shattering stories. Their two sons were killed during the war, they had a daughter that had died young, and their entire livestock was either killed or taken from them by the Germans and Russians. They had just been able to start rebuilding their lives. A portion of their strength to move on, came from a priest in a distance parish some twenty kilometers away. He had walked the distance to speak with them and to let them know that they were not alone.

The locals were aware of the passing trains and knew they carried prisoners and equipment taken from German and Polish factories. They too were all too aware of how many prisoners had tried to escape and were shot trying. Soon it became clear that we could not over stay our welcome and we knew we had to leave this charitable couple behind. They gave us directions to our destinations and warned us of the Russian outposts around the towns. The farmer told us that on the north and southeast borders of Poland were eleven Soviet divisions, on the east border about fifty kilometers of Warszawa twelve divisions, and on the west side bordering Poland and East Germany there were rumored to be nineteen divisions. The farmer's wife provided us with some crude baked sourdough bread, dried wild mushrooms, carrots, and sunflower seeds. We said our goodbyes with heavy hearts.

Franek and I remained together for a while. He tried once more to persuade me to come with him to Warszawa and I almost consented to his offer rather than chance getting lost on my way back to Genthin. Going to Warsaw was impossible; the prospect of living under the complete control of the Russians was absolutely out of the question. I think he finally understood when it came time to part. We went our separate ways after the town of Elblag. Franek's journey would take him another 200 kilometers to the south while mine would be approximately 485 kilometers. My life felt like one big loss. My mother and sister, my family, my friends from Genthin, and now Franek who had been like a big brother to me. I knew I had to stay focused and press on no matter what if I wanted to stay free. My strength came through prayer and I had no doubt in my mind that this would one day all be behind me and I would be happy at last.

From time to time, I imagined machine gun fire behind me, I knew it was not real and had to physically block my mind against those images and sounds. I nibbled on my rations so they would last until I was able to find someone who would help me out again. To say the least, there were times when I wanted to give up. When those feelings overwhelmed me, I would ask myself what kind of man I was. If I gave up after all this, who was I? I might as well have let them shoot me on the train. Giving up no longer became an option and I trudged on.

The Race to Escape

Two days after Franek and I parted, leaving the town of Elblag behind, I was now on the run on my own. My destination was Genthin. Darkness overcame me as I walked down a country road deep in Poland. Suddenly, I noticed an engine noise in the far distance. Turning around I noticed two large headlights heading toward me. I started to panic, these were truck headlights, was it a Russian army truck or a Polish farmer? I started to run frantically looking for cover. My heart was pounding to its limits, soon I discovered a huge pile of brush near the road, and I scrambled behind it just in time. As the truck neared, I heard the engine slow down. I was almost beside myself when the truck stopped in the road near where I was hiding. All I could see were boots getting out of the truck. Russian soldiers! There were two of them, they walked to the front of the truck, one called out "pree ha dee t'yehsno va!" (Come back again!) The other soldier came back with a flashlight and shined its beam on either side of the road, he ran it over the brush pile in which I was hiding, but apparently could not see me.

They became frustrated when they couldn't seem to find what they were looking for. Were they looking for me? My heart was ready to jump out of my chest. They stood there looking in my direction for what seemed to be an eternity, until one of them said "Ee d yom t yeh!" (Let's go!) Finally, they got back into their truck and drove off. My hands were moist, my body was trembling. I don't remember how long I remained in the brush pile, all I remember is that I prayed that they would not find me. There was no doubt in my mind that if they did find me, it would have been my last night in that desolate countryside in Poland. If I would have been caught my family would have no way of knowing it, I had no identifying paperwork of my person.

It took quite a while for me to pull myself together enough to emerge into the ever-growing darkness of the evening. I was reluctant to leave its security, but I had to move on. As I walked along, I assured myself that my faith and prayers had gotten me out of yet another narrow escape. Not many days go by that something doesn't remind me of that nearly fatal night.

Cautiously, I walked down the dirt road. A rather cold wind started to blow from the east making walking difficult, I needed to find some shelter until morning. In the near distance, I could see some buildings. In Poland, small hamlets are scattered throughout the countryside. As I got closer, I could see that it was indeed a small village. On its outskirts, I came upon a small shed, its door was missing, as were some of the boards on one side, but it was bigger than I had anticipated it to be. There seemed to be enough room among the farming implements for me to make a bed out of a pile of straw, which I found in one of its corners. My exhausted body collapsed into the little nest I had created, but as the wind picked up and started rattling the boards, I was afraid to go to sleep. I knew I had to leave the safe haven at the first sign of light to avoid being discovered. Could I sleep light enough to make it out in time? I had to trust my internal clock to wake me. Stories abounded in this area about Siberian wolves that roamed the thick expanse of deep forest that surrounded this countryside. These wolves were fearless and would attack anything or anyone that crossed their paths. Despite all this, I somehow managed to fall asleep.

I woke up long before dawn and felt somewhat rested. My feet no longer hurt and I was able to will my body to move on. I was concerned about my food stores, I was down to a stale hard piece of bread and a few raw potatoes. Besides keeping an eye out for any Russian soldiers, I needed to find some more food. I headed west based on the directions we got from the farmer and his wife two days before. I figured I had about 485 kilometers to go to get back to East Germany. Right now, I was looking for a river. By the time I got to it , it was dark. I was scared that I would be seen or heard by locals in the area. For three days, I had not encountered anyone. Most Polish people did not own vehicles or could afford to run them during the war, so the engine I now heard had to belong to the Russian army. I had just crossed the bridge and was scrambling down the embankment when the truck started to cross. From my vantage point, I was able to see the now familiar insignia. My heart was pounding, but they continued past me. Once again, I had tempted fate and won.

After a brief rest, I forced my already emotionally exhausted body up off the ground and continued on my journey. I had no real idea of where I was, I just knew I had a long way to go. I stayed mostly on back roads and avoided contact with people unless it was unavoidable. I tried to rest close to farms, because farms meant food and shelter. I kept my thoughts focused on my destination and most of all, kept repeating to myself not to give up.

Some days later, I came to the proverbial fork in the road. I figured I had to continue west to reach East Germany so I chose the road that veered somewhat to the left. The road seemed endless. I was past exhaustion, I needed food and rest. It was almost noon on an exceptionally sunny day, when I noticed in the distance a farmer plowing his field outside a small hamlet. The last time I had encountered a Polish farmer, Franek had done most of the negotiating. This time it was up to me. I was very happy I knew how to speak Polish, because this would be my lifesaver. I cautiously approached the farmer calling out "Dobredzien Panu!" (Good Day Sir!) In Polish, 'pan or pani' accompanies any greeting (sir or madam). He smiled and called out good morning in response. He was an older man, probably in his sixties. We exchanged pleasantries and I noticed that he was looking me over as we talked. It did not take much for him to realize what I was and what I needed. I had not been able to clean up in several days and my clothes were filthy. He made the comment that he needed to give his plow horse a rest. As he unharnessed the horse from the plow and hooked it up to the wagon, he told me how he had had other horses, but that the Russians had confiscated them. As we rode toward his small farm, he asked me many questions about where I came from and where I was going. I had to be very careful about what I told this man, since I was not sure where his loyalties lay.

When we arrived at the farm, I helped him unhook the horse and feed it. The smell of sweet hay was very comforting and it made me even more tired. His little farm was about two kilometers from the village. I felt fairly comfortable as we neared his house. The old farmer made the sign of the cross before he entered, which reminded me that most Poles were devout Catholics. He invited me in to meet his wife, Maria. She greeted us at the door, she was wearing a 'babushka', a kind of headscarf as most women do in Poland and Russia. I was shown to a small shed outside where there was a pump and water basin where I could wash up.

A short time later I learned they had lost three sons to the war. Grief had left them unable to part with some of their personal possessions, so I was given a change of clothes from one of the boys. I was overwhelmed by their generosity. Refreshed and cleaned up. I felt like a newborn baby.

While the farmer and I talked, his wife prepared a meal for us. The 'zupa' a mixed vegetable soup along with potatoes made me feel like I had died and gone to heaven. It satisfied every need my famished body was longing for. The couple warned me to be very careful. They reaffirmed where the area was occupied by the Russians. They told me horrendous stories of heinous crimes committed against the Polish people and about how innocent Poles had been killed. He gave me new directions to the East German border about twenty kilometers away. My next destination was to be a town called Butow, where I should try to cross the Poland-German border. He asked me why I wanted to go to East Germany. I told him my sister lived in Berlin and I wanted to try to find her. The couple insisted I spend the night in their sons' loft. What bliss it was to sleep in a real bed! I took off in the morning after an early breakfast. Armed with new provisions of rye bread, carrots, and boiled potatoes. We parted with misty eyes. It was an experience I would not soon forget.

Refreshed and revitalized I hit the road once again. I came upon Butow late that afternoon and crossed into East Germany undetected. I walked quickly but not so quick as to draw attention to myself. I did not speak to anyone unless I initiated it. As I entered the town of Bummelsburg about eighteen kilometers from the border, I heard the happy voices of children playing 'fussball' (soccer), but most of all I heard the sounds of the German language. An older gentleman came my way and I said good morning to him. I asked him if he could tell me the time. After scrutinizing me and seeming to find me no threat, he told me what time it was and went on his way.

It was late afternoon when I entered the town and after a little while, it began to rain. At first lightly, and gradually progressing into quite a heavy downpour. I welcomed the rain at first, because I was parched and needed to be rehydrated. At first, it felt good, but I soon realized that I needed to find shelter or keep moving. As I walked through the town, I noticed the telltale signs of war everywhere; burned out buildings, damaged churches, and homes. I would stand out and be noticed if I continued to walk through the now deserted streets in the heavy downpour. The sky looked ominous covered in dark heavy clouds, it did not look like the rain would stop any time soon. It also was dark out and I knew I needed to get inside somewhere quick.

I was becoming nervous. My legs began to ache, I was frightened. The farmer's words came back to me about how heavily guarded the border towns were by the Russians. I needed to be careful. I was cautious with every doorway I passed and every corner I turned. Ahead of me, I could make out the figure of what seemed to be a person hunched over. As I neared the figure, I realized it was that of an older woman. As we approached each other, I took the chance and said good evening to her. She looked at me with a sparkle in her eyes and retorted with "Grüss Gott!" (God Bless You!) She asked me what I was doing out in the rain and chastised me for being so wet. She told me I should go home because the Russians would be coming out soon. I told her I had no home to go to and no one to go home to. She told me to follow her. I was amazed at how quickly this old woman could walk. She looked frail and forlorn, but with a mission, she could really move. Several times, she would look over her shoulder, I think to make sure I was still following her and that no one else was. We slowed only when we reached a small house. She quickly unlocked the door and motioned me to come inside. With much aggression, she pulled the curtains shut, voicing that she did not want the Russians to be able to see through the window. I was a little apprehensive about taking the woman up on her hospitality when she did so without much provocation, but my body won out and I allowed myself to be comforted by her actions.

She insisted I take off my wet outer clothes and hung them by the oven to dry. I was becoming accustomed to having to answer the litany of questions I would be asked by whoever took me in about where I was from, what had happened, and where I was going. She chastised me for being out in the dark, in the rain, and out after curfew. She told me about a boy (one of many) who had been shot by the Russians for being out after hours. I told her I did not know about the curfew and then asked her why she was out after curfew. She answered that she knew the patrol routes and chanced rushing home in hopes she would not be caught. The Russians had taken over a large school building and several homes in the area so they had a place to stay inside the city. One could hear shots being fired all the time. While we talked, she prepared some food for us. She told me how scared everyone was, how the farmers were robbed of their livestock and food. Some farmers who withheld what the Russians wanted were taken away from their homes. My head was spinning, I had experienced the Russian form of punishment, and it made me more determined to get back to Genthin. Once again, I was thankful to be out of the harsh elements and gave in to the irresistible aroma of the food she was preparing. She eventually called me into her small kitchen and invited me to sit at her table. I bowed my head as she raised hers to face the heavens and thanked God for allowing her to share what little she had with me. She had made 'kartoffel-suppe und brot' (potato soup and bread). It was the best I had ever had next to my stepmother's.

She seemed to be a nice gentle woman, yet you could see that the war had made her bitter. We talked endlessly. Her name was Anna Goffka. She told me that her sons had been killed in WWII and her husband had been killed by invading Russians. She had a daughter, whose husband too had been killed during the war, leaving her with two small children to raise on her own. She told me she was coming from her daughter's house when we met on the street. I asked her what had happened to the church I had passed in town, its spire was missing. I asked if there were still services held there. She told me the church had been damaged during a bombing and the priest had been arrested. Her story touched me as much as the pain that showed in her eyes. It was evident that this woman had suffered much. We talked until midnight, suddenly the night's quiet was broken by gunfire. She turned off the lights in the house and in a short time, we heard the sound of trucks in the streets. She told me the soldiers would fire at anything that moved and would arrest anyone who survived. The soldiers were singing and laughing aloud. You could tell they had been drinking which was not unusual. She told me this happened every night, sometimes making sleep impossible.

I told her I should be going, the food and rest had revived me. She insisted I spend the night. She was afraid I would be seen by the Russians and either killed or captured. By morning, my clothing were dry and the rain had stopped. She made me a most wonderful breakfast 'kartoffelpuffer und brat kratoffeln' (potato pancakes and homefries). She apologized for not being able to do better, but I was not complaining. I was however, anxious to leave. She practically begged me to look for work in town and stay a while. It was heartbreaking to have to leave this nice woman. It was a tempting offer, but I had this drive to get back to Genthin and to be finally free.

With tears spilling onto her cheeks, she pressed a bag into my hand with food she could spare to help me along on my journey. Her blessing on me carried me out the door, "Gott beschutze dichmein junge." (May God watch over you, my boy) I never saw her again, but just writing these lines, I can see her mother like face in the doorway, and her waving goodbye, wishing me luck and safe passage.

As I left her house, I realized that I had been walking for six days. I silently prayed that God would look over this sweet lonely woman and her family. My next destination was Neustettin about 45 kilometers away. I stayed to the side roads and avoided contact with the locals. It was early fall and the colors and beauty of nature helped me find peace. The countryside was bucolic as I walked along the back roads. I felt refreshed and reconnected with the earth and because of this, I made good progress. I passed by a nearby lake and marveled in its pristine water and the serenity it offered me. There was so much beauty around me I could only praise the Lord for all the things he had done for me so far, and for all the help I knew he would give me along this arduous journey.

If you did not know this land and its cities had been ravished by war, the countryside I was passing through would not have let on to it. I passed farms in the distance with farmers working their land. Everything looked peaceful and pastoral, yet there was no denying that it was still a very dangerous and precarious time. These people lived in fear and uncertainty. Would their families be spared? Would the soldiers pick their farm or business to raid? Would they lose their possessions? These people lived only day-to-day, not knowing what the next day would bring.

I had started this trek near the Gulf of Danzig and had headed west, according to my calculations, I had logged about 135 kilometers, I knew I needed to pick up my pace. My goal was to walk about 40 kilometers a day and I was nowhere near logging that kind of distance. I reassessed my situation and figured that now that I was on the open road, the weather seemed to be better that I should start making better time. I thanked the Lord for the kindness the strangers I had encountered had bestowed on me, with their help, I had renewed my spirit, my body, and my mental condition.

The weather turned for the better. The sun began peeking through the soft huge cotton like clouds, warming the indolent gusts of winds that buffeted me as I walked along. The old woman had given me a gift, a pocket notebook in which I could record my journey home, I knew tonight that I would make use of it while the memories were still fresh in my mind. I came upon a small wooded area where I decided to rest a minute. The sound of the wind moving in and out sounded like a melodious symphony. While I sat there, I wrote down this hymn remembered from my religion classes (A tribute to Holy Mary).

O Maria, meine Liebe! Denk ich recht im Herzen Dein:
Schwindet alles Schwer und Trube,
Und, wie heller Morgenschein, Dringts durch Lust und irdschen
Schmerz Leuchtend mir durchs ganze Herz.

****

(O Maria, my Love! As I think quite of your heart, everything heavy fades. Like the bright morning light penetrating through clouds, my desire and pain illuminates through my whole heart.)

The resplendence of my surroundings was so unimaginably peaceful, it was almost impossible for me to will myself to leave. I ate a little and continued on my way. I was now approaching a small village and noticed a large church with a large steeple. In it was a built in clock, this was somewhat unusual, but I was grateful for the opportunity to know what time it was. It was noon, as the clock's strokes soon told me with its resounding chimes. I was able to pass swiftly through the town unnoticed while the few people I encountered went about their daily business not giving me a second glance. Outside the town, I neared the lake I had noticed earlier, its clear waters tempted me to set aside my agenda and take a refreshing swim, but my will power won out and I continued on my way.

As I walked along I, thought about a poem I had once read by Johann Wolfgang (von) Goethe:

Wilkommen und Abschied
(A Poem to a Lady)
Dich sah ich, Und die milde freude
Floss von dem süssen blick auf mich
Ganz war mein herz an deiner seite
Und jeder atemzug für dich

*****

"I saw your Coming and Departure"
I saw you and balmy joy flowed from your sweet look at me. My heart was completely at your side and each breath was for you.

The fair temperature and sunny conditions sent adrenaline throughout my body. At times, I could not contain my energy and would run down the country roads. Soon I came across another set of farms, some with women and children behind the farm implements. As I came closer, I noticed they were harvesting 'pommes de terre' (potatoes). Food was always sparse and this was a good opportunity to replenish my supplies. I mustered up my courage once again and approached one of the farmers. "Guten

Tag, Mein Herr!" (Good day, Sir!) I asked if I could have some of their crop. At first, they looked at me with some disbelief and finally asked why I wanted potatoes. I explained my situation briefly as I could and to my surprise, the farmer said I could take as many as I wanted. As I got ready once again to set out, the farmer provided me with better directions on how to get to Neustettin. He filled me in on where the Russian troops were and with that wished me a good day and a safe journey.

I figured I had enough food to last me at least two days. I was overwhelmed with the generosity I had encountered so far. I told myself that despite all this country had endured, there were still people in it who had good hearts. The words my father once told me rang in my ears, "You could always trust a farmer to share what they can with you, if you ask they will seldom refuse you." How true this has been. I thanked the Lord for once again steering me in the right direction. I was very very grateful.

With the new directions and the information of where the Russians were camped out, I made sure I avoided as much contact with settled areas as possible. It would have been devastating to have come this far to be captured. It was getting late and the sun was beginning to set as I passed through a small village. I noticed that the main street was paved with cobblestones, which reminded me of our streets in Tarnowskie-Góry where I had grown up, it brought back good memories. I became somewhat anxious, as it got darker, because of the curfew the old woman had told me about. I kept my eyes focused as much as possible to eschew any encounter with the Russians. One could feel the threat of death in the streets. Stories of the random shootings by the Russians made me fear the dark.

I figured I must be about five kilometers away from Neustettin and felt determined to make it despite the odds. My body was telling me it was time to rest, I had no idea of where I could, but I was sure, when the time came that I could indeed stop, I would find shelter as I had in the past. In the darkness, I soon saw lights flickering above what I could only assume were Neustettin. Within minutes of seeing the lights, I came upon a sign that confirmed my assumption. My body told me I was there, but my mind told me I had to make it to my finish line in order to truly finish my goal. As I neared the town I congratulated myself on my perseverance, I had walked approximately 48 kilometers that day. I knew that if I actually went into the town at night it would be suicidal, because of the Russian patrols, so I set out to find somewhere I could bed down for the night. My dilemma soon solved itself as I came across a fairly large dilapidated barn with half of its big doors missing. I rejoiced silently and cautiously entered the cavernous barn. I stopped to listen to see if it was inhabited, and the only sounds I heard were those of pigeons in the loft. They scolded me for intruding on their private space; crying out and flapping their wings, sending clouds of dust around my head.

My eyes soon adjusted to the darkness and I was able to find my way around with a minimal amount of difficulty. I heard other sounds of owls and possible rodents, I was a little apprehensive, but felt we could make do without causing any of us undue harm. I took a good look around at my surroundings in case I had to make a quick escape. There was some damage on one wall, obviously by artillery, and there were doors at either end of the long barn. I opened the opposite door from where I had entered in case the need arose that I would have to leave that way. There were two wagons in the barn in one of them was straw. Even though it was prickly, somewhat musty and a little damp, I knew it would afford me comfortable bedding for the night. Even though I was tired, a realization kept me awake a little longer. A few days ago I had turned 18, I had been captured, interrogated by the Russians, sentenced to a prison camp, loaded onto a train destined for Siberia, escaped from the train, and now was running for my life across Germany. The only gift I had was the fact that I was still alive and that was the most precious gift of all. With those thoughts now in my head, I fell asleep with a soft 'nordlicht' (aurora) in the evening sky.

The new day dawned. A typical autumn day, crisp and chilly. I checked over my directions and confirmed that I was on the right track. My next target town was Pyritz and I had to cross another river, the Oder, which would turn me in the direction of Berlin. As I left the barn, I could see that I was indeed on the outskirts of Neustettin, but I had no time to sightsee, Pyritz was about 70 kilometers away and I had to move on. Time was a precious commodity and I could not waste it.

I entered the town noticing only a few people moving about their business. Energized I walked almost gleefully across the main street, slipping on the dew wetted cobblestones just as I had as a child back home. As the sun rose higher in the sky, I assured myself it would be a good day. I had a long walk ahead of me, but I prayed that it would be a good one. A group of children with their mothers passed by me, excited by the prospect of another day and school ahead of them. I wanted to reassure my directions, but did not want to bother the women. I soon came across an elderly man with a cane and a long white beard. I wished him good morning and proceeded to ask him for some directions. Slightly suspicious of my directness and of how I looked, he answered my questions without much hesitation. I knew I did not really have time to stop, but I asked the old man anyway where there was a church. He pointed one out to me, but unfortunately it was locked and I could not get inside. Next door to the church stood a small brick building, which I could only assume was the rectory. I knocked on the door and was warmly greeted by the priest who answered it. Without any hesitation, he invited me inside. His name was Father Anton and he was from Poland. I told him that I too was from Poland from the town of Tarnowskie-Góry. His eyes brightened like two diamonds. He replied that he had grown up in Czenstochowa about 40 kilometers from my hometown. He asked me to sit down and to tell him about myself. His rectory was moderately furnished, but comfortable. I knew of where he grew up, I went there on one of our class trips when I was in school, before Hitler invaded our country. We had visited the Mother of Jasna Gora-Our Lady of Czenstochowa. I told him my story since those idealist days and the only comment he had was 'Ach die Russen" (Yes, the Russians). The priest was amazed at the distance I had left behind me. When I told him my destination was Genthin, we looked it up in the atlas and he exclaimed that it was over 200 kilometers away.

He asked if I was hungry and I told him, I was, having lived on raw potatoes, carrots, and bread over the last few days I yearned for hot food. The priest made me scrambled eggs, tea, and rye toast. We talked about where I would head once I made it to

Pyritz and that the next stop would be Potsdam. He was doubtful that I could walk that far given my physical condition. He also voiced his concern that I had a high probability of being arrested again by the Russians, since they were in every town I needed to go through. Without any identification on me, I could get lost in the system if I was arrested and no one would ever know where I was. The priest thought for a while and said he had another plan he would like me to consider.

Not far from the rectory was a train station. Each day a train came in from Neustettin and traveled from there to Berlin. It sounded ideal. I wanted so very much to see my sister, Anna again, but I had no money whatsoever. I hadn't even seen money in the weeks since I had been arrested. He told me not to worry. He said he needed to leave me for a little bit while he went to the train station and that I could take the opportunity to clean up. He was back quicker than I had expected. He informed me that there were Russian soldiers at the station and near it, but he added the train was usually on time so I should not have to wait around long.

Having cleaned up, I realized that my clothing was looking worn; he was able to provide me with a warm parka and a better cap along with a rucksack in which he put some provisions, bread, boiled eggs, carrots, and potatoes along with a small blanket. I was dumfounded with all he was doing for me. Too soon, it was time for me to leave. Before we headed to the train station, he said we would go to church. We prayed together, he blessed me and we left for the terminal. I was scared, my heart was pulsing rapidly.

As we walked to the station, we didn't talk much. I had much on my mind. Father Anton told me that the train pass would not only take me to Berlin, but also on to Potsdam. I was profoundly grateful for all he was doing for me. As my time neared to leave, we shook hands. Father Anton said his final goodbyes to me with the words, "Möge unser Gott mit dir sein mein sohn" (May our Lord be with you, my son). With that, we parted. I walked down the endless terminal and turned around to wave goodbye, but the gentle soft-spoken priest was nowhere to be seen. Today, as I write this book my thoughts still wander back to the time, however short, that I spent with Father Anton and what he did for me.

I boarded the train without incident. As the train began to pull out of the station, the conductor came through the cars and checked our tickets. With a slight amount of trepidation, I handed him my train pass and having found everything in order, he moved on. I found it incomprehensible that I was sitting in a train car heading for Berlin. For a short time I would not have to fight the elements, wonder where I would be sleeping, or have to worry about the Russians picking me up off the streets of some dark town. The train was crowded with both Polish and German passengers. Although, the train stopped several times we moved quickly toward my destination. Once again, I thanked God for all he had made possible for me. An ancient prayer begins: "We should at all times and in all places give thanks to thee the Lord God, Father Almighty." Of all the places in the world. I have been more blessed than any other. Yes, although hunger and fear were stalking me at all times I knew that at the end of the dark tunnel there must be light. Because I knew I was never alone, I was grateful to my God that he looked after me during those rough times.

I passed the time watching the different people on the train. Those that left and the new ones who boarded the train. As we neared Pyritz about 70 kilometers from Neustettin, the day had turned rather gray and grim. For the time being, the weather did not matter to me, I was alive. At the station, I noticed Russian soldiers patrolling the platforms with machine guns at their sides. It was a reminder of what I had to be careful to avoid. I did not get off the train there, but stayed on to its final stop in Berlin. The scenery outside brought back the reality that the war had touched this area also. Damaged, burned out buildings sped by as the train picked up speed. We crossed the Oder River. It was an awesome expanse. I could not help but wonder how I would have crossed it safely on foot. Being on this train was simply a miracle. God must have been looking out for me again.

As we picked up speed, again after crossing the river I couldn't help but remember the last time I was in Berlin. It was at the end of March in 1945. I was in the German Wehrmacht and had been ordered to deliver an interintelligence from Mutzel to Potsdam. I covered the 90 kilometers on bicycle. Once in

Potsdam, I was to deliver this missive to the high command of the German army. I had seen much of the country before.

The beautiful autumn day had turned into a foggy and drizzly late evening. This time of year when it got foggy, it was hard to tell when the day ended and the night began. As I drowsed in the warm train car, I couldn't help but thank God, for all the amazing things that had happened to me good and bad. For the bad times had given strength I didn't know I could possess and the good times gave me peace that I knew I had earned and deserved. I must have fallen asleep, Before I knew it I was being awakened by the passenger sitting beside me whom I had told I was going to get off in Berlin.

Anxiety took over my body as we neared Berlin. I had let myself feel sheltered and protected during the train ride. Soon I would have to face the reality of the outside world. I was somewhat familiar with the city for having lived there in 1943. I knew that the Berlin I once knew had changed since the war. The city was divided and occupied by the Russians, British, American, and French troops. Again, having no identification of any kind was a serious detriment and therefore I had to avoid any encounter with the occupying forces of the city of Berlin as well as the police. When the train finally stopped, it did so outside a burned out building. Someone had painted on it 'Veritas – Justitia – Libertas' (Truth – Justice – Freedom).

With the city as occupied as it was, I chose not to look for Anna, but to move on toward my next stop of Potsdam. It was late in the evening when we entered the city. I had been there before, but this time things were quite different. This city too had been affected by the final days of WWII. I was disorientated in this devastated city. Most of the streets were dark or sparsely illuminated. As I moved down the streets, I came across an elderly couple. I said good evening to them and asked them for directions and if there was a Red Cross Station somewhere close. They told me there was one about five blocks from where we were. I pushed my exhausted body through the darkened streets as quickly as I could.

The Red Cross Station was my only hope to find shelter. I found the building, but the door was locked. I nervously knocked several times. Cautiously, the door was opened, I could not blame them, and it was very late. The man at the door told me that there wasn't any more room. I explained to him that I would not require much and would leave very early in the morning. After some hesitation, he told me to wait outside the door. Closing it in my face, I heard the door latch on the other side. Fear rippled through me. Would he let me in? My situation only declined further, when it started to rain. I pressed my body under the short canopy that framed the building's doorway.

The night had turned rather chilly and my now wet exhausted body started to shiver. I began to think that the man would never come back when to my surprise, I heard the door being unlocked once again. This time a different man opened the door. I could tell in an instant that this was a man who had compassion for his fellowman. With a smile and in a soft voice he welcomed me inside, "Guten abend, komme herein" (Good evening, come in.) I stood in the small vestibule and was told to wait there. After a few minutes, I started to feel warmer. I was soon approached by yet another Red Cross officer and he asked me to follow him. He took me to a small office and told me to have a seat. Panic seized me when he asked me for identification. I quickly told him my situation. He asked me where my parents were, I told him that the last time I knew they were still in Tarnowskie-Góry. Both he and I knew it was impossible for me to return to that part of Poland at this time. He explained to me that due to the bombings in Potsdam, many buildings had been damaged and the shelter was full, but he would find a space for me tonight. I expressed my gratitude and realized that once again my prayers had been answered.

A new day dawned, full of anticipation and anxiety. Early in the morning as I was getting ready to leave the Red Cross Shelter, I was called into the office. The officer behind the desk was the same one I had spoken to the night before giving me permission to spend the night. From the look on his face, he had good news for me. We talked a little and I found out he had been working for the Red Cross during the entire war. He asked me what my destination was and I told him it was Genthin. We went over my directions and routing. My next stop would be

Magdeburg An Der Elbe River. He cautioned me again that Genthin was occupied by the Russians, I was undeterred. I had about 90 kilometers to go and he was impressed that I had made it this far and had not known anyone who had made this type of journey alone.

After breakfast, I was given some nonperishable food: can goods, dry bread, and crackers. I thanked the Red Cross officer warmly, and left the shelter. The late fall morning was chilly and my breath left trails of fog in the air. As always I prayed, "Lord help me to stay alive and guide me!" My goal was to get to Genthin in two days. As I walked through the city of Potsdam, I was overwhelmed with the evidence of tremendous amounts of devastation left behind by the war. Potsdam was once a proud beautiful city. It once had been a garrison town under the great elector Frederick the Great, to whom the city owes many of its fine buildings. It was also once the summer residence of the Hohenzollerns, but now lay in rubble and ashes.

As the day progressed, the mercury rose and it turned out to be a beautiful day. My feet wanted to run, but I knew I had to ration my energy for the long and arduous day ahead of me. The officer had given me directions on how to safely get out of the city. These became invaluable to me. He had cautioned me to be on the constant lookout for Russians. Their unpredictability was always on my mind.

There was not a single day that I did not pray, "Lord, help me to start each day by listening to You and listing the wonderful blessings You have provided that make me content." I still pray this little prayer today.

The journey was daunting at times, but I was determined to make it to Genthin. I figured that I had already logged approximately 360 kilometers since my journey began. Many times, I had to fend off sad thoughts that I knew would deplete my spirit. I had to think of only the good times with my family, not the fact that I missed them. I had to focus on the fact that I was alive. I thought of the giant willow trees I passed along the way, I looked at the clouds; I let myself be mesmerized by the tall blades of grass that swayed in the autumn breeze. All these little things and hundreds like them made me forget my troubles. When I felt down, I would chastise myself. I told myself to grow up and to stop thinking of defeat. I wrote this sentence in my little diary and read it over many times throughout this ordeal. It became my mantra and in some ways made me content. Gradually, this call to courage replaced the negative voices in my head.

The weather stayed balmy and I made great progress. I had passed two small towns and now approached what seemed to be a stretched out village dotted with farms. My tired feet were weighing me down, letting me know I needed rest. As I approached the village, I noticed some of the barns and homes had thatched roofs, a sight I had not seen in years. They reminded me of my grandparents' farm in Poland and homes in Lüneburger-Heide in Germany, where I was stationed in the Wehrmacht. As I neared one of the farms, I noticed two men cutting clover and tall grass. Their heads were donned with old and dilapidated hats, the rhythm of their scythes proved to me that they were skillful long-term farmers. Nearby a wagon with a team of oxen stood ready to be loaded. I called out good day and they responded with "Grüss Gott!" (God be with you!) It was a good omen.

I was now accustomed to the question and answer session that would preclude any hospitality until their curiosity was quenched. I told them what they wanted to know and offered to help them load the wagon. I was given a pitchfork and started loading the wagon with fresh cut clover. The sweet smell of the clover was wonderful and it made me feel good to actually work for any assistance they were willing to offer me.

It was early afternoon, the sun felt warm on my back, I was in my bliss. I had not felt better in months. From time to time, I would go over to the oxen and feed them from my hand some of the fresh cut clover. It did not take long for me to make some friends. I felt like I was back home on my grandparents' farm, for a moment I forgot my troubles and I forgot I had many miles to go. The two farmers continued cutting wide swaths of the tall clover. The sun began to set, the wagon was almost loaded, when one of the men came over to me and said, "Mein junge du hast gut gearbeitet" (My boy, you've worked well.) He said it was time to go home that they would finish cutting tomorrow. I really did not want to stop. The two men introduced themselves, they were brothers (Adam and Gustav). They invited me back to their home and I gratefully accepted their invitation. I let myself daydream on the ride to their home. I could see my grandparents' beautiful old farmhouse, the huge barn, the stable, and the cow barn. What I liked the most about this vision was the thatched roofs on the buildings, it gave everything such an idyllic setting.

Immediately upon our arrival at their farmhouse, an older woman came out to greet the men. It turned out she was Adam's wife. I found out later that Gustav's wife had died during the war. I helped the men put the oxen away in the barn and unload the wagon. Soon Adam's wife called out that it was suppertime and I realized that I was famished. Over the meal, more questions followed about my journey and plans. The brothers were impressed with the way I had pitched in, helped in the field, and told me that they had a lot of work to do. The Russians had taken most of their livestock and hay reserves and they could use my help. I was flattered. They put me up in a spare room and I eagerly fell into bed and soon was sound asleep.

The next morning after a good night's rest, I awoke to a glorious sunrise. Over breakfast, I learned that Gustav was a skilled blacksmith and the only one in the vast area. He was already outside working on one of the big wagon wheels, which was in need of repair. Forging and fashioning a broken part, swinging his hammer skillfully against the heated part on the anvil reminded me of the blacksmith in my grandparents' village.

Adam's wife radiated love and compassion, she was a wonderful woman. Everyone was very kind to me. It was so enigmatic to me and I could not stop thinking about it. Once the wagon wheel had been repaired and the oxen hooked back up to it, we left the farm. The day was sunny and had promises of growing quite warm. It would be a productive day cutting hay. The brothers skillfully cut while my job was to spread the fresh cut grass thin and evenly so it would dry faster in the warm sun. It was good work and I enjoyed it. For at least a little while, I forgot my loneliness and homesickness.

Before I knew it, Adam's wife was bringing us lunch, we sat in the shade of the wagon and ate, while the oxen filled their bellies with fresh grass nearby. They told me how much they had suffered when the Russian armies moved in. They told me of the German Wehrmacht retreat. When the Germans left, they took most of the livestock while the Russians took the horses and what was left.

I did not want to leave and stayed with them for three days. We had replenished the hay supply for the winter months, I was refreshed, and it was time for me to move on. The brothers did not want me to leave and convinced me to stay yet another day and help them cut wood for their winter. The feeling of being needed made me feel good again. They not only provided me with shelter and food, but companionship, which I was so dearly lacking over the past several weeks. It meant a great deal to me.

When I finally convinced these wonderful people that I had to move on, they provided me with food, water, money, and a pair of boots. My clothes were extremely worn through by now and I knew that I would draw attention to myself if I looked out of place. The farmer's wife embraced me with tears in her eyes as I said my goodbyes. The four days I spent on the farm and the way they accepted my fate and me are still deeply ingrained in my soul to this day. They were a godsend.

As I set out on the country road in the chilly fall morning, I couldn't help but look back and thank them once again, as I continued toward Genthin. I carry a picture of them in my mind, standing there the three of them waving to me as I walked out of their lives. They, like the others cautioned me about the main roads, the trucks, and talking to people. My next destination was Brandenburg on the Havel River about 34 kilometers from their village. I had been to Brandenburg before on my secret mission when I was in the German Wehrmacht. The brothers had told me to be careful since the Russians heavily occupied the city. I headed west and made good progress.

I was walking out in the open with no trees, no homes, or habitation around when suddenly I heard barking and howling; was it wolves? Dogs? It frightened me somewhat. Soon I could see them coming toward me, dogs! Their barking and growling escalated as they started to circle around me. They looked ready to attack. They darted in and out at my body from every direction. I was petrified. I knew I could not panic or they would tear me apart. They looked hungry, I could see the outline of their bones as they walked around me. In my attempt to fend them off, one of the dogs got a hold of my boot and tried to pull me to the ground. I regained my balance, pulled my rucksack from my shoulders, and dug in it for food that I could throw for them to run after. It worked. While the dogs gorged themselves on my precious rations, I ran as if my life depended on it. It did. Fortunately, they did not follow me.

This episode made me realize how fortunate I was to have escaped and taught me not to be caught unarmed again. I promised myself I would find a stout stick so I would have some type of defense if this should happen again. I soon came across a grove of trees, I sat down in their cool shade and thanked God for rescuing me from the dogs. I took a moment to see what I had left in my rucksack. It wasn't much. In my panic I had thrown out just about everything I had. What I had left was a loaf of freshly baked bread. Not knowing where my next meal would be coming from I knew that I had to make it last as long as I could. I left the soft wind soothe my jangled nerves until I felt I could get going once again.

It was late in the afternoon, having passed two towns; Grosskreutz and Jeserig without any difficulties that I realized I had to pick up my pace if I wanted to make Brandenburg before nightfall. My only concerns were the Russians. As I neared the city, I could see tall factory chimneys, which emanated light and dark smoke. This gave me hope, that at least this city was alive. The brothers had told me that Brandenburg had been severely damaged toward the end of WWII.

Tired and exhausted I was determined to pass through this city before it was too dark. This city had a curfew also and one could be shot if found outside after dark. Several blocks down, I could make out a group of Russian soldiers strutting around boisterously in their boots, with their machine guns at their sides. I quickly found a way around them. At times to avoid being seen or heard, I hid in doorways or stopped dead in my tracks. I seemed incapable of grasping the implications of what would happen to me if I actually encountered them face to face. I moved on as quickly as I could. Even in the dark, I could see the vast destruction the war had caused to this once prosperous city.

In its glory, Brandenburg had a port, industries (steelworks and manufacturing of tractors), machinery, textiles, leather goods, as well as rolling mills. All this now lay in ruins and rubble. Among the town's historical buildings was a cathedral on an island in the Havel River. This building was rebuilt in a gothic style of the 14th century. As I passed by many of the burned out buildings, I could still smell the acrid and permeating fumes emanating from them.

As I moved on in the now almost dark city, I came upon a road that was blocked off by two Russian tanks. I quickly backtracked and crossed over a block to avoid the soldiers. The street I came out into was lit by streetlights, which cast ghastly shadows of the burned out buildings into its wide-open expanse. The stillness and silence of the night made it hard for me to keep my emotions in check. I prayed as I walked. This gave me courage to continue on and was my only comfort.

It had been a long day, my legs had begun to tell me that they needed rest. I was forced to find a place for the night lest I make a crucial error in judgment, which I could not afford to do so close to my destination. I was hoping to find a barn. I actually found something better. A lone streetlight illuminated a badly damaged two-story house, its windows and doors had been blown out from bombings. The streetlight gave me just enough light to pick my way through the rubble. Once inside I was apprehensive, but what choice did I have? Carefully, I walked around the first floor and found a small room that would serve me best.

I reached into my rucksack for my precious blanket and made myself as comfortable as I could on the floor. I had not planned to go to sleep, I just wanted to rest. My last thoughts were contemplating the moth that fluttered lazily against my cheek on silken shadowed wings. I listened to the sound of the Russian soldiers patrolling the streets. My body stiffened as I heard machine gun fire in the distance. Despite all this, I allowed my mother's voice to once again calm me, "Fear not because He is always with you." With that, I must have fallen asleep. Sometime later, I do not really know how long I actually slept, the sound of a truck passing the house woke me. I woke as a new day was dawning. I could not fathom how I could actually have slept in such a situation, but realized that my body would override anything my mind could tell it to do.

My stomach growled, I had less than a quarter of the bread left and very little water in my canteen. I ate and felt somewhat nourished and felt I could get started on what I hoped would be the last leg of my journey.

The day turned out to be foggy, cold, and dreary. In the daylight, I could see how badly the city had been ravished by the war. Whole buildings, apartment complexes, and historical buildings that once were known for their magnificent architecture were now collapsing burned out piles of rubble. It was horrible to behold. It was early, the streets were desolate which was just right for me. I had no idea in what direction I was heading. I was still concerned about the curfew. I had no idea of what time it was.

As I moved along the fog seemed to lift, maybe the day would not be bad after all. My stomach reminded me that the meager breakfast I was able to give it was not enough. At times, it growled so loudly I thought others would hear. Suddenly, I noticed a large group of people coming my way, not knowing if they were civilians or soldiers, I quickly found a doorway in which to hide. As they neared me I could tell what they were; workers, men and women. They carried shovels and picks over their shoulders. My instincts told me to join their little group. I would be safe in their numbers. As we walked, one of the men realized I was not a regular to their group and started to ask me questions. I answered him as best I could, and he told me that they were the "rubble people," organized by the city of Brandenburg to clear the rubble throughout the city. They were paid a stipend and were given one meal a day at noon. Most of the group had brought food with them; sandwiches wrapped in newspaper. My decision to join them had been a good one. Furnished with a shovel, I set to work along side those men and women. Again, it felt good to work, to earn my way even though I was hungry and had other places to be. I was amazed at how hard these people worked. It became apparent that they were tired of looking at the devastation around them every day.

My plight had spread through the little group and when the mid morning break was called, they shared some of their food with me. How lucky could I have been, the Lord once again had come to my aid. After the short respite, we resumed our tasks and before I knew it the city's soup kitchen showed up with Red Cross volunteers to feed us. We worked side by side for the rest of the day clearing away the debris. The rubble was loaded into old trucks, piles of steel, bricks, and concrete. It was backbreaking work, but it felt good. It helped me clear my head.

There was a sort of comradeship amongst the group and my hard work had won me their admiration. I was offered shelter for the night from the foreman and accepted it. The walk was long to his house, but we made it before nightfall. Along the walk, he wanted to know more about me, I told him as much as I could. His wife was at their door to welcome him home after his long day. If she was surprised to see me, she did not show it. Her eyes sparkled as she invited me to come inside.

Above her head on the lintel in the rear of the kitchen were the words "Grüss Gott" (Hail to God.) I had a warm feeling and felt safe. The meal consisted of a vegetable and a small piece of meat. I had not had meat in several weeks and relished the taste of it with every bite I ate. We talked of the war and the tragedies we all had suffered until the foreman said it was time to go to bed. What a night! I could sleep in a safe bed. It was more than I could have dreamed of.

I had chosen to spend another day with the group, helping them work. As we waited for the rest to join us, he told me that jobs were hard to find and throughout the day, it was not uncommon for people to flock in to get the meager wage and the meal. No one was surprised to find themselves working next to teachers, office workers, professors, etc. The foreman himself was once with the Hitler regime, a government official, now he picked rubble. No one was better than anyone else was. Everyone was in the same condition. I was told there were hundreds of groups such as this throughout the city. These people understood that they could not just give up. If they wanted to rebuild the city, it would be up to them to make it happen.

I was told about the horrible atrocities, about genocide, which had taken place during the last days of the war. I knew some of what had happened, but it still appalled me that this lack of respect for others could cause such pain. I wanted to share my thoughts and plans with these people about escaping from East to

West Germany, to be free but I dared not. The less they knew the better it would be for them.

The group was concerned for me, I had grown very thin, but I worked along side them without complaint. I spent another night with the foreman, I felt stronger and less fearful on the new day. The breakfast of potato pancakes, fried potatoes, and coffee curbed our overnight fasting as we set out to tackle another day of labor. As we neared the already gathered group of workers that morning, we were accosted by a truckload of Russian soldiers. My heart dropped in my chest. I thought I would be ill. I hid myself behind the group of older people and hoped I did not stand out. There were about ten soldiers in the truck, four of them got out; one was an officer. To my astonishment, the officer spoke German, I was about twenty meters away as he approached the foreman and they seemed to be discussing something.

I was able to learn that these soldiers were searching for former German Wehrmacht officers, fugitives, and Nazi government officials. The Soviet officer mentioned several times during their conversation that the city's major office was under Soviet control and even though the war had been over for five months, they did not neglect their duties. How well did I actually know these people? Would they turn me in? Having come this far, been through so much, would it end here? The officer scanned the group, scrutinizing each of us, he focused in on two of the men. The soldiers immediately arrested them and took them away. The foreman was visibly distraught. I knew at that moment that I could not stay here any longer. I feared that they would come back next time for me. My head was spinning, my blood was rushing through my body. I had to move on. How? When? Where? The horrible war had made me homeless once again. I had to struggle every day to survive. My life had been redefined in terms of my liberty and pursuit for freedom.

There was no time for weakness or complacency. The day passed quickly and by the end of it, I had made up my mind to leave the following morning. I knew that no matter how hard it would be to give up the new friends I had made, they would understand that it was safer for everyone if I left their company as quickly as possible. My fears of not making it back to Genthin were growing with each passing hour. After the evening prayer and meal, I told the foreman and his wife of my decision. I told them of my destination, my goal of finishing my education, and ultimately finding my family again. They understood and wished me luck.

The last night in their house was probably the longest one I had spent yet. My desire to be free and to reach Genthin was like burning embers inside me. The events of the day kept flashing before my eyes and I couldn't help but marvel that it could have been me. Once again, the Lord had spared me. We all woke early, his wife had made a warm breakfast. They had found me a pair of boots and clothes from one of their sons (who had been killed in the war). The foreman gave me fifty marks that he said I had earned and that he could collect from the city on my behalf. My rucksack was filled with food and my canteen with water. They gave me new directions and instructions on how to get out of the city. Before I knew it, it was time to face reality and step outside the door to once again continue my journey.

After all the aid I had been given over the weeks, one would have thought saying goodbye to those who helped would have gotten easier, but it had not. Tears were shed by all as we said our farewells. They said "aufwiedersehen" (until we meet again), but we knew that would not be until our deaths. I reluctantly left this loving house.

Autumn was in full swing this crisp October day in 1945 when I left this couple. My fear of the unknown ahead of me did little to shake off the chill that invaded my body as I walked down the deserted streets. The reality that I could be snatched off the streets at any time almost paralyzed me. I had no identification, if caught I would become just another statistic of the war. If Stalin didn't hesitate to shoot his own officers who failed to perform according to his plans, it was no wonder that civilians lived in fear for their lives. The fear inside me kept driving me, I would not give up!

My mind was lucid, my body was refreshed. I was determined to make it to Genthin that day. According to the foreman, I had about 32 kilometers to go. I had three options as a mode of transportation that would assist me on this leg of my journey. I was told I could get a ride on a barge that left from a dock in Brandenburg, which would bring me into Genthin through a canal. He also said that there were trains that ran between the two cities. Lastly, there was always walking. This chilly morning I chose the first option. I quickly walked to the port occasionally asking passersby for directions. As I neared the area, I could hear the shrill sounds of the ship's sirens denoting, I just followed those sounds. The smell of the water filled my senses to the brim. Much to my chagrin as I turned the corner I noticed not only the men loading and unloading the large boats, but also Russian trucks and tanks as well as the soldiers who manned them milling about inspecting all that went on. I knew immediately that attempting to come any closer would be suicidal.

Immediately, I turned around and backtracked from the way I had come. My body wanted to run, but I knew doing so would cause suspicion. With the greatest amount of willpower I had, I forced myself to walk. Regaining some composure I chose to check out the train, after all, I felt like a rich man; I had fifty German marks in my possession. I hoped I had enough money to buy a train pass to Genthin. Too much time had passed since I set out from my benefactors' house, it was already late morning, and I had not even made it out of the city. In my panic, I had lost my bearings and had to ask for directions to the train station.

Once at the train station I found the stationmaster only to find out that the train for Genthin had left at six o'clock that morning and another was not scheduled until six o'clock that evening. I could not wait that long, I would have to walk and I would have to walk hard and fast to make up for all the time that I had lost already. I could not wait to get out of this sadly depressed city. I again asked for the quickest directions out of the city and soon found myself in the open countryside. The last clock I had seen told me it was around eleven o'clock, with no one around I felt safe to run a bit to put some distance between Brandenburg and me.

When I settled down, I took a minute to thank the Lord for the last three days and for having protected me over the past twenty days since I had escaped the Russian death train. Grateful for the good boots and coat I pushed my body against the increasingly ceaseless groaning, biting, dust spitting wind; it was a miserable day. By mid afternoon I reached Bensdorf, I was half way there, the next town I would pass would be Brettin.

The weather fought me every step of the way. I fought against and was constantly buffeted by the wind, copious with dust that clogged my nostrils making it hard for me to breathe as I trudged down the country road. The northeast wind was bitter cold, after all, it was the end of October, and there was no doubt of the type of winter that would follow. I needed a short respite from the wind; I had to find shelter. The skies took on an ominous appearance, lightening flared and thunder sounded; it began to rain. I desperately needed shelter. In no time at all I was wet through to the skin, my body began to shake from the bitter cold and ice-like pellets piercing any exposed areas. Visibility was limited even though it was only mid afternoon, the dark clouds made it appear as if it was early evening. I pressed on and through, squinting my eyes I could make out the low black shape of a farmhouse against the horizon. If there was one building I hoped there would be more, but looking around I could see none.

The fields were now white with frozen rain, I could barely open my eyes because of the biting freezing rain. When I forced myself to look up I noticed smoke coming from the building, it was occupied! My spirits rose as I inched my way forward. As I cautiously approached it, I could see it was a wretched and dilapidated place. It was a low stone building with a barn next to it, an empty sheep pen and a broken down wagon stood outside now covered with ice and a light drift of snow. There was no evidence of cattle or farm life at all. The silence was absolute and almost frightening. The building had a thatched roof that had been damaged, the front door of the house had what looked like bullet holes in it. Except the slight trickle of smoke from the roof, there were no other signs of life. The Russians apparently had taken everything.

It was freezing cold and I was soaked through to the skin, I could not will myself to knock; I found a stick and banged on the building hoping to draw someone's attention. There was no response. I called out "Hallo! Ist dort jemand? Lass mich in!" (Hello! Is there anyone? Let me in!) The door remained shut, I knew if I did not get my exhausted body inside, hypothermia would set in, I could already feel the cold seeping ever deeper inside me.

I tried to call out again, but all that came out was a sob. Helplessness swept over me. I stood close to the door and called out that I was not a Russian soldier that I was a German refugee and needed help. A roaring sound rushed through my head, I feared I would pass out. I shut my eyes fighting down this horrible sensation and prayed that I would not freeze to death out here. Slowly the door opened and on the other side stood an old man whose face was deeply ingrained with furrows, which showed the ravages of war. His sad eyes looked at me with suspicion as he asked me who I was. I explained myself in German as best I could, and he invited me inside. He took my hand in his and I could feel the leathery toughness of his skin, this was a hard working man. To express my gratitude to this man was impossible.

As the warmth of the cabin seeped into my body, he explained that he had just recently been ransacked by the Russians. Two days prior, they had taken his last horse and good wagon. They took a sack of potatoes, the only food they could find. What they were actually looking for was his granddaughter who he was hiding under the floorboards of the farmhouse. Her father had been killed in the war and her mother had died a couple of months before.

I could have embraced the crude iron stove, but chose instead to stand with my back in front of it, forcing the warmth directly into my body to drive the cold out of it. The farmer told me to strip down so that I could lay my clothes out to dry. I could not afford to let myself become sick. I took off what I felt comfortable with and he gave me a warm coat to put on. As my senses returned, I took stock of my surroundings. It was a small, but cozy cabin; a kitchen, living quarters, and probably a bedroom in back. The old man left me only to return with a young woman about the age of twenty and introduced her as his granddaughter, Maria. She was painfully thin, even though her head was covered with a light shawl I could see that she had chestnut brown hair, her eyes showed only the sadness she felt and had endured over the past months. Her truly endearing feature was her warm smile, she whispered "Good evening." I thought at that moment how sad it was that people like her had to live in fear and obscurity. I hoped that one day these people would be able to live in peace instead of having the threat of being constantly hunted and violated.

Even though his food was in short supply, the farmer and his granddaughter made a simple meal of boiled potatoes, cabbage, and turnips for us. Maria fully understood their situation and looked at me warily. I always thought and still do that hunger must be the heaviest and loneliest burden one must bear next to homelessness.

The loathing for the Russians from these people seeped out of their pores. After a long conversation about the war, I told them of my plans. Even though they did not know me, I could tell they were concerned about the plans I had made. The warmth of the room had made me extremely tired. They arranged a pile of straw, covered it with a blanket, and made a bed for me in the corner of the room. I laid there in the darkness and listened to the crackle of the wood in the stove. It began to lull me to sleep. I snuggled under the heavy goose down quilt and fell asleep.

Early next morning, I heard a whispered conversation between the farmer and his granddaughter, but what they said I could not make out. As I got up, I was told I could go out to the water pump in the adjacent shed. When I came back in, the farmer had revived the fire in the stove, and they had prepared a light breakfast of 'brat kartoffeln and rogenbrot', a coffee-like brew made with chicory along with heavy rye bread. The farmer asked me if I wanted to stay another night, but as much as I wanted to stay, I reluctantly insisted that I had to move on. My clothes had dried over night. A short time later, I was ready to leave. It was painful to leave these people behind; I could feel their sadness and destitution.

The farmer told me that I was about five kilometers from Brettin and warned me about the Russian outposts. Expressing my gratitude, I took leave of these kind people. The farmer had confirmed to me that it was November 1, 1945. I could not believe it. Refreshed and full of energy, I was ready to face the new day, the day that would hopefully end in Genthin.

Stepping outside I was amazed at the contrast between this day and the last. A soft breeze was blowing in from the northeast and it had promises of being a warm November day. As I walked down the snow covered country road, I prayed that God would not only look after me, but all my benefactors throughout this long arduous journey. I would not be going into Benthin for fear of encountering the Russians, but would be passing by it. As I neared the town, I could see people. Not being able to make certain they were civilians and since I could not hear their conversation, I felt it prudent that I avoid them altogether. I decided to cut across the field, stumbling over rocks and ruts I moved undaunted putting distance between me and the group of people. I forged my way forward and came across a ravine with a shallow stream running through it. I was fortunate to find a place to cross. A tree had fallen creating a makeshift bridge over which I could make my way to the other side. I was pleased with my progress and moved on.

I also had to avoid the Haval Canal. It was the only waterway that linked the cities of Magdeburg, Genthin, Brandenburg, and Berlin; it leads eventually to the Baltic Sea. There would be much travel on this waterway and with travel came the threat of Russian troops. The biggest risk I now faced was not coming too close to the canal, but how could I avoid it? Continuing on my way I came across a sign that read – Genthin fifteen kilometers. I was relieved knowing I was still on the right path. Although I was familiar with this area from my mission to Potsdam, it all seemed different now. When I had passed through this region in March of 1945, I had used the main roads, now I was forced onto backcountry roads and had to make my way with apprehension filling each step I took.

I had not made good time, due to the road conditions, but with my rucksack over my shoulder and the sun on my back, I forged on. I passed burned out farms with no sign of cattle or other life. Here too the war had left its mark. My spirits rose with each step I took, knowing with each step that I was that much closer to my destination. I knew the Lord would not let me get this far only to let something happen to me when I could almost touch my goal. By early afternoon my body demanded that I take a break, I was in open country, and the wind had picked up and I wanted to find shelter from the chill that was invading the afternoon.

After about two more kilometers, I came across a cemetery with a small chapel in its center. To my disappointment, the doors were locked, but I took the opportunity of its seclusion to lay down my blanket and eat my meager meal of rye bread, boiled potatoes, and water. Sitting in the shade of the trees, surrounded by tombstones it was very serene. After a short respite, I was ready to move on. I neared another small village and had to make the decision as to whether or not I would pass by it or through it. This enigma I alone had to solve. Did I come this far to jeopardize my situation? I prayed and asked for guidance. I wanted to reaffirm my directions and with some trepidation decided to walk towards the village. At the first house I encountered I knocked on its door.

There was no answer, I knocked again, and this time I was rewarded with a woman's voice calling out "Who's there?" I tried to explain my situation and she told me to go away, to go to another house, because her husband was ill. I reiterated that all I needed were directions. I waited awhile listening to the movements inside the house. Finally, the door opened a crack and on the other side of it stood a sad old woman. Her wariness vanished as she looked at my condition and her compassion for my situation made her open the door wider. She explained that from time to time, the Russians would bother the outside villages and it was always better to pretend that no one was home.

Once inside, I noticed that her husband was indeed ill and was lying in bed. She introduced me to him and I was again besieged with many questions. I told them about my journey and about my desire to reach Genthin. I only stayed a short while. They gave me the directions I needed, let me refill my canteen and warned me about the Russians and I left this caring couple.

Back on the road, I seemed to move at warp speed. I was only eight kilometers from GENTHIN! Now being truly fall, November's nightfall came quicker and I had to make it to shelter before dark to avoid the Russian curfew. I started to count my steps, calculating them into minutes to help me determine how long it would take me to cover this distance I had left. It was like a dream coming true. The bitter wind made travel difficult, but I knew it was nothing I couldn't handle with God's help. As I neared the town, I couldn't help but revisit all that had happened here that had kicked off this chain of events. This is where I lived, where I was arrested by the KGB, sentenced to the labor camp, and put on the train heading for Siberia. Not withstanding all of that I wanted to come back to this town to reconnect with the people I knew and loved. I wanted to restart my life and one day make my way to West Germany and eventually to freedom.

I was able to slip into the town unnoticed and with a watchful eye for any Russian patrols; I carefully made my way to the Schützenhaus, which was on the outskirts of town. This is where I worked before I was arrested. I knew the owner Herr Neumann well and was sure he would welcome me warmly. As I approached the huge building with its iron fence and tall chestnut trees, I was overcome with emotions. The trees now devoid of their foliage gave the atmosphere a desolate appearance. I tried the gate, but it was locked with a chain and padlock. I stepped out of the glow of the streetlight to a darkened area, threw my rucksack over the fence, and climbed over it myself. Dropping to the ground, I found I had attracted the dogs, who barked to alert their owners of an intruder. I stopped frozen in my tracks. I knew that Frau Neumann used to keep pit bulls for security, even though she herself had been attacked once while feeding them. I was relieved to see that they were in their dog pen and I was safe from them. There was a light in one of the second floor windows and I had to get inside in order for the dogs to quiet down. If I didn't, the noise might attract Russian patrols who would want to see what was going on.

I knocked and then pounded on the door. After some minutes, someone finally called out from the other side asking who was there. I said it was me, Günther; that I was alive and to let me in. The door opened and there stood Herr Krause, Herr Neumann's brother-in-law who had lived with them ever since the war. Dumfounded he looked at me, obviously, he did not recognize me, and the past weeks had indeed changed my appearance. Finally, something about my appearance struck him as familiar and he told me to come inside quickly. At the same time I heard Herr Neumann calling out from the second floor, "Who's there?" Herr Kraus called back up to him that it was "Günther, it's Günther!" I heard him exclaim "Mein Gott!" and he and Frau Neumann flew down the stairs and embraced me. It was a very emotional moment for all of us. They had given me up for dead or imprisoned, but I had never given up hope that I would return to them. I silently took a moment to thank God again for all He had done to watch over me, to direct me, and for giving courage to those who helped me over this long, dangerous, and arduous journey. God had been good to me and I trusted in Him completely. I was home. My journey was over. My anxieties had left me at least for a short time. The Neumann's accepted me back into their life.

However, my journey was not truly over. Over the next year, my thoughts were consumed with planning my escape to West Germany. However, for now I was content to be back where I called home.

Genthin

After my arduous journey across Poland, I was very grateful that Herr Neumann reemployed me at the Schützenhaus. I had nowhere else to go and I had always enjoyed this rich historically intoxicating city. After the war it evolved from a Slavic settlement to becoming part of East Germany and things had changed somewhat. I would rather had gone on to my home town of Tarnowskie-Góry in Poland, but it was still occupied by the Russians and I would not be able to return there for some time.

I was somewhat hesitant to return to the city where I had been arrested by the KGB, but I was under the hopes that they would be gone or had lost interest in me; it was a risk I was willing to take. I came back to Genthin, simply because I knew people there, people who I could trust. Sentimentally, I could look at Genthin and see similarities between it and the town in which I grew up. Both had rich architecture, historic buildings, and a great deal of history surrounding their beginnings. It saddened me to come back to the destruction, which had occurred during the end of the war and saddened me further to imagine what had happened to Tarnowskie-Góry.

Herr and Frau Neumann were good people. They had always treated me with kindness and I enjoyed working for them. I showed up at Herr Neumann's door a penniless emaciated human being now I had food, a room, clothes, and I felt safe with good people with whom I worked. I felt very lucky indeed. The inn's staff consisted of several older men and women who often times treated me like their son, which would push my homesickness momentarily away. It did not take long for my life to level off and for a routine to develop that would consume my day. Nevertheless, no matter how busy I was there were times that loneliness still managed to creep into my thoughts and I would find myself missing my family who I had not seen in almost three years.

I worked in the kitchen as well as in the restaurant, waiting on civilian patrons as well as Russian officers. The officers frequented the inn because of its warm and cozy ambiance, they seemed to enjoy the relaxed atmosphere, which was such a contrast to their daily harsh regimen. However, for several weeks I would not allow myself out in the restaurant out of fear that some KGB officer might be around I didn't feel safe until Herr Neumann assured me that just weeks before my return, the Russians had rotated the entire KGB staff housed at the villa, which was within walking distance to the inn, this news left me feeling relieved and a little bolder to venture out from behind closed doors. Relieved by this news I began to work almost daily in the Restaurant and when they needed me to help out in the kitchen I put my time in there.

Most of the officers spoke German and when I could, I eavesdropped in on their conversations so I would not be caught off guard. The majority of them were polite with a few exceptions of course and I became comfortable around them with time. I served them politely drawing as little attention to myself as possible and my efforts did not go unnoticed, many times I was tipped quite well, this money I put away so I always had money in case of an emergency.

As peaceful as the days were, our nights were often disrupted by the sound of gunfire coming from the Russian Kammandantura. Only six months had passed since the war had ended and things were still very unstable. At first, Herr Neumann would not tell me very much, but the more concerned I got the more willing he was to discuss matters with me. Many nights after the Inn would close he would invite me up to his second floor apartment where we would have tea and talk. Herr Neumann was indeed one of the many unsung heroes of the war and one of the many who I can truly say saved my life on more than one occasion. During one of our nightly teas, they confided in me that the situation in town was a little unstable. There were problems with the new communist government and the town's future did not look very bright. They told me if they were younger, they would move and leave everything they had built behind, this is how seriously they felt about the changes. I felt sorry for them and stored this information away for later when I knew I had to make the decision to leave or stay.

Life in East Germany was unpredictable and the presence of the soviet army made life for the people precarious. There still was a curfew making walks at night out of the question. It was imperative that I be very careful and watch the daily activities at the inn regarding the Russian officers, after all it was the KGB who had arrested and sentenced me to hard labor and had deported me to Russia. As I said before, I got along with the Russian soldiers who frequented the restaurant and I got the impression that they liked me as well. I could speak and understand Russian and was able to communicate with them fairly well, they liked that, but I always made sure I made mistakes so I was able to learn things I probably shouldn't have known. Herr Neumann cautioned me about who I spoke to, reminding me that often times the KGB would dress as civilians to flush out those they were looking for. You never knew whom they would arrest next. Herr Neumann was in a precarious situation, he was not a member of the communist party and for a businessman in the "ost-zone" governed by the communists, this was very unusual. He was one of the few who stood up to his beliefs that he should not be forced to belong to a party or regime that he did not believe in. There were times I would hear parts of conversations between these 'civilians' and the Russian soldiers, I would see maps being looked at and furtively pocketed, during these episodes I would get a real uneasy feeling. I often walked away from their tables wondering who would be arrested that day.

My situation put me in jeopardy as one day I was approached by a man who was about forty years old, he had been wounded in the war and now walked on crutches. He told me flatly, that he needed my help. I was shocked at his forthrightness and asked him what kind of help I could possibly offer him. He confided in me that five months ago, the KGB had arrested his seventy-one year old ailing father and were holding him at the villa, he asked me if I would be willing to help him look for his father.

To say the least I was stunned by his request and did not know what to say. He asked if I would accompany him to his house where he and his wife could explain the situation in more detail. I found myself in a very unusual predicament. After thinking it over for a minute, I told him I would come to his house on my next day off.

A couple of days later I met him and his wife at their house. I learned that his mother had passed away just a few months ago just after his father had been arrested. His father was a businessman who had lost everything to the communist regime. He was a member of the NSDAP (Nazis Party) during the time of the Third Reich and now he was a prisoner. It came as no surprise that he was a member of the NSDAP nearly every man had to be in order to survive. If you weren't Hitler would have them arrested and sent to prison or a labor camp, now the KGB's goal was to search the town to find those who belonged to this organization. I had heard horror stories about what happened to those prisoners and hoped that nothing had happened to this man's father. I was not sure if I could or should help him, I had my own problems to deal with and I was not sure if I should let myself become involved anymore than I already was. It was extremely hard for me to look at this couple who were clearly in pain and tell them I could not help them. As we parted on the chilly December day, he begged me to try to find out anything I could about his father. I walked away from them with a cold and heavy heart.

Christmas of 1945 was approaching, this would be the third one I had spent away from my family. Christmas time at home was always a special time for us. Even during the war time years and when we didn't have much, our parents were always able to make it special; we would attend masses in our beautifully decorated St. Anna church and later we would spend time with close friends. Those times seemed like eons ago. I had no fond holiday memories since I had been forced to leave home, as Christmas drew nearer the more withdrawn I became. I forced myself to live in the present and to be thankful that I was alive and well, that I had a good job and nice people to work for and with, and that I was safe at last. Yet, no matter how I tried to focus on the positive things in my life, something was missing and that was my freedom. Christmas came and went with little fanfare. As 1945 came to a close, it was mostly the Russian soldiers who celebrated bringing in the New Year with lots of vodka, champagne, and Russian caviar.

One day in the spring of 1946, the man who had approached me the previous fall about getting his father out of the villa once again approached me for help. He practically begged me to help him, he was at his wits end not knowing what he should do. He had no one else to turn to, he had already gone to the Genthin police, and they were not able to help him. I asked him how he thought I would be able to help him. He did not know, but for some reason he saw me as his savior in this situation. After the confrontation I could not sleep, his pleading haunted me as the days crept by. One day a man dressed in civilian clothing came into the restaurant and pulled me aside and I was told to report to the kammandantura within the hour. I asked why and asked what they wanted with me, and I was told I would know once I got there. After the man left, I sought out Herr Neumann and told him about what had happened. He was just as stunned as I was. I had no choice but to go, we both knew it was better I go without them having to come and get me by force. I loathed the idea of stepping foot inside the villa, I knew once I was inside all the events from ten months ago would come rushing back at me.

The Kammandantura was only a short distance from the inn and I walked to it with an immense amount of trepidation. It was a crisp early spring day, just right for taking a walk and I would have enjoyed it had it been under different circumstances. By the time I arrived at the headquarters my body was quivering all over. When I approached the gate, the guards stopped me and asked for my name and upon telling them, I was led by one of the guards inside the villa. I was handed off to two Russian soldiers and very cordially taken to the second floor of the villa. As I walked along, I could not help but wonder what they wanted of me. I thought I would pass out from the stress that was building inside my brain. As I walked I noticed to my amazement that the once darkly painted walls had been painted white giving one the illusion of a more friendly inviting atmosphere. I was taken to an office where I was handed off to yet another officer and a man in civilian clothing. I was asked to take a seat and offered a cigarette, I told them I did not smoke, but I could use a glass of water. I was very nervous and still did not know why I was there. The officer sat behind a huge and beautifully adorned desk. He lit a cigarette and drew a long draw and exhaled a huge cloud of smoke into the room, this seemed to take forever. He looked me in the eye and explained that he knew who I was. He thanked me for coming and added "Wir brauchen ihre hilfe" (We need your help). I was speechless! At this point, the man dressed as a civilian took over the conversation. He indicated that I was to keep this meeting strictly confidential and I was not to talk about anything that was discussed with anyone outside of this office. Finally, he told me what they needed. They needed me to find them a German doctor, not one from Genthin, I had to get one from out of town, and I had forty-eight hours. They confided in me that the Kommandant was ill; to be precise he had a venereal disease. They could not procure a Russian doctor, because if his superiors found out about this he would be demoted or face execution. Inside I had to allow myself a small sense of enjoyment at this man's predicament. In broken Russian, I asked them very politely, why they had picked me for this 'mission'. I took a deep breath and took a chance by requesting that I would help them out if they would help me out. I gathered my courage and indicated that I knew they had an innocent man locked up and his only violation was the fact that he was a member of the NSDAP and that if I found this doctor for them they would release this man to me. To my amazement, they agreed to honor my request as long as I returned with a doctor within forty-eight hours.

I left the villa not really knowing how I was going to pull it off. My only thought was to go see the one doctor that I was familiar with in Genthin and that was my dentist, Dr. Stenner. I told him what I needed and he promised that he would be able to find someone who could help me out. He contacted a doctor in Brandenburg who was willing to help us out and treat the Russian officer. Two days later, I reported to the Kammandantura and was once again escorted inside with a degree of importance. I told the officer who he needed to see in Brandenburg and the details were mapped out, I would accompany him and his driver to assure he was not being set up.

The next day I reported to the villa and the three of us crammed ourselves into a small German sports coupe, I was given a warm coat to wear, I knew it would be a chilly forty-kilometer ride. There was not enough room for me to ride inside the car so I was forced to make this journey in the rumble seat. I had never ridden in one before and was fairly comfortable in it until we hit the open road, where the driver decided to drive at an incredible speed. The wind whipped around me trying desperately to tug me out of the seat on to the roadway. I scrunched down as much as I could to avoid being tossed out. At one point, I peeked out to see how close we were to our destination and to my chagrin noticed dark ominous clouds forming and within seconds, we were in the midst of a snowstorm. Thankfully, the driver had to reduce his speed when visibility became so poor that he could not see. Fortunately like so many April storms, it did not last. However, I was covered with so much wet snow, that I could have made snowballs.

We ended up late for the appointment due to the weather and not being able to find the address given to me, but after some misdirection, we found the doctor's office. I was glad to unfold myself from the rumble seat and stretch my legs. I went in with the officer so I could interpret what was being told to him, he was treated and told that he would have to return at least two more times. The drive back to the villa was uneventful. The officer was greeted by his command after which he asked me to join him in his office. He asked if there was anything else he could do for me and I reminded him about releasing the old man, and he promised to do that, but he asked if there was anything, he could do for me. I told him about my watch which had been taken from me when I was held as a prisoner ten months prior.

Within minutes of returning, I had accomplished my second 'mission' and that was taking custody of an ailing elderly gentleman and after ten months reuniting him with his family. It is impossible to describe the joy of this father and son reunion. They commended me on my courage to make such a demand of the Russians and then holding my ground to see that it was carried out.

I was surprised when a week later upon our second visit to the doctor he presented me with a Swiss made Omega watch, which I still have today, along with other Russian memorabilia. I accompanied him on his remaining visits and he recovered fully. I had become quite a fixture at the Kommandantura even having the opportunity to dine with them on one occasion during which time they introduced me to the art of drinking Russian vodka and caviar.

I continued to work at the Schützenhaus, days passed by and I began to focus on my future. I wasn't sure where to begin, but I knew it had to start with leaving East Germany. I knew I could not continue to live under a communist regime.

As I reflect on the events that took place several decades ago, I remember all this as well as if it happened just yesterday. I have never felt such satisfaction as when I freed that old man and returned him to his family. I felt relief that I could help that ailing officer even after all that had been done to me. "Turn the other cheek" the Bible says, and I did that on that day. I think of that officer every time I pass that framed Omega watch that hangs on my wall. After all, I had been through those months I never let go of the words from my stepmother to pray and keep my faith. I truly believe that God has always been with me, I do not doubt it for a minute. *"Non estad astra millis terries via?"* (Our life is a warfare and who knows it or not?) Regardless of whom we are, where we are from, or where we are going we must remember that we are all human. It's the way God wants us to be, because "He said by their fruits you will know them." How true it is. Wars have always produced good and evil people. "As gold in the fire, so men are tried in adversity." *Tribulatio ditut;* and which Camerarus shadowed in an emblem of a thresher and corn. *"Si tritura absit, paleis abdita granda nos crux mundanis separate a paleis"* (As threshing separates straw from the corn by crosses from the world's chaff are we born. Corn is not separated but by threshing nor men from worldly impediments, but by tribulation. (The Anatomy of Melancholy by Robert Burton)

Asking God and engaging Him in this difficult situation has been nothing but a spiritual quid pro quo. The Russian commandant not only got his health, but his life and I was able to have this ailing old man released and all with God's help. "With God nothing is impossible."

In our dangerous world of today, with many
of our young people in harms way, I am sure we all
know someone for whom we can pray. A prayer is very
powerful, one of the most powerful forces on this earth.
Trust me I know it.

"Tri bulatio di tat"
Some men are tried in adversity

"Our lives are but a very dream,
and while we look about,
immortalitas adest, eternity is at hand"

"Quicquid vult, habere nemo potest"
No man can have what he will

"They that sow in tears shall reap in joy."
— Psalm CXXVI

Escaping East Germany

I continued to work at the Schützenhaus. Herr and Frau Neumann were glad that I came back to Genthin. Prior to that, I had stayed at the home of the former teachers who were employed by Herr Kleinert at the restaurant outside of Berlin. I had left Frau Meier's home in such a hurry that I had left some of my belongings behind. When I unpacked my 'koffer' I realized that I had left my diary under my mattress and that troubled me somewhat. I knew it was important that that diary not be found, especially by the East German police. I was not concerned with Frau Meier finding it, but I did not want any trouble to come to her because of me.

It was Christmas Day, my third away from my family. The Neumann's did their best to comfort me, mostly by keeping me busy. Christmases at home had always been a very special occasion. Our mother was able to produce the finest meal and desserts out of what appeared to be a near empty larder. Her luscious baked goods still make my mouth water to this day. Christmas 1946 came and went without much fanfare. New Year's Eve at the Schützenhaus, was for the most part celebrated with lots of champagne and Russian caviar, and singing by primarily Russian officers and a select party of civilians. New Year's Eve for me was just another working day, however, this time I made myself a resolution; that this would be the last one I spent in East Germany. I needed to finish my apprenticeship per my written agreement with Herr Kleinert, but I was not sure how I would, now that he too had been arrested. I was worried about not finishing my education and decided to focus on my immediate situation with Herr Neumann and my plans to escape from East Germany. The staff liked me and I liked everyone I worked with at the Schützenhaus, but something was missing in my life.

It was not easy living in East Germany during these times. Life in a Russian occupied zone was difficult. People could not congregate freely on the streets and our movements throughout the town were limited. Everyone had to be careful when talking to strangers for fear you were conversing with the KGB in plain clothes. Women were in danger daily from soldiers who still operated under the mindset that they could abuse those they wish at any time and for any reason; the police had no authority to stop any attacks so we were in essence powerless against the Russians. Innocent people were arrested on trumped up charges or for forced associations over which they had no control. They were detained and many times never seen again. At times, I thought that there was a measure of hope and that things might improve. However, even though we all knew that, the war was over; we could see that another was on the horizon.

Living under a communist dictation, by Stalin, showed no future for me. I lived in constant fear and therefore became a prisoner by it in my own head. I had been living in Genthin on and off for just about a year and a half and I knew the surrounding area quite well. I had been listening to many people about the political developments and things did not look good. The only place I felt safe was inside the Schützenhaus. My plan was to escape to West Germany, it was the only way I could finish my education and apprenticeship and fulfill my dream of going to college. My nights became restless, my plans rolled around my head and needed to be voiced, but I knew I could not talk about this with anyone. I knew when I finally did decide to make my move; I would probably have to leave some of my already meager possessions behind. I was frightened of the actual move though, I had heard many stories about people being caught by the Volkspolice, or "Vopos," or by the Russians who guarded the borders between east and West Germany. I knew I would have to travel under the darkness of night and that it would be a daunting task, but it was worth the risk to me to remain safe. Over and over my thoughts returned to what I had to accomplish before I could leave:

> Foremost, I could not discuss my plan with anyone, not even my closest confidant.
> It could not take place in winter, it would be too cold, it would be slow traveling because of snow, and snow would allow anyone following my tracks to lead right to me. I had also heard stories about people freezing to death trying to cover the miles and miles to the border.
> I figured on late spring, when the weather was a little more stable.

I would only be carrying my rucksack, so anything I wanted to take had to fit in there and I would have to purchase or find whatever else I needed along the way through whatever means were available to me.

I needed a good road map even if I had to sketch it myself; I needed to find a compass with which I could navigate if I needed to.

I had to wipe traces of me clean from my room so no one would be able to find clues as to where I had gone.

Even though most of my travel would be at night, I had to leave the city itself before curfew without being seen.

I studied this plan daily and made changes to anything that looked lacking. I intentionally listened to some of the older patrons who dined with us, sometimes asking what seemed to be stupid questions regarding a specific conversation in order to glean more information about nearby towns or the actual boundaries of East and West Germany. What aided me most during this planning phase was my ability to speak German, Russian, and Polish; these languages enabled me to converse with just about everyone with whom I came in contact. I heard stories of people being shot, or taken prisoner, or sentenced to hard labor. There was one story that struck a chord with me. It was about a young man, around my age, who while in his attempt to climb the barbed wire fence was shot by the Vopo, badly wounded he lay calling for help on the East side of the wall, no one came to help him and he simply bled to death.

As much as I was able to plan about the actual escape, I could not map out what lay on the other side of the border. I did not know how I would live, find work, or even continue my education. Despite all the trepidation that lay before me, the thought of escaping hit me like a blitz throughout my entire body and would not leave me. It came down to timing, good planning, coordinating all the details, and faith in God.

I valued my work at the Schützenhaus; my time in Genthin had given me a chance to feel safe enough to work on my plans and to analyze my situation. Everything that I had endured up until now had also aided me in being able to formulate this expedition.

I felt more confident of my capabilities through my time in the Wehrmacht. My life from the point I left home has been one of struggle and faith; I was no longer a young boy without a care, but a young man living in fear with a dream to be free.

As I worked on my plan, I had to be careful not to arouse any suspicion among those I worked closely with on a daily basis. I had to be very careful whom I talked to or with, for fear I would have been talking to a German who belonged to the communist party, just waiting for the opportunity to have the chance to arrest one of their own countrymen. I was aware of the countless others who had fled the communist regime before me that had indeed made it across the border and knew that if they made it so would I. Daily, I strove to keep a positive attitude and focus on the date I had picked to make my move. "The clock only moves in one direction," therefore I had to move on with my plan and not look back at what I was leaving behind. I could not afford to be bitter or disappointed about what had taken place, I had to focus on the now and my future.

I continued to work and was very watchful of any activities that were new or out of the ordinary in our small network. I took note of any new KGB agents or Russian soldiers that I saw in the area and tried to find out if they were here to stay or just passing through without drawing notice to my questions. When I saw a new influx of KGB agents, it worried me a great deal.

My days off consisted of many hours sitting at the railroad station watching and making notes of the trains that came and went. I noted the Allied trains, mostly British or American that traveled to the west with only a brief stop in Genthin. I talked with the older men who came into the terminal to kill time. From listening to these men, I gleaned vast amounts of wisdom and experience. Several conversations stayed with me, I learned there was a no-man's land between East and West Germany, this is where many died in their attempt to flee. Another time, I found out that on all trains leaving Genthin, that at the last stop before Helmstedt, all passengers' train passes were scrutinized by the Vopos, to avoid that, I knew I would have to get off the train at least two stops before the border to avoid any contact with the patrolling guards and walk the remaining distance. It never bothered me to spend my time there; I had always enjoyed the sound of locomotives so my time passed quickly. I often times had a hard time sleeping after these afternoons. My head would be racing with all I had learned and I would often wake in the middle of the night panic stricken and shivering from the sweat that covered my slim body.

My time was set in stone; as soon as all traces of snow were gone, I would make my move. There was a myriad of things to be taken into consideration so as not to endanger my plan. I went out of my way to keep the Russians, especially the KGB officers happy so I would stay in their graces and from under their microscope. I was in a unique position being able to be around them on a daily basis. I knew some of them were just doing their jobs in fear of Stalin's heavy hand; we had heard of officers and soldiers who without hesitation were eliminated for not following orders.

The seasons soon changed and spring had started to move in. Before I knew it, my plans would become reality. Despite the fact that I was alone, I truly was not alone, because God was always with me and He protected me and spoke to my heart; He said, "Follow me and I'll lead you." I had lived in fear for so many years, now I was on the threshold of a new life. The task in front of me was daunting, but my determination never wavered.

Finally, the day came; I packed my rucksack with all the essentials I thought I needed, extra socks, notes, a small blanket, making sure I left nothing behind that would identify me. I wrote a note to Herr and Frau Neumann about how much I appreciated all the things they had done for me and how sorry I was to be leaving them behind. I knew that Herr Neumann would understand my reasoning about leaving and would agree that I needed to move on. I felt like a coward leaving them without saying goodbye face to face after all they had done for me, but I also knew this was the best way to do it. This way they could truthfully say they knew nothing of my plans until after it had happened. I had filled my sack with dry bread, crackers, carrots and dried beans, I had filled my canteen with water, wore my warmest jacket and my best shoes.

It was mid afternoon in mid April of 1947, when I was able to slip out of the Schützenhaus undetected and took in every aspect of that long beautiful chestnut lined avenue as I walked down it for the last time.

Crossing into West Germany

I made it to the train station on schedule; I had purchased the train pass three days before so I did not have to wait in line with the other passengers. I removed my rucksack so I looked less obvious. I was seriously over dressed; I had on my long underwear, two shirts, a heavy sweater, coat, and a wool hat. I could not carry a koffer and I didn't want to waste what little space I had in my rucksack with clothing so I had no choice. I didn't look altogether out of place though, most passenger trains were poorly heated so many people dressed warmly for their trip. I on the other hand had prepared myself for a very different trip and the apprehension of what lay ahead once I stepped off that train raised my body temperature even higher.

As I stood there waiting for the train to arrive, I could not help but ask myself repeatedly if this was all real? Once everyone heard the locomotive's whistle announcing its pull into the station, there was a rush to the platform. When we were able to board the train, I made sure I sat at a window seat so I could see the names of the towns we passed and pulled into. Within minutes, the train was packed to its capacity. Across from me sat an old man donned with a dilapidated hat and an older woman, whom I assumed was his wife. As the train pulled out of the station, all I could think of was that I was embarking on the most important ride of my life, one that would take me west into the unknown.

As we rolled along, I could not help but think that I had left this station on a train once before over a year ago. That train took me east to a Russian labor camp; I praised the Lord that the one now was taking me west toward <u>freedom!</u> I knew the road ahead would be a rough one, but I hoped I had prepared myself for what I knew and imagined I would have to endure. As the train picked up speed, it was comforting to know that with each passing kilometer I was that much closer to the western border. I desperately wanted to leave all the bad memories of the past five years behind me. Even today, I have a hard time finding a good memory from those years between 1942 and 1947. Now sitting on the train, I prayed that this would be the start of a promising and better future.

To my dismay, the couple across from me attempted to engage me in a conversation. I had hoped that I would not have to talk to anyone for fear of saying the wrong thing. How was I to answer the simplest of questions without looking like I was hiding something? I answered their questions as briefly as I could, trying to memorize what I was saying so it would come out naturally if asked again. I realized that they didn't want to seem rude and just wanted to pass the time chatting with me, but I really did not want to talk to anyone. I wished I could be like some others on the train oblivious to the world, sleeping peacefully even snoring. Some ate homemade sandwiches and talked with their families. I was afraid to open my rucksack for fear of exposing its contents and giving away my intent.

Shortly after the train had left the station, the railway official came to check our train passes. It was a well-known fact that they were all communists and kept an eye out for any traveler that looked suspicious, especially those traveling west. Their arrogant faces gave them all a sort of family resemblance. He checked everyone's passes even those who pretended to be sleeping. When he came to me, a sweat broke out all over my body, he took the pass looked at it and looked at me and to my surprise smiled at me and wished me a good journey. My mind was crowded with the thought of "I've got to be FREE." I know it sounds like a Sammy Davis tune, but I, like so many others who thought it long before he put those words to music, had a very different reason. To have my freedom meant a great deal to me.

The locomotive snuffed, puffed, and occasionally gave out her resounding shrill whistle. Before I knew it, we were making our first stop. I must have been daydreaming and realized I had missed the sign, telling me where we were, I asked the old couple across from me and they told me we were in Parchau. My destination was Bebertal, this is where I planned to get off the train, and I could not go on to Beendorf, which was right by the border for that would be suicidal. After a short stop, the train jerked forward and was once again on its way west.

As the night crept in the train car, the smell of sweet sausages, hard-boiled eggs, strong smelling onions, and the clean crisp smell of cucumbers filled the air as people prepared a picnic sort of supper for themselves. Again, I felt reluctant to open my bag and tried to block out the rumbling in my stomach as the aroma tickled my nostrils.

I couldn't help but think of my note and how the Neumann's had handled my disappearance. I felt sadness in my heart and could only hope that they understood. For a brief moment, I wondered what indeed I had done. I had left a good job, a place to stay, food to eat, people who liked me and cared for me for a fate truly unknown and unpredictable. I visibly shook myself to disperse any ill will, forced myself to look out into the orange sunset of that night in mid April, and imagined my years to come. Little did I know that I would never see Genthin or those that I loved in that town again? I pray that even today, Herr and Frau Neumann are looking down on me from heaven, for that is where they belonged. Holding myself together so as not to cry was a challenge, but I knew that I must remain strong and not give up. At that moment, I was not tied to anybody, and I was almost free.

It was long past midnight when the train finally pulled into the station at Bebertal, where I had decided to get off the train. I asked one of the passengers how far it was to Beendorf and he told me only about seven kilometers. When I asked him more about the town and directions to it, he looked me up and down and commented that he hoped I wasn't planning to go there yet tonight. He added that if I understood that it was close to the East German border and that it was very dangerous. He said that the Vopos and Russians guarded the border, after we were all done talking; he had actually told me more than I wanted to know, but I was glad he did. After we finished talking, he walked off into the night and so did I. This was the start of my walk to freedom. The night was crisp with a full moon shining down to light my way. Through everything I had been told about crossing the border, it was best to do it between two and five o'clock in the morning. I clocked myself, and figured I was able to walk about a kilometer every ten minutes. I estimated that I would be at the border about three o'clock.

I was very aware of my surroundings and always was on the watch for people and for any strange noises. Suddenly, I heard a noise behind me, I saw a pair of headlights, whether it was a car or truck, I did not know. I figured whoever was coming up behind me had to have been either the Volk police or Russian soldiers. On each side of the road was an embankment with low growing shrubs; I quickly made my way into the cover. I prayed I was hidden enough that the headlights would not pick me out as the vehicle passed me. From my hiding place I could make out that the truck was a Soviet Army one, to my relief it kept going on by, once they were farther down the road I made my way onto the roadway again and tried to make up time; minutes had passed and I wanted to be at the border by three o'clock. When the dawn came, I wanted to be in Helmstedt; which was the first city on the west side of the border.

I was full of anxiety; I was on the threshold of a new chapter in my life. As I walked along, I came across a sign that told me I had about two more kilometers to go; I focused my entire energy on that walk. I did not know what to expect at the end of those two kilometers, but I knew that my destiny was to get there. It was about two o'clock now, I wondered whether the guards were sleeping, I sure wanted to. I knew I needed to rest for a moment or two so I could collect my thoughts and regain a little energy. I decided to find a place where I could sit down and eat a piece of dry bread and maybe a carrot. I found a huge tree and arranged myself under it so I was somewhat comfortable. I sat down, took a minute to pray to God for getting me this far, and prayed that He would look out for me the rest of the way.

"Freedom" to me meant more than precious jewels; the road to it required patience, perseverance, courage, faith, and endurance. My life had been full of obstacles, setbacks, mistakes, and disappointments which wore me down and yet I was able to overcome all that. I did not know what lay in store for me. No one does; only the strong survive and move on. I decided it was time for me to get going; I packed up my blanket and my foodstuffs. With my hunger pains satisfied for the time being, I was ready to take on my next challenge and that was to circumvent the village of Beendorf. I wanted to avoid all human contact; my only thought was to cross the border. I inched myself closer to the goal line. In front of me, I heard gunshots and I threw myself to the ground. My imagination took over and in it; I saw dozens of people being gunned down as they tried to run across the no man's land. Was this really happening? Would I make it? I was scared. In the distance, I could see powerful searchlights sweeping the landscape.

These beams swept in a full 360-degree circle illuminating everything in its path. I lay there frozen too scared to move, even to breathe. What was I going to do? I had come this far I knew I did not want to go back. How could I face Herr Neumann if I went back, would he even take me back in? I was sure by now the KGB or the Russian regulars to the restaurant had asked about me, I was sure I would be arrested by the KGB if I went back to Genthin; I had to go through with what I had started.

The night rapidly changed, the clouds and stars had gone away along with the moonlight, and I was left in utter darkness. Despair had overcome me to the point where I had to sit or lay down to gather my nerves together. I came across a cluster of pine trees, in which I took refuge. I knew I had to regain my composure in order for me to cover that last kilometer. It had been a long tiring day. My brain was crowded with millions of thoughts and questions spinning around it. If I was able to cross the border safely, I had about six kilometers to go on the other side before I came to Helmstedt; I figured I had about an hour and a half to go. My courage or lack thereof would not let me walk that last kilometer that night, it sickened me to be that close and not be able to finish my task, I told myself I would have to wait it out. The night became eerily silent not even the trees made any noise.

In the silent darkness, I heard the sound of a train. I knew that freight trains as well as passenger trains went into West Germany, maybe this was my chance. I figured the train was no more than a half-kilometer from me, but jumping onto a train was risky and I knew there were soldiers guarding the trains, this was not a good idea. I knew I would not be able to spend the rest of the night out in the open I needed to find some shelter. A new day was almost dawning, the village of Beendorf was on my left, and I could see its scattered homes dotting the horizon. I faintly hear the crow of a rooster, which brought back fond memories of my grandparents' farm; it had to be a good omen. Where there were roosters, there were barns. Barns meant shelter for the night, shelter where I could spend the night undetected and undisturbed.

I told myself to be patient that something would come along. God had once again answered my prayers. As I walked closer to where I had heard the rooster crow, I did indeed find a barn, albeit a little worse for wear from artillery shelling. Even though it was missing some of its fundamental structure, the shelter it provided was immensely better than sleeping under a pine tree. To me that night, it was like being in a palace.

As the sun crept up to greet the new day I inspected my temporary lodging and found it to be quite a bit bigger than what I had thought it to be from the outside. I was grateful for that, the size of it would allow me to hide out and rest until I was ready to move on. As I looked for a place to lay my tired body, I inadvertently startled a set of doves, which sent up a cloud of dust and feathers. They cooed excitedly at me and I whispered that I was sorry and would try not to bother them again. I found my way to the hayloft. The hay smelled musty, but I did not care, I was safer than being outside or even being on the ground floor where I had a better chance of being found out. My chief concern was would I be able to stay out of sight once the day came into full swing. I settled into a little nest I had made for myself and was within seconds asleep. I don't know exactly how long I slept but when I woke up, it was late afternoon. To say the least I was extremely relieved to have slept that long. That meant I had not been found out and my goal was once again within reach. My body was now recharged, but I was hungry. My food supplies were low and without a clear idea of where my next meal would come from, I ate sparingly. As I ate I watched the sun set and once again thanked the Lord for getting me this far.

Now that I was rested, I knew nothing would keep me from crossing the border bar being shot. I wanted to reassure myself of my position and the area and that meant I needed to talk to someone, so I could reinforce my plans. I cautiously left the barn, doing a visual swipe of the exterior before I stepped foot out of the barn. My father had always told me that I could trust a farmer so I decided to approach the nearest farmstead. As I neared the property, I heard the mooing of cows, which meant there was life and that there probably was someone home. As I neared their gate, I noticed an older woman coming out of the cow barn. I called out "Guten Abend" (Good Evening) and asked if I could speak with her and she told me to stay where I was, that she would get her husband. A short while later he came out and told me that this area was patrolled by Russian soldiers at all hours of the day because of its proximity to the border. He stated that it was not a good idea for us to be talking outside, and we went into a small shed. We stood inside this wood filled shed and he asked me my name, what I was doing, where I came from, and many other questions, which I cautiously answered. He was surprised that I was willing to take the risk of crossing the border. He recounted that just the day before two people had been shot while trying to cross, one was killed and the other was wounded. When happenings like this occurred, the word spread quickly in the small village, mostly, so farmers as these could pass the warnings along to those who got the bug to flee.

Our conversation was interrupted when his wife called for him to come inside. He was gracious enough to invite me in to his home. The farmer's wife was taken aback when I walked into their home. They had just about been ready to sit down to their evening meal and invited me to sit and enjoy their meal with them. The only payment they would accept was answers to questions that they had. I knew that if I told them too much, about what I was planning to do, I would be putting them in danger, so I answered their questions with caution. As I discussed my predicament, I could see that the farmer understood my determination. To my amazement, he informed me that he knew the area around the border and the guard activities pretty well. He told me that the best time to cross was after midnight and to keep to the northwest once I was on the other side. Once across about two more kilometers, I would come onto a bend in the road and that is where the trains slow down because of the danger of derailment, I could jump the train there if I wanted to. He indicated where I should plan to cross the border, which was as far away from the watchtowers as I could get and still get across. The farmer had helped many others cross, but he was careful to tell me that this was not a foolproof plan, just one that had helped in the past.

The farmer's wife while we had been talking put together a bag of food for me to take along until I got myself settled. Just before it was time to leave, we all said a prayer for my safety and that of others who had this need to be free. I left the farmhouse with tears in my eyes and determination in my heart. I followed the directions the farmer had given me and it was almost midnight when I set out on the last part of this journey. Under the cover of the night sky, I walked down a narrow country road and across a field. Tonight I would have liked the night not to have been so illuminated by the moon and stars. I would have preferred to have been crossing these open spaces during a night of low visibility. With each step, I prayed that I would take another.

With about two hundred meters to go, I came upon the searchlights I had seen the previous night. As bright as they seemed from two miles away, it is almost impossible to describe how bright they were this up close. I was sure I could never escape their stark white fingers that seemed to reach for me that night. Just as my courage seemed to slip away from me, a cloud covered up the moon; once again, God was looking down at me; it was as if He had covered up the moon with His hand. With my next step, I figured I was in no man's land and I quickly increased my pace, staying low, I covered the open area. Soon, I came across the markers denoting that I was at the border, my heart was pounding sending adrenaline to my legs, and I started to run. I had to run across a great expanse of open area to be out of danger. Before I knew it, I had crossed the border and I was in West Germany, my legs hadn't gotten the message as quickly as my brain did and for a moment, I could not stop running.

I tripped on something and went down. I scrambled to a nearby tree and lay on the ground thanking God over and over again about how grateful I was for all His help. I thought at that moment my heart would jump out of my chest. I don't know how long I sat there, but the sound of gunshots in the distance brought me back to reality. I quickly prayed that whoever was being shot at had survived and would live to see the <u>freedom</u> and feel the sensation of crossing that imaginary border.

With each step I took, the reality that I was free sank in. I slowly regained control over my body. It had been a grueling journey, but one of hope. As I walked down the road, I thought of this proverb:

> *"In his mind, a man plans his course,*
> *but the Lord directs his steps."*

Proverbs 15:9

The Road to Freedom

Freedom is not really free. It has its price and everyone who wants it has to pay. For generations countries have strived and fought for their freedom only to pay a high price for it. I left my footprints in East Germany forever; I remember Genthin and my time there very vividly. Now that I had gotten this far, my next goal was to get to Helmstedt. According to the directions the farmer had given me, I only had a few kilometers to go. To get to the bend where the trains had to slow down, I had to go to the northwest. I was relieved that in this foreign terrain, I had my compass, or so I thought I did. I searched my pockets and my rucksack, but to no avail. I retraced my steps in my mind and surmised that I must have lost it when I was running those last meters. I was now forced to rely on the sun as my guide.

I had kept the Omega watch that the Russian Kommandant had given me and I checked the time. It was only two o'clock in the morning. I quickly worked my way down the road. Every so often, I had to stop because my right leg was bothering me from when I fell. It was an annoying pain. To describe it would be to say it was a stinging biting pain. I had to take my rucksack off my shoulder in order for me to sit down under a tall pine tree. I leaned up against the trunk so I could support my back and stretch out my legs. The area on which I was sitting was soft with pine needles and very comfortable. The tension my body had been holding in for the past several months just seemed to seep out of me into those pine needles. I don't remember the last time I felt this sense of relief. I knew I wasn't totally out of danger but for the time being, I allowed myself the rest.

The approaching rumbling of an oncoming train shook me out of my revelry. That train was due around three o'clock; I forgot the pain in my legs and started to run in the direction of the sound. As I came around the bend, I had to slide down a slight embankment toward the tracks. I was happy that the moon had come out again and my way was illuminated. I knew this had to be a freight train, because passenger trains did not run at night. As it started to round the bend, I could see it was a long train and the thought of what I had to do made my heart pound. I stepped back out of the sight of the locomotive and waited in the shadows until enough cars had passed me that the engineer would not notice me hop onto one of the platforms between the cars. I had never done this before, but I knew I was to run along side the train matching my speed to its, and then when I found my chance to hop sideways into an open train car. Before I knew it, I had done it! I was exuberant! Out of all the train rides I had been on in my young life, this was the most exciting one I would ever experience. I was on my own type of "freedom train."

I sat there clutching my meager possessions and reflected on how I was heading west into a future that I hoped would be bright, yet very unknown. I stood up and held onto the edges thinking of the words my mother often told me, "Don't ever give up!" I never did. I took a moment to reflect on all those who gave up their lives in the quest for freedom and those who fought and won the right to be free. After I said a little prayer of thanks, I thought of the Chinese proverb that reads; "The journey of a thousand miles begins with the first step." I took this step and was on the road to fulfilling my dreams. Riding on that train car on that early morning, I took the opportunity to breathe in the fresh air, I was too excited to sleep; I was afraid I would miss something. I was not sure if the train actually stopped in Helmstedt, I had to be ready to jump from the train if it came to that.

I had hoped to see the sunrise on my first day of freedom, instead as the train clacked along down the tracks the rain started to fall. I was distressed to see the rain turn into a downpour, would I be able to see my 'stop'. I wasn't sure and I did not want to miss it, for I was not sure where I would end up. I looked at my watch and to my astonishment a great deal of time had passed, I was sure we had passed by Helmstedt. Well, we were still heading west so at least that was okay. Where we stopped, I would have to figure it out when the time came. My patience was finally rewarded, the rain stopped and I was able to see the last seconds of the sunrise. I took a deep breath and decided to jump off the train. When I landed, it was near a small wooded area. I wished I had my compass, but I didn't have it and would have to rely on my instincts. I moved on down the tracks in the same direction in which the train went. The sun felt good on my back and took the dampness out of my clothing. As I walked along my leg once again began to bother me. I had been on the go for almost twenty-four hours and I was exhausted. A soft wind had begun to blow sending the huge boughs into motion creating a nature's symphony. It was very soothing. I decided to get off the tracks in case another train came along, I still had no desire to be seen by anyone out here in the open; to do so I had to climb up another embankment.

I decided I had to play it safe, I had no clue where I was, all I did know was that I had to get somewhere comfortable so I could take care of my aching leg. I found a comfortable spot, removed my blanket from my rucksack, and wrapped it around my rapidly chilling body. I must have dozed off. A rustling in the brush woke me. I looked at my watch to find it was mid afternoon. The sound that had woke me, I heard again, I sat upright and looked around me and was startled to find an old man with a long white beard walking in my direction. For some reason his sudden appearance seemed to paralyze me. He was soon standing in front of me. He must have realized that I was frightened and was quick to assure me that everything was going to be all right. He explained to me that he often came to this secluded area to meditate in the beauty of the valley spread out below us. Slowly I took in what he was saying as I forced myself to wake up.

I waited for the inevitable question as to what I was doing sleeping in the open. I am sure he knew why I was there, but I did not want to jeopardize anything so I just stated that I was taking a rest after a long walk. He called my bluff a little by stating that he had seen me walking earlier along the railroad tracks and had wondered where I had disappeared to. I could not help but wonder who this man was and what he wanted of me. I decided I wanted to be on an even playing field with this man and attempted to stand up, but my leg betrayed me and I stumbled backward against the tree. The man looked worried and asked me if I was hurt. He asked me if I had hurt myself jumping from the train. I asked myself again, who this man was. He stated that he had seen people seriously hurt and even occasionally killed jumping from the trains that ran into West Germany. I decided he knew enough about me to explain my situation to him.

He told me I had nothing to be afraid of, which relieved me somewhat. I asked where I was and what the next town was that I would be coming to. He told me the village in the valley was Bockboden, which was on the outskirts of Harzmountain, which coincidentally was where his farm was. He asked where I was headed and when I told him Helmstedt, he informed me that I was about twenty-five kilometers south west of it, I knew I was going to veer somewhat off course without my compass, but I had not thought I would get that lost. The man asked me to trust him and to come with him down to the village. I agreed to accompany him and we slowly made our way down the hillside. As we walked along, I realized why I had not noticed the settlement; it was on the other side of the hill and through a dense stand of woods. By the time we made it to the bottom, it was late afternoon and the sun had started to set. I looked back to see this huge fireball sinking into the horizon, quietly putting an ending on another day of freedom. I caught myself looking over my shoulder frequently, as did my companion. He assured me I was safe and that there were no Russians here. As we navigated our way through the trees, I could tell that the man obviously knew his way around the area pretty well, which put me at ease. As we neared the hamlet, I took a moment to reflect on its beautiful setting; a few scattered homes, a small lake with its mirror like surface reflecting the thatched roofs and setting sun.

We walked down a well-trodden path, before entering the small village. He stopped and asked me if I was still afraid, I answered without hesitation that I wasn't. The thatched roofs reminded me of back home. As we neared the homes, I could make out the soft lighting emanating from inside them giving the area a warm welcoming atmosphere. By the time we reached his small farm, I was limping pretty badly. As we walked up to his door, his wife opened it for us, having watched us come down the lane. Excitedly she asked her husband where he had been. He admonished her with a single glance and a quick acknowledgement of my presence by stating that he had brought a guest home. Just like that, she turned to me and graciously welcomed me into their home. Once inside she asked her husband where he had found me. He told her where and that I needed help. She held her hand out to me and I gratefully took it in both of mine.

The wonderful smell of supper made my mouth water. The man's wife told me to have a seat, she stated she had made her husband's favorite stew and I was welcome to share it with them. We sat at a small table and bowed our heads and the old man said grace. I could not believe how fortunate I was, my last hot meal was almost forty-eight hours ago. It took all my restraint not to devour the delicious plateful of food like a savage. By now, I had grown accustomed to divulging my story to strangers and after supper, I told my story. They asked me many questions about the war and the Russians and we compared stories about those that had suffered. The night grew late and they without question or hesitation insisted that I spend the night with them. I felt at peace with them and accepted their invitation.

By the time, I had finished my stories; I realized that my leg no longer hurt me. Having eliminated a serious injury, I figured I must have pulled something and would heal given rest. The next morning I helped with simple chores and over breakfast learned that they had lost their son in the war. I stayed with this wonderful couple for two and a half days, after which I had become restless, wanting to continue my journey toward my new life. They were saddened to see me leave, but willing to help in whatever way they could. I once again set out with food and essentials I would need until I could fend for myself.

I felt like a shard that has been tossed from shore to shore endlessly drifting until fate determines its final destination. The farmer knew I wanted to get to Helmstedt and intuition must have told him I didn't have enough money for a train ticket and he pressed a few German marks into my hand and after one last request that I stay with them a little longer, he wished me a safe trip. He walked away. It was a glorious day as I walked the four kilometers to the train station on that chilly April day in 1947. It was almost impossible not to skip down the road as I realized that it had only been three days since I had crossed the border.

My fate rested once again like the rucksack on my shoulders. It had been almost four years since I had left my home in Tarnowskie-Góry. I had been forced to leave my parents and my brother and sisters. As I rode along I could not help but wonder if they were alright, and if they wondered about me. These thoughts were never far out of my head, but I had no way of learning the answers. I once again thanked God for all the help I had gotten over the past four years from people who had nothing to gain by helping me, but a place in heaven. I was now in a country where I could start over without fear and without attachments. My mother's words echoed in my head forcing me never to give up no matter what. I soon was in Helmstedt, penniless, but with hope and the knowledge that I was free; I had accomplished my mission. The impossible had become the possible. Perseverance had paid off; my life was now to change forever.

Alone in Helmstedt

Helmstedt was founded in 900 AD and was located in the British zone, after the partition of Germany following World War II. The city was located in lower Saxony in the Federal Republic of Germany. What was amazing is that it was virtually untouched by any bombings, mostly because there was no significant industry in the city. It was a beautiful old city, which housed the oldest university in Europe. The school was built in the sixteenth century in the Renaissance style. Helmstedt served as a frontier post and a checkpoint between East and West Germany near the main autobahn to Berlin.

I had chosen Helmstedt to be the location where I would start my new life. I had to set my priorities and make the most important decisions of my young life. Some of these choices were spontaneous while others required some thought; some were satisfying and some were not. I had no home to go to and was starting out with nothing, my provisions were gone and I had begun to wonder where I would find my next meal, but I did not let any of this create any roadblocks that I knew I could not overcome. Helmstedt became the crossroad of my new life. I began to wonder how I would find work or continue my education without any personal identification, I had no way of proving who I was; this indeed became a major concern for me. I had all these concerns and very few answers to any of them.

I wandered around the city and during one of my excursions I came across a large container in the back of a small hotel. Today it would be called a dumpster. I had never seen one before, and after struggling to lift the lid I climbed into the container only to find to my salvation; it contained cast off food. I picked out what I was familiar with, but I was stupefied by a strange item. I could tell it was some sort of fruit and I took a chance and tasted it; later I was to find out it was a banana. I had heard of bananas, but unlike today they were not very popular and their availability was limited in Poland. Another piece of strange treat I came across was sour yet sweet. It was a grapefruit. You might think that this is a juvenile recollection, but you have to remember this was a different world. Back then, everything was limited and new. As I was feasting on my dumpster buffet, I happened to look up and noticed I was being watched by a British soldier on the second floor of the hotel. He called down to me in English; all I could make out was hungry. Of all the languages I spoke, English was not one of them. I looked up at him and answered, "Ja, ich bin hungry." With that, he disappeared inside his room only to reappear with an armload of food which he showered down on me. It was as if I was receiving 'manna' from heaven. What a lucky day it turned out to be, and how grateful I was.

With my hunger satisfied, I took up my task of looking for work. Unemployment was the common state here as it was in every other town in Europe after the war. As I checked out the employment situation in Helmstedt, I found my choices to be rather limited. The city only housed two small hotels, one really was not a hotel, but more like the British headquarters, and the other was not hiring. I had checked in with the police to see what kind of options I had and to my surprise, they found me a place to stay. It was a homeless shelter. They also suggested that I venture outside the city limits to the British army base about four kilometers out of the city, there I was told I might find work.

The next day I set out with an air of confidence with the expectation of finding a job. As I approached the compound gate, I took a moment to compose myself. I summoned up my resolve and confronted the sentries on duty. The two British guards stood next to a wooden booth and were armed with rifles. One walked the front of the fence line making regimented sharp turns at each end of the gate. I walked up to the soldier standing guard at the gate and asked to see the director of personnel, he replied in a language I did not understand and I again stated my reason for being there. I realized that the language barrier would be a major problem in me getting inside these gates. The police had told me that the building I was looking for was at the far end of the base and the director's name was Herr Muller. Over and over, I repeated that I needed to see the personnel director, Herr Muller. The guard finally became frustrated with me, stepped inside the booth, cranked up a strange looking device, and spoke into it. I was not afraid, just frustrated. I had no reason to fear these soldiers as I did the Russians, I just had to be patient and wait for someone to come who could help me. After what felt like an eternity, the guard stepped out of the booth and told me that Herr Muller would be coming up directly. Even though he spoke in English, I listened to his words and realized what he was telling me was what I wanted to hear, so I relaxed and waited.

It did not take long before I saw a man exiting one of the buildings. He walked across the expanse supporting himself on two crutches. After speaking briefly to the guards, he motioned to me to come with him. As I passed the sentries, I remembered my manners and said thank you. I followed the man, who I could only presume was Herr Muller to his office. He indicated I should sit down and proceeded to ask me a whole list of questions, such as how I got to Helmstedt and the like. It turned out to be a long interview by the time I was able to answer all his questions. He sat there a moment seemingly to take it all in, when at length he indicated that he had a position for me, if I was willing to take it. He told me I would be working in the base kitchen and made me promise to learn to speak English, so I could take direction with little supervision. I promised I would do my best, and felt it could not be that hard, since I already knew three languages, I was sure I could learn English too. We talked a lot that afternoon, I was surprised to learn he had been a major in the Luftwaffe and had flown ME-109s. He lost his leg when he was shot down at Normandy on D-day and the result was a lifetime disability. I shared the horrors of a POW camp with him although mine was in the hands of the Russians and his time was under British rule, which I was to learn was much more humane.

I was given a space with another German, who I was to learn had served the war on a u-boat. He spoke English well and it was part of his job to see I learned as much English as I could as quickly as I could. He too had survived a POW camp and the Holocaust. His parents had been killed during the war and this endeared me to him. We got along well and I absorbed the English language like a sponge. During the days that followed, I marveled once more at my great fortune of finding work as well as a place to stay in a strange country.

My time in the camp's kitchen was one marvel after another. I was exposed to food I never knew existed and quantities for which most Germans I knew had never seen. After a few days I was summoned to the director's office and told that I would be assuming new duties in the 'officer's mess'. He was pleased with the progress of my English. I was outfitted with a very formal stylish uniform and told to report to the quartermaster, Major Taylor; at this point, I became an official employee of the second South Staffordshire Regiment. I learned a great deal professionally during my time on that base and that knowledge contributed immensely to my career.

I was liked by most of the officers, but one, Captain Smith always seemed to have something to complain about. One day his toast would be too light and the next too dark, he constantly yelled at me about one thing or another. One of the most fascinating events that I was allowed to witness, as a spectator was their polo matches. It was exciting to watch the officers riding their horses, swinging their long handled mallets in attempts to drive a small wooden ball through their opponent's goal. I felt sorry for their horses, however, they often rode them to the point of exhaustion. I was allowed to watch the games as long as I waited on the ladies who attended. I served them English tea and French pastries on the patio of the officer's quarters. These women, this culture fascinated me. I loved their way of dress, very formal, very colorful; many times, I felt as though I was walking around in a dream.

My days were long and full, my roommate made sure I was on time even on the days when I wanted to sleep in. He taught me punctuality, dependability, and above all to be immaculately presentable. As fast as I was picking up the new language, I wished sometimes that I had a magic wand that I could wave which would make my English flawless, so I sounded as professional as I hoped I looked and acted. I liked my job and was able to save up the money I earned so that someday I would be able to support myself. With the encouragement of my roommate, I studied harder and made good progress.

Several weeks into my time there, rumors began to spread that the base would be shutting down; I began to wonder what would happen to me if this became a reality. Over the next few days, I realized that many of the British officers were already gone. Finally, the day came when I was told the Officers Mess would be closed, I cannot say I missed Captain Smith with his constant demands from me, but I did miss my work. Eventually, the base did finally post its closing date; Herr Muller met with me to give me my last paycheck and I thanked him for giving me the opportunity to get my feet back on the ground. With a sad heart and weary mind, I once again found myself on the move into an uncertain future.

I walked those long four kilometers back into Helmstedt and made a stop at the Hotel Petzold hoping that there was an opening there I could fill, but I had no luck finding work. The owner suggested I head over to Brunswick about 35 kilometers northwest of Helmstedt. I had been able to save some money working on the base and put it towards a train ticket. Brunswick or Braunschweig as it was known then was one of the oldest cities in Germany dating back to 1031. I did not know much about this city nor did anyone who I talked to about it; but to be honest, I really didn't care; I just wanted to find a way to support myself and needed a place to live. When I arrived in Brunswick, I was shocked to see there was no railroad structure there. The terminal or station lay in ruins; another example of the devastation of the war. Everywhere I looked, I could see evidence that this city had not been spared and if I stayed here, I would be around constant reminders of the horrors these people too had suffered. I knew I had to forge on, whether it be here or somewhere else, I could not go back to where I had come from. Experience had taught me that perseverance would pay off and I would indeed find a way to make it.

I asked people I came across where the police station was and once inside prepared myself to tell my 'life story' once again to strangers. Germany was still a police state and people had to register when they moved to a new town. I recalled that the people for whom I worked in Mutzel, Herr and Frau Georg Kegel, once said they would someday move back to Braunschweig. I told the police officer this and he looked their names up in the large ledger that was kept for this very reason. Within minutes, he found their names and wrote down their address for me. As I walked through the city, I was saddened to see this obviously beautiful city reduced to rubble and ruin. The horrible war screamed out at you with every turn. I came across war wounded limping around the streets or trying to maneuver in wheelchairs among the debris. I wondered if this war ravaged city had anything to offer, but I had faith that it did and was not about to give up until I had exhausted every opportunity.

As the sun set, the shadows cast grotesque images against the buildings from the misshapen piles of bent metal and brick. I was glad it was not yet dark or traveling through the city would have been a horrifying ordeal. Following the directions given to me, I came to what looked like a desolated street. Every building I passed had windows broken out and cracks running down the walls. I had to question myself whether people were actually living here. Just as I was about to turn back a woman exited out of one of the buildings, I rushed up to her and asked her if I had the right address. She looked at my slip of paper and confirmed I was in the right place, I asked her if she knew Herr Kegel. Obviously she did, her eyes lit up like diamonds. She told me they were her friends and lived on the fifth floor of the building. She said she had to rush off to see her daughter and left me standing in the street looking up at the building.

I started up the formidable task of climbing the five flights of stairs and finally rested on the last landing letting my heart rest after this arduous workout. I was appalled at the conditions in which these people were living and once again wondered if there was anything here for me. I hesitantly knocked on the door, having gotten no response I knocked again a little more forcefully. I was just about to leave when a timid voice called out from the other side, "Wer ist dort?" (Who is there?) I said Günther, you knew me in Magdeburg. The door opened and there stood Frau Kegel. She cried out in surprise and quickly invited me inside the apartment. I asked her where her husband was and she indicated that he was working at a restaurant as a waiter about three blocks away, but I could wait for him and that he would be home in a few hours.

Frau Kegel was amazed to see me again. We relived some of our experiences at the Hotel in Auschwitz back in 1943. Herr Kegel was the hotel reception manager and she was Herr Kleinert's secretary. It was a joyful reunion albeit bittersweet. She apologized for the cramped quarters in which she and her husband now lived, but I thought she had done wonders with what little they had. She explained to me that this apartment used to take up the whole fifth floor, but with the current housing shortage, it had been renovated into three smaller ones. She related to me how many families were crammed into almost impossible living conditions many times without heat or electricity. She warned me that food was in short supply and in order to buy even the basic staples one had to stand in long lines hoping that there would be some left when it came to be your turn.

We had just started to talk about all that had happened over the past three years when we heard footsteps in the foyer. She got up stating that that should be Herr Kegel and rushed to open the door for him. She whispered to him that they had a guest and when he rounded the corner, I could see he was surprised to see me sitting there in his little apartment. He hadn't changed too much over the years, a few more wrinkles perhaps and a little less hair, but the same sparkle shone out of his eyes as he greeted me. His wife left us alone to catch up as she set about putting together their evening meal. As we caught up on everything, I expressed my condolences when he told me his only son, Winfred had been killed just six weeks before the war had ended. I felt a pang of sorrow when I heard this; this young man and I were the same age. Without hesitation, he insisted I stay with them for as long as I needed to, that somehow they would make room for me. I had known this family for a long time and I knew he was a kind and generous man, someone I could surely count on. Just before I laid my tired body down on what would be my bed for a while, Herr Kegel assured me he could find me a job at the restaurant and I should accompany him the next day when he went to work.

The following morning I woke full of hope and energy. After a light breakfast, Herr Kegel and I walked the short distance to the restaurant where he worked as the headwaiter. He took me at once to the owner and after introducing us, left us to have our first conversation. After a short interview, I was told I would work in both the kitchen and in the restaurant as a waiter. I thanked the owner, Herr Krone and practically skipped with joy back to the apartment. The next day I arrived at the Restaurant Krone to work my first day in the kitchen. I was surprised despite the shortage of supplies that they served many meat dishes. Little did I know at the beginning that the Salisbury steaks, meatloaves and in even the cut steaks were indeed horsemeat. I was a little apprehensive about serving it, but the people did not seem to mind and I got over it. The restaurant was very popular; in fact, people would stand in lines well before it opened. People from every walk of life stood there with their 'food stamp' in hand and waited until they could be seated. Without this food stamp, they could not have a table. The government at that time allocated only a precious few of these stamps, only the amount they deemed necessary, but more could be found on the black market like so many other things one could not buy out in the open.

I was thankful for what I had and made sure to let the Lord know it daily. The Kegels' had made a spot for me in the foyer and even rigged up a curtain so I had a sense of privacy. I was thankful that I had a place to sleep and a job with which I could support myself. I insisted that I pay the Kegels' rent for my space and reluctantly they took it. I walked to and from work with Herr Kegel each day over which time we became quite comfortable around each other.

As I became more familiar with the workings of the restaurant's kitchen the chef taught me the art of cutting proper steaks out of huge sides of horsemeat. They left nothing go to waste, what could not be cut into steaks or roasts was ground up for patties or loaves. I never really got over serving horsemeat at the restaurant, but I figured that if hundreds of people could eat it every day, I could too. As much as I enjoyed the chaos in the kitchen, I equally enjoyed my time on the 'floor' with the public. I was quick with my service and seemed to be an asset to Herr Kegel. I became friends with many of the patrons and was rewarded with a good deal of tips. I made enough money to pay my rent and support myself comfortably; I didn't need much to get by. I took pride in being able to outfit myself with clothing bought on the black market, I had always liked to look my best.

Over the weeks, I learned more of what had happened to this historical city. Braunschweig had been hit by repeated heavy air raids, which left over ninety percent of the city destroyed; over 3,000 people were estimated to have died during those raids. There was no way this city could ever be rebuilt to its former glory and that was truly a shame.

With each day that passed, I grew to care deeply for Herr and Frau Kegel. They were good to me and supported my decisions as though I was their own son. What they could not do however, was relieve the pain and loneliness that constantly plagued me deep down inside. I hadn't seen my parents now for almost five years and from what I had been hearing I was not certain when the time would come that I could safely travel to Poland to reunite with them. It was difficult to cope when I would turn melancholy over these thoughts, but I did the best I could.

After a few weeks, I was granted a day off and took this opportunity to travel back to Helmstedt. I needed to escape from this ugliness if only for a day. I liked Helmstedt and would have preferred to have stayed there had circumstances been different; it reminded me so much of my hometown. I went back to the Hotel Petzold in hopes that there was a job opening and to my astonishment, there was. The owner, Herr Duebner, indicated that they needed help in the kitchen and if I would be willing to help them out. What could I say?! I loved this city; I jumped at the chance to leave the dreariness of Brunswick. I told him I would be able to start in two days and caught the train home.

Once back at the apartment I had the awesome task of informing the Kegels of what had transpired. I felt sorry for them and almost wished I had not made the commitment I did, but I knew I had to do what I thought was best for me. I thanked them repeatedly for all they had done for me and they understood. They were wonderful people who had suffered so much, yet were willing to help those in need. The next day I left this caring couple never to see them again. I think often about them even after six decades, they were truly people of God and one more set to add to the list of unsung heroes who helped without a thought for themselves.

Helmstedt 1947

Once I arrived back in Helmstedt, I knew immediately that this was a town I was going to like. I reported that very same day to the owner of the Hotel Petzold, Herr Karl Duebner. I was expected and greeted warmly. While standing in the hotel lobby, his wife joined us and she too welcomed me to their staff. I was little disappointed that I would not be living in the hotel itself, this always had made for convenience on everyone's part, but they explained that they needed all of their forty-eight rooms for guests. I was not to worry though; Herr Duebner had arranged for me to board with a nice older couple that he knew. I would be renting a small room on the second floor of their spacious three-story house. My quarters were within walking distance to the hotel, only approximately fifteen minutes away.

The hotel was charming surrounded by chestnut trees with carriage buildings on the backside where in years past, guests could park their carriages and board their horses as well. What made the hotel so inviting was its lobby. It housed a small concierge desk and behind it, one could see the hotel's telephone system with the plug-in and plug out cables. The rooms were charming and each uniquely furnished. The hotel had been put together with care and with thoughts geared toward the guest's comfort. The hotel had maintained this look for years and the owners were certain of the fact that if they were to change even the smallest detail, they would lose business. The hotel had a very unique personality. Above the reception desk a sign hung suspended from the ceiling which stated that English was spoken there which made it appealing to travelers from every country; France, Britain, Germany, Poland, the Americas and of course Russia. Helmstedt had become the city of hope.

As the day wore on, I realized that I wanted to see where I would be living and whom I would be living with. I had an overwhelming desire to be settled once again. I walked along the road toward this house and marveled how this small town differed from Brunswick, it was like a day and night comparison. Where Brunswick had been ravaged by the war and still bore its scars almost two years later, Helmstedt had been spared. I had had a brief time when I was last there to find out some of the city's history. I knew it housed a museum and had been built in the medieval times and still sported very beautiful rich architecture of the time. I easily found the address of my new residence and took a moment to step back and take it all in. The house sat on a hillside with other buildings around it. The houses were set in a circle with the open space to be shared by the neighborhood. I found out later that this space housed an open-air market during the day.

I knocked on the door and a very pleasant couple opened it to me. I was invited in and found I liked them from the very moment I laid eyes on them. My room as I was told was on the second floor of the house. It was a small room, but I liked it a lot. They had set me up with a large feather bed with two large pillows, a table and chairs, and a tall wardrobe, and a pitcher and bowl with which I could wash up, I had to go downstairs to use the bathroom. This would take some forethought on my part, but I did not think there would be a problem attending to my personal needs in this arrangement. My accommodations greatly exceeded any expectations I had; I was to live in luxury. I took my time getting settled in for I did not have to report to work until the next day.

The next day I reported for work in the hotel's kitchen, I was to assist Herr Duebner's mother and aunt; the two women ran the kitchen. I had never worked for women before and figured that it would take a little time getting adjusted to it. During my interview Herr Duebner had promised me that if I worked for him for two years without any problems, he would see to it that I would be able to attend college in Switzerland. My goal now was to impress this man with what I could do and to learn everything that his establishment could teach me. One obstacle was the fact that I did not have my high school diploma and I had yet to complete my apprenticeship.

I needed a plan and a means to achieve it. Herr Kleinert often said to me, "Implementing ideas without a plan is just plain foolishness." I knew I could not waste my time; I needed to take advantage of every opportunity I got and stay focused.

First and foremost, I had to work hard and follow instructions, so Herr Duebner would not find a reason to let me go.

Second, be the most dependable and loyal employee he had ever had.

Third, study and learn as much as possible through those around me.

Fourth, earn my high school diploma.

Fifth, complete my apprenticeship.

Sixth, save money for college.

Seventh, prepare for college,

To accomplish all this I had to use my time very wisely. Over the months, I found it took a lot of work and a great deal of perseverance. My fears about working under the ladies in the kitchen worked out quite well. I learned quickly to follow their orders to the letter for if I didn't, I was given additional chores; the chore I disliked the most was scrubbing the pots and pans.

Herr and Frau Duebner were the salt of the earth. They were compassionate, honest, professional, and articulate. They had a wonderful sense of humor and everyone who knew them respected them immensely. They helped me overcome my shortcomings. With their help, I further developed my proficiency of the German language. They boosted my self-esteem and confidence level. My life was very fulfilling and rewarding in many ways. Each day I took a new breath of "Freedom" and savored it as it coursed through my body.

For the first time in a long time, I could truly support myself. I knew I did not have to beg or rely on anyone to provide for me. Each day became precious to me with each new thing I learned and each step I took closer to my goal of going to college. I strove to remain true to my core values and ethos my parents had instilled in me with their words and through their actions. Never giving up had become the very foundation I had built on since I was forced to leave home and has stayed with me all these years. Prayer had gotten me this far and I knew it would get me even farther. I had faced challenges and mastered them. My faith stayed firm and with it, I knew nothing was impossible.

I was happy with my job and enjoyed working with those around me. I knew I had to look out for myself; I had no one else to do it for me. I knew my parents had their own lives to deal with and I had to do things for myself. Sometimes, I had to force my courage to the top of my personality and I allowed my enthusiasm and faith to be my stepping stones; without them I would have never been able to achieve all I had set out to do. To fulfill my agreement with the Duebner's I was to work six days out of the week; they were long days, sometimes too long. I tried never to complain as I didn't want anyone to know I had weaknesses.

It was now December of 1947, another Christmas was fast approaching, and it would be my fifth one without my family. It had been difficult sleepwalking through the holidays, while those around me celebrated with friends and family. The war had so drastically changed my life and it took all my will to overcome it. Loneliness at times is a soul's greatest enemy and I tried to fight it off as best I could.

Herr and Frau Duebner kept true to their promise and enabled me to continue my education. I was making good progress and Herr Duebner was pleased with my overall performance and I was enrolled in the Helmstedt Gymnasium (an academic high school) so I could prepare for college. Through his tutelage, I was able to complete my apprenticeship, which consisted of working in my field for the required three years, having finally achieved this I submitted my documentation to the chamber of commerce and in turn received my certificate. At that time, I felt very empowered and relieved that it was finally over.

One evening in my room I went over my list of goals and realized that even though I was working long hours in the restaurant, I had been able to finish high school and complete my apprenticeship. I had been putting my 'college' money into a special savings account, which Herr Duebner promised to match toward my higher education if I continued to work for them for two more years.

I enjoyed my work in the kitchen alongside the two fine chefs with which I worked. I also enjoyed working in the restaurant itself. The Hotel Petzold had a reputation for fine cuisine and excellent service and wonderful accommodations. My time there seemed to fly by in a blink of an eye, and the world around me continued to change.

In June of 1948, the German mark hit an all time low. It had been devalued and no matter how many thousands of the old marks one had. Every citizen was given forty 'new' German marks. The once empty shops now were stocked to the brim seemingly overnight; the black market was out of business. The hotel took advantage of this and bought the finest products it could find to continue to produce the finest dishes in the area. The hotel was located near the autobahn to Berlin and anyone who traveled it would surely stop in Helmstedt and would have to stay at the only functioning hotel in town.

We had the reputation of being a melting pot of nationalities and strove to live up to our draw. That summer we had the honor of having a renowned Russian born actress staying at the hotel, her name was Olga Chekhova. She and her entourage took up several rooms in the hotel. Every day we had to work around the onslaught of reporters who jammed our lobby hoping to catch a glimpse of this actress and anyone else of importance that ventured off the autobahn in search of a good meal and a place to rest. To say the least, the experiences I had the fortune of working at the Hotel Petzold were some of the greatest of my life.

I truly felt that God had a purpose for me being there, not only was I helping people, but most of all through Him, they were helping me to recover and regain my composure and ability to move on with my life. This time here provided for my future and helped me put my past behind me for a while.

When the Iron Curtain fell after World War II reporters flocked in from every country and gathered in or around the hotel to report on the latest and dramatic developments on the East German border. When there were no rooms available, they gladly paid to sleep on the floor in the lobby and sometimes in their cars so they would not miss anything. There were times during these two years, when I thought another war was ready to break out. Relations between the two super powers, the Soviet Union and the United States, were strained and everyone had to work through the cold war. No one knew how long any of this would last, only time would tell. Trains with British and American soldiers frequently passed through Helmstedt only to be held up for hours by the Russians at the border checkpoint. People in Helmstedt had reason to fear that their close proximity to the border could bring repercussions down on them. I was worried that my situation could turn for the worse and I might not be able to go to college. I confided my fears to Herr Duebner who assured me that everything would work out and that I should not worry so much. We were filled to the brim with reporters; they had even camped out in tents just to be close to any developments on the autobahn or at the border.

I had accomplished just about all my goals and had added one, and that was to learn French. In my studies, I had excelled in German as well as in the culinary arts. With having such a strong background in the hospitality industry and apparently I had a knack for it, I wanted this to be my long-term career; everything I had accomplished so far was simply a stepping-stone towards my future. I was impressed with the patience afforded to me by Herr Duebner; this made me work and study even harder so I would impress him in whatever I did. Without my parents to guide me, I only had Herr Duebner to rely on and I trusted him without hesitation. I knew the best person I had at my disposal to teach me French was our Maitre D' at the Hotel, Herr Helge; he had become my confidant when I needed to talk. My greatest enemy was my loneliness, I had written my parents in Tarnowskie-Góry, but I had yet to hear from them in return. I knew my letters would be censored, so I was extremely careful of what I would write, often times when I could spare it, I would send along with the letter a little money, which I later learned they never received.

I knew that at some point, there would be a light at the end of this dark tunnel, but I had the determination to forge on with my life and toward my goals. My mother had ingrained in me four words, "truth, honesty, respect, and integrity" (THRY). She had told me time and time again that if I followed her advice I would be able to make it through anything no matter how difficult it got to be. It was now the end of the summer of my second year in Helmstedt and it was time to start making plans for my college education. Herr Duebner was a graduate of the renowned Ecole Hoteliere de Lausanne Academic and Executive Programmes, and he recommended that this was the school in which I should enroll. The Ecole Hotelier was founded in 1893 by the Swiss Hotelier, Jacques Tschumi in Lausanne Switzerland. Students attended the school from all over the world, but there was one hitch, in order for me to be considered I had to have a solid knowledge of, and be able to converse in the French language. He did some asking around and found a couple that frequented the restaurant who would help tutor me in the language. Three times a week I would attend 'classes' with this couple. The Pohl's were both Professors and Dr's of philosophy and taught at the University of Prag. They had escaped from Czechoslovakia to Germany before Hitler invaded their country and had at that time settled in Helmstedt. Madam Dr. Pohl spoke impeccable French and three days a week she had me mimic her pronunciations repeatedly until I got them perfect; she was a very good teacher. The Ecole Hotelier was and still is one of the world's most respected schools majoring in hospitality management. Madam Dr. Pohl shared Herr Duebner's and my dream that I attend the school and because of that, she was extremely strict with me and my lessons. I have to give her credit though; she had an enormous amount of patience with my French grammar, which I sometimes confused between the Russian, German, and my parent language, Polish. She was always there, would quickly correct me, and kept me in line. Madam Pohl greatly influenced my life and to a great extent reinforced the importance of me continuing my education. I have to admit that I wasn't always a diligent student; my studies often times took a distant second place behind my work. I had to work, I had no one else to support me, and I had to keep my commitments that I had made to Herr Duebner. Madam Pohl understood my priorities and found ways that I could work and study at the same time or in the time I had to allow for it.

There were many nights I would get home after ten o'clock and have to stay up for hours studying my lessons, which my teacher had left for me. I was determined to master this language. However, with all the hard work and studying there suddenly was a huge cloud overshadowing Helmstedt as well as West Berlin; another war looked like it was on the horizon. The Russians had imposed a complete blockade on West Berlin and had cut off access to Berlin from West Germany, which cut off supplies of food and other commodities to West Berlin. In the summer of 1948, General Lucius Clay, the Military Governor of the American troops issued a declaration that with the aid of the British and French troops they would organize the largest airlift operation to bring supplies to West Berlin. As a result, over a thousand cargo planes both American and British flew over the skies of Helmstedt every minute; this went on for sixteen months. Their mission was to supply West Berlin with food, medicine, coal, oil, and fuel. The drone of the cargo planes was awesome and sometimes I feel I can still hear them flying overhead. Many American and British pilots lost their lives in the call of duty. I don't know what was more fascinating, watching the planes or the reporters scrambling over each other as well as rooftops in an effort to get that one 'money shot'.

Over time things got back to normal and people went on with their lives. I had submitted my application to the Ecole Hotelier de Lausanne, but it was rejected on two grounds; as I had feared, my French did not meet their standards and the other was because I had served in the German Wehrmacht. Both Herr Duebner and Madam Dr. Pohl were very upset by this and they both wrote letters to the German ambassador in Switzerland explaining my situation. Finally, after several long excruciating weeks, Herr Duebner received a letter back from the German ambassador my application had been reconsidered and I had been accepted, but there was a catch, I had to pay the entire two years tuition in advance. I was elated that I had been accepted. With the tuition money I had from my tips and earnings, along with the money that Herr Duebner had put away, I had more than enough in the bank to cover it. After we figured out how much I needed, we found that I had enough to purchase a motorcycle, which I had had my eye on; it was a Horex Regina 400 ccm, with lots of chrome. I wanted transportation that would be fuel-efficient yet powerful enough to navigate up the steep Swiss Alps with ease.

I could hardly believe that I had achieved this major goal in my young life. All the hard work and patience on everyone's part had paid off. The Duebner's were extremely proud of me, they had no children, and I became like a son to them. I cannot say enough about Professors Herr and Madam Pohl; to do them justice they actually need a chapter all to themselves. Before I left for Switzerland, Madam Pohl presented me with two books from her private collection; "Les Femmes, *Leur Condition*." They are leather bound with gold accents; they were printed in France in 1803. I still have them today in my own library of over 2,000 books and every time I see them, I think of her and everything she did for me to get me where I am today.

When it came time to leave, I found it extremely difficult. Out of all the people I had known over the past five years, this town and these people seemed to have gone way beyond what they had to, their efforts changed my life forever. As I packed my belongings, I tried to 'pack' the good memories of all the people who had opened their doors and hearts to me. People whom without their unfailing support and encouragement I would have never made it. Most of my possessions I shipped by rail to Switzerland; I only took with me what I could fit into the saddlebags of my Horex Regina. One cool morning, I mounted my motorcycle and with a gentle kick, I drove off, and with tears in my eyes, I left Helmstedt behind me. Mark Twain once wrote,

"Courage is not the lack of fear; it is acting in spite of it."

Switzerland 1948-1953

After a nerve-racking battle for an entry visa to Switzerland and the acceptance to the Ecole Hoteliere de Lausanne, I was now on my way to Switzerland. My Horex Regina became my companion and I trusted her with my life. Since I had left Helmstedt, I had crossed the major part of West Germany into Baden-Baden, a luxurious spa resort and then through the mountainous Black Forest to Switzerland itself. Crossing the border from West Germany to Switzerland presented no problem whatsoever, the border guards found my passport and visa in good order and I was now in a country that only God could have created. Everywhere I traveled, I found nothing but beauty, such as I never knew existed. There were lush green forests, against the brilliance of the peaks of the Swiss alps, it was all so exhilarating; I relished every moment of it, but most of all I relished my freedom.

I remember vividly crossing the border. It was a gorgeous day with deep blue skies laced with light cotton like clouds moving across the Swiss Alps. I told my Regina that we had to stop and admire the spectacular work of God. I paused for a moment and I actually thought I was dreaming. I had lived in Poland and I had seen the invasion of our country by the Nazis army and subsequently lived through the horrible war, but it seemed that my reward was the beauty I was now witnessing. There was so much to see and absorb. When I crossed the border I have to confess, I considered myself the luckiest man in the world.

Switzerland rode into the twentieth century still on bicycles, steam trains, and steamboats; wondering about the horseless carriage and dreaming of vehicles that could fly; that was Switzerland in 1949. Switzerland lived in tranquility despite the developments, which surrounded this country. It was a quiet country of slopes, lakes, and whose people enjoyed living in seclusion. Even though the country had its industry, some still tended their goats on mountainsides. The people I met spoke a mix of languages Italian, French, German, and something called Romanch. I could speak German and French, but how was I to hold my own with Italian and Romanch?

I enjoyed riding as the day ended; riding into the spectacular rays of the setting sun was exhilarating. One evening I found a small hamlet where the curling smoke from their chimneys dissolved into the crisp clear air. I had no idea how long I would be staying in Switzerland, but I hoped this was an omen of things to come. I let the beauty awaken my spirit. The towns and villages were adorned with flower boxes overflowing with radiant beauty. I thanked the Lord with every kilometer I added to my odometer for this wonderful gift He had allowed me to see.

Soon I passed St. Gall; it was named for an Irishman, St. Gallus who as a missionary came to this mountainous region in 614 AD to live out his days. The area I learned was a mix of Catholic, Protestants, and Jews, but unlike many places at this time in our lives, these people found a way to live in peace with each other. I was told by the natives not to miss the abbey of St. Gall, so I made time for a visit. I could not wait to see the architecture, the Swiss acclaimed that this was the finest Baroque church in Switzerland; the abbey did not disappoint.

From there, I drove on to Zurich. Zurich was the Bohemian capital of Switzerland. This city was the home to many famous outlanders such as Thomas Mann, Wagner, Lenin, and

Einstein. This city was big enough to get lost in and I did. Instead of letting me stay lost and alone, I let the friendliness of the Zurich people put me on the right track and draw me out of my shell. I wanted to stay, but this was not my destination and I had to move on. From here I was to go on to Bern, I had almost taken another route, and I am glad I didn't. Just when I thought I would not see anything more lovely than I had already, I came to Bern. Its vistas of pleasant hill suburbs were visible everywhere. The mountains that surrounded it were dotted with vibrant green forests standing out against the white peaks of the Oberland. I was mesmerized and actually found it hard to move on. I took stock of my timeline and realized that I had two days until school started, so I decided to stay the night just outside of Bern. I found a small boarding house, which let me park my precious Horex under their porch. One of my lessons with Professor Pohl was the study of Swiss hotels. She impressed on me that no matter how large or small the hotel was, they took pride in their establishments and I would have a hard time putting one over the other. The Pension where I stayed that night was clean, comfortable, and well serviced. Refreshed after a good night's rest, I woke in time to watch the glorious sunrise setting the peaks of the mountaintops on fire, it was an awesome sight.

As I neared my destination of Lausanne, in the French side of Switzerland, I could eventually make out the cathedral of Lausanne in the distance. It seemed to pull me toward it. It was early September of 1949 when I drove around the Lac Leman with the cathedral in the background, I was amazed at its beauty; it was like being in a totally different world. In Lausanne, almost everyone spoke French. Once again, I was eternally grateful to Professor Pohl for her tutelage. My command of the language allowed me to move around this city undeterred. I had to rewire my brain immediately, so as not to stand out as a foreigner does. Streets became "rue d bourg," avenues "de la paix"; thank you was "merci bien." For a while, I let myself forget the German language, to enable me to engulf myself in the culture completely. I enjoyed the French language, it sounded like music to my ears. Lausanne called itself the city of youth; it attracted the offspring of potentates and the children of cinema 'royalty'. Education was its major business, which attracted students from every corner of the world. I learned later that as a lad, Adlai Stevenson attended a school nearby in Ouchy on Lac Leman, Hercules is even credited for founding the city "eh bien!" (So good!)

I could not wait to enroll in my classes. My admission papers were checked and rechecked and my life was to change drastically. All the students were called by their last name, which I found a little odd, I evolved from Herr Skaletz into Monsieur Skaletz, and it took some getting used to. At nights, I often marveled how far I had come from a naive boy in Tarnowskie-Góry, almost six years ago. All I had was my faith and prayers to keep me going, I definitely was not preordained from birth to make a success of myself, but I knew if I was going to make something of my future it was totally up to me to do it.

Ecole Hoteliere de Lausanne

I faced all my courses with anticipation and a desire to excel; one course stood in my way and that was swimming. I had never swam much as a child and hadn't at all as a young adult, this course was mandatory and I had to face another daunting challenge that I knew I would do whatever it took to learn how. I took the initiative to go to the city's public pool in my free time to take lessons. When our swim classes began at the university, we were taken to a mountain lake; there was no tippy toeing into the lake, we were to jump in from a high board into the icy water. It was to say the least extremely invigorating and rewarding to be able to do it at all.

At school, I was interested in and challenged by all my studies. Our instructors taught in either the French or the German language it took a lot of effort to keep up. I knew my money would not hold up forever so I set out to find a part time job, I found a position at the commons, working in the kitchen, this meant free meals, which was a relief from my tight budget; it didn't pay much, but it supplemented my meager savings and lifestyle. When I wasn't working at my job or studying, I helped out in the school library, this fed my addiction to the printed word; I often times was found reading instead of doing the task assigned to me and would get in trouble with my supervisor because of it. Sometimes I was envious of my fellow students who came from well to do families who did not have to work to support themselves, but I found that book learning is not enough to get by in the world. One needed knowledge of the real world if they were going to make it in life.

I enjoyed my time in the library and even enjoyed the quirkiness of the head librarian, Madam Chapuliere. She would sit behind the pulpit shaped desk tapping the tops of the library cards, adjusting her nameplate and staring out at the patrons over her spectacles; her glare could scare any seasoned soldier. She had been in charge of the library at that time for forty-one years. My goal was to appease her with my work and my knowledge of the inventory and where the books were located so when someone needed assistance I could provide it without hesitation. I had heard rumors that Madam Chapulier rather enjoyed running shivering assistants home in tears for something as trivial as a book out of line on a shelf. Very often, she would launch her corseted figure to the magazine rack to check if any of the slick publications were slipping from their designated slots. She could move around the library without a sound and would often be up behind you before you heard even a rustle of a petticoat. She was meticulous in everything she did whether it was the orderliness of the main room or the calligraphy on the index cards. Penmanship was a highly treasured skill and represented the person who could accomplish it a true artist; I have often tried to replicate it, but I never achieved her level of expertise. Mostly, she was a wonderful woman and I valued the experience of being surrounded by so many books, which gave me a life long appreciation for literature of every kind. Even today, to the dismay of my wife Elaine, I hate to part with a book and if I have to it puts me into a type of depression. My time there wasn't always stressed, there was another librarian, we called her Madam Joyeux, and she was always a joy to be around. Whenever she would catch me reading when I was supposed to be working, she would 'walk' the other way. I enjoyed my time at the library, it paid for the cost of textbooks and then some.

There was no on-campus housing; I found a small room to rent on the Rue de la Cathedrale near the beautiful cathedral. The landlady was Mademoiselle De Duvalle, a spinster with a good heart and a soft smile. She called me by my middle name, Franz or Monsieur Françoise. I had been very fortunate in my selection of benefactors, so many of them filled the void in my life left by the absence of my parents, and Mademoiselle was another one that fit this image.

The university opened my eyes and soul to a completely new world; this was my new beginning, I had put a period on my past at last. It didn't matter where you came from once you stepped foot into the school's domain, everyone was given duties to perform in the kitchen as a cook's apprentice; peeling potatoes, cleaning vegetables, setting the tables in the dining room, washing and sanitizing the wares, etc. Our formal dining room accepted guests from the outside. They expected and were served only the best. Which we provided in a very professional manner. Our professors impressed on us that there was only one way to do things and that was the right way. In the kitchen and dining areas, we learned by actual hands on experiences; one couldn't learn these skills from a book or lecture hall.

Academically I struggled, but I tried every day to live up to the expectations of everyone who had gotten me to this point, especially Herr Duebner. I persevered and made my grades. What I truly enjoyed doing and what I excelled at was dealing with people. My classmates urged me to run for class president, I threw my name in the ring. This was a new challenge for me; I was never really political, but like everything else, I had accomplished so far, I found out what I had to do to succeed and I did it. I campaigned and was voted president of my fraternity. During my reign I developed organizational abilities, planned various school activities, and encouraged students to work together on some school related extra curricular activities. All these skills helped me later, I was to find, in my management positions.

The two years I spent at the Ecole Hotelier De Lausanne were well spent. I not only learned the culinary arts, but also the basics of accounting, marketing, production, finance, behavioral science, and management control. I was able to hone my analytic skills and it sharpened my communication abilities.

There were times however, when I admit I became star struck by some of my classmates. I had never been this close to those in the limelight. Many of the students were sons of luminaries and famous hotel business leaders, I read about their families all the time in the Swiss newspapers. While at the school I met a fine young man named Kurt Ason whose family owned two hotels in Austria. We became inseparable friends. He was Austrian and even though I could speak German, we both struggled with our French so we had a common bond between us, which enabled us to get along quite well.

During the summer break, he asked me to come to Austria to spend the vacation with him and his parents. I had to turn down his invitation however, I needed and wanted to work for the summer and had found a position as a waiter at a resort complex called the Montreux there in Switzerland. This lakeside Rivera was set in the midst of rolling meadows in the shadow of sheltering mountains. In Montreux, there were numerous hotels, but I was fortunate enough to find a position at one of the most prestigious the Montreux Palace. Many days, the loneliness would seep into my body, when I allowed myself to give in to the self-pity of having no family to go back to during the off months. However, as always I survived these soul-wrenching attacks and moved on with my life.

I was content with riding to work each day on my trustworthy Horex Regina enjoying the freedom of the open road. After only one week at the Montreux Palace, I was promoted from 'demi chef de rang' to 'chef de rang' by the general manager, Monsieur Pezzola. Since my motorcycle was frowned upon by the elite clientele of the area, I was given a room in the attic of the hotel and my meals were included in my wages, allowing me to save time and money by not having to commute or pay for food.

I worked there for two months of the summer break and made enough money to pay for my final year of tuition. Soon it was time for classes to resume and I looked forward to catching up with my friend Kurt as well as my other classmates who had left the area for the summer.

With Kurt's arrival back on campus came an offer to come work for his family at one of their hotels once I graduated; I was honored at the offer, the Sacher Hotel in Austria was well renowned. With this possibility came the responsibility to focus all my energy on my education. I needed to use my time wisely and acquire as much information as possible in the short time I had at this institution.

On my days off, which there were few, I would often stroll down the Place St. Francois, the Place du Chateau to the place de la Palud, and eventually end up at the Rue de Bourge the main street of shops in the town just bustling with life. The shops that lined this area were stocked with the finest merchandise from all over the globe. What a treat this was to be able to select what you wanted out in the open, there was no need for the black market; everything was legal and legitimate. As always I was in awe of the architecture that surrounded me, having only vivid memories of destruction and hunger in my young life, this was a refreshing change.

I looked forward to the new semester. What I enjoyed the most was that there was a great deal of reading assignments, both in German and French, which allowed me to strengthen my proficiency in both languages. My favorite subject was mathematics. Product knowledge was stressed with great importance, as it was one of the major areas of a good executive chef or manager. Being able to stay within one's budget and getting the best quality and value of a product was an integral part of anyone in the hospitality business. One of the most important required courses to be sure, was Food Safety, I remember a statement made by our professor, "Where there is no food safety, there is death." How true this was then and in today's technically advanced age. Over my career, I had witnessed many a foolish food safety decision on the part of an establishment's management or head chef, some resulting in serious consequences, but the lessons taught through these mistakes in judgment were more valuable than any classroom training session. During my time at the Ecole De Lausanne, I managed to take just about every course offered on its curriculum; I wanted to be the most trained chef or manager entering the arena. The motto I chose to live by was, "No matter how much you know there is never enough of what you know."

All too soon, we were counting down the weeks until graduation. It was truly hard to believe I was even here, much less finishing my education and mapping out my future. I had planned to pass on the offer presented to me by my good friend Kurt, and had decided to move on south into the Italian part of Switzerland. I felt confident that I had studied hard, even though I had not made the honor roll, I felt I had built a solid foundation for my future. During the last year at the school, I worked at the Excelsior Hotel in Lausanne, as a waiter. This allowed me to put money away to achieve my goals.

The experiences and skills I acquired in Switzerland were embedded in my very core. Our teachers stressed this point over and over again that, "Discipline molds a man's life. To be disciplined means to be self-controlled." The Ecole de Lausanne had a reputation for producing great chefs and managers and being disciplined is a major component to their successes. The four years I spent at the Lausanne were great ones and I hoped I had used my time wisely. I had a treasure trove of knowledge and was eager to use it.

When I had a chance I made the effort to visit Herr and Frau Duebner and Professors Pohl, they were pleased with my progress and I professed my extreme gratitude to them for allowing me this opportunity. The day of my graduation came and I walked away with a Bachelors Degree in the Science of Culinary Arts and Management. I was now able to venture out into a world with hopes of achieving dreams that my parents never had a chance to living in Poland. I had made many friends during these past few years and many of them invited me to visit them. If I would have accepted them all, I would still be traveling all over the world today. After graduation, I took some time off to enjoy the company of my friend Kurt. We traveled the countryside of Switzerland.

Switzerland
(Loosely based on the *"The Pathless Woods,"* by Lord Byron)
There was a pleasure in these pathless woods,
there was a rapture in great and lonely hills,
there is a society where none intruded.
By the cascades and music in their Alps,
still I liked a place a damn sight!
More when it has cows, a chapel to pray,
some homely cots, a library of lore

Kurt and I canvassed the country. From Lausanne, we visited Lugano, Locarno, onto Monaco, then to Milano and Insbruck and eventually into Salzburg and Wien. I was constantly struck by the beauty of this region, which had no fame of yielding gold or silver, but only its wealth of natural radiance. This area with its bursting abundance of emerald forests, turquoise waters fed by nearby ageless glaciers, endless pastures of blooming radiance all highlighted with brilliant startling sunlight. Gazing upon this beautiful, magical landscape it was easy to believe that God's power had been at work painting this magnificent canvass for all who ventured to share in it.

After graduation, I spent a few weeks in Wein (Vienna) at the Hotel Sacher, which was owned by Kurt's parents. They allowed me to work in all the areas of the hotel where I was able to hone my skills and find my areas of weakness. I reveled in the musical ambiance of Johann Strauss it was a wonderful experience. After a few weeks, I decided it was time to leave, I was eager to begin my new life. As much as I was looking forward to getting out on my own, it was hard to say goodbye to my dear friend and confidant.

After my 'vacation', I found a position at the Davos, one of the largest Alpine resorts in Europe. The Davos boasted that it had one of the longest ski runs and one of the largest ice rinks ever; its ski instruction included many of the area schools even I learned to ski and enjoyed the recreational sport. In the winter, the population of the town doubled the villages combined and became as international as London, Paris, or Cairo; along the promenade, all the Berlitz languages could be heard. I also worked in some of the resorts in St. Moritz. One season I worked at the Wagnerian Castle, it was one of the greatest experiences of my life. I relished the atmosphere in which I had the pleasure of working, its great lounges magnificently paneled and chandeliered, amidst it all were many treasures among them a controversial Raphael Madonna and child. I thanked God every day that I had this opportunity to living a life that many only hope to.

My sojourn in Switzerland had been very rewarding, very fulfilling, intellectually challenging and stimulating. Before I left Switzerland, I had yet to accomplish one more goal and that was to have the watch, which was given to me by the Russian officer as a gift, appraised. I went to the famous Omega watch company and talked to one of the sons. He was astounded that someone as young as I was possessed a watch as fine as this one. He asked me how I came upon having it and I told him it was a gift from a KGB officer. He asked me if I wanted to sell it, even though I could have used the money, I declined his offer. I still own this watch and it hangs framed in my 'library' in my home.

From here, I moved on to Paris and found a position with the Hotel Ruiz de Paris where I continued my formal education in the hospitality realm. I worked under the renowned Maitre de Cuisine who taught me the finer arts of nouvelle cuisine, as well as the basics of making the fine sauces. Cooking is truly an art as well as a science and I had the privilege of working with some of the best 'scientists and artists' around. A master chef and excellent professor de cuisine, Sigmund Freud once said that a well-spent life rests on successful engagement with arbeit and liebe – work and love. Both require difficult choices and neither is made easier by the abundance of possibilities open to those of status. For me, finding my life's vocation was crucial and had been my goal since I was a young teen. No matter how difficult times were for me, I stayed focused on my future. I did however, find a chance to revisit Helmstedt in 1953 for its 1000th anniversary. I received a special commemorative plaque from the city's Burgermeister. I relish it to this day, I owed a lot to this city, it gave me my new life after my escape from East Germany; I should have been giving them a plaque.

The Tree
By Günther F. Skaletz

The tree
That never had to fight
For the sun and sky and the air and light
But stood out in the open plain and always got its
Share of rain, never became a forest king.
The man who never had to fight
To win his share of sun and sky and air and light

Never became a manly man, but lived and died as he began.
Good timber does not grow easy
The stronger the winds, the tougher the tree
(Adversity isn't always all bad)

E Plu-Ri-Bus U-Num
(Out of many, one)

"Talent develops in quiet, alone; character is sharpened
in the torrent of the world."

A New Start in Frankfurt

My next step was to move on to Frankfurt, to learn more and to craft a better professional future. I arrived in the city of Frankfurt Am Main in September of 1953. I rode into the city on my trusty Horex Regina, and reported to the well-known Hotel Frankfurter-Hof. I was to check in as soon as I got to town and in doing so presented my credentials to the director of the hotel who I met in his spacious and elegantly furnished windowless office. I was met by an impeccably dressed man, Herr Wachs in many ways reminded me of my first boss and guardian Herr Kleinert. He took his time looking through everything I had documented over the past few years; the places I worked at in Switzerland, my graduating from the Ecole de Lausanne. He stopped looking at my accomplishments when he got to the Hotel Beau Rivage; he sat there looking at me without saying a word. Slowly and deliberately, he removed a cigarette from an etui and causally tapped it on his fingernail before lighting it. I racked my brain to think of a reason why he would have a problem with anything in my portfolio. The silence in the great office was suffocating; I loathed the feeling of sitting in this tomb of a room. Herr Wachs finally broke the silence with a question, which he asked me in French, "Ah bien, sie haben gute refrences." I was startled to hear him speak in French and answered "Merci Monsieur." The next time he spoke he did so in German, I was relieved that he did not throw English at me, for I knew very little of that.

Our conversation was cordial and rather lengthy. He asked me many of the same questions to which I had quickly become accustomed to answering. Herr Wachs politely indicated that even though my credentials and references were very good, he was reluctant to hire me because of my age. After a slight pause for inward cogitation, he said that he would be willing to help me find a job in a smaller hotel. With indignation in my voice, I let him know how disappointed I was with his decision not to hire me. He sympathized with my situation and assured me that he would make some phone calls on my behalf and asked that I wait for him in the grand lobby. I sat in the enormous elegantly styled lobby as though I was sitting on hot coals. Here I was, ready to enter the field of my choosing with a degree from one of the finest schools in Europe and I had been turned down for a job I truly wanted and deserved; I was devastated. Where would I go from here, I didn't want to be without work long, I didn't want to use up my savings and prayed that this was only a minor set back.

Just when I thought my nerves would snap, a bellman dressed in an impeccable uniform approached me and asked me if I was Mr. Skaletz? I answered that I was and he motioned for me to follow him. Once again, I found myself in the director's office. When I approached Herr Wachs, with a smile he apologized for having made me wait so long. He told me that he had contacted a colleague of his who was the director of a small but very prestigious hotel in Konigstein Im Taunus. He told me where I was to go and that I was to report to a Herr Jordan who would be expecting me. I thanked him for all his help and once more was on the road to places unknown. The town of Koenigstein was about forty-five kilometers north of Frankfurt Am Main. I was relieved to have a job waiting for me, but I had to admit that I was extremely disappointed with the turn of events. At first, I thought that maybe I should go back to Switzerland, where I knew I could find a job without question or reservation, but I decided along my drive to accept my commitment and move forward. Along the drive, I stopped at the Carlton Hotel in hopes there was an opening, but to my dismay, I was told there were no openings and that unemployment was very high due to the war. If the wind was right, one could still smell the acrid smoke that drifted off the ruins and destruction left by shelling. As much as I thought I wanted to go back to Switzerland, I really couldn't since my visa had expired.

After talking to some of the town's folk in Frankfurt I learned that there was a housing shortage as well as high unemployment. Sometimes I wondered if the war would ever stop haunting me. Soon I was on my way to Koenigstein in the Harz mountain region. It did not take me long to get there and I rode into town just as the sun had begun to set. The sight I beheld was like holding a jewel in my hand; I thought I was dreaming as I rode into town. As the sun went down, it set the mountaintops on fire putting the countryside in a golden glow. Riding into town, I could see that the war had not touched this hamlet and I reveled in the lure of the ancient magnificent buildings that rose up on either side of me.

I found the hotel with little effort. The Haus der Lander was situated so that it overlooked the medieval village below it. I later learned its legacy was that it was once the summer residence of Baron de Rothschild's family. They lived most of the year in a chateau in Frankfurt, but summered in this beautiful home in Koenigstein. Current history was that for a short time, it was occupied by the American army, but they had left it virtually undamaged; upon their leaving, it was renovated into a hotel state. It became popular when it started to host meetings of various ministers from West Germany and the United States.

The hotel's director, Herr Jordan greeted me cordially. I know I mention how people were dressed back in those times, but it always amazed me that despite all the hardships, people still stuck to their dress codes and requirements no matter how much it took to do so. Herr Jordan's 'uniform' was black striped trousers, white shirt, silver tie and a black jacket. He confirmed that I had a position with the hotel, which included room and board as long as I worked for him. I would be sharing a room with a young man from Barcelona, Spain; he too was a graduate from the Ecole de Lausanne, his name was Fernando. Quickly, I realized how fortunate I was once again. It did not take long to realize that the detour I had to take from Frankfurt was worth the 'pain'.

Once again, I was surrounded by delicious and impeccably prepared dishes full of unexpected flavor combinations. I later learned that these combinations would become a true chef's cuisine signature. The chef's main objective was to provide the best in culinary arts and I knew that my time at the Haus der Lander would prove to be a true privilege. I came out of school thinking like many new graduates, that I knew it all, but as time went on, I realized I still had a lot to learn. Like one of the great master chefs of France, Monsieur Escoffier (chef of the kings), once said; "It's not the food that makes the plate, it's the art in the way it is presented." I was determined to chart my own course, to watch and learn each day. I never let myself get overwhelmed, I did not give up when I had nothing, and I was surely not going to give up now that everything I had been working for was within my sight. I never questioned whether I could do it, but always how I would do it.

Two thousand years ago, the prophet who said, "Man doth not live by bread alone" knew that man always had a need for spiritual sustenance. Down through the ages when men gathered around a table to eat, they gathered together for more than food. There is the social aspect of it whether it be casual, formal or an occasion; everything we did had to fit one of these purposes. Managers and chefs worth their salt understood this truth and strove to fill the needs of their patrons. Cooking definitely is an art and rightfully so. It draws on imagination and skill of the well-trained chef in order to achieve success. Not everyone though reaches that pinnacle. Many feel that the art has been sacrificed to the scientific community; I agree to a point, but a true chef will still rely on his experiences and preferences; hands on is still the best policy of a great culinary maestro.

At the Ecole de Lausanne, we studied animal anatomy to better understand the different parts of an animal in order to cook each part to perfection. Learning the techniques as I did was one thing, but I had to put it into practice and make sure people liked my output. What made the process of learning this complicated craft even more interesting was learning how the various equipment worked and of course learning new techniques to accomplish old standards. I remember as a child I always hung around in the kitchen helping my stepmother prepare the meals whenever possible. I cleaned vegetables, helped with the prep work for potato pancakes and dumplings, which we served the family. I not only was allowed to help cook, but I was also made to help with the clean up as this was and is a large part of the process.

While in Koenigstein at the Hotel Haus der Lander, my life took another turn. The atmosphere was more sophisticated, intimate, and elegant. My role there was a dual one; this was part of the agreement. I was to work for three days in the dining room or at reception and three days in the kitchen. I knew I was going to love working there. The people were interesting and the job was challenging. What I enjoyed most were the people who frequented the hotel, on one occasion the German Chancellor himself, Konrad Adenauer dined there. On this occasion, I not only helped prepare the final formal dinner, but I was chosen to supervise the service of the seven-course dinner that was served. From start to finish this was a rewarding challenging assignment.

I mentioned earlier that I had a roommate, Fernando, even though he spoke very little German we somehow managed to communicate quite well. What drew us to each other is that when we worked together we had a good time doing anything that was assigned to us. I was surprised to learn that he had been sent here to learn, his parents owned a hotel in Barcelona, and he extended to me a job offer many times during our time together. No matter how interesting my job was here at the Haus der Lander, I had my eyes set on the Hotel Frankfurter-hof. It held one of the highest rankings in Germany.

Before I knew it, I was celebrating my three-month anniversary at the Haus der Lander and once again, it was Christmas time. On one of my days off, I jumped on my Horex Regina and drove back to Frankfurt to check in with the director, Herr Wachs at the Frankfurter-hof. The day I set out it was a cold and snowy day, but I was determined to cover the distance on my motorcycle even though it would be a rough ride. Once there I asked if I could have a minute or two of the director's time. I waited and allowed myself to warm up in the beautiful lobby. It did not take long and I was ushered into his office. He was surprised to see me and asked what he could do for me. I took the moment to express my gratitude for all he had done for me and told him how my job was going at the Haus der Lander, but I also took the opportunity to tell him that I still wanted a position at his Hotel. He listened to me with a stony look on his face, after I finished he let the silence gather between us, after a moment I realized that I was holding my breath waiting for his response. Finally, he took a deep breath and indicated that maybe he had a job for me after all at his establishment. No one could have given me a better Christmas present. We talked a little longer and I decided I had better head back before it got too dark and the weather turned for the worse.

I drove back to the Haus der Lander without a second thought to the road conditions. All the way back, I was thinking how I was going to break the news to Herr Jordan. Immediately upon my return, I sought him out and explained what had been offered to me. I gave him my two weeks notice, which allowed me to work through the Christmas holiday for him, which he appreciated.

I left the Haus der Lander for Frankfurt in January of 1954. Frankfurt had endured Allied bombing raids and about eighty percent of the city had been flattened in 1944. The inner city still showed vast destruction and the rebuilding was a slow process. After the war, Frankfurt became the 'Cradle of Democracy' in Germany. I would be working at the historical hotel, which was owned by the Steigenberger family who founded the Frankurter-hof at the turn of the century. The Steigenberger family had deep roots in the hospitality business and the hotel had lodged many luminaries such as Konrad Adenauer, Chancellor of Germany; Willy Brandt, the Ober Burgermeister of West Berlin who later became the Chancellor of Germany; just to name a few. I was excited at this opportunity and I knew that it would have an enormous impact on my career. However, my first priority was to find a place to live. In the cold, I scoured the city, but there were few places available. For two days, I rented a small room in a partially damaged hotel. I was finally able to find a place to stay just outside the city limits, about five kilometers from the hotel.

I got settled in and tried to figure out how I was going to get around in the winter, I knew I would not be able to continue to travel the roadways on my motorcycle. When I posed my dilemma to my landlord, he suggested a place where I could store my bike for the winter. I then found I was able to use the streetcar to and from work in the mornings and most nights, on the nights I had to work late, I had no choice but to walk the five kilometers back to my room. I didn't mind walking, usually I enjoyed walking through the brightly illuminated inner city, however the part I did not relish was the walk outside the city limits where it was pitch dark. I had heard reports of people being robbed and sometimes killed walking alone, and I never dAllied around, I was extremely relieved when I would be sitting on my bed in my room. I knew if I intended to stay at the Frankfurter-hof, I would need to find a place to stay inside the city limits. After several months of walking too and from work, I finally found a large room in the center of the city about fifteen minutes from the hotel. The building held three families who shared one kitchen and a single bath. I felt fortunate however to have stumbled upon this opportunity and paid dearly for the convenience.

I liked my job at the hotel and I liked Herr Wachs who seemed to be very pleased with my performance. I tried exceptionally hard to not give him a reason to doubt his decision to give me a chance. I had started at the hotel on February 1, 1954 and by April 1 of that same year, I had received two promotions.

The Frankfurter-hof had a very fine reputation for excellent accommodations and for its eclectic cuisine and service. It was no secret that this hotel was frequented by businessmen from all over the world. Since this was the case, all the employees were required to speak French, some English as well as their native language so they could converse with just about anyone who entered the establishment. Every day we were put to the test, one day rumors started to unfold that we would be receiving a very notable guest and within a few days, it became a reality.

Our celebrity guest was King Ibn Saud of Saudi Arabia. He arrived with a complete entourage of at least a dozen princes and aides. They emerged from a caravan of black Cadillacs and were whisked away to their rooms without much of a wait in the hotel's spacious lobby. Security was extremely tight; men in dark suits were visible throughout the hotel. Crowds of people impatiently waited for a glimpse of the King and to personally witness this remarkable historical event.

I was fortunate to have been put to work in every department at the hotel reception, kitchen and in the restaurant. I soon was appointed Chef de Rang; which meant I was responsible for overseeing all the food service activities. Since I held this position, I was privileged to be in charge of coordinating requests made by the king through his personal aide and the Maitre de Cuisine, Herr Perl. I worked around the clock to be at their disposal, since it seemed they never slept. I was to report to Herr Wachs as to their activities and requests, so he was never out of the loop; he was extremely concerned that the King's stay went without a hitch. We had the pleasure of their company for several days. As exhausting as it was to take care of their needs, it was an extremely rewarding experience. After things quieted down and regained a sense of normalcy, I was called to the director's office and he promoted me to Chef d Etage of the hotel.

We no sooner regained our composure, when we accepted the request for a visit from a young 'king', King Hussein from Jordan. We only had a few days to prepare for his stay, but having survived the experience of the King of Saudi, we knew we could handle it. When King Hussein arrived at the hotel it was in a very modest fashion; only a few limousines and only a few aides had accompanied him. Since I had proved myself in the past, I was once again put in charge of his care.

I remember as a student at the Ecole de Lausanne, one of the teachers told us that to get to the top, requires hard work, patience, and determination; no truer words were ever spoken. Your days were long, but rewarding. It was imperative that your patrons came first and it was important to make them feel comfortable and pampered to the best of your ability. I felt and still do that the hospitality business was the most interesting profession next only to the entertainment field. Both professions required that you make a great first impression so the 'audience' would come back to see you again. As in the entertainment field, a good 'performer/chef/concierge' could earn high pay, but along with that, salary comes numerous sleepless nights and long work weeks; one's social life suffered as a result. However, the awards and publicity one receives as a result are worth the work.

As satisfied as I was with my position at the hotel, I wanted to make it to a management level, but in order to do that I needed more experience in finance, strategy, and marketing. My knowledge and experience in these areas was extremely limited and I needed to find ways to expand my resume in these fields. I decided to continue my education, by finding a business school where I enrolled in a business course and attended day and evening classes; after a few months, I had a better understanding of Finance and Marketing.

No Longer Alone

I was now twenty-seven years old, I had been working since I was fourteen. I had served in the German Wehrmacht and had survived the Holocaust. My life had been full and at times, I felt truly blessed, yet I was overwhelmed with loneliness. I had a good paying job and had been saving money for my future; I now was thinking of settling down. I took a chance and invested some of my money with a financial institution that was building condominiums in a suburban wooded area near Frankfurt-Main. It proved to be a good investment.

I had made many friends in the two years at the Frankfurter-hof Hotel, but I needed more, I needed family, I still could not go home to Poland. Whenever I had two days off, I would jump on my motorcycle and drive the 300 kilometers across the autobahn from West Germany through East Germany and from there to Berlin just to visit my sister Anna. Anna was the youngest sibling and now married to a very nice young man, who was a true 'Berliner'. He was born and had lived in Berlin all his life. He had served in the German Luftwaffe, his name was Wolfgang, and he became like a brother to me. These small reunions were always special even though the rides home at night were a little precarious. I never saw any cars on the autobahn at night, so the long stretches of road just seemed to go on endlessly into the black of the evenings.

My career at the Frankfurter-hof was going well, I could not complain. When I wasn't able to visit Anna, I spent my free time polishing my trusty Horex Regina and touring the streets of Frankfurt or the surrounding towns. My Horex Regina was my most prized possession and I had dubbed her 'my bride'. After all, she was always there for me and she took me wherever I needed to go. However, at night I realized as I lay in my bed, that I needed a companion.   One beautiful day while cruising around my neighborhood I decided to stop in at the flower shop on the corner, I had always enjoyed the freshness of floral arrangements and on impulse went inside to buy some for my apartment. A lovely young lady behind the counter looked at me with a pair of luminous green eyes and asked me how she could assist me.   I was mesmerized. This fair-skinned beauty moved with grace and spoke with the usual Hesse, Frankfurter accent. I broke from my trance, ordered a small bouquet, and walked on air back to my room. The world around me seemed to have changed; I couldn't get her face out of my head. Two days later, I went back to the shop just to see the vision, which had consumed my every waking, thought for the past forty-eight hours. She greeted me with a warm smile and I mumbled something about needing daffodils. After paying for them I stated that I had to run that my 'bride' was waiting, I handed her the bouquet and practically raced out the door, jumped on my trusty Regina and sped away. All day at work, I kept asking myself what had happened to me, what had I done? I had never felt this way before and it scared me a little, yet at the same time, I was tingly with excitement. I could not wait to see her again.

I could not afford flowers every day, so I gathered up my courage, walked in the shop, and introduced myself. Her name was Ursula Weiss. She nervously asked me what I meant by my bride and I stammered out that it was just something I called my motorcycle, which caused us both to laugh. We started to see each other as often as time permitted us to. Some evenings we would take long walks and just enjoy each other's company. Ursula was refined yet fun to be with and she soon became my friend and confidant. One day after a bit of courting, she suggested that maybe it was time I met her parents. I was anxious to meet them but with some trepidation, I agreed to it and set a date. It turned out to be a gorgeous spring afternoon when I arrived at her parents' apartment, I was greeted by her mother and father who seemed to be genuinely nice people; Ursula's younger sister, Eda was also there. We had some tea and once more, I seemed to be under interrogation by her father. I had the feeling that her mother approved of me, but I had yet to pass muster with her father. He was not altogether thrilled with my chosen profession or the fact I worked in a hotel; like many fathers, they wanted to make certain their daughters could be taken care of. When he found out I had been born in Poland, he didn't much seem to like that either. Herr Weiss was a big, deadly serious man who did not mince words. Despite my shortcomings, I seemed to win him over.

It didn't take long for us to realize that we were in love. Our dates often consisted of simple things; walking in Rothschild Park watching the swans gracefully swimming on the lake, sometimes we would attend a concert or go to a movie, or to the Palm Garten Café where big bands would play popular tunes from Glenn Miller or Harry James. A few of our dates were even chaperoned by her father so he could keep an eye on her and observe me as I courted his daughter. After a few months, we realized that we wanted to be together always and we announced our engagement. To say the least Herr Weiss had to digest this information a bit before he gave his blessing. We set a date for January 8, 1956. I bought the engagement rings, two simple gold bands, which we also used as our wedding bands. I surprised my future bride with a trip to Switzerland as an engagement gift. I had purchased a sidecar for the Regina and we traveled together through the warm summer days in the open air. We had one close call on this vacation, while traveling on the autobahn, passing Manheim about forty kilometers from Frankfurt a semi truck cut us off as I was passing a car. I stepped hard on the brakes and lost control of the bike, Ursula grabbed me in panic. I regained some control, but as I was pulling the bike over to the median, I lost control and flipped the bike upside down trapping us both under the bike. The battery dripped acid onto my pinned legs and I started to panic. Fortunately, my arms were free and I was able to flag down a passing vehicle. In one of the cars that stopped was a doctor and he along with others managed to maneuver the bike off the both of us. The doctor checked us both over. As a precaution, he suggested that it might be best if Ursula went to the hospital to be thoroughly checked over. A passing highway patrol car of the ADAC, which patrolled the autobahn, stopped and was able to telephone for an ambulance. My legs were bruised and I had a few acid burns, but other than that, I seemed able to limp away and did not require any real medical attention. By the time the ambulance arrived, we were both feeling much better, but he insisted that we still go get checked out. I was forever grateful for his assistance and hope that all has gone well with him over the years. Once at the hospital Ursula was checked in for observation for the night, my legs were treated and I was discharged. I rented two rooms at a nearby hotel and fretted all night long as to her condition. When I arrived the next morning to check on her, I was relieved to find her waiting for me ready to leave. We contacted the police to find where my motorcycle had been taken and where I could get it repaired. We had a day to relax as the mechanic worked on the bike. The next morning after I was assured with a test drive that the bike was in excellent running condition, we paid the bill and once more took off on my beloved Horex Regina.

We crossed West Germany through the Black Forest – stayed at the Baden a luxurious spa resort and from there went on to Switzerland. We stayed overnight in a little inn, we were pleased to discover that they too enjoyed food and richly pampered their guests with their dinners and breakfasts. We spent some time in Bern, a small but lovely capital in Europe. We learned that a good part of Bern was constructed out of wood and in 1405 burned down. It was eventually rebuilt out of stone. What we most enjoyed there was the art and architecture, there was a famous fountain ornamented by gaily painted figures; there were many of these types of fountains in the city. Bern houses the finest collection of Baroque art in Switzerland, most of it from 1550 made by a fine sculptor in Fribourg.

We traveled on to Interlaken, which was in the Middle Ages just a stopover point for travelers on foot or traveling by horse for one of the many mountain passes. As we drove along on the Horex, we could admire the Jungfrau. The Jungfrau shares with the Matterhorn the honor of being the most admired mountain of the Alps. The Matterhorn is a fierce solitary exclamation point, where as the Jungfrau builds to its climax with its lofty white fluent lines, this mountain range dominates the more dramatic peaks with its sheer beauty. Interlaken is a true tourist must see with its well-groomed streets. Horse drawn carriages clop clopping along the streets is definitely a must see. We enjoyed the majestic Lake Thun and the Lake of Brienz, as well as the nearby River Aare, and marveled at nature's creation of the ragged hills that formed the v-frame of the Jungfrau; with reluctance, we had to move on. Robert Frost wrote about his visit to Interlaken:

"The hotels along the WEG all sit and look one way, they turn their backs on the Aare and they stare at the Alps all day."

We cruised through Gstaad bordered by snowy alpine peaks and wished we could afford to stay at its fashionable and expensive hotels, especially the Palace Hotel. Gstaad was and is the place to come if you want to see Hollywood royalty, it's set within the border of the gentle Gruyere countryside and stormy mountain Alps. I worked a winter at the Palace Hotel while at Ecole de Lausanne, skied its snowy slopes, and found it an excellent place to vacation. I had chosen to take Ursula on this trip to show her the beauty of this country, she had never been out of Frankfurt, and she was beside herself with the bounty of what she beheld.

In the small town of Altdorf, we stopped at a wonderful bakery, which was famous for its masterfully sculpted bread; scenes of planting of the seeds to the meal in a peasant's cottage were depicted with great care and pride. We did not want to go inside, but looked inside with awe with our noses pressed to the window; the proprietor came out and invited us to come in. He brought us out two large bars of chocolate, which we ate like little children. In Switzerland, when people try to give you a piece of their life to savor, it is best to take it and when you do, they thank you! You are always treated as if you are someone special with a bow and a polite yet heartfelt "Aufwiedersehen, au revoir, arrivederla…"

When we arrived in Geneva we immediately sought out the fountain that depicted the story of the boy who stood on his head, walked the top of a fence, and then leap-frogged a hydrant back and forth to show off for his girl friend, which upon seeing his antics told him she couldn't love him. We found the 'Jet d'eau' in the Lac Leman and it was spectacular. Internationally, Geneva is a highly distinguished city. Tourists from all over rushed to and fro; even with the abundance of activity, the city gives off the impression of great emptiness. We drove the Rue Farel and enjoyed the carved capitals of the cathedral we passed. We were taken aback by the quiet prettiness of St. Pierre Square.

From Geneva, we drove on to Lausanne. It felt to me like a homecoming of sorts. The city is very hill and dale like, knitting itself together with long flights of stairs and bridges that spanned valleys of streets far below. There are rivers that run through the town but they are subterranean covered by paving which allows traffic to move unobstructed throughout the city. Lausanne housed a cathedral that was considered Switzerland's finest. It was started in 1175 and is a remarkable work of architectural art.

Our time had run out and we had to get back to Frankfurt-Main. We wanted to make one more stop in Montreux, but we had run out of time and regretfully headed back home. We had spent ten days in Switzerland and had enjoyed beautiful weather as well as breathtaking sights and scenery. I was proud of my little Horex Regina; it never let me down through all the traveling we put on it over those ten days. As we once again drove onto the autobahn, flashbacks of our accident made us apprehensive, but the Lord was watching over us and we made it home safely. Little did we know, but the accident report had been sent on to Ursula's parents and once back home, we had a lot of explaining to do.

I had the thrill of planning my wedding with my mother-in-law and things seemed to work out fine. I had written my parents about our plans to get married, but unfortunately, they were not able to come. Anna, however, along with her husband accepted our invitation and arrived in their vintage Volkswagen. A friend of the Weiss' a Major in the U.S. army stationed in Frankfurt accepted an invitation and arrived in a huge street cruiser, a Pontiac Starchief – the biggest car in Frankfurt at the time. My best man was a colleague of mine from the hotel, Heinz Eifert and Ursula's sister Eda was her maid of honor. Ursula's father hired a four-wheeled enclosed carriage drawn by a team of white horses. The wedding was to be small and intimate; we would hold the reception in her parents' second floor apartment, the official wedding was held at city hall on January 8, 1956. The next day we had a ceremony at the Katharien Kirche in the town center, but that morning I had to work at the hotel. I rushed home at noon to shower and change into my white shirt and starched collar, white bowtie, and formal suit complete with tails and a top hat. Before I knew it, my landlady was knocking at my door telling me the carriage was waiting on the street for me. I yelled down to the driver to wait, with trembling fingers I attempted to get my tie tied, but I couldn't. Running down the stairs, I flew expectantly out the front door, only to find the driver and the carriage gone. What was I to do? My father-in-law already did not think much of me and here I had already screwed up one of the most important days of my life. I stood there shivering in the cold, trying to figure out what I should do next, when around the corner came the army major in his huge car. He pulled up beside me and asked me in jest, if I was lost. I leaned into the window only to find my brother-in-law, Wolfgang also in the car. I quickly told them what had happened and with a hearty laugh at my expense, they told me to get into the car and off to Ursula's parents' apartment. When we got there, of course, I had to explain what had happened and to my relief they did not give me too much grief over the incident. The carriage was waiting at the apartment and my day old wife and I boarded and we took off for the church, needless to say, we were late. The priest and guests were patiently waiting for our arrival. I was amazed at the number of people who filled the church. I had no idea that so many people knew and cared about the two of us this much. The ceremony was beautiful and from there, we headed back to my new parents-in-law's apartment where dinner was served for a small group of intimate friends and family. As the night drew on, I realized that I had truly found my 'family' again and I felt at home.

Ursula moved in with me in my small apartment the next day. We honeymooned in Berwang, Austria at a ski resort in Tyrol near Innsbruck. There was always snow and the skiing was wonderful. While we were gone, Ursula's father was able to find us a two-bedroom apartment, which we moved into when we returned. Within a year, we had our first child, a girl that we named Anemone, just like the flower I had first seen in the wild where it grew in the Swiss Alps. About a year later, the condominium, which I had invested in, was complete and we moved into a suburb of Frankfurt, Sprendlingen that was located in a wooded area. With a wife, child, and living a little farther from my job, I had to make the decision to sell my most prized possession, the Horex Regina. I bought a small car a Fiat Torpolino. It was only a two seater, but it served us fine.

The car enabled us to visit Anna in Berlin, often. The only thing we did not like about the trip was the checkpoint at the East German border, the border guards were usually pretty efficient in checking over the necessary papers needed to travel between the two divisions, but it was the VOPOS that could be unpredictable. The smallest infraction could mean a lengthy delay at the border. There were times it seemed like they made people wait just because they had the power to do so. Sometimes our vehicles were checked down to the smallest cranny. We were always in fear that something unbeknown to us would turn up and we would be detained. You could not help but breathe a sigh of relief when they finally opened the gate and you could drive through. Often you would also be checked before entering Berlin. The Vopos would take your papers behind a wall and check to see if your name was on their 'most wanted list', if it was you could be arrested immediately.

During one of my visits to Anna, we discussed the possibility of us visiting our parents in Poland whom we had not seen in thirteen years. Anna and Wolfgang said they would look into the possibility of obtaining a visa from the Polish consulate. I was beside myself with anticipation that this trip was a possibility and looked forward to the day when Anna had everything arranged.

Going Home

My hometown of Tarnowskie-Góry (Upper Silesia) was still occupied by the Russians in 1955 and I was not sure at all when we would be able to go back home. Anna had applied for an entry visa so we could both go visit our parents after almost thirteen years of being apart from them. Our initial request was denied by the Polish Consulate, therefore we could not travel to Poland, we were extremely disappointed, and we were not sure why we were refused, for no reason was given. Devastated we waited for another chance.

The Cold War created by Stalin intensified and later lead to a complete blockade of commerce between West and East Germany, including West Berlin. There were two events that had great impact on the beginnings of the Berlin Blockade, they were; when a British military train coming from West Germany to Berlin, after passing Helmstedt – West Germany was detained at the Russian checkpoint was forced to declutch and remained there for many hours. A few days later, a train with American soldiers was forced to do the same and with that, the Cold War between the Allies and the Russians escalated to the point, which ultimately lead to a full scale Berlin Blockade. Consequently, General Lucius D. Clay, the commanding officer of the American forces in West Germany and West Berlin, with the approval of the Pentagon informed his counterpart the Russian commanding officer in East Berlin, General Major Alexander Kotikow, that the American forces would supply West Berlin with all the necessary goods by air, and with that the biggest airlift in history began and the reality of the Cold War came to the front. These developments were a detriment to both Anna and myself and our efforts to go back to our hometown. Just simple travel between the two factions soon became very difficult and complicated. Eastern Europe was still controlled by the Soviet regime, these people who wanted to be free, had lived through the worst to get to this point, and still were denied their freedom by the Russians as well as the East German Communist Regime. Despite all this, I held on to the dream that things would eventually improve and that Anna and I would be reunited with our family. Wolfgang was very supportive of our plan to visit our family and he made some inquiries to the East

German Embassy as well as the Polish Embassy and found that only a very few restricted visas were being granted and those went for the most part to high ranking government officials or businessmen. Nevertheless, Wolfgang would not take no for an answer. One day Anna wrote and told me to gather together and send to her; my, Ursula's, and our daughter's birth certificates, vaccination documentation, proof of employment and a few more necessary items so they could resubmit an official application for the entry visa. We were going to need one for East Germany and another for Poland, the wheels were set in motion; I hated to get my hopes up, but it would be a long time yet until we would obtain those elusive visas.

All those years Anna and I were hoping to go home, but now our dreams were shattered. I could not sleep for weeks, I was tormented by the thought that I could not go home. I was angry. Nevertheless, my mother's words came back to me time and again. Keep praying and to never give up hope, those were the words my mother lived by. Somehow, I knew the day would come when I would be boarding that train to Poland.

I wrote a long letter to Anna and Wolfgang in Berlin. We decided to let the holidays pass and to reapply after the holidays for the entry visa. My mind was set; we were going to be able to go home somehow. I wanted to see my parents, my brother and sister; and I wanted to see my hometown again. I needed to see the house in which I grew up and the countryside where I played as a child before it was too late. I had somehow survived numerous setbacks and always landed on my feet. Some things mostly require patience and faith, no matter how enigmatic they may appear. As the New Year dawned, Anna and her husband tried for the visas again. To request the visas took a lot of paperwork and I was grateful that Anna lived in Berlin where the consulate was so she was able to hand deliver all the documents that were necessary in order to apply.

I knew Anna would be relentless in her quest to fulfill our dream. She had survived WWII in Berlin, I knew she would persevere. In October of 1958, she received another rejection, but this time it stated what was wrong with our application. We had to correct the mistakes and submit pictures along with the application.

We jumped through their hoops once more and she once again hand delivered the application. We had hoped that we would receive the ultimate Christmas gift, that of the visas, but it wasn't to be. We somehow made it through New Years and again were let down.

March came and so did a call from Anna, she was beside herself with excitement. The visas had been approved!! I should be getting a letter soon. I could not wait! What news! We were going home! Before we could travel though, there was a lot of work still ahead of us, but for the most part, the red tape was over. Planning and anticipating this trip home had consumed me for the past sixteen years. Every soldier young or old when they are in the field wants to go home. We soldiers spoke of it in reverent, terms building it up to almost mythical proportions. We called it 'the world'. The world was a place where people slept in real beds, took hot showers every day, and didn't have to keep their steel helmets and rifles within arms distance. In the real world, buddies had nothing better to do than pack sandwiches and go hunting or fishing. Girls looked and smelled pretty and wore dresses. We discussed going home all the time. You could start a conversation with anyone, by just asking, "What are you going to do once you get home?" However, for me going home did not happen for sixteen years.

When I left home, I was a teenage boy, now I was a grown man with a wife and family. I wanted to go home and touch my past. I wanted to see my small room that I shared with my brother Bernhard. I hoped to find my old rocking horse still up in the attic. I wanted to go down into the basement where we hid the Jews and marvel once again, at how they stayed down in that room where the spiders overwhelmed it and they never complained.

It was in June of 1959, when I loaded Ursula and our daughter, Anemone into our car and headed out on the autobahn to meet Anna in Berlin. We stayed overnight at her apartment. That night was one of celebration and a lot of talk, we thought we were dreaming. The almost impossible had become the possible. We checked and double-checked our visas and passports for fear something would turn up missing. Anna and Wolfgang had arranged train passes for us and we would be leaving at noon.

Since we would be traveling all night, we had arranged to have a Pullman car so the children would have a place to run around or relax when they got tired or antsy. It was hard to sleep on the train, for the "VOPOS," Russian soldiers with their ready machine guns at their sides, would always be coming around checking our visas, etc. Our nerves had begun to fray. Anna was on pins and needles to see our mother again, Wolfgang and Ursula couldn't wait to meet the family we unendlessly talked about and I wanted to shake my father's hand and sit down so I could finally get answers to so many questions I had.

When we made one station stop the train was boarded by what seemed to be hundreds of people. Along with those new passengers came an escort of armed Russian soldiers. The soldiers moved around the train, asking everyone for their passports and checked our papers mercilessly. All this brought back bad memories and I broke out in a light sweat. One of the soldiers found a Polish to German dictionary in my suitcase and started to ask me a lot of questions. We were scared to some degree for there always was an air of unpredictability with Russian soldiers, depending on their mood; you had to be ready for anything. He started to ask me questions and even though I could have answered him in Russian, I chose to answer in German. I must have satisfied his curiosity for soon they left our compartment. A couple of hours later, our belongings, and papers were checked again by Russian soldiers, but we passed their inspection too.

By mid morning, we were pulling into Tarnowskie-Góry. We were HOME! Tears were rolling down my face. Soon I was stepping down off a train onto the platform where I stood sixteen years ago when my father handed me off to my new life in April of 1943. I looked for familiar faces and soon found the one of my mother. I stood to the side and watched her scan the crowd looking for us and while she did, I noticed all the changes these past years had left on her beautiful face. I quickly realized that my father was standing next to her. Standing there as he had the last time I saw him. Wearing his wide brimmed hat, his sarmatian moustache, gentle sad eyes. Soon his eyes found me and a smile spread across his face. It was a smile of love and relief as he realized I was okay and the world would be right again. There was no doubt in my mind that he knew I had scars of some kind, if not on the outside in the inside. Having lived through the war he knew what it did to a person.

I was still that soldier, tired from all those years of dreaming about going home. Then it hit me, it wasn't the hot showers, soft beds, the fishing trips or the pretty girls. The world was our parents and our loved ones. The world revolved around them getting letters to us and ours to them. The world was the one they prayed in for our safety. The world was the one they lived in waiting for us to return and my world now stood on this train platform waiting for the sea of people to part so we could embrace each other.

I had missed out on a lot of Christmases, but the best one was happening in June of 1959 right there. There were many wounds inside me that had to heal and I could almost feel the old wounds clearing up. We rushed to each other, not wanting to let each other go. Everyone tried to talk at once, trying desperately to fill in all the years in a few rushed minutes. Father came to his senses first and he took us home.

At nights, I tried to stop the clock with my mind so it would quit ticking off the time we had left, but to no avail. We visited with old friends and family, laughed and cried. On quiet nights after everyone was asleep, my mother told me how my father had suffered once he learned about what had happened to me at Auschwitz. Mother cooked the meals I remembered and father and I had long talks in the barn. It seemed the days got shorter and I still had so much I wanted to discuss with both of them. I assured both of them that I harbored no hard feelings about any decision they made on my behalf. They did what they thought was best and put me with people who would help me, and they did.

Bernhard arranged for us to visit Krakow to do a little sightseeing of the Wawel Castle with its renaissance courtyard as well as the St. Barbara Church. It was a memorable experience. I had visited them as a child back in 1939 while attending school and this visit allowed me to reflect on those times. Bernhard took us to the coalmines where our father worked for years, thousands of feet below the surface.

Father asked me many questions about the war, what I saw, and how I managed to survive it. I answered him as well as I was able to. I would have never received the Purple Heart from the German Wehrmacht, since my records had been lost. My father, however, having listened to my stories, went to his closet and brought out a box which contained the Iron Cross which he had been awarded for Distinguished Conduct in WWI. He told me that I deserved this as much as he did and gave it to me. I still have it today and will treasure it always.

I took long walks around the farm, and relived the times on the farm. I thought about how much work it took to till the soil and plant and reap the crops. I thought about the animals I tended and the fences I helped him repair over the years. On one such walk, I came across my father lying beneath a tree with his wide brimmed hat covering his eyes. I stood there as he rested, not willing to interrupt this serene moment. I wanted to get his attention, so I started to whistle as I approached him. He pushed the hat off his face and called out to me. Hearing him call me his son warmed my heart to the very core. I went over to him and told him that it was time for lunch and I helped him to his feet. He looked older and moved a little slower, I could not be certain whether it was because his bones ached or because he realized it was our last day there. He told me on the walk back to the house that the past ten days had been the best days of his life. He was so happy to have all his children around him that at times he could not contain his emotions. He told me he was proud of me and asked if I would try to come back the following year and I promised to start the paperwork immediately upon my return home.

I felt so close to my father during that visit. I had proven myself to be a brave man, but when I was up against my father, I realized that I had not yet shown his type of courage. The evening before our departure, my father had invited our old parish priest to supper. It was a great honor to see him. We talked and laughed, and after a blessing, we ate a wonderful meal which mother had worked all day on. The dinner started with fresh bread, which we topped with paper-thin slices of salo, a peppery fatback, which was a specialty of our father. The second course was cold salads of cabbage, carrots, and beets; an aspic of pork studded with garlic, cloves, and a platter of sliced sausage and homemade goat cheese. Platters of meat stuffed rolls of cabbage followed this, and by the time the evening ended, we had drunk two bottles of vodka along with a towering bottle of Crimean Champagne. There were enormous tortes made with sweet-layered dried fruits and blackberry jam. We toasted the night away as we talked about whatever subject came to mind. We talked a lot, laughed a lot, and cried until there were no more tears. It was a wonderful memorable evening. We were all touched by this visit for we learned so much about each other and how we had grown. We relived the past so we could put it finally to rest.

Before we left for the train, we made a stop at the cemetery to pay our respects to our biological mother and older sister Agnes. That afternoon with heavy hearts, we said goodbye to our parents and siblings. My heart was sad, but there was also a great sense of closure, rejoicing, and contentment. I had accomplished yet another goal, to go home. Reluctantly, we boarded the train back to Berlin. All the way back, we prayed and thanked the Lord for giving us the privilege of seeing our parents again.

My Vater

Bernhard Skaletz
May 11, 1888 to December 31, 1959

My father once said, "The depth of a talent is measured by its longevity. Slow and steady wins the race."

As I reflect on him today, I recall him being a driving dynamo. Never did I hear him say he was tired. He was a good provider and a good father. His Christian beliefs and conduct exemplified the vision of a man who believed in his country and God.

He served in World War I, as a major in the Cavalry under Kaiser Wilhelm. He was wounded twice and nearly died of yellow gas poisoning. He finds himself after the Plebiscite in 1919 as a Pole and after the invasion by Hitler in 1939 becomes a German again.

My father held a great passion for his family and worked hard to provide for their daily needs. He was concerned about the environment and how the land was worked where we lived. He worked long days to make certain there was food on the table, especially during the Great Depression. He rose long before the sun and rode to work on his bicycle rain or shine, through sleet or snow to the train station where he would catch a train that would take him to the mines.

He taught us how to choose our friends. He taught us to respect one another and those we associated with no matter what race or creed they were. We had Jewish friends, but we never thought of them as Jews, they were just neighbors and were always welcome in our home and we in turn in theirs. They inspired me a great deal and showed us the greatness of their culture. Our father once told us that we would find all kinds of people in the world and we would find we could not get along with all of them, but we should always give them the benefit of the doubt.

He was strict, but fair. Punishments or admonishments fit the infraction and I loved him for it. He believed in discipline, hard work, and respect for authority. He was an extraordinary man and a role model for all of us. He was a religious man. He reminded us that even in the face of great losses look for life and to relish the gift of it.

I remember on my tenth birthday he gave me a gift of a bar of fine chocolate (chocolate at that time in Poland was a rare treat), and a notebook; this was an exceptional birthday gift and I considered myself extremely lucky that he took the time from his day to think of me. He taught me to be self-sufficient at an early age and for that, I am grateful.

He was a pillar of strength and a paragon. His legacy will live on forever in my heart. Without his advice, I would not be able to write this book. He will always remain my hero.

"Wisdom and inspiration are a dynamic duo and the right attitude can create miracles."

My father was defined by his work ethic. When he wasn't working at his regular job, he would hire out as a handyman to the neighborhood. We helped him when we could, by doing chores around the farm and lending him an extra hand at some household project. He loved to work with his hands and had a small workshop where he restored furniture and built toys for us.

This was not unusual of his generation though. Many men and women who grew up during those times of the Great Depression and WWI built the countries we know today. I've met many successful businessmen who worked as teenagers to the point of supporting their families or saving for college, more so than just earning spending money as so many young adults do today. These life lessons are not soon forgotten and can be ingrained in future generations if preserved correctly.

During my childhood and that of my father, there were very few labor saving devices compared to what there is today. Most things were done by hand and it was hard backbreaking work. The home I grew up in had no indoor plumbing and our water needed to be pumped from the well and carried by buckets into the house to either be used for cooking or heated for washing. Cows were milked by hand, implements, combines, and plow horses pulled plows. Hay was baled and pitched by hand, no mechanized machinery for this arduous task. This all seems so primitive compared to modern day technology.

Because of these early experiences, this generation was drafted young to fight for their country. They believed in what they were doing, for they were taught to love their country and the freedoms it provided. The war forced women into factories where they made weapons of destruction. Those women, who had a stomach for it, became nurses and in many ways, fought alongside their loved ones. My sister, Maria in fact became a nurse in World War II. When the war ended, this same generation was ready to rebuild the devastated cities of Germany, Italy, and France to name a few.

Time never erases the ravages of war and the horror it brings. No one from that generation or who lived through those times can forget the tragedies; ration stamps, standing in bread lines, and watching their friends and family being torn away from them. No one quit a job back then. If you did not like your boss or job you toughed it out until you could find something else. Work was hard to come by and those who had jobs stuck to them with a discipline that is unmet in today's world.

His Untimely Death

We were back in our new home in Sprendlingen, a suburb of Frankfurt-Main, still overwhelmed by the visit to my hometown in June of 1959; I promised my parents that I would visit them again the following year. It took at least that long to get a travel visa. We weren't settled in completely yet and before we knew it Christmas was approaching and my wife, Ursula and I needed to shop for presents for our family and loved ones back home. I enjoyed putting together care packages and sending them home, in comparison to my family in Poland, we felt so blessed with the array of items we could choose. I knew what they needed and did my best to find the items that they could no longer either afford or find.

We celebrated the New Year with Ursula's aunt in Bad Hombrug about forty kilometers north of Frankfurt and stayed there overnight. When we returned home, we checked our messages and found a telegram from my brother Bernhard, informing us that our father had died New Years Eve. To say the least I was in shock. Six months ago when we visited, he had not complained about ill health or any concerns that would have lead us to believe his end was near. How could he be gone? We had so much yet to catch up on. I was inconsolable. Life was not fair; I had lived this over and over again. I am an optimist by nature, but at times, you need more. As the minutes passed, I pulled myself together and began to come to terms with my father's death. I had learned to live with fear, but not with the loss of a loved one, especially one I considered a hero. I put everything in God's hands for I knew He would pull me through this.

I called Anna in Berlin. She asked if I would be attending the funeral, which was in three days. I told her I wanted to, but she would have to go to the Polish consulate and apply for an emergency entrance visa for me. I wanted to call Bernhard, but he did not have a telephone and I had no way of contacting him on short notice. I sent him a telegram confirming that I had received the news and that I was planning to come home.

I requested time off from work to attend the funeral and canceled our plans for a ski vacation in Austria. After several calls to Anna and three telegrams to Bernhard, I had my travel visa and I was ready to go. Ursula and our daughter chose to stay home, Anna's husband too chose to stay home with their daughters for fear the funeral would be too much for the girls.

On January 2, I climbed into my Borgward Goliath and drove the 400 kilometers to Berlin. I had planned to meet Anna at seven o'clock that evening and calculated that it would take me about seven hours to get there. When I set out on the Autobahn, it had begun to snow. I wasn't overly concerned since I had quite a bit of experience driving in wind and snowy conditions. I began to get concerned however, when the light snowfall turned into an all out blizzard. Visibility was poor and I had to reduce my speed to 30 mph to be safe. I came across cars that had driven off the road and it made me nervous. One car caught my attention. It was on its side and I thought I saw movement. I pulled over and found a man and woman desperately trying to free themselves. The door was jammed; I got my tire jack and smashed the window freeing the man who helped me get his wife out of the car. With no other cars in sight, I told them I would take them to the next town. We drove carefully bracing ourselves when a car would pass us and occasionally go into a skid. I got off at the next exit and drove the couple to a hospital where I left them off. Shortly after, I was once again on the autobahn. The blizzard did not want to let up. I passed through the check points with minimal intrusion, it seemed no one wanted to be out in the storm; I had about 90 kilometers to go.

I did not get to Anna's until 10:30 that evening a full three and a half hours after I told her I would be there. Everyone was worried including Ursula, I called her right away and told her I was well and what had happened. Anna told me we had a meeting at the Polish consulate in the morning so we could get our visas. I was exhausted and gratefully fell into a deep sleep. The next morning we went to the consulate armed with our passports and the telegraphs from Bernhard. The agent looked at our documentation and to our surprise told us that the telegraphs were not sufficient for him to issue an emergency visa to us. We needed to get the doctor who had attended to our father to telegram attesting to the fact the he was indeed dead. We quickly went to the post office and cabled this request to Bernhard telling him too to postpone the funeral for a day, since we would not be there in time.

Despondent we went back to her apartment to wait for a response. Anna told her husband what had happened and suddenly began to cry, her daughter hearing her mother's sobs, started to cry and before I knew it, I was too. Poor Wolfgang had his hands full trying to console us all. Around midnight we got the confirmation we needed to attest to the death of our father and after a sleepless night, first thing in the morning we went back to the consulate. We did not even have to wait, the person who had dealt with us the other day was expecting us, and within an hour, we had our visa. We still had to get the visa from East Germany and quickly headed over there. We telegrammed Bernhard again telling him that all was well and that we were leaving. By three that afternoon, we were boarding a train from Berlin for Tarnowskie-Góry and expected to be there before noon.

In our compartment, we both broke down and we cried the tension and sorrow out of our bodies. Soon we regained our composure and waited out the night. Our passports were checked during the night and having found everything in order, we were left alone. The next morning we listened carefully when the stops were called out. Tension immediately hit us when we were down to our stop of Tarnowskie-Góry. When we pulled into the station and got off the train, we looked around and found Bernhard waiting for us. We rushed straight from the terminal to the funeral ceremony, which started at noon.

Our father's funeral was at St. Anna Church. Father had helped build this church back in 1919, when he returned from WWI. It was not surprising to see a large turnout for the man that was well liked and admired by many of our town. Even the superintendent of the coalmine was there in a ceremonial uniform that he wore on special occasions. Polish miners are among the last groups in Europe who had a trade 'uniform'. I took one last moment to lay my hand on his to thank him for what he had done for me and to say a final "Lebewohl" (farewell.) A one-horse hearse took my father to the cemetery where he was laid to rest. The coal miner's band played "Ich Hat Einen Kameraden" (I had once a comrade). I had taken pictures of the events of that day, but through subsequent moves, I somehow lost them. Anna and I stayed overnight to help our mother cope with the grief of losing her life partner. Before I left Poland, my mother gave me a box which my father wanted me to have, inside it was his dress ring with a very unusual gem set in 14k gold, a timeless clock that had been in our family ever since I was a small boy; it always sat on our mantle but no one ever wound it except our father. Inside were his pipe, cigar cutter, and his walking stick. I held these items dear to me for they remind me forever of my beloved father. These items are invaluable and I hope to one day hand them down to my children.

Our trip back to Germany was a solemn one, we said little. Our lives were forever changed. I made extra efforts to keep in touch with Anna, my one link to our family, by traveling from Frankfurt to visit her. My younger sister was and still is very special to me. Our mother eventually moved from Tarnowskie-Góry. I left the town and never returned, I wanted to leave everything I knew so well, behind. We had our land there, it is being held by the city in our names, and all we have to do is reclaim it. I think sometimes about going back and building a memorial of sorts to our parents commemorating all they did for us, but I am not sure I could do it. Anna and her husband went back several times to visit the gravesites of our family. She was able to do what I could not.

My Big Break

The hospitality business has such a breadth of offerings that for a guy like me, eager to learn all the aspects of it was like being a kid in a candy store. I never felt satiated. Although generally speaking, I had been content with my job at the Hotel Frankfurter-hof. I enjoyed working with my colleagues and in an establishment where a high standard of 'esprit de corps' had been maintained between the staff and management. However, no matter how hard I tried to be satisfied, there seemed to be a void in my career. I needed to make a change. Professionally, I had made good progress and yet there were still areas in which I needed to excel.

This renowned hotel had clients from all over the world. Frankfurt-Am Main had been and still is today the capital city of commerce and financial institutions. It was not until around June of 1961, when a man who had been staying at the Hotel, approached me and involved me in a short conversation. He introduced himself as Mr. Reber and told me he was from New York. He explained that he had been watching me work and wanted to offer me a position with his hotel. I was simply dumfounded. could not believe I had heard him right. I repeated back what he had said to me and he confirmed that I had indeed heard him right.

I told him that this was not the right place to have this conversation and he agreed. We arranged to meet in two days. I needed tó discuss this offer with my wife, Ursula and wanted to have enough time to think about making such a drastic move. Two days later I met with Mr. Reber and I have to say I was tempted by his job offer, however, I told him I needed more time to think everything over. He understood my position and before he checked out of the hotel and got ready to leave for New York, he made sure I had his contact information so I could stay in touch with him.

Over the next few months, we corresponded back and forth ironing out the details. Finally, the ball was in my court and I had to make my decision of whether or not I would indeed take him up on his offer. After talking about it with Ursula and my sister, Anna I decided to accept the position at his hotel and the plan was to be in New York in May of 1962. There was a great deal of red tape that had to be processed and many aspects that had to be considered before I could make the trip. The first thing I had to do was check in with the American Embassy in Frankfurt-Main. I was given instructions and the guidelines I had to follow on how to obtain a visa. We had a year to make sure all our paperwork was in order and that we were in order. Mr. Reber had a great deal of experience with work visas and he helped out as much as he could. To get the visa we had to be in good health, this required a physical to be performed by an appointed American doctor. I knew we did not have a criminal record and that we were politically pure. The visa would only be good for one year.

As a boy, I had always wondered what the world looked like on the other side of the vast Atlantic Ocean. I had always liked history and was interested in other cultures. How different could these people be than us? How little did I know. It all sounded so enigmatic; soon I was to realize first hand what was on the other side of that big body of water.

I needed to give Herr Wachs a three-month notice and in return, he agreed to keep my position open to me when I returned from the States. On April 29, 1962, my wife and I boarded the gigantic S.S. America in Bremerhaven, Germany. The crossing would take a little over seven days if the weather cooperated and would cover a distance of 4,000 miles.

Ursula made arrangements for our daughter to stay with her parents and with heavy hearts, tearful goodbyes, and great anticipation, we boarded the ocean liner. Once on board, before we left port, we were taken on a tour of the vessel. We were shown our cabin, some of the more pertinent sections of the ship such as the elegant dining hall and the captain's deck.

We stood on deck and listened to the band play farewell tunes while thousands of us waved goodbye to our loved ones on shore. I can still hear the three mighty blasts of the sirens as it signaled that the boat was ready to leave the dock. It was an awesome experience and we hadn't even made it to the open sea yet. I thought I was dreaming.

In the quiet of our stateroom, my imagination started to run wild. Were there still Indians? Did they still hunt with a bow and arrow? I know this sounds juvenile, but I had no way of really knowing what I was getting into, but I was soon to find out.

Crossing the Atlantic Ocean

The S.S. *America*, the mighty vessel had left the port some time ago. It was approaching the enigmatic English Channel. It had been said that the channel could cause more havoc for a ship than the open sea. We were just about to find this out. I for one could not get enough of the magnificence of the open water. I explored as much of the ship as I was allowed to and enjoyed every minute of it.

I was fascinated by the hordes of seagulls that followed the ship's wake. They accompanied this monster with crying out at us as they flew alongside. This type of bird was new to me. There weren't many of them in Germany. Their gray and white bodies along with the way they could maneuver in the air reminded me of the German Stukas. Once we crossed some imaginary boundary the birds one by one dropped back so they could alight once more on dry land only a few diehards stayed with the ship a few miles more and then they too were gone.

Over dinner, we were told we would soon be entering the English Channel. The meer, now slightly swollen made this colossal ship to rock. Anyone who has ever passed through the Channel during the spring knows what I am talking about. The huge waves would mount up high and after running out of space and having nowhere to go would crash against the steel hull of the boat. These repeated blows caused the boat to rock, even experienced captains were glad to have the Channel behind them.

Ursula and I stood on deck and admired the sun as it set over the ocean horizon. It seemed to touch the swells of the ocean as it descended. It was an awesome and unbelievable sight. The weather had been relatively balmy with a soft wind blowing from the west, as we stood there on the deck. We looked back at the Port of Bremerhaven and admired its skyline, its lights glittering in the dusk. There was no turning back. There was a scary uneasy feeling in my stomach. Neither of us knew what lay ahead of us across the wide expanse of the Atlantic Ocean. As a boy growing up, my brother and I had heard stories about the ocean, how it could become violent with its powerful waves at a moment's notice. All I had to go on were stories I had heard as a child and facts I had been taught in school. Now I was standing on the deck of one of the largest boats in the world, the *S.S. America.*

I looked back and found that I could no longer see Bremerhaven and that we were now on the open sea. After about twenty-one hours, we had traveled about 520 kilometers and were at our first port of call in South Hampton. Passengers boarded and departed and we were soon on our way to the French port of Le Havre about 98 kilometers away. The next stop would be in Cobh in Ireland, another 385 kilometers, and about seventeen hours steaming time from Le Havre. The *S.S. America* now had over two thousand passengers along with its crew of nine hundred. We were told that from this port we would be heading for New York.

On the second night of the voyage, the captain announced that for those who wanted to see the *S.S. France* pass by our boat on its way back from New York, they should come up on deck. Over a hundred passengers climbed up on deck to witness this spectacle. It was an awesome sight to see this slick huge sailing vessel cruising over the waves like a floating light show. Its lights illuminated the water and the darkness around it. It stayed far enough away from us so its swells would not rock our ship.

There was always something new to see or do on the ship. We could hear the steady and monotonous drone of the ship's powerful engines, especially at night. As exciting as all this was, we did manage to sleep. As this magnificent vessel forged its way across the vast expanse of the Atlantic, my wife and I stood on deck and watched the waves chase each other without ever seeming to catch up with the ones in front of them.

During one of our times on the upper deck, we noticed that the weather had seemed to take a turn for the worse and ominous clouds were filling the sky. A deck guard came up and politely suggested that we leave the deck for the comfort of our cabins. By dinnertime, the boat had begun to definitely sway. After dinner, we noticed that the crew had put up ropes between the steel columns of the long hallways. I asked what they were for and was told that they would aid us passengers by giving us something to hold on to, when we needed to navigate back to our rooms. We had no idea how rough the sea could get, but for movies and films in the theater. We were soon to find out first hand though.

The crew kept us occupied by providing the scheduled entertainment as though nothing was happening outside. Ursula and I decided to go to the ballroom to have a dance or two before retiring. It was then that the ship indeed began to roll. At this point, we decided we would be safer and would enjoy the night better in our stateroom. We used the ropes provided to move down the hallways and sat in wonder as the ship really began to roll. It was mind boggling how just drops of water could make a boat this massive to be tossed about like it was a toy boat for your bathtub. Being new to this experience, we were not sure we would survive the ordeal and soon found ourselves huddled in the corner of our cabin, as the tempest outside howled like a wild beast, praying that all would be alright and that we would survive the storm.

The night passed and the mighty *S.S. America* kept true to its course. The next morning over breakfast, the ship once again began to move side to side. Our breakfast was swept away from us; plates, coffee cups, etc. all falling to the floor. People began to panic. Once again, we heard the captain's voice over the public address system, announcing once again that we were in another heavy storm. He assured us not to be concerned and to stay calm, but suggested we go back to our staterooms. We could see the ship cruising through an ocean smoking white with spume. It heaved and shrieked under the power of the winds. The meer was foaming mad as the ship battled its way through the raging sea. The gale force winds whipped up monstrous walls of water that threw them against the fourteen-story high ocean liner.

We had friends that had traveled the ocean several times, who warned us of the rough seas, but we never expected it to be this bad. We tried to cope with the conditions as best we could. Just the simplest traveling in the halls took great effort. When it came time to eat, for those who had the stomach for it, only a dozen or so made it to the dining hall. Ursula was one of those who succumbed to seasickness, I on the other hand had a true desire to get a picture of the raging storm, which I managed to do.

As night fell, once again the ship's band played in the lounge in an effort to keep the passengers calm. One couldn't tell if people were dancing or just swaying with the rock of the ship. During one roll, our luggage opened up in the stateroom and our possessions were strewn across the room. That night we found it impossible to sleep and decided instead to just wait out the storm and pray that God would see us through the night. Late that night or it might have been early morning, we could tell that the boat had begun to manage to steady itself and the winds had started to die down. We could also tell that the ship had begun to slow down. Soon we heard a large rumbling sound and I quickly found a seaman who told me that the ship was dropping anchor. I wondered aloud why a ship would choose to anchor in the middle of the ocean. He told me to go back to my cabin. I went back inside and managed to fall asleep. Morning came and we decided to go down to breakfast. As we moved down the hallway, the captain came over the speaker informing us that they had received a distress call from a Russian Freighter and had had to change its course to aid the ship. The Russian ship's captain had suffered a heart attack and needed immediate attention. The *S.S. America* dispatched a lifeboat overboard with a rescue crew. They would in turn bring the ailing captain back to our ship where we had the facilities to help him. I do not recall if we had breakfast or not that day. My journal I had been keeping does not say.

Hundreds of people jammed the upper deck to watch this truly humanitarian turn of events unfold. The bravery of those men who donned life jackets and allowed themselves to be lowered into the still raging seas was beyond comprehension. They had to cross about 400 hundred yards before they reached the freighter. We watched and held our breaths as that lifeboat was tossed about in the rough sea on that cold morning. What seemed to take hours was over in minutes and they returned to our ship safely with the captain in tow. They hoisted him up in a rescue gurney and through one of the loading portholes of the boat. I don't know if the Russian Captain survived the ordeal, but it was remarkable to witness.

As severe as the first part of the crossing was, the second part of the crossing was smooth and unremarkable. Many hours were spent scanning the empty seas with my binoculars or camera in hopes that I would catch a glimpse of anything of interest that I might be able to record on film. I have to admit that what I enjoyed the most was the wonder and glory of God's sunrises and sunsets.

He used the skies as his canvass and colored with rich colors of oranges, yellows, purples, and blues. If you have never been on the water at night, you have missed one of nature's true visions; that of the night sky illuminated by billions of stars with the effervescent moon superimposed on its velvety black backdrop.

During these quiet times, I often let my mind wander to what I would be doing once I made it to the states. What was at the end of this voyage? What was next for me? Would I find what had been promised? I had a job lined up, but I had not met these people? Would they be as accommodating as those I had left behind? So many questions, but no answers. I knew Mr. Reber, my sponsor in the states, would be waiting for us in New York. I had seen pictures of the city, but knew very little about it.

I was relieved, yet apprehensive as the ship picked up speed and plowed its course through the Atlantic Ocean. I liked the steady drone of the engines, it seemed like they were humming some tune that only they knew the words to. Due to our delay caused in the rescue of the Russian Captain, our arrival in New York would be delayed by several hours. I was concerned whether or not Mr. Reber would be aware of this and if he would be able to wait for our ship to dock.

Day six was smooth sailing and even though there was nothing happening to hold ones attention; if you allowed yourself to be caught up in the beauty of the expanse of blue water all around us, you couldn't help but feel satisfied. It seemed now like the ship actually was gliding across the water. The ship's crew was always visible and willing to help its passengers in every possible way.

For the past ten years, I had been working in hotels with my body and feet always in motion. This was my first real vacation, where nothing was expected of me, except to relax and enjoy myself. Although, I was enjoying this journey, I was beginning to feel the need to be productive and get back to work. As I stood on deck that day, I was relieved to see a seagull come out to meet the ship. Was it a good omen? I hoped so.

I scanned the horizon and soon in the distance, I could begin to make out the mighty Statue of Liberty. I had only seen pictures of her on postcards in Germany. I knew she represented Freedom for all nations' peoples. As she came into view, the ship reduced its speed in order to enter the harbor. The sight of her as we pulled up along side was indescribable and overpowering. The crossing had taken seven days and nine hours. I was now to begin a brand new chapter in my life. As we docked, I read the sign that stated, "Welcome to America" tears welled in my eyes.

As we began to leave the ship, we had to go through the necessary formalities, such as: meeting with the inspectors of the Immigration and Naturalization Department who checked our papers, visa, and luggage. It was a time consuming process. I had learned enough English, so there was no language barrier. We passed through the process without any problems and found Mr. Reber. He had been patiently waiting for us and quickly whisked us away in his huge Cadillac.

Ursula stayed in New York for two weeks before returning to Germany. Before she left, we were able to see much of the 'big' city of New York. We wanted to visit the Empire State Building and almost couldn't find it. After walking for blocks, we asked a police officer where it was, he told us to lean back and look up, and we might be able to see its spire. Much to our chagrin, we were standing right in front of it. We went to concerts and saw the Rockets perform at the Radio City Music Hall. We listened to the biggest organ in the world with its innumerable pipes creating an unforgettable sound. This alone made the crossing of the Atlantic Ocean worthwhile. We went window-shopping at Macys and Tiffanies, but our budgets forced us to settle for J.C. Penney. The two weeks flew by and before I knew it, I was waving goodbye to her as she boarded the *S.S. Hanseatic*, which would take her back to Germany.

I had begun my career in the States at Mr. Reber's Hotel and Resort. I worked hard to improve and extend my professional skills by relearning many things the American way. I learned the American culture, history, and habits. Sometimes I had trouble understanding the mentality and the American way of life. So many things seemed different, but I learned to cope with it.

I met a great many fascinating people. I took time to travel a little and the area I liked the most was up-state New York. The Catskill Hills with their rustic views and surroundings. I enjoyed the valley of the Delaware River, where George Washington crossed. Everywhere I went and every place I visited, the beauty and history embellished my horizons.

Mr. Reber was very supportive of my work in every way possible. He was an hotelier extraordinaire. He made sure I learned as much as I could during my time there. He taught me the many fine points of the hospitality business. All his training became invaluable to me in my subsequent career. The time passed all too rapidly and before I knew it I was about to leave.

As I reflect back on my time at the Frankfurter-hof, I thought I knew it all, but it wasn't until I had this experience that my life had been opened up to what my profession really had to offer and gave real meaning to my chosen field. I couldn't thank Mr. Reber enough for the opportunity he had afforded me and the position I held at the Waldorf.

I had grown quite close to him and his wife, Erica. We often got together; they were both very caring and loving people. They were so cordial to me and this was a feeling that I seldom experienced. As a farewell gift, they took me to the Radio City Music Hall to once more enjoy a spectacular evening of fine entertainment.

On December 15, 1962, I boarded the *S.S. United States*, which was the fastest ship at that time and had won a blue ribbon for the feat. By noon that day, I was once more on my way over the Atlantic Ocean, but this time I was going back to Europe.

My time in the States, had not only contributed to my experience in the 'arena', but it also enriched my English language skills. I took the time during the crossing to sort things out. I needed desperately to absorb all that I had accomplished.

Even after a year, I was constantly amazed at how the American people lived. They worked and played hard. They had a freedom that I was not used to. They took this freedom for granted and I found I wanted to have that same ability. Even after all this time, I recalled the words of my vater, "Do what you need to do, but do it right." I read my journal at night, which I had kept during my time at the hotel. I knew somewhere in this diary were the answers to the questions and concerns that raced through my head. I was in agony over the decisions I was facing. I wondered how they would affect my family and the rest of my life. I knew having experienced the Americas that I would now have to make a choice between them and Germany. It was a very difficult situation to be in. I was confused, bewildered, and somewhat overwhelmed.

Mr. Reber had made me a promise that if I returned to New York, that I had a job waiting for me. It once again, made me realize that I had been fortunate with the type of people that I had the pleasure of knowing. I truly had a great treasure of friends, now on both sides of the Atlantic.

The voyage back was rough, but not near what I had experienced on the first voyage. Crossing alone afforded me the opportunity to make shipboard acquaintances. By pure happenstance, I bumped into a Mr. Whitenhall, the vice-president of a major company who often frequented the Frankfurter-hof. Upon meeting up with me, he exclaimed, "Günther, what the hell are you doing on this ship?" After a brief conversation, he invited me to join him for dinner in his private first class dining room. I of course, could only afford tourist class, so this was to be a real treat. We had a good time and a great meal. It was nice to have a friend on board.

Back in Germany

I was relieved and excited to be back on German soil and to be back with my wife and daughter, Anemone. I could not wait to visit family and friends. It was a wonderful Christmas. That year we took a ski vacation in Austria. I had always enjoyed skiing even as a small child. Back home, Bernhard and I would make our skis out of wooden barrel staves. After soaking them in water, we would set them in a vise for a few days to bend them until the tips were bent enough to slide through the snow with ease. What fun that was.

After we returned from our ski trip, I began my new job at the Rhein-Main Hotel near Frankfurt-Main. When I had returned from New York, I had decided not to return to the Frankfurter-hof. I had been offered the Executive Director of day-to-day operations at the Rhein-Main and after some negotiations; I accepted the position and was to start in February.

This hotel was located near the airport and therefore I had the pleasure of serving people once again, from all over the world. It was expected that we had excellent accommodations, as well as fine cuisine. I had to know every aspect of how the hotel operated. It was imperative that I knew and over saw how the food was prepared and that the facility had the safest sanitary conditions possible.

I remember one episode, which stuck with me all these years. It was at the Hotel Beau Rivage in Geneva, Switzerland. While working at that French restaurant, we had a group of celebrities come in to dine; among them was the renowned German movie star, Willy Burgel. I took great pains to prepare the famous French dessert: Crepes Suzzette. This dessert took a lot of work and involved flaming it in the end. It was to be the grand finale of an extraordinary dinner. It was obvious that the party was looking forward it, and it was to be the highlight of the evening, but it turned out to be a disaster. While flaming these almost transparent crepes, everything went well and I served the group. When I served the host of the party, Herr Willy Burgel, one of these crepes slipped out of the tongs with which I was serving them and fell into his lap. He was dressed in an elegant tuxedo, I was mortified. It was all I could do to stay there and help clean up the mess. He graciously stood up, brushed himself off with his napkin, and to my relief laughed about the incident. I apologized profusely and he told me not to worry about it.

I was fortunate to have had formal training in the financial side of a hospitality business and I realized how important it was to understand this side of it. I knew the kitchen was the heart, but the 'body' would die if the soul (budgetary side) were not tended to with as much diligence. I drew on the various job skills I had gleaned from all the different positions I had held over the years. I called upon those closest to me in the business to get me through the rough spots and worked long hours to prove myself.

The reward for all the hard work, no matter how large or small the operation was, was to have satisfied clients who returned because they wanted to, not because it was the only place left. In order to do this, it requires great attention to daily details, patience, and determination. As good as my education was at the Ecole De

Lausanne, it did not entirely prepare a person with everything one needed to know to be successful in this profession. Most of the knowledge gained came from experience in the field whether it is good or bad, success or failures.

Immigrating to the United States

If anyone had told me in 1939, following the unexpected invasion of our country, Poland, that I would be one day living in America, I would have never accepted this theory. Little did I know that it did happen, in 1964.

After my return from New York, I worked for a year at the Rhein-Main Hotel near Frankfurt Am Main. During my tenure there, I had kept in contact with Mr. Reber, who in turn kept me abreast of job opportunities, should I become interested enough to make the change he knew my life needed.

However, I was enjoying my job at the hotel. We liked our condominium and lifestyle. Our daughter was now in second grade and doing well in school. We were close enough to Anna and her husband and daughter that they could visit whenever they had a chance. Despite the inconvenience of the checkpoints, we visited often. That was until the Soviet Premier, Nikita Khrushchev's approval in August of 1961. With this event, over two million East Germans escaped to West Germany. The Berliner Wall was erected and with that, it became impossible to visit with the only link I had to my family, Anna.

In the fall of 1963, Mr. Reber again offered me a position at his Hotel and resort in New York. After careful consideration of this proposition, my wife and I decided to apply for a permanent immigration visa for the three of us. I contacted my former boss of our decision and he was very happy with it. He promised to meet us when we arrived in New York and would make the necessary arrangements for us on his end, so we had a place to stay when we got there. Once again, we had to navigate the seemingly endless hurdles that needed to be jumped in order for us to obtain those pieces of paper. Everything went well and we were granted the visas. I resigned from my job at the Rhein Main Hotel. My employer, Herr Siegert and the staff there were sad to see me leave.

They held a farewell party for us and all our friends and family came to wish us good luck. We found renters for our condominium and before we knew it, we were boarding the train for Bremerhaven.

On April 29, 1964, we were leaving the port of Bremerhaven on the S.S. *United States* heading for New York and our new life, which awaited us there. This time with tears and heavy hearts, we waved goodbye to those well-wishers; my in-laws and our best friends, Liesel and Rolf Barner who stood on their pier wishing us the best, until we could no longer see them.

With both my wife and I having had crossed the Atlantic before, we were prepared for the journey. We were, however, concerned for our daughter, Anemone who had no idea of what to expect. We hoped the crossing would be a smooth one. As I revisited my diaries as I write this book, I came across an entry of something she said to me. "Dad, it has been an awesome experience." She traveled well, with only a slight case of seasickness. While my wife and Anemone sunbathed on the upper deck, I explored the ship's endless decks and poked my nose in wherever I could and asked questions of the staff. No one ever seemed to mind my inquisitiveness. Now a-days one would not be able to do this without causing suspicion. It was a much simpler time then.

We had the pleasure of meeting an elderly couple from New Jersey. They had been visiting relatives in Germany and crossing the
Atlantic had become old news to them. It was their eighth time. They admitted that each crossing was different and they loved them all. I cued Anemone in to the beauty that was all around her. She came to admire the open sea and how the skies complemented its beauty. She especially enjoyed the sight of the moon in the pitch black of the ocean nights and how it shimmered off the inky water.

Having worked in some high-end establishments, I of course, took great interest in the food and service on board the ship. The meals offered were beyond anyone's imagination and the wealthy as well as tourist traveler ate the same, unless a meal was special ordered. We all enjoyed ourselves immensely.

The ship took the rough seas at times with ease as it plowed its way toward the east coast of the United States. We passed our time playing shuffleboard on deck and shopping in its gift stores. Soon we were able to make out the unmistakable outstretched welcoming arm of Lady Liberty. As we glided into port, I realized that I had a different current traveling through my body, that of confidence in my decisions I had made. Even though we would have to find a new home and friends, which was a little intimidating, we had each other.

As we stood on shore, having passed through all the immigration stations, I realized that another dream was becoming a reality. As scared as I was, I took comfort in all those who had come before me and had been able to fulfill their dreams as I was about to. It wasn't long before we found Mr. Reber and loaded our belongings into his shiny black Cadillac and drove off to his Hotel and resort in Barryville. I remembered the Hotel's setting very well. It sat in a valley along the Delaware River with seemingly untouched forests surrounding it.

Within days, we rented a cozy log house in the woods. We enrolled Anemone into a school in Eldred, a short distance from Barryville. I admired that little girl, a great deal. She faced a far bigger challenge than I had ever done. She had to somehow contend with her fellow classmates' snickering, for she spoke absolutely no English. With her mother's help, she picked up the English language quickly and soon fit in with ease.

I started my new job and things were going along quite well. Soon we were able to purchase our first American car, a 1964 Mercury Comet. At times, I couldn't help but think this was all a dream. This reality held more responsibilities. I was a true family man now, I had no one to back me up except for Mr. Reber. I felt a great obligation to him and sought always to do my best.

On my days off, we would take excursions around the Delaware region, which is located in the tri-state wedge of New York, Pennsylvania, and New Jersey. Words do not do justice to the beauty that surrounded us on these drives. I remembered, that we had friends outside of Barryville and that was the now retired major who had attended our wedding, Robert Wrynn and his wife who lived in Texas. We had been exchanging letters and talked often by telephone. We had gotten along since the first moment we met and his wife, Astrid was a sweetheart. They invited us on one occasion to visit them in Texas. Along with the invite to visit, came the offer of a job at one of the leading hotels in Austin; the Commodore Perry Hotel. I was not sure if I could take the position. I felt a loyalty to Mr. Reber and his establishment. Summer was just beginning and I knew he would appreciate my help and experience.

I took the summer to glean as much as I could from my position at Mr. Reber's Hotel and resort. I knew that by Labor Day, the travelers would have had to return home and his season would be drawing to a close. Before I set any type of decision into stone, I knew I would have to discuss my job offer with Mr. Reber. My wife was all for us moving to Texas, since she had not really made any friends where we were now.

Toward the end of September, I knew my mind had been made up and I summoned all my courage to go to Mr. Reber and tell him of my decision. To say the least, he and his wife were disappointed that I had chosen to leave his establishment, but he asked if I would consider staying until the end of October. I assured him this would not be a problem. We contacted our friends in Texas and informed them that we had indeed accepted their offer. On November 2, 1964, we said our goodbyes. Mr. Reber, left a job offer on the table for me, should I decide to return.

We hooked up a rented a U-haul trailer to our Mercury Comet, loaded it with our few possessions, and took off. During our short stay in our small cottage, we had acquired a cat, which we named Billy Boy. We were not sure how he would travel, but decided to take him along, to pacify Anemone. We made an early stop and that was to get a map from our local AAA agent. As we traveled the highways, I could not help but reflect on the freedom that was to become a way of life for me. I thought often about how difficult simple travel between Frankfurt and Berlin was back in Germany, with the checkpoints and papers you always were required to carry. Here, all one needed was either a drivers license or an identification card to move from one area or state. One did not have to check in with the local police departments and you were free to roam at will.

By the time we hit Columbus, Ohio, we had our first taste of an American winter. Even though it was early November, we had driven into an unexpected blizzard, which temporarily shut the city down. Unaccustomed to driving in this type of weather with a trailer in tow, I pulled over under an overpass to wait out the storm. It did not last long. We were relieved to leave the heavy blanket of white snow behind us.

One night in Illinois, we rented a room in a small motel, which was set off in a wooded area. Sometime during the night, Anemone for some reason had opened the motel door and our cat, Billy Boy had gotten out. Anemone was distraught. She woke us exclaiming excitedly that the cat had gotten out and we quickly dressed and started looking for it. Soon we heard the motel owner's dog starting to bark, guess what he was barking at; our cat. Billy Boy was high up in one of the trees. It was a good thing that we were in no real hurry and we assured our daughter that we would do whatever possible to get her precious Billy Boy down. She called out to him, my wife and I called out to him to come down, but it only seemed to drive him higher up in the branches. Suddenly, the motel owner came over and stated he had some fish in his truck and thought possibly he could entice the cat down with a tempting treat. He cut up a fairly large trout, placed some on a stick and held it up so the scent of it wafted up into the foliage of the tree. It became too much for Billy Boy and he slowly made his way back down to the ground. He was rewarded for returning to us with a meal of fresh trout with Anemone watching closely over him. When he was finished eating, she picked him up and we were once again on our way.

In early May, 1964, Herr Kleinert appeared at our front door just before our immigration to the United States. At this time he needed my help. I had not seen Herrn Kleinert for over 16 years since my escape from East Germany. I had been the only one out of the 24 employees who had been arrested in Auschwitz at the hotel which Herr Kleinert owned along with two other establishments.

The purpose of his visit was to ask if I would be able to make a deposition at an attorney's office stating that Herr Kleinert actually did own all three properties. With my deposition he was able to submit documentation to the German government for which he would receive reparation. He was extremely pleased that I was still alive and could provide the written testimony.

This was the last time I saw Herrn Kleinert. However, he did write me a few months later in 1965 while I was living in New York, to inform me that he did indeed receive compensation for his properties from the German government.

I still treasure his letters, which he wrote to me in German and he expressed gratitude for what I had done for him. It was my obligation to do this for Herrn Kleinert because I truly believed deep in my heart that he had saved my life.

Honing My Skills in Texas

As we drove along, I could not help but realize that just this past spring we had crossed the Atlantic, some 4,500 miles and we did it in a little over five days, but this trip to Texas, which was only 1,000 miles would take the same amount of time. I didn't complain though, I enjoyed immensely the beauty of this country as we drove across it.

Our destination was Austin, Texas. Not knowing where we needed to get off, we traveled the highway at a slow rate of speed. We must have been traveling too slow for traffic and before we knew it, we were being pulled over by a State trooper. I panicked. However, it turned out to be a routine stop, I had to show him my driver's license. After radioing in my information, he asked what the problem was and after I told him our situation, with a smile on his face he welcomed us to Texas and gave us directions as to where we should get off so we could contact the major. Unfortunately, we got lost and found ourselves on the outskirts of the city and not knowing where we needed to go, we called our friend and tried to explain to him where we were. Laughing a little at our predicament, he indicated that he knew exactly where we were and that he would meet us in a few minutes. What a relief it was to see him pull up in his Ford Fairlane. What a joyful reunion it was.

We followed him to his home in University Hills, a suburb of Austin. Arriving in Texas, probably is comparable to arriving in a foreign country. After a wonderful reunion with our friends Bob and Astrid Wrynn, I reported to the job, which he had arranged for me at the Commodore Perry Hotel in Austin. The General Manager was a Mr. Ronald Morgan. We hit it off right away. I was put in charge of the 'Deck Club', which was a private club within the Hotel. You had to be a member to use the facilities of this operation. I met powerful politicians from within the state of Texas. I had a wonderful staff working for me. It was my first time working with a very diverse ethnic staff and I found them to be very loyal, dependable and extremely friendly.

We stayed with the Wrynns for a short time until we could find a place of our own. We were fortunate to find a house close to them which made our stay there all that more enjoyable. I enjoyed working at the Commodore Perry. I came to realize more and more that the hospitality business was similar to showbiz. Everyone likes to be entertained. I believed that if you did your job right, you would almost be able to hear the applause, but if you failed the boos would resonate throughout the establishment. My main objective was that my staff did their job well with everyone pulling their weight and that we provided the best service possible.

We enjoyed living in Austin along the Colorado River. We ended up living in Texas for ten years. It was the longest I lived in one place, since I had left my home in Tarnowskie-Góry.

Once more Christmas rolled around. It would have been my twenty-second one away from my hometown. What surprised me most was the Texas way of life. I was used to cold weather, snow and a brilliant atmosphere at this time of year. However, my first Christmas in Texas was to be green with its natives dressed in short sleeves as they promenaded the streets of this beautiful city. We spent a wonderful holiday season with our friends. Anemone was disappointed that there was no snow and even more distraught when our friends told her that it rarely snowed in Texas.

After a few months at the Hotel, I attended a mandatory conference for all the managers, which was held in Fort Worth. While I was there, I met a fine gentleman, Leo Meyer, former alumni of the Ecole De Lausanne. He was the Director of Food and Beverage operation at the Dallas Hilton. I still do not understand what drew people to me and what made them take interest in my talents, but before I left the conference, he offered me a position at his hotel. I thought about it for a short time and decided that I was not ready to make a move at this time, so I declined the offer.

However, I was never content to stay in one position for very long. There were still many things that I did not know. I had learned so much since my arrival in the States. I truly believe in the adage that learning is an ongoing process. I also believe that one never really finishes learning, no matter how long one lives.

During that same time period, while I was back at the Commodore, I was approached by another person who gave me the opportunity to consider a position with the Six Flags Inn in Arlington Texas. This offer was tempting. He extended a generous salary in conjunction with wonderful benefits. After talking it over with my family, we decided that I should take this offer and we were soon moving to Arlington. This was one of the biggest establishments for which I worked and it aided me in perfecting my talents in America.

The Wrynns were disappointed that we were moving away, but they understood that I needed to acquire more experience in my profession, and Arlington was not that far away. We were still able to visit each other on a regular basis.

We bought a large three-bedroom home with a two-car garage on a corner lot for only $15,000. This also included to Anemone's delight a membership to the local swimming pool; which was right across from our home. With temperatures usually around ninety degrees this was a nice perk for all of us.

My job kept me busy, I had been appointed as the Food, Beverage, and Service Manager. I managed one of the biggest staffs that I ever would; two hundred employees. One of my first changes was to hire a new executive chef. I had heard of a fine German chef who was working in Houston. I offered him the position and he immediately accepted. His wife and mine became friends immediately.

We liked our neighborhood, I had a good job. Overall, we were doing quite well. We were blessed and very grateful to God for what he had done for us. As I said before, I believed that you never stopped learning. During my tenure at this Inn, I joined an organization called the Food and Beverage Association. Members had to attend workshops and seminars with an emphasis on management. Meetings were held monthly and the quarterly seminars usually lasted three to four days. Each seminar accumulated credit points toward a certification in Hospitality Management.

In 1966, we had convinced my in-laws to visit us in Texas. Ursula and Anemone were beside themselves with joy during their stay. I was able to take some time off from work and arranged to show them around this state which we had grown to love. With a little research, I found that Texas was the home of some German settlements such as; New Braunfels, San Marcos, Fredricksburg, and Castroville. We visited Bob and Astrid in Austin, the Alamo, and Corpus Christi. It was a very memorable time for all of us. After several weeks, we had to say goodbye to them.

Up to this point, we were all doing well, but after Ursula's parents left, we noticed that Anemone seemed to be losing weight. She was already a slight child and we immediately became concerned and took her to the doctor. She was diagnosed with diabetes. She would require insulin shots for the rest of her life. She quickly accepted her fate and to this day, I am amazed that she is able to poke herself without so much as a second thought to test her blood and administer the medicine that allows her to live a relatively normal lifestyle.

After about two years in the States, I came to find out that many top chefs and managers in the Hospitality field came from European countries or were trained in Europe. This could explain some of the interest that seemed to follow me wherever I went. During yet another seminar, I met up with Mr. Meyer again, and he offered me a position with his thousand-room hotel in Dallas. I was flattered and he said he would be willing for me to join his staff when I was ready. I talked it over with Ursula and she had no objections to me taking the position. We would not have to move, since it was only a twenty-mile trip from our home to his hotel. I was familiar with Dallas and eventually we decided I should accept his offer.

I resigned my post at the Six Flags Inn and in February 1967 moved on. My new position would be that of Director of Catering, which would involve overseeing the food and beverage activities of the banquet department. Since we had had the same basic training in Switzerland, I quickly developed a wonderful rapport with Leo Meyer who was my immediate supervisor. I had a spacious office and for the first time a secretary. My days were extremely full. Each day I had to routinely go over the daily business activities, communicate with the kitchen staff, and keep on top of the banquet facilities. The ballroom was elegantly designed and could easily house over three thousand people, along with numerous meeting rooms for smaller gatherings. I relished every hour of my working day, and strove to make every day a productive one.

During my time there, I had the pleasure of overseeing an event, which was being held for German Chancellor, Ludwig Erhard. Due to my command of the German language, I was to be in charge of all the formal and informal food activities during his stay at the Hotel. When he arrived at the Hotel, I greeted him and welcomed him to Texas and specifically Dallas. I introduced him to the managers of the Hotel and escorted him to his suite. Several formal dinners took place while he was in residence. My French came in handy during one dinner where it was attended by representatives from Britain, the United States, and France. It was a very exciting time, but I paid for it by putting in extremely long hours. The Hotel seemed never to sleep while the Chancellor stayed with us. Along with the hustle and bustle of the Hotel, we had to contend with reporters, news crews, and cameras who were everywhere and often times in the way. Before the Chancellor left, he presented me with an autographed picture, which hangs in my library at home to this day.

As enjoyable and grateful I was to have had this experience, I was relieved when it ended. The commutes back and forth between home and work with few hours of rest in between had started to take its toll on me and I looked forward to being able to rest.

It was early in 1967, when my wife realized that she was expecting our second child. We had come to accept the fact that we would only be blessed with one child since Anemone was already ten years old, but that was not to be. We figured out that the baby was due in October and each day I waited on pins and needles for my pager to go off, alerting me to the fact that she had gone into labor. I was probably in the Hotel's cavernous halls when she summoned me. Well, I did not hear the page and in turn, I missed her 'call'. It wasn't until I came out into the lobby, where I found one of the resident managers calling out to me that my neighbor had called to tell me they had taken my wife to the hospital. I left everything and practically flew to the hospital. I definitely was exceeding the speed limit, when I realized that the sirens I was hearing were meant for me. Looking in my mirrors I finally noticed the squad car with its revolving lights following me. I decided I had better stop and explain my situation before I got into real trouble. The officer asked to see my driver's license. I was nervous and excited. I was having a hard time getting it out of my wallet. The officer told me to calm down and asked what was wrong. I tried to explain about my wife being in labor, but he did not seem interested or did not hear me. He asked me again for my license. Precious minutes were passing and I wanted to be there when my child was born. Finally, I found my license and after checking it, he asked me if I was indeed on my way to the hospital. I reiterated that I was indeed to be a father soon, if I hadn't already missed the blessed event. He seemed to accept my story and after handing me back my license told me to drive a little slower, follow the traffic laws and to drive safely. Well, I didn't listen to him and within a short distance, I was stopped again by an officer. Unfortunately, the same one had stopped me earlier. Again, he let me go, but with a stronger warning. It took me an hour to travel the twenty miles to the hospital. Once there I found the maternity ward and my wife and daughter, Anemone. Just before midnight on my birthday, October 10, our second daughter was born. We named her Bettina.

It was in the spring of 1968, when I received an unexpected call from San Antonio. I had met a Mr. Bailey at one of our seminars and after a lengthy discussion, he offered me the position of General Manager at his establishment. I asked how he had heard of me, but he refused to disclose who had dropped my name. He invited me down to meet with his board of directors, the chairman, and the president of the Argyle Club. I was aghast, I asked him again who he was and he told me that he was the chairman of the club's search committee. I told him I would have to talk to my wife and would call him in two days.

We had visited San Antonio about a year ago and had found it to be a beautiful city. Its European architecture, historic buildings, and rich culture (which were influenced by the Spanish) drew me to it. I loved the softly rolling hills, which were covered with blue bonnets giving a serene view wherever you looked. My wife and I talked about the move and it was decided that I should take the position. I called Mr. Bailey and within two days, I received a letter not only confirming my job offer, but also round trip airfare from Dallas to San Antonio. On my next day off, I got on the flight to San Antonio. I was greeted by Mr. Bailey himself. We rode in his Mercedes Benz Limousine. We drove to the Alamo Heights, a small community within the city of San Antonio. We drove to a secluded area surrounded by extremely tall trees. As we drove through the gates, I was in awe at the sight that was before me. We were headed toward one of the most majestic buildings I had ever seen. It had tall columns, which supported three étage, I was overwhelmed. A valet at the entrance attended to his Mercedes as we entered the building.

Once inside, I was stricken by the interior, its furnishing, and ambience. I thought I was in a different world. A lunch was waiting for us after which I was introduced to five gentlemen, apparently members of the board of directors. After a long discussion and many questions, they summed up what they were looking for. They needed someone who was well versed and erudite in the hospitality field. Someone who could provide good leadership. They needed someone who had experience in all facets of a food operation. The ideal candidate would have worked in many social settings. After this speech, three of the men left the room, while the other two engaged me in a casual conversation. A short while later the three returned, asked me a few more questions after which, the president offered me the position. My head was spinning, It took all the courage I had to tell them I needed to think over the offer. I explained that I could not make this type of decision without talking things over with my wife and family. They seemed to appreciate my predicament and said they looked forward to hearing from me soon.

I flew back to Dallas and from there drove back home to Arlington. As I deliberated over this magnificent offer, I received a letter from Mr. Bailey again stating how pleased they would be to have me on their staff. In the letter, as the saying goes, "they made me an offer I could not refuse." It wasn't that kind of offer, but nonetheless I felt I could not pass it up. Not only was the salary and the position one that I wanted to add to my resume, but they also paid for my moving expenses.

It was heartbreaking to think of leaving all our new friends and neighborhood, which we enjoyed, but I felt it was the right decision. Mr. Meyer was supportive, albeit he didn't want to see me go. It was an emotional situation, one I think of often.

We sold our home in Arlington and moved to San Antonio. Mr. Bailey invited us to spend a night at the Villa, in order for us to get first hand knowledge of the atmosphere.

With his help, we found a beautiful home. I have to admit that I admired the fact that my wife was willing to put up with the numerous times I asked her to move so I could obtain experience in another aspect of this field. Whenever a position sounded right for me, we would discuss it and take a family vote. Anemone also had a say in these decisions and they always were supportive of these moves. This was our fourth home in four years.

The Argyle was and still is an exclusive private club with about six hundred members. All social activities were arranged by or with the general manager. The initiation fee was high and only the well-to-do or influential were invited to join. Its membership includes: doctors, lawyers, community leaders, as well as politicians. Most of the members lived in Texas, but there were some from other states as well. The Argyle is affiliated with the Foundation for Research and Education, a branch of the Medical Institute of San Antonio. Through the years very little has escaped the Argyle in way of recognition and honors.

Almost all the members were world travelers who had discriminating culinary tastes. The main challenge I faced as the General Manager was to provide them with the best menu and a wide variety of items, which changed frequently. It was a challenge I enjoyed immensely. The eclectic menu was fantastic and at one time, a gourmet magazine had requested some of my recipes.

Antique silver cutlery and furnishings complemented the atmosphere. The cypress floors were impressive to say the least as were the eighteen-inch thick stone walls. The décor represented the motifs and period of the six flags of Texas.

On one occasion, I was summoned personally by the president of the First National Bank of San Antonio, who wanted to arrange an intimate dinner for twenty people. The setting would involve the entire second floor and one of our elegant private dining rooms. I was to keep these arrangements as confidential as possible, for the guest of honor was to be none other than President Lyndon B. Johnson. All the details were worked out and I was attentive to every detail of the affair. I was very impressed with my staff that day for the service and the food was impeccable. After the dinner, I received a visit from the President's secretary indicating that the President himself wanted to speak to me. Quickly, I went over in my head if something had gone wrong. I couldn't think of anything. I was coiled tight as a spring as I approached his table. I introduced myself again to him, and to my relief he complimented me, "Mr. Skaletz, I've been dining all over the world, but this has been one of the finest dinners I've ever attended." All I could say, was "Thank you." Before his party left the Argyle, he signed my private guestbook. He was a very cordial man and even shook hands with some of the members in the lower dining rooms. With that, he was whisked away by men in dark suits and sunglasses. I was relieved that this event was over, but before I left, I personally thanked each of my staff for a flawless evening.

The following day I took off to relax. We had installed an in ground swimming pool and I was playing with my daughter Bettina in the pool. Suddenly, my wife ran out onto the patio, exclaiming that a Mike Howard wanted to talk me. I didn't know who he was and she stated he was the President's secretary and that he was on the telephone. Not thinking, I asked how he got our telephone number since it was unlisted, but the President I am sure can find out anything he wants to about anyone. I grabbed a towel and rushed to the telephone. Upon greeting him, he informed me that the President of the United States wanted to speak with me. The President was then put on the line. In shock, I listened to him compliment me once again on the dinner and the service. He told me it was one of the most eclectic and well-prepared events he had ever attended. I thanked him again for his compliments. I thought that would be the end of the conversation, but it almost became too much to bear as he went on about the night. All I was able to say was thank you repeatedly. Suddenly, he changed the subject and asked if I had done anything that someone would have considered impossible in my lifetime. I replied that I was an optimist by nature and that nothing was impossible. I noted that I had faced many difficult situations and had mastered most of them. We talked for a while. He seemed to be in no hurry to end the conversation. He indicated that he was planning a surprise dinner for his wife, Lady Bird Johnson with about forty or so guests in attendance. He wanted to know if I could duplicate the menu, I had served him just two days ago. I replied that of course I could. That may have been the biggest mistake I had ever made, I had not asked him when he wanted to do this. To my chagrin he told me he needed it that evening. I couldn't say anything, my mind was racing. I had no idea how I could pull this off in the manner I needed to do it. He wondered aloud if I was still there, and I replied that I was. He rattled off the details that he wanted fulfilled and I silently made note of them. My head was spinning, much like the Sputnik, which orbited the earth. All I could do was reply yes to each request he made. I stood their oblivious to the fact I was dripping water on our hard wood floors, gradually I became aware of Ursula trying to wipe up around my feet. He ended the conversation with "Are we all set then?" I replied, "Yes, Mr. President." With that, our thirty-minute conversation ended. I don't think I ever showered, shaved, and dressed as fast as I did that day. I drove at a frantic speed to the Argyle all the way trying to figure out how I was going to do this.

When I arrived, my secretary met me and explained that the President had called for me. I told her I knew that and proceeded to tell her what the conversation entailed. The club was closed that day, so this was going to truly be a daunting challenging task. I called in as much of the staff as I could muster up and we set about duplicating the meal. I even had to arrange for a Mariachi band to provide entertainment; to my relief they showed up on time. By six-thirty that evening, the guests started to arrive. The evening and the dinner was a success. I had created an extraordinary dessert called the Scotch Irish Symphony. After dessert was served, I was once again summoned to the President's table. To my delight, Lady Bird Johnson exclaimed that the dessert was the highlight of the evening.

During my time at the Argyle, I had the pleasure of serving the President many times and got to know him quite well. I even served him at his Texas "Whitehouse." To describe my experiences with the President would require me to write an entire new book. He was a great man. He loved to listen to my stories about my background and how I came to this country. On one such occasion, he exclaimed to me, "Mr. Skaletz, you must write a book!" I received numerous calls from Lady Bird, requesting my services. I remember one in particular, I was to make the President's favorite roasts, the Argyle whole rib eye. She told me that no one could make it like I could. I told her of course I would do it, but I couldn't leave the hotel that night for it was extremely busy. We made arrangements for me to meet his secret service men at a highway motel and they would transport it the rest of the way. What a night!

My time at the Argyle was never dull, that is more than true. One other extraordinary event was an elegant dinner for a three star General and Commanding Chief Officer, Harry Critz at Fort Sam Houston. I also served General Coiner and General Walton E. Harris. This was the norm at the prestigious Argyle Club.

I was to organize a three-day outing at the ranch of Attorney General, John Hill. The ranch overlooked the valley of the Pedernales River. When I arrived at the ranch, I was not greeted by the Attorney General's wife, but by their three flesh eating vicious pit bulls. It was a harrowing experience. They circled my car, I sounded my horn several times and was relieved when Mrs. Hill finally called off the dogs. She apologized profusely for having lost track of time and escorted me inside. We discussed the details of the three-day event. Everything was to be catered by the Argyle: On Friday an informal dinner, Saturday there would be a black tie dinner, and on Sunday a brunch. When I looked at the dining hall, I was amazed. It was cavernous and could easily accommodate two hundred people. I was soon to find out that everyone and anyone of importance was to be there including President and Lady Bird Johnson. When the President spotted me, he came over and playfully commented, "Mr. Skaletz, I thought you 'worked' for me!" I told him, politically I needed to remain in the middle. He said I should have been a politician. The weekend went off without a hitch and everyone was satisfied.

I presided over yet another elegant affair hosted by then U.S. Attorney General, John Mitchel. This night I arrived to find my reserved parking space taken. Indignantly, I approached the men standing next to the vehicle to find out who had parked in my space only to find that they were secret service agents. They asked for an ID and I told them I was the general manager of the club. This didn't faze them one bit. I felt in my pockets only to find that when I had changed into my tuxedo for the evening's event, I had not brought my wallet with me. I explained again, who I was and that if they didn't let me in, the President would not be getting his dinner. After a bit one of the agents decided, it was in their best interest to verify my identity and he went inside. He soon came back and with a sheepish look, I was allowed into the building. After dinner, I was asked to bring my entire staff into the elegant dining room and introduce them to the President. He greeted each one with a handshake and cordial comment, after which the entire party broke out into applause. I could not have been prouder of my staff and what we had accomplished.

I have two treasured books in my private library at home that were given to me by the President and Lady Bird Johnson, they are *The Vantage Point: Perspectives of the Presidency 1963-1969: Lyndon Baines Johnson*, signed by him and *The White House Diary* which she signed. I treasure them both.

In 1972, I was scheduled to attend a convention as a member of the CMAA (Club Manager Association of America) in London, England. Since this trip could turn out to be a vacation of sorts, I opted to bring my family along with me. While I attended the seminars, my wife and children shopped and did some sightseeing with friends. While we were there, we took the opportunity to visit with my wife's parents in Frankfurt-Main. It was a nice trip, but short lived and we were soon back in San Antonio. There are many times I reflect back on how many opportunities I had during my career and the wonderful people that I had met since I had immigrated to the United States. It was the best move that I could have made. I considered myself extremely blessed, not only with good health, but with a good education fostered by those who cared about my welfare.

I sometimes thought I could stay at the Argyle forever. Even though not all the experiences were good ones, the Argyle was an extremely good stepping-stone for me. However, the clock moves only in one direction and I soon realized that days, weeks, and months were passing by at warp speed.

My Life is Turned Upside Down

With the passing of President Johnson, I accepted a position as General Manager at the Whitehall Club in Oklahoma City. It was set on top of the Fidelity Bank of Oklahoma City, with a spectacular view of the surrounding architecture. The Whitehall was a prestigious club, however, it was in poor financial shape. I was told by the then chairman of the board that my task was to resurrect this operation. After settling into the community, I set about tackling the mountain of problems. Being an optimist, I knew nothing was truly impossible and I hit each obstacle running.

Once again, I stuck to what I knew best and that was the European trained professionals. I hired a German trained chef who had spent some time in Paris, London, and Austria; his diverse experience would only serve us for the better. I needed to not only improve the bottom line, but to turn the reputation of one's dining experience around 360 degrees. I fine-tuned the staff so that we were soon able to offer the best in culinary arts and service. After only a few short months, the operation's financial situation improved substantially. I trimmed out unnecessary 'fat' our financial statements proved that what I was doing was working.

Word of mouth and the new reputation of the club increased the membership and we were soon in the black. The Whitehall soon became the talk of the town.

During my time at the Whitehall, I had started taking evening classes at the University of Oklahoma City. Over a relatively short period of time, I was able to obtain my Masters Degree in Business Administration and Business Law. I looked into the latter, since most of my current positions consisted of contracts and financial activities on a greater scale than I was used to.

Time flew by and before we knew it our oldest daughter, Anemone fell in love and decided to marry an Australian professional tennis player. She had met him at the Oklahoma Tennis Club where she often played. We were doing very well financially and we were able to give her a beautiful wedding.

Wherever I worked and whatever type of staff I had, I always strove to make them as professional as they could be. I developed training programs and manuals to help them. I got a great deal of satisfaction as I watched them grow and improve. I believe what helped me reach these young minds, as many of them were much younger than I was, was the fact they knew I was once one of them.

I had only been at the Whitehall three years, when I heard from a friend of mine from Texas. He was now the director of sales at the Tan-Tar-A Resort in Missouri. He told me that the owner, Mr. Duenke had heard about me and wanted to offer me a job. I was speechless. The opportunity was enormous. This resort was one of the largest in America. It had five restaurants and enough banquet facilities to accommodate thirty five hundred people. I respectfully told him I would have to think about it, but that I was settled and just getting comfortable with my position at the Whitehall. He knew me from Texas and also knew that I could not resist an opportunity to better myself. A few days passed and I received the formal job offer in the mail along with round trip airline tickets for myself and my entire family. He was right, I couldn't resist. I requested time off and flew out to the Ozarks. The Ozarks in the fall are magnificent. You have never seen colors such as these if you haven't traveled there. We were met at the airport by Mike Delacy, my colleague and friend from Dallas and were given accommodations in the Governor's suite at the resort. We dined in their four star restaurant. It was wonderful. The next morning after breakfast, I met with the board. The interview lasted for almost two and a half-hours. After lunch with my family and the owner, we took an afternoon cruise on the Lake of the Ozarks. As we watched the sunset during dinner, we could not help but have our breath taken away by the beauty of our surroundings.

The following day after more 'wining and dining' I met with the owner and the vice president of the resort. They offered me the position of director of food and beverage of the <u>entire</u> resort. I was by now gasping for breath. I could not believe that they had this much faith in my abilities. I asked him to give me at least two days to think it over and discuss it with my family. He understood and left me to make my decision. That afternoon we left for Oklahoma City. In February of 1976, I left Oklahoma and moved to the Ozarks. This time, I had decided to make the move alone. This position had a great deal more responsibility and I did not want to uproot everyone if it did not work out. For about ten months, I worked at the resort. I had been living in a rented condo and every other week either my wife and daughter, Bettina would come to see me or I would go out to see them.

This position did prove to be extremely challenging. It took a great deal of my time and effort to manage all the different aspects of it. In my department alone, there were over two hundred and fifty employees. I had to revamp the menus in all five of the restaurants, and recalculate the costs for banquet activities. I had much larger budgets to manage and to balance. There was an extreme amount of responsibility. I had two secretaries who helped me manage my daily needs, correspondence, meetings, etc.

During one of my family's visits, Bettina ran into my office exclaiming they had finally found a home they liked. I dropped everything and we went together to check it out. It was indeed a large beautiful home overlooking the lake. My job was going well and I had exceeded Mr. Duenke's expectations. Financially the resort was doing well and the operating costs were down. With all this in mind, my job secure and the fact that I desperately wanted my family with me, we put an offer on the house and bought it. Unfortunately, the house needed some remodeling to make it suit our needs more. The existing carport was to be replaced by a two-car garage, we wanted to add a large deck to the back of the house, and the second floor layout was changed. Money was not an issue, what we needed were good contractors to do the work. After some looking, we found someone who we thought would do a good job. With the remodeling completed I was looking forward to what I thought would be yet another happy chapter in my life. However, unbeknownst to me, I was to find out that my wife was <u>not</u> happy and she asked for a divorce. She left our daughter with me and moved away. Bettina and I were devastated. How do you explain to a ten-year old girl that her mother had left? I couldn't explain it to myself.

Not only was my life in shambles, but my job was soon to be disrupted also. The resort had been sold to the Marriott Hotel Corporation and I was transferred to the Dulles Airport Hotel in Washington DC. I didn't like the city at all, I quickly put my networking skills to work, and before I knew it, I was contacted by the president of the Highland Country Club in Omaha, Mr. Sidney Abraham. After a visit with the board, I was offered a job, which I accepted on the spot. Ironically, I Günther Skaletz, of German descent became the general manager of a Jewish Country Club. It proved to be one of the most interesting positions I have ever had. I got along famously with the board of directors. It seemed my war experiences only proved to bring them closer into my life. Often times during the monthly board meetings, we would get off the subject of the club and discuss my experiences in the war.

I had the run of the place. Cart-blanch, whatever I wanted. As a young man, I remember vividly eating out of garbage cans and now I had all the lox and bagels I could eat. It was a nice way to work my way out of the misery that seemed to swallow me whole. They were a down to earth, unpretentious people and I served them well, I gave great attention to every detail I was overseeing and they showed their appreciation for my efforts.

That was until I received a call from a Mr. Lahey from Oshkosh, Wisconsin. He was the president of the Miles Kimball Corporation, which owned a restaurant in Oshkosh. He offered me the job as general manager. As much as I liked my job at the Highland Country Club and its members, I was antsy to get away and make another change in my life. My problem was, that I had never heard of the city and only had a maps image of where Wisconsin was. I asked a well-traveled friend where Oshkosh was and he replied "Oshkosh B'Gosh!", now I really was confused. We looked it up and found that it was on Lake Winnebago and when Mr. Lahey called again, we arranged for me to fly out and meet him for an interview. I flew into Wittman Field where I was greeted by Mr. Lahey. He drove me out to his house so I could freshen up. He promised to take me to a landmark in the area that he thought I might enjoy and that was the farm of Mrs. Krantz, the widow of the famous violinist Herr Krantz. Visiting the farm brought back dear memories of my grandparents' farm back home in Poland. We had breakfast the next morning at the Pearl Coffee Shop and dinner that evening at the Gray Fox restaurant, which is the restaurant that the company owned. He definitely wanted me to accept his offer. After a brief meeting, he drove me over to meet Mrs. Kimball. Her husband had founded the Miles Kimball Company. I found her to be a charming lady. Over dinner that evening, we talked out more of the details to this position and over dessert, we were joined by Mrs. Kimball. I had already decided to accept the position and did so formally.

Regretfully, I resigned my position at the Highland Country Club. Bettina and I packed up our belongings, our two cats; Pasha and Snoopy, our dog; Heidi into our Chevy Blazer and drove straight through to Oshkosh.

Everything is Right Again

Shortly after my arrival I started to experience excruciating chest pains; I consulted my doctor immediately. After a thorough examination and a short stay in the hospital, they found that the pain was actually coming from a large tumor in my right lung. The operation would prove to be complicated and risky. I said a prayer with the hospital chaplain and I was soon on my way to surgery. They had to remove a rib and the tumor was about the size of a polo ball. To my relief the tumor was benign. I spent twelve days in intensive care. No one is sure why I developed this tumor. It could have been from the war and all the acrid smoke I inhaled or it could have come from simple second hand smoke in the establishments for which I worked for so many years, I will never know for sure. All I know is that I survived and for that, every day is a miracle.

When my wife and I divorced, it was agreed that Bettina would live with me, but over time, our daughter decided she wanted to live with her mother in Missouri. Wanting her to be happy, I consented. I visited her as much as my scheduled allowed.

It was upon my return from one of the visits that I was to meet the woman who would take away all my heartache. She turned out to be the true love of my life, the ying to my yang. When I returned from one of my weekends with Bettina, I noticed a new employee at the restaurant. I found out that my assistant manager had hired her. I introduced myself to her and she told me her name was Elaine. She was beautiful, all I could say at that time was "Nice to meet you." I have to admit I am not a very smooth talker when it comes to women, especially beautiful ones. I stopped in as often as I could and after a few weeks asked her out on a date. It was the best personal thing I had ever done.

It was love at first sight. We worked together for a year and dated almost that entire time. On July 23, 1981, in a simple ceremony, we were married. It's been a blessing and I thank the Lord every day of my life that He made all this possible for me.

Shortly after, we moved from Oshkosh to Oconomowoc where I had accepted a position as the Food and Service Director of the Olympia Resort. Elaine was able to get a job there too as head hostess. After a year and a half, the resort went through some changes and our positions were eliminated. Jobs were hard to come by and we moved to Milwaukee. I worked for a year at the Marriott Hotel in Brookfield. While I was there, I attended a meeting of the managers at the Pfister Hotel in Milwaukee. By pure happenstance, I ran into an acquaintance I knew from Fort Worth Texas. He asked me what I was doing in Milwaukee and I told him where I was working. I hadn't seen him since 1966, but I remembered that he was a well-established businessman and when he offered me a position with his operation, I jumped at the chance. I resigned my position at the Marriott Hotel and became the Director of Food and Beverage at the Sheraton Hotel.

Things were picking up and Elaine and I bought a very nice home, an English Tudor. Elaine loved the place. She took great pains to restore it to its original splendor. She wanted its natural beauty to shine through. She did a splendid job, making this house into a home for us. This house was the first one I had that had a working fireplace. It was very relaxing to come home after a hard day's work and sit in front of it with a cup of hot tea and honey. We were very happy.

Violence in the States was something I had never experienced until one night when I returned home from work. I was surprised to find that our backyard light was not on. Normally, Elaine left it on for me when I was working late, so I would not have to walk from the garage to the house in the dark. Not thinking anything of it, I parked my car in the garage and headed toward the house. On most nights the neighbors' dogs on either side of us would announce my arrival, but on this night, they were silent. This concerned me somewhat, but I ignored it. Just as I was about to approach the house a man's voice stopped me in my tracks. Not knowing what was going on, I turned around and when I did, I saw a heavyset man donned with a mask standing in the dark behind me. He assaulted me by hitting me on the head. I struggled to get away, but he pushed me backward and I fell on our concrete steps. Bleeding from the wound on my head, I managed to get up. I was carrying some clothing to the house on hangers. I grabbed one of the wooden hangers and started to beat the unsuspecting assailant over the head with it, all the while yelling for someone to help me. No one came. I then noticed that the dogs were still not barking. What was the matter? My cries soon reached Elaine and she came out to the second floor balcony. She started to call out for help. When the man realized he wasn't going to get what he came for he let me go and ran away. I climbed the stairs and Elaine helped me into the house. Seeing my face and hands covered with blood, she collapsed. I managed to make it to the telephone and called the police. When they finally arrived, almost a half hour later, they searched the yards in vain. They did however find a long heavy screwdriver, which had been used to break our basement window. It was evident that he wanted to get into the house. I thank God daily that I had come home earlier than usual on that fateful night,

I am sure if I hadn't, my wife Elaine would not be with me today. For the next two weeks, a police car escorted me home from work at the Hotel. Every sound at night woke us up, it was a harrowing experience.

Our Final Move

Following this incident, we decided to sell our home and move away from Milwaukee. We had on numerous occasions driven through a small city north of Milwaukee, Two Rivers. We liked this quaint city on beautiful Lake Michigan. Elaine was familiar with the area too. As a child, she and her parents would drive through the city on their way to a cabin up north. She had always thought she would settle here when she grew up and we jumped at the chance to make the move.

We often ate at a small hotel on the lake and during one of our lunches, I made contact with a gentleman who suggested we dine at a local supper club in a small town just outside the city. He drove us into the country not far out of town and we were surprised to find out that Shoto really was not much of a 'town', more like a tavern, supper club and a firehouse. The supper club was set along a peaceful river, which spilled over a small dam right outside the dining windows. The food was fine and I could see myself working there. I liked the quiet ambiance, which was such a change from my last positions. After our lunch, I requested to see the owner. Shortly after, a tall man of imposing stature appeared at our table and introduced himself as Mr. Gene Holly. He asked what he could do for me and I asked to speak with him in private. I went with him to his office and told him I was interested in working for him. Not knowing who I was, he asked me what I could do. I told him, "Anything." He asked me to be more specific and proceeded to ask me if I could cook. I said, "Of course, and much more." By the time I left, I was assured that I indeed had a position as an assistant chef at the River Falls Supper Club.

We drove back to Milwaukee and submitted my resignation at the Sheraton. We put the house on the market and sold it within three months. We found a lovely small house on Lake Michigan. Elaine's dream had come true, she would have her dream house on the lake. In September of 1987 we moved.

The entire Holly family worked at the supper club. His daughter, Janelle was my administrative assistant. She made sure I presented the best to our customers. Sherie Holly was the office manager and Sandy Holly did the payroll. Mrs. Holly, was probably the best baker I had ever encountered in my very long career. His sons, Mike and Fran, helped out during the holidays when we served hundreds of people. We were quite the team. Everyone took their job seriously. By January of the next year, I was promoted to general manager of the facility and Elaine took the position of head hostess. We enjoyed working there; this was truly a blessing. I had been thinking about going into retirement, but did not want to entirely stop working.

In 1994, I retired. I managed to take about a month off. Elaine and I took the time to travel a little and relax with our gardening and sometimes just to watch the traffic go by. One day I received a call from someone I had worked with at the supper club and he asked if I would consider coming to a small private country club just outside of town to fill the position of a sous chef. I discussed it with Elaine and even though she would have liked to have me at home, gave her blessing. For four years, I worked with my friend, Thomas Hessel, at Branch River Country Club. I enjoyed my work and the intimate setting of the club and its members and their families. Being such a small club, one was able to get to know most of the members, which I liked a lot. I served heads of industry, doctors, lawyers, and bankers. Though it was not a large club, we never skimped on the menu. The head chef, Brian and I worked well together and prepared spectacular meals and events. We put on poolside lobster parties as well as multi station banquets. The annual high point of the club was a black tie affair held during the holidays. The club would be decorated beyond description and people called months in advance to get the best seating available. Elegantly dressed hostesses seated you and the staff was on their best behavior. Another high profile event was hosted by the local Catholic high school. It was their annual Wine Auction, which raised money for the school. It would start with a wine tasting in the afternoon after which we would have to reset the areas to accommodate a hundred or more guests for a formal dinner. This event paired selected wines with an intricate seven-course meal. Just the place settings alone were a work of art. I made a great many lifelong friends who still to this day say they miss my presence at the club.

I work now and then at the Manitowoc Holiday Inn as an assistant chef. People ask me why I don't just stay home, but something inside me continually draws me to this field and my need to stay active, forces me to help out whoever asks.

A Look at My Family

In November of 1989, when President Ronald Reagan told the Soviet leader, Mikhail Gorbachev to "tear down the wall." My sister, Anna and her husband were very relieved. I had not seen Anna for almost thirty-four years, but now I could make plans for a visit. I made arrangements to travel to Berlin, April of 1998. We reminisced and talked about the war, our family, and our lives. We had a lot of catching up to do. It was a wonderful visit. When I had last seen her, she only had one daughter. Now she had two and they were both married with children of their own. It made me realize how fast time flew by without one realizing it.

Both our parents are gone now, and so is our loving stepmother, as is our brother Bernhard and our sisters Agnes and Maria. We are the only two left, Anna, and I. During my visit, we went back to see all the shops and places that were leveled by the bombardments. I was amazed at how well everything had been rebuilt. If you did not know the history of the Berlin, you could not tell it had been so badly damaged not that long ago. Wolfgang took me back to Potsdam, to the Cecilien Hoff-Castle where I had been during my secret mission. After forty-nine years, it was and is a museum. After the war, this was where President Truman, Prime Minister Churchill, and Soviet leader Stalin held their conference. One room housed an oval table surrounded by high backed captains chairs and you could almost see those powerful people debating the demise of Germany. It was an awesome historical site. I stood there and reflected that as a young soldier, I had delivered intelligence documents to this place of power.

Reflecting on My Career

I was asked once, what the proper time for supper was. The ancient Greek philosopher, Diogenes the Cynic is reputed to have replied, "If you are a rich man, whenever you please; but if you are a poor man, whenever you can."

It is fitting to say that I've enjoyed working in the hospitality industry. It has become my passion and it was just like falling in love. Some things you liked about it and the things you didn't, you learned to live with the things you didn't. I seemed to have a knack for it; I seemed to have a great rapport with those I came in contact with. Very seldom did anyone leave without a smile. That's what this business is all about, making people happy. One needed to provide them with eclectic food, but also with extraordinary service. During my career, my culinary philosophy has always been, "Believe in the integrity of food and service, make it second to none."

I tried to leave food in its natural state as much as possible. I try to draw out the flavors, but basically, the idea is not to manipulate the product. The key is to find really good products to start with so they can stand on their own.

I've often thought what made me pursue this field and the answer is a self-imposed question. When I left my home and the security of my family in 1942, things became so different.

I have to admit that hospitality nor gastronomy (the art or science of good eating) wasn't what I thought I would be doing with my life. As the son of a 'baumeister' or master builder, I felt I wanted to be a forest ranger. I'd always enjoyed nature and the outdoors. I loved to roam through the countryside and in the forests surrounding my home. I thought at one time that I would follow the traditions of my grandparents and that would have been to run a farm, since all three sets had working farms and I had spent a great deal of time on them during my childhood. Life on the farm became almost second nature to me. However, with the invasion of our country by Adolf Hitler, on September 1, 1939, everything changed. With this invasion, my plans and dreams of attending the Jagiellonian University in Krakow were dashed. Despite my successes, I still regret never having had the opportunity to follow those early dreams.

I knew though, no matter what I decided to do with my life, I wanted it to be in a profession that would last a long time. Having always liked working in our kitchen back home, I realized that maybe the hospitality field was indeed the right one for me.

"One man in his time, plays many parts . . ."
William Shakespeare, <u>As You Like It</u>

During my apprenticeship, I met many people with whom I felt safe. The camaraderie in the kitchens and among the restaurant staff became like family to me. Even as I endured the trials and torment of my arrest, the labor camp, and the war, my escape from the death train, I longed to reinstate myself with those I felt comfortable with. I often times silently thank that barber in Genthin for suggesting that I go to the "Das Schützenhaus "to see Herrn Neumann about a job; that is when things started to change for me. All those years, separated from my family; I found my family in those I worked with.

During my long career, I always believed that everyone deserves a second chance, not to mention a first one. In this industry, you learn quickly, that you cannot do it alone. It's like the military. One soldier doesn't fight the enemy, it takes a whole platoon.

I have met thousands of interesting and awe inspiring people of every race and found that they each had something different to offer in their own ways and from their own cultures. I have traveled through most of the European countries and marveled in the beauty that is everywhere you cared to look; whether it is architecture or in nature alone. I traveled more than three times around the world, only to settle down in this unique city of Two Rivers, on the shores of Lake Michigan. I thank my wife Elaine for that. For without her I would never have found this caring community.

In the culinary arts, the challenge is to honor the ingredients, but at the same time to be able to respond to the more diversified palates of the diners. One had to also become part of the community in which you lived and worked. It has always been my goal to demonstrate to those I worked with or those who worked under me, the importance of community spirit. It makes you become a better professional in any field of endeavor.

I loved to teach and develop young minds. This has always been my priority. One of the fundamentals I teach is common courtesy. Anyone who knows me, knows they should extend a welcome to me before we commence any type of project whether it is formal or informal. A simple "Bon jour" or "Bienvenu" is all it takes sometimes to make someone's day. Learning is a never-ending process. It is what keeps us young.

Traveling and living in the different cultures around the world teaches you respect and tolerance. Without these experiences, I do not believe I would have the self-confidence I have today. It gave me the chance to change my life and the world around me.

I've learned over the years that I can find happiness in poetry, prose, and in music and this keeps my heart and soul healthy. I struggle every day not to let loneliness and despair get into my life for it breaks one's spirit and brings death so much closer to you.

These last twenty-five years the one special person in my life has been my wife, Elaine. She has always supported whatever endeavor I wanted to pursue. She cares for me and my family as if they were her own. Elaine has more strength and reserve in her body than most people would give her credit. This remarkable woman lost both of her young children, at a young age. It is unbelievable to me how she managed to live through losing them both at the same time and still managed to find love in her heart for my children and now our grandson. She is an inspiration to me and to others who know her. She deserves a very special place in heaven.

This page is dedicated to my wife Elaine
For her patience and unending
Love, which she has always given me.
Over the twenty-five years, I have known her
She has never given up on me, on life, or on her own happiness.
She has suffered tragedies and illnesses that
Would have weakened less people.
She is truly a remarkable lady and I admire her greatly.

To my daughter Bettina,
son-in-law Glenn, and grandson Grant Günther.
May they never experience war.

As long as you live, the shadow of my biography, <u>Life on Both Sides of the Wall</u> will brush you. In every pair of eyes that rests on you, you will see compassion, like a cloud passing behind woods in winter. The memory of your father dissembled in friendly and unfriendly eyes. Sometimes you might wonder which is harder to bear. Friendly forgiveness or outright hate, you be the judge. In time, therefore, when the sum of your experiences of life gives you authority, you will ask yourself the question, "What, and who our father was?" I give you the answer in this book. I have faced torture, hunger, and loneliness, and at times, I was homeless. I had to struggle to survive. Faith, prayers, and hope were my constant companions. I survived extreme darkness during the war. My reward was being able to bring and hold my two children in my arms. I wanted to make sure you had everything you wanted and needed to have a happy life. A home, family, and love until you wanted to leave and pursue your own lives. I wanted this for you, for I had these things torn from me. You might not agree with all my decisions then and now, but do know that I did what I thought was best and that I have always and will always love you.

May the echoes of your past, present, and future be kind and gentle.

With all my love, your dad and friend

This book is affectionately inscribed by your Vater and friend.
With all my love, your Vater
"In Perpetum"

Herald Times Reporter

May 27, 1992

Manitowoc, WI

Diners Get Presidential Preference From German Chef

by Kim Stephens, news editor

Reprinted with permission by Herald Times Reporter, Manitowoc, WI

SHOTO - If it's impossible, it's possible for Günther Skaletz.

Just ask him about a dinner he organized for President Lyndon B. Johnson's wife, Lady Bird.

The morning after LBJ had attended a dinner Skaletz did in San Antonio, Texas, the president called, said it was one of the finest dinners he had ever attended, and asked the cook to prepare the same menu for a dinner his wife was planning.

"I said, 'Why yes Mr. President, when?" Skaletz recalled. "He said, 'tonight.'"

"When dinner was over he was very impressed," Skaletz said. "Nothing's impossible — I'm a very positive person."

That positive attitude eventually brought Skaletz to River Falls Supper Club, where he serves as manager. The road to Shoto has been varied and busy, because as Skaletz says, "in this business, you have to move."

The Frankfurt, Germany native graduated in 1958 from the Culinary Institute in Switzerland and worked in Paris, London, and Germany before coming to the United States in 1962. His U.S. tenure has taken him to New York, Texas, Oklahoma, Missouri, Milwaukee, and finally, Shoto.

"After living in big cities, living in a small town is more comfortable and less hectic," Skaletz said.

Being in Shoto, however, hasn't cut his scope of the food and beverage business. Skaletz pitches in whenever necessary to ensure the supper club presents its best face and fare to his guests. Skaletz said local dinner guests are intermingled with guests from big cities, and the club works diligently to provide a pleasant dining experience for each guest.

"We call it downtown Shoto, but when it comes to experience, that's what counts," he said.

His daily experiences may take him to the phone placing orders, worrying about landscape or helping people prepare menus for an upcoming dinner. The office phone rings constantly with customers or vendors vying for a little of his time — and he keeps one step ahead of them all, asking the right questions and taking down pertinent information.

He even manages to average about two hours a day in the kitchen, supervising, making special desserts or helping get a jump on a dinner by cutting meat.

"It's very relaxing," Skaletz said about the kitchen time. "Office work is very stressful sometimes."

Being in the restaurant business means working weekends, and Skaletz is used to having Monday as his usual day off. When not at River Falls, he and his wife enjoy skiing, walking the beach in Algoma, and sharing a half gallon of ice cream.

Skaletz, however, saves his culinary cap for the office kitchen, shying away from menu planning at home.

"I don't cook at home," he said. "My wife does the cooking...I leave it up to her."

Editor's note to clarify: The President asked Mr. Skaletz, the chef, to prepare a dinner he was planning for the First Lady, Lady Bird Johnson. Also, Skaletz's tenure took him to New York, Texas, Oklahoma, Missouri, Washington D.C., Nebraska, Milwaukee, and finally to Shoto.

CHEF SHARES SECRETS FOR BON APPETIT

PORK TENDERLOIN PROVENCALE
4 (3 ounce size) pork filet medallions
1/2 clove garlic or garlic powder
1 medium size onion, diced
2 tablespoons finely chopped parsley
1/4 pound sliced fresh mushrooms
4 ounces butter
1/4 pint half and half
1 hard-boiled egg
Fresh parsley

Place the butter in a skillet and melt. Take the pork filet medallions, sprinkled with salt and pepper and sauté until well done (dark golden brown). The filets shouldn't be thicker than 1/2 inch. Sprinkle medallions with parsley while sautéing.

In a separate skillet, smother the onions in butter or margarine, until they are done. Add the mushrooms and blend with the onions, until slightly done; however, they should remain crisp after five minutes. Add the half and half and blend everything together and let simmer for 10 minutes, stirring constantly. Add some of the finely chopped parsley and season with salt and pepper to taste.

Remove the medallions from the skillet and place in a separate plate. Add the butter which the medallions were sautéed in to the sauce in the other skillet. Blend together, but do not let the sauce boil.

Serve on parsley rice or mixed rice. Top the rice with the pork medallion and pour the sauce over the medallions. Garnish with two slices of hard-boiled egg and fresh parsley.

You may serve this dish with a boiled half tomato, broccoli, or green asparagus.

Serves two.

BAKED LOBSTER SAVANNAH

Use 3 pound lobster. Boil off the tail, remove from heat and cut into chunks. Place in a buttered baking dish, dot with butter and add salt to taste. Bake for 20 minutes, slowly.

Sauce:

Make 1 cup cream sauce enriched with egg yolk and add 2-1/2 tablespoons sherry (not too dry), lobster meat, 1/2 cup diced mushrooms and ¼ cup diced green peppers. Cook by stirring constantly for 15 minutes.

Remove from heat and stir in 1/4 cup diced pimento, a dash of paprika, salt and white pepper.

Fill lobster shell with mixture and sprinkle with 1/2 cup bread crumbs mixed with parmesan cheese.

CHICKEN BREAST A LA MAISON

Two chicken breasts
Flour, salt, white pepper
Diced shallots
White wine
1/4 cup fresh cream

Dust chicken with flour mixed with a little salt and white pepper and sauté in butter or olive oil until golden brown, turning two or three times.

Add a few diced shallots and a pinch of dry white wine. Remove the chicken breasts and place on a platter. Add 1/4 cup fresh cream, blend mixture and turn off heat. Stir mixture for a moment and pour over the chicken.

Serve with rice or pasta.

ESCALOPES DE VEAU CHASSEUR
(Veal cutlets, hunter style)
6 veal cutlets
Butter
9 ounces sliced mushrooms
1/4 cup green onions
1/4 glass of white wine
2 tablespoons tomato puree
chopped parsley

Flatten cutlets and sauté in butter, without breading them. Remove from sauté pan and place them on a platter.

Into the hot butter used for cooking the cutlets, drop the mushrooms and green onions. Add a little olive oil and brown them in the pan. Cook for a moment and moisten with the white wine and let it reduce by 1/2.

Add the tomato puree. Blend together and pour over the cutlets. Sprinkle with chopped parsley.

Serve over rice or pasta.

Serve three cutlets per person.

A Note from the Author

Writing this book was a labor of love. I suppose that this is true of most books. This autobiography spills as much from my heart as it does from my memories. Even though it was daunting at times, I pushed through the painful memories and continued on with what I had started.

I grew up during the Great Depression, I served in World War II. I risked my life to escape East Germany in the cover of darkness, alone without any idea of where I was going or what I was going to do once I got there. These experiences made me strong.

I was blessed with wonderful parents, who died way before I could show them what I had done with my life. Even though they may not be able to return to this earth, they can live again and be reborn in this book.

I cannot measure the true gratitude to all the wonderful people who helped me along the way through all my journeys in good times and bad. I have met many people who have touched my life deeply and gave meaning to my life. Without these people, this book would not be complete or have become a reality.

Sometimes God prepares us to perform some extraordinary mission in our lives. More often though, he prepares us for a greater mission for that will benefit all mankind.

As I reflect on the evil and horrendous years during WWII and how it robbed me of the vital years of my childhood, I remind myself that I need to be grateful that I indeed survived them when so many others didn't.

No one, regardless of their ethnicity, color, or gender should have to suffer for the decisions outside their control. I cry at night for the homeless and the hungry for I know first hand what they are going through. I feel for those who have lost their FREEDOM and hope that they find peace and contentment.

Günther F. Skaletz

Remember When . . .
In the Year I was Born – 1927

It was the year that a World Conference on Faith and "Ordus" was held in Geneva, Switzerland

Lindberg flew across the Atlantic in the *Spirit of St. Louis*

Ford introduced the Model A

Television was introduced and CBS was founded

Sculpting of Mount Rushmore began

Calvin Coolidge was President of the United States

The Holland Tunnel opened

Popular Songs were: *"Old Man River" and "I'm Looking over a Four Leaf Clover"*

Best Selling Novel was: *Elmer Gantry*

Celebrities-to-be were born: Doc Severinsen, Pope Benedict XVI, Erma Bombeck, Rosalynn Carter, John Chancellor, and Sidney Poitier

And In...

1929, the New York Stock Market Collapsed, which lead to the Great Depression of the 1930's

Totalitarianism was beginning in Italy

Economic problems in Germany paved the road for the rise of Adolf Hitler and the Nazis Regime, which would spread over Germany and eventually into Poland by 1939.

A Special Dedication to

~Herrn Otto Kleinert who saved me from the
gas chambers of Auschwitz.~

~Herrn and Frau Neumann~

~The Polish and German farmers who provided me with
directions to <u>Freedom</u>, shelter, and food~

~Professors Dr. E & Paul Pohl who made it possible for me to
attend the Ecole De Lausanne in Switzerland~

~Herrn Karl Duebner – the hotel owner, who has been very
instrumental in rebuilding my future and endeavor~

~The innumerable people who helped me to survive
the grueling Road to <u>Freedom</u>~

Without the above, I would never have made it.
"Nothing is impossible with faith, hope, prayers, and God."

Je me souviens – Genthin
(I remember Genthin)

*Goethe, the great German Philosopher and Poet in 1817
wrote this about life and nature:*
"Nothing should be more highly prized
than the value of each day."

Life and nature. Life is a constant reminder that we should not
overlook the beauty, which surrounds us.

*"Die täler, hügel und felder, das getreide, die pflanzen, bäume
und blüten, ja die farben die erde und steine."*
(The valleys, hills and fields, the grains, the plants, trees, and blossoms,
and the colours of the soils, and rocks, all these, represent life.)

Tom Brokaw said in his book, "The greatest generation," this
generation is fading away at a rate of 1,100-1,200 people a day.
Therefore this generation of World War II will soon vanish forever."

Therefore may this story remind us, that one should not take
'FREEDOM' for granted.

G. F. S. (2006)

"Rarely does a book offer two lessons in life. "Life on Both Sides of the Wall" is a testimony to man's indomitable will to live and that of a free man...This book serves as a witness to others how faith in God can lead us through life's many difficulties and challenges."

Larry Wojick

"Only rarely does a book of this quality appear – an inspired work."

"A remarkable work, gripping ...from first to last page."

"A fascinating book."

"It was a pleasure working on this project. I feel privileged to have been asked to help him write his story. With each word I realized what a truly remarkable man I have as a friend."

Dianne Stewart

"Heart stopping."

school teacher

Your book brings to the forefront how faith, hope, prayers, and hard work can be your guide to a good future.

I've just finished reading your book. What an exceptional story of hope and faith. Thank you so much.

Having read your book Life on Both Sides of the Wall, it was hard to put it down once I started reading.

- A reader from Kewaunee, WI

Your book emphasizes basic humanity and how important it is. There are many lessons in your book which I would love to share with my students.

Your book, Life on Both Sides of the Wall, is very powerful. Thank you for writing this book.

A retired teacher

"Absolutely inspiring. I could not put the book down once I started. God Bless you!"

A monetary contribution to The National World War II Museum in honor of Günther F. Skaletz Survivor-Author of "Life on Both Sides of the Wall" was made by Lewis Post – Tina Shine's brother, friends of Günther Skaletz